THE OXFORD CHEKHOV

VOLUME II

PLATONOV

IVANOV

THE SEAGULL

THE OXFORD
CHEKHOV

VOLUME II

PLATONOV
IVANOV
THE SEAGULL

Translated and edited by
RONALD HINGLEY

LONDON
OXFORD UNIVERSITY PRESS
NEW YORK TORONTO
1967

Oxford University Press, Ely House, London W. 1

GLASGOW NEW YORK TORONTO MELBOURNE WELLINGTON
CAPE TOWN SALISBURY IBADAN NAIROBI LUSAKA ADDIS ABABA
BOMBAY CALCUTTA MADRAS KARACHI LAHORE DACCA
KUALA LUMPUR HONG KONG TOKYO

© *Ronald Hingley 1967*

PRINTED IN GREAT BRITAIN

To

VALENTIN KIPARSKY

CONTENTS

PREFACE

(a) Contents of this volume

THE present volume contains Chekhov's first two long plays (*Platonov* and *Ivanov*), together with *The Seagull*. Thus all the full-length plays are presented in volumes ii and iii of this edition in what is basically their chronological order. However, the need to have the comparatively early *Wood-Demon* in the same volume as *Uncle Vanya* has led to a deliberate break in strict chronological sequence,[1] and in any case the disputed dating of *Uncle Vanya*[2] has made some compromise with this principle inevitable.

(b) Platonov

For reasons of convenience, and in accordance with the practice of several other translations and editions, the title *Platonov* has been given to the posthumous play, probably written in 1880-1, with which this volume begins. However, it is not clear by what name Chekhov himself would have wished the play to be known (assuming that he would have wished it to be known at all), since the only extant manuscript lacks a title page. Nor is there any firm evidence linking the play with the title *Fatherless* which occurs in Chekhov's correspondence and has been attached to *Platonov* by one Russian editor.[3]

Until recently *Platonov* was known only to a few enthusiasts for Chekhov's work, but the situation has now changed. In fact my translation happens to be the third into English to appear in the 1960s, following those of Mr. Dmitri Makaroff and Mr. David Magarshack, in addition to which Mr. Alex Szögyi's adaptation, *A Country Scandal*, must also be mentioned. So *Platonov* can no longer be offered to the reader as a new discovery. Recent interest in the play must be welcomed, since it is all too easy to think of *Platonov* as an extravagant juvenile exercise. Having once dismissed it all too easily myself, I was a little daunted by the idea of translating it. But *Platonov* certainly grows on one, especially if approached with a close knowledge of the text of Chekhov's later plays. The echoes of it in Chekhov's later work are very numerous indeed. A comprehensive exploration of this aspect of

---

[1] See *The Oxford Chekhov*, vol. iii, p. ix.
[2] Ibid., p. 300.
[3] See below, p. 282.

the play would have involved too much technical detail for the present edition, but some of the more obvious points are discussed in the Introduction below. Quite apart from its technical interest, *Platonov* has its own literary merits, as it is hoped users of this translation will discover for themselves.

(c) The text

The translations in this volume are based on the Russian text as printed in volumes xi and xii of the admirable twenty-volume *Complete Collection of the Works and Letters of A. P. Chekhov* (Moscow, 1944–51). This edition is here referred to as '*Works, 1944–51*'.[1]

(d) Treatment of proper names

The treatment of names of persons follows the lines laid down at some length in the Prefaces to volumes iii and viii of the present edition.[2] Briefly, the aim has been to convey the relationships between the characters by stylistic means rather than by mechanically reproducing the names as they occur in the Russian text. Rather free use has been made of English Christian names where these seem appropriate, i.e. in the following instances:

Anglicized form	Russian form	Anglicized form	Russian form
Abraham	Abram	Matthew	Matvey
Constantine	Konstantin	Maxim	Maksim
Cyril	Kirill	Michael	Mikhail
Eugene	Yevgeny	Nicholas	Nikolay
Gabriel	Gavrila	Paul	Pavel
Gregory	Grigory	Peter	Pyotr
Isaac	Isaak	Sarah	Sarra
Jacob	Yakov	Simon	Semyon
Martha	Marfa	Timothy	Timofey
Mary	Marya		

The affectionate form Зюзюшка (for 'Zinaida', in *Ivanov*) has been rendered 'Zizi'.

The policy of austerity in rendering Russian names, as adopted in this edition, seems more and more justified in the light of increased

[1] For a longer note on *Works, 1944–51*, see Preface to vol. iii of the present edition, p. ix.

[2] See *The Oxford Chekhov*, vol. iii, pp. xi–xvii; vol. viii, pp. ix–x.

experience in translating Chekhov. It is surely preferable to present your audience, as here, with 'Paul Lebedev' and 'Michael Borkin' rather than with 'Pavel Kirilych Lebedev' and 'Mikhail Mikhailovitch Borkin (Misha Mishilitch)', as the same characters appear in the programme to a recent performance of *Ivanov*.

(e) *Rendering of terms of abuse*

Belonging as they do to the early and more exuberant period of Chekhov's career, *Platonov* (especially) and also *Ivanov* abound in terms of abuse which pose a difficult problem to the translator. What, in particular, is to be done with the recurrent key word подлец? The dictionaries give such equivalents as 'scoundrel' or 'rogue', but the most superficial knowledge of Russian nineteenth-century literature is enough to show that подлец packed a much heftier punch than such semi-archaic or quaint British allocutions now carry. When, in Act Four of *Ivanov*, Dr. Lvov calls the hero a подлец, he is immediately challenged to a duel by two of the other characters. Moreover, in the first extant draft of the play (see pp. 325–6) this insult alone was enough to cause Ivanov to die of shock without needing, as in the later drafts, to have recourse to his revolver. 'You are a scoundrel' is in any case wholly inadequate as a rendering of Lvov's words, and I have settled on the italicized '*you are the most unmitigated swine!*'—after rejecting 'bastard', 'bloody swine' and the obvious 'four-letter' words with some regret at abandoning epithets of greater force and brevity.

Another problem is the rendering of the angry taunt жидовка, which Ivanov addresses to his wife at the end of Act Three. 'Jewess!' alone is quite inadequate and is in any case not a term of abuse at all, while 'Yid!' is much too forceful, apart from being excruciatingly wrong in tone and obviously out of the question. Here 'You Jewish bitch!' seems to strike the happy medium.

In general the problem is to find such a happy medium for each of the very numerous terms of abuse. In a given instance this involves choosing between the competing claims of such words as scoundrel, rogue, blackguard, mountebank, cad, rotter, crook, twister, bounder, hound, swine, scum, bitch, cow, drip, squirt and so on. Some of these have lost their force in English, others have too strong a period flavour, while others again may be enjoying a temporary vogue as forceful insults, yet be liable to lapse. Some care has been taken with the choice of such terms in the hope of finding a compromise, the aim being to steer a course between the under-forceful and the over-slangy. In earlier English versions of these texts little attention seems to have been devoted to this minor, but important, aspect of translation. Chekhov's taunts should strike with a force equal to that which they carry in the original. It is a pity to water them down.

(ƒ) On adapting Chekhov

In the not so distant past some well-known actors or producers have made a practice of 'adapting' English texts of Chekhov's plays for the stage. This was an understandable, indeed necessary, procedure at the time when translators of Chekhov did not, so far as one can judge, even aim at writing lines which should be 'speakable' on the stage. Several such adaptations have enjoyed well-deserved success. However, these productions tend to be more remarkable for the skill of the acting and direction than for the faithfulness to Chekhov's word and spirit of the English texts on which they are based. To adapt Chekhov is to risk doing violence to his work, and it is also to do a grave disservice to the cause of serious translation. Now that better translations from the Russian, conceived in stage terms and written for actors, are becoming available, it is to be hoped that the need for adaptation will be re-examined. The adapters concerned are certainly much more skilled at adapting Chekhov than I should be at producing or playing Hamlet, though one suspects that some of them are not entirely (or at all?) at home with the original Russian. Anyway, I think there is a strong case for each of us sticking to his last. From this pious hope one play—*Platonov*—must be partially excepted. Since it would take rather longer to stage than Wagner's *Götterdämmerung* or *Tristan*, while being on a somewhat less sublime artistic level, it must obviously be cut before it can be staged, and earlier translators have very naturally either abridged it or indicated optional cuts in the body of the text. However, to adopt either practice would be inconsistent with the general policy followed in the present edition, and it has therefore been decided to translate the text in full just as Chekhov left it, allowing any producers of the play to determine their own cuts.

(g) Dates

Dates relating to Russia before 1918 are given in the 'old style'—that is, they lag behind the calendar in use in Western Europe by twelve days in the nineteenth century and by thirteen days in the twentieth century.

(h) Acknowledgements

Mr. I. P. Foote has continued, as in earlier volumes, to compare my draft versions with the original Russian and has contributed most valuable suggestions and criticisms of style and interpretation. Dr. A. J. Krailsheimer has given further help in purging the text of 'translationese', as has my wife, besides affording encouragement and assistance with proof-reading and secretarial chores. Mrs. Olga Bowditch continues to convert tape and much-corrected typescript into impeccable copy. It is a pleasure to acknowledge their kindness and help.

RONALD HINGLEY

Frilford, Abingdon
1967

INTRODUCTION

THE plays in this volume show three very different phases of Chekhov's work as a dramatist and span a decade and a half of intense literary activity. *Platonov* represents his period as an apprentice author and *The Seagull* his mature craftsmanship, while *Ivanov* comes between the two, showing affinities with both past and future. Each play is typical of its author, but each also has markedly individual features. All three works provide valuable insights into Chekhov's development, and they take us from early experimentation over the threshold of his greatest drama.

Platonov is the most exotic item and hardly looks like a work by Chekhov at all. A huge drama, almost as long as *Uncle Vanya, Three Sisters* and *The Cherry Orchard* rolled into one, it seems to bear few traces of Chekhov the master of hints, half-statements and eloquent silences, being as exuberant as the later plays are concise and austere. Can a work so lush and repetitious really point to the subtlety of Chekhov's maturity? True, such a progression is a feature in the development of many creative artists, and can be studied in the work of figures as different from Chekhov as Pushkin and Verdi. But rarely are the poles between youthful *élan* and the wisdom of maturity spaced so far apart as they are between *Platonov* and *The Cherry Orchard*, Chekhov's first and last full-length dramas.

Next to length and exuberance, the most obvious difference between *Platonov* and Chekhov's mature work lies in the part played by action. Notoriously the writer in whose plays and stories 'nothing happens', Chekhov himself admitted as much when he stated that his *Seagull* contained 'little action and a hundredweight and a half of love'.[1] *Platonov* may not be exactly packed with thrills, possessing as it does more than its share of garrulous characters. But it does have its moments. It is at least the only play by Chekhov in which a heroine tries to throw herself under a train on stage and is prevented from doing so by a horse-thief who is later lynched by infuriated peasants. The same heroine also saves her husband from being knifed on stage and later attempts to poison herself by eating matches, all this while remaining the most phlegmatic character in the play. Apart from these excitements *Platonov* is full of quarrels, denunciations and confessions of love

---

[1] See below, p. 332.

or hatred. Nor is it easy to believe that there exists any other dramatic or fictional work containing so many lines in which one character tells another to 'get out of here', 'leave the premises', 'run along with you' or 'buzz off'—or in which so many changes are rung on the theme of 'stop talking', 'be quiet' and 'shut up'.

Platonov ends with a murder, a crime of passion in which the hero is shot by one of three discarded or would-be mistresses. Such an episode has its parallels in Chekhov's later work, where murders and scenes of violence are not unknown—the other two plays in this volume both end with a fatal revolver shot. All the same, violence was steadily declining in Chekhov's writings, and the most effective ending to any of his plays is surely that of *The Cherry Orchard*—his only full-length play to eschew gunfire altogether. As will be remembered, it just leaves the audience with an old man accidentally shut up in an empty house. One is reminded once again of the intermediate position occupied by *Ivanov*, whic his less rumbustious than *Platonov*, but in which Chekhov makes a point of giving the audience a 'punch on the nose' at the end of each act.[1]

The steady decrease in violence in Chekhov's drama can be briefly documented by reviewing in chronological order the main violent episodes in the full-length plays.

Date	Title of play	Items
?1880–1	Platonov	Two attempted suicides—one on, one off stage; an attempted knifing; a lynching off stage; murder by shooting.
1887–9	Ivanov	Suicide by shooting (on stage).
1889–90	The Wood-Demon	Suicide by shooting (off stage, shot not heard by audience).
?1890 ?1896	Uncle Vanya	Attempted murder by shooting on stage.
1896	The Seagull	Attempted suicide; an actual suicide (off stage, shot heard by audience).
1900–1	Three Sisters	Death by shooting (off stage in duel; shot heard in distance by audience).
1903–4	The Cherry Orchard	No shooting (but Yepikhodov carries a revolver so that he can commit suicide if necessary).

This progressive decline in violence suggests a contrast with Dostoyevsky, whose evolution went in the opposite direction and whose attainment of maturity as a writer coincided with his discovery

[1] See below, p. 285.

that murder was a necessary ingredient in his plots—as it became from *Crime and Punishment* onwards. His mature fiction is all built around crimes of violence and includes, in *The Brothers Karamazov*, a distinguished 'whodunit'. Though Chekhov has also contributed to the same genre his own detective story *The Shooting Party* (1884), that is his first (and only) novel, whereas *The Brothers Karamazov* is Dostoyevsky's last and most celebrated work. Thus Chekhov moved in the opposite direction to Dostoyevsky in his use of fictional violence. Murder, so fruitful a topic to the earlier writer, did not give Chekhov what he wanted. His experiments took him further and further in the direction of inner drama, admittedly with exceptions such as his fine story *Murder* (1895).

There appears to be no evidence of any serious influence of Dostoyevsky on Chekhov, who apparently disliked Dostoyevsky's novels, and was in any case not greatly interested in them. But it is worth charting some striking similarities between *Platonov* (as opposed to almost all Chekhov's other work) and Dostoyevsky's writings— even though these affinities are probably coincidental. In *Platonov*, as in Dostoyevsky's work, the characters are under exceptionally heavy emotional and psychological pressure during much of the time. They oscillate between extreme expressions of love and hatred and are always liable to perform the sudden volte-face, that characteristic ploy of Dostoyevsky's. The plot of *Platonov*, like that of almost all Dostoyevsky's later novels, is a web of intertwined financial and amorous complexities. The characters of *Platonov*, like those in Dostoyevsky, are constantly liable to 'blench', 'flare up', 'blush' or 'stand rooted to the spot'. There are the frequent quarrels, denunciations and outbursts—and all the 'guffaws' and samples of heavy sarcasm. These features make *Platonov* the most Dostoyevskian of Chekhov's works. But the main value of the play to Chekhov was surely that of an experiment which failed. His full exploration of the technique of overstatement in this early experimental work may well have helped to turn him—on the rebound, as it were—into the most laconic of the great Russian prose writers.

'Chaotic, unconvincing, and tedious', according to one useful recent study of Chekhov,[1] *Platonov* is a great deal less facetious than many of the early comic sketches which Chekhov contributed to the Russian press. That its composition was an immensely serious exercise to its twenty-year-old author is a safe assumption, though (as shown in

[1] F. L. Lucas, *The Drama of Chekhov, Synge, Yeats and Pirandello*, p. 23.

Appendix i) there is an almost total lack of evidence on the origins and history of the text. One serious theme in the play has inevitably attracted attention: the loss of the Voynitsevs' estate, sold by auction under somewhat indecorous circumstances, like the Cherry Orchard a quarter of a century later. The loss of a family home was a theme of permanent fascination to Chekhov, who had himself experienced it at first hand as a boy on the humble level appropriate to the son of a provincial shopkeeper—the Chekhovs' lodger, one Selivanov, tricked them into allowing him to buy up their small house. This theme also appears in an early story of 1882, *Belated Blossom*, where Chekhov links it with a study of the Russian gentry in decline, as in *The Cherry Orchard* and *Platonov*.

The loss of the Voynitsevs' estate is not the main element in the plot of *Platonov*, which chiefly revolves round the hero's amatory misfortunes and might be summed up as 'hell hath no fury like several women scorned'. Platonov is irresistible to all the women of his circle. As Chekhov apparently conceived the matter, this was an extreme form of misfortune, for he seems to be implying that a love affair must inevitably be a profoundly gloomy experience. That fornication is morally wrong has been the contention of many sages—the proposition that it is unenjoyable has found fewer supporters. But such does seem to be Platonov's own view, and perhaps that of his creator. Platonov cannot reconcile the conflicting demands of his wife Sasha with those of Anna and Sonya Voynitsev who both compete for his favours, quite apart from his love-hate entanglement with Mary Grekov and the involvements of the cuckolded or ousted Sergey Voynitsev and Nicholas Triletsky.

Thus the central situation of *Platonov* presents a parallel with that of *Ivanov*. Each play is dominated by a single hero to a much greater extent than any of Chekhov's other full-length plays. And the two heroes have so much in common that it is not fanciful to regard *Platonov* as a kind of preliminary sketch for *Ivanov*. Perhaps the very speed with which Chekhov threw off the first draft of *Ivanov*—in two weeks—was only possible because he had already spent so much time developing a similar theme a few years earlier. Each hero is a young man possessed of a fascination for the opposite sex literally fatal in the sense that it leads to the murder of the one and the suicide of the other. In each case the hero's love brings frustration and misery to himself and his female admirers, of whom Platonov has four and Ivanov a mere two. And each hero behaves with gross selfishness and inconsiderateness amounting to cruelty, yet seems to enjoy the sympathy of Chekhov himself. This sympathy, or at least absence of condemnation, can be documented for *Ivanov* (see the letter quoted on pp. 291–5), but seems to be implied with no less force by the text of *Platonov*.

Both heroes thus exemplify a tendency of Russian fiction which has continually fascinated its Anglo-Saxon readers: a broad tolerance and refusal to strike moral attitudes. To do evil or behave badly in Russian fiction is not necessarily to be an evil person—rather the opposite, one sometimes feels. Thus, being a prostitute (admittedly an unenthusiastic one) only reinforces the status of Dostoyevsky's Sonya in *Crime and Punishment* as the representative of his ideal of good, whereas the arch-bogyman Svidrigaylov represents evil—yet has little impact on the action of the novel apart from distributing largesse to various deserving causes.

Not that Ivanov represents a Chekhovian ideal of good or stands in any simple good–evil confrontation with his enemy, Dr. Lvov. Lvov is at least superficially well intentioned and does his best to help Anna, but he is put forward as detestable. He is one of those 'do-gooders' whom Chekhov liked to show spreading alarm and despondency as a result of their activities—Lydia Volchaninov in *The Artist's Story* (1896) is another example. Thus *Ivanov* points a simple lesson: the danger of making facile moral judgements. ('No, Doctor, we all have too many wheels, screws and valves to judge each other on first impressions or one or two pointers'—Ivanov to Dr. Lvov in Act Three.)

One of Chekhov's preoccupations was that Ivanov should not be dismissed as a 'superfluous man', the term commonly applied by critics to a succession of heroes in Russian literature who include Chatsky (in Griboyedov's play *Woe from Wit*) and several heroes of novels: Onegin (in Pushkin's *Eugene Onegin*); Pechorin (in Lermontov's *Hero of Our Time*); Rudin (in Turgenev's *Rudin*); and Oblomov (in Goncharov's *Oblomov*). Like Ivanov, these are all young married men of the gentry class—the idea of a superfluous *woman* does not seem to have occurred to Russian critics and writers. Like Ivanov, they easily attract the love of desirable young women, with whom they can only form frustrating relationships. They are all able to support themselves more or less in idleness even if, as Rudin, they are poor men—or they have some at least nominal profession, the army or civil service. But they cannot find any satisfactory goal in life, all tending to be over-talkative, indecisive and introspective. Each is to some extent a self-portrait of his creator, but deprived of a main characteristic: creative

talent. They are all men of superior intelligence and potential, and the
prevalence of the literary type was widely interpreted as a criticism of
imperial Russian society, especially of the 'stifling' atmosphere under
Nicholas I, during whose reign an intelligent and sensitive young man
could find no suitable field in which to deploy his talents—as was
claimed frequently, vociferously and only too truthfully.

Ivanov possesses most of the above characteristics, but Chekhov
went out of his way to maintain that his hero was no superfluous man.
He gave two reasons for making this distinction. Firstly, Ivanov
blames himself, not society, for his predicament.[1] And secondly,
Chekhov felt Ivanov to be more closely observed from life than the
superfluous men, and had conceived, he told a correspondent, 'the
daring ambition of summing up everything so far written about such
Dismal Desmonds and of putting an end to these writings with
Ivanov'.[2]

One could wish that Chekhov had expounded the differences
between Ivanov and the superfluous men at greater length, especially
as his correspondence is so eloquent and revealing on other aspects of
the play. It is tempting to defy his wishes and say that Ivanov does in
fact exhibit most of the 'superfluous' characteristics and is not the least
interesting specimen of the type, being at least a more fascinating study
than Rudin. Chekhov's dislike of hearing his hero dismissed as another
superfluous man no doubt derived from his endearing distrust of
clichés and literary stereotypes, especially of those which, like this one,
had been made the peg for the politico-social harangues which he
found distasteful. Incidentally, Platonov, too, possesses most of the
'superfluous' characteristics, but fits less easily into the category because
he has a wife and child, admittedly more or less abandoned by him.
The other superfluous men are all not-so-gay bachelors.

Social satire is another feature common to *Platonov* and *Ivanov*.
This is particularly outspoken in *Ivanov*, where the ménage of the
Lebedevs enables Chekhov to castigate features of provincial Russian
society against which he continued to inveigh throughout his life.
These include an obsession with eating, drinking, making money,
playing cards and gossiping about the neighbours, as well as empty-
headedness and frivolity. Much of this comes under the heading
of the Russian word *poshlost*, which can be roughly translated as

---

[1] For the passage 'When narrow, unreliable people get in a mess like this, they usually
put it all down to their environment' etc., see p. 292, below.
[2] See below, p. 296.

'complacent acceptance of the second-rate'. These features occur in other full-length plays, for example in *Three Sisters*, but are more prominent and are exposed in a more ruthlessly satirical spirit in *Ivanov*. One of Chekhov's reasons for approving of Ivanov himself was presumably that he was not just another drunken, greedy, gossiping, card-playing provincial bore, which seems to have been the supreme crime in Chekhov's eyes. Badly as he behaved, Ivanov was at least superior to his environment.

The Seagull, together with *Uncle Vanya*, begins Chekhov's period of maturity as a dramatist, yet is in many ways the least typical of the four plays of his maturity. A feature of the play is its exploration of the problems of pen and stage in the persons of two writers and two actresses. One member of each pair is mature and established (Trigorin, Irina), while the other two (Treplev, Nina) are younger, and are not acknowledged successes, though neither is a total failure. Chekhov uses Trigorin to paint what is to some extent a self-portrait, especially in Trigorin's attitude to the problems of authorship. This makes his lines particularly interesting material, all the more so as this 'author's confession' represents a departure from Chekhov's usual reticence on such matters in his imaginative work. Other biographical echoes in *The Seagull* include the eccentric use of the play to convey a message to a young woman in the audience, and also the two episodes involving the painter Levitan which probably first suggested to Chekhov his use of the lake and of the symbolic seagull.[1]

The play is also distinguished from Chekhov's other dramatic work by the symbolic use made of the shot seagull, wantonly destroyed like Nina's life. This has naturally given rise to comparisons with Ibsen and particularly with *The Wild Duck* (1884). Chekhov himself did not see *The Wild Duck* until 1901, long after his *Seagull* was written, and (according to Stanislavsky) he expressed a low opinion of Ibsen's play. Whether or not the symbolic seagull is a lineal descendant of Ibsen's duck is not known.[2] And in any case, though the seagull is an effective symbol on the stage, the effect is a crude one, judged by Chekhov's normal standards. Nor can he have been very satisfied with the device himself, for his later plays lack any comparably blatant symbol.

Of the four plays of Chekhov's maturity, two (*The Seagull* and *The Cherry Orchard*) are described by him as comedies in their sub-titles. His use of this word has perhaps created more problems that it has

[1] See below, Appendix iii, pp. 335–6.
[2] See further, *The Seagull*, ed. Henry, p. 29.

solved and is briefly discussed in the introduction to volume iii of this edition.[1] Whatever the rights and wrongs of the argument, *The Seagull* is at least less of a comedy than *The Cherry Orchard*. Not that the earlier play lacks amusing scenes and characters. The clash between Irina Arkadin and her son Constantine gives rise to rich comedy of situation in the quarrels which take place between the two over Constantine's play and his mother's attachment to Trigorin. The second of these quarrels delightfully echoes the flare-up between Trofimov and Mrs. Ranevsky in Act Three of *The Cherry Orchard*. Two skilfully drawn elderly men, each essentially a Chekhovian stage-buffoon (Sorin and Shamrayev), collect their quota of laughs. But the highly charged emotions surrounding Nina's misfortunes and Constantine's suicide hardly accord with the label 'comedy', even when one remembers Chekhov's loose and idiosyncratic use of the word. Of all Chekhov's plays *The Seagull* is the most sombre in tone and even *Ivanov* has a lighter touch, though sub-titled a 'drama'.

In *The Seagull* Nina and Constantine's miseries certainly strike home, but here too one feels that Chekhov was not operating quite inside his own proper territory. This is far from calling the play morbid or unsuccessful. But it does convey an overall impression of pessimism such as has sometimes been too readily associated with Chekhov himself and with his work as a whole, as indeed has the opposite label of effervescent optimism. Perhaps *The Seagull*, a justly famous item in the international theatrical repertoire, contributed something to creating this impression in the first place. To a very large extent it is a study of frustration, much admittedly comic, but much undeniably tragic and with a special flavour of hopelessness.

Some critics have attempted to rescue the play from charges of undue pessimism by reading qualities into Nina which hardly seem present in Chekhov's text, and the same has been done—less absurdly, but also unwarrantably—for Anya in *The Cherry Orchard*, and even, tentatively, for Sonya in *Platonov*. Thus Nina has been interpreted as radiant, starry-eyed, confident and forward-looking, a sort of idealized Komsomol girl before her time. But this is to go far beyond what Chekhov wrote. It seems more consistent with the text to accept *The Seagull* as a pessimistic work, which is very far from saying that either Chekhov himself or his work as a whole is pessimistic—or that it would necessarily matter all that much if it was.

[1] *The Oxford Chekhov*, vol. iii, pp. 8–10.

PLATONOV

(?1880–1881)

CHARACTERS

ANNA VOYNITSEV, a general's young widow

SERGEY VOYNITSEV, General Voynitsev's son by his first marriage

SONYA, his wife

PORFIRY GLAGOLYEV ⎫
CYRIL, his son ⎪ landowners,
GERASIM PETRIN ⎬ neighbours
PAUL SHCHERBUK ⎭ of the Voynitsevs

MARY GREKOV, a girl of 20

IVAN TRILETSKY, a retired colonel

NICHOLAS, his son, a young doctor

ABRAHAM VENGEROVICH, a rich Jew

ISAAC, his son, a student

TIMOTHY BUGROV, a businessman

MICHAEL PLATONOV, a village schoolmaster

SASHA, his wife, daughter of Ivan Triletsky

OSIP, a horse thief, aged about 30

MARKO, a court messenger, a little old man

VASILY ⎫
JACOB ⎬ servants of the Voynitsevs
KATYA ⎭

Guests and servants

The action takes place on the Voynitsevs' estate in the south of European Russia

ACT ONE

The VOYNITSEVS' *drawing-room. A french window opening on the garden and two doors leading to other rooms. Mixed modern and antique furniture. A grand piano. Near it a music-stand with a violin and some music. A harmonium. Pictures (oleographs) in gilt frames.*

SCENE I

[ANNA *sits at the piano, head bent over the keys.* NICHOLAS *comes in.*]

NICHOLAS [*goes up to* ANNA]. Well?

ANNA [*raises her head*]. Nothing. I'm rather bored.

NICHOLAS. How about a smoke, my pet? I'm dying for a cigarette. Haven't had one since this morning, don't know why.

ANNA [*hands him cigarettes*]. Take plenty, so you needn't bother me later. [*They light up.*] I'm bored, Nicholas, bored and fed up, with nothing to do.

[NICHOLAS *takes her hand.*]

ANNA. Feeling my pulse? I'm quite well.

NICHOLAS. Not your pulse—a little kiss. [*Kisses her hand.*] I like kissing your hand, it's like satin. What soap do you use, they're so white? Wonderful hands. I'll have another, actually. [*Kisses her hand.*] Like a game of chess?

ANNA. All right. [*Looks at the clock.*] Quarter past twelve, our guests must be ravenous.

NICHOLAS [*sets the chess-board*]. No doubt. I'm starving myself.

ANNA. I don't care about you—you always are starving, though you keep stuffing yourself. [*They sit down to play chess.*] Your move— oh, he already has moved. You should think first. I'm going here. You always are starving.

NICHOLAS. You've moved? I see. Yes, I'm starving. Is dinner soon?

ANNA. I don't think so. The chef celebrated our arrival by having a drop too much, and now he's out cold. But we'll get lunch before very long. Really, Nicholas, when will you have had enough? Stuffing yourself like that, it's ghastly. What a big stomach for such a little man.

NICHOLAS. Pretty remarkable, I agree.

ANNA. Barges in here and scoffs half a pie without asking. You know it's not my pie, don't you? You're a pig, dear. Your move.

NICHOLAS. I don't know, I only know the pie would go bad if I didn't eat it. Have you moved? Quite good. Here's mine. I eat a lot because I'm healthy—you don't mind that, do you? *Mens sana in corpore sano.* Why think? Move without thinking, dear. [*Sings.*] 'I could a tale unfold——'

ANNA. Be quiet, I can't think.

NICHOLAS. It's a pity—a clever girl like you, and no idea of gastronomy! A poor eater is a monster, a moral freak, because—. Hey, you can't go there, what do you think you're at? Oh, that's different. Now taste's a natural function like sight and hearing, in fact it's one of the five senses, old girl, and thus an integral branch of psychology. Psychology, I said.

ANNA. You're about to be witty, I do believe. Don't, dear, it bores me and it doesn't go with your face. I never laugh at your jokes, you may have noticed that—if not, it's time you did.

NICHOLAS. Your ladyship's move, and look out for your knight. You don't laugh because you always miss the point, see?

ANNA. What are you goggling at? Your move. Will your young woman come today, do you think?

NICHOLAS. She did say she would.

ANNA. Then it's time she was here, it's gone twelve. Are you—I'm sorry if I'm being indiscreet, but are you just friends or is there more to it?

NICHOLAS. Meaning what?

ANNA. Be frank, Nicholas. I ask as your friend, not so I can gossip about it. What are Mary Grekov and you to each other? Be frank, and please don't be funny about it. Come on, it's just a friendly inquiry, honestly.

NICHOLAS. What we are to each other no one yet knows.

ANNA. At least——

NICHOLAS. I visit her, talk to her, bore her, put her mother to the expense of serving coffee, and that's all. Your move. I go there every day or two, I might add, and stroll along their shady garden paths. I talk about my interests, and she talks about hers, holding me by this button and taking the fluff off my collar. I'm always covered with fluff, aren't I?

ANNA. Go on.

NICHOLAS. That's all. It's hard to say what attracts me about her. Am I bored, am I in love, or is it something else? I've no idea. I know I miss her terribly in the afternoons, and from a few random inquiries I know she misses me.

ANNA. It's love then?

NICHOLAS [*shrugs*]. Very likely. Do I love her or don't I? What do you think?

ANNA. A charming thing to say! You should know best.

NICHOLAS. Oh, you don't understand. Your move.

ANNA. There. No, I don't—few women would understand such behaviour. [*Pause.*]

NICHOLAS. She's a nice child.

ANNA. I like her—a bright little thing. Only mind you don't get her into any trouble, my friend, because that's a failing of yours. You'll hang around, talk a lot of hot air, promise the earth, get her a bad name—and then simply drop her. I'd be sorry for her. What's she doing these days?

NICHOLAS. Reading.

ANNA. And studying chemistry? [*Laughs.*]

NICHOLAS. I think so.

ANNA. Good for her. Steady on, mind your sleeve. I like her and her sharp little nose, she might make quite a decent scientist.

NICHOLAS. She doesn't know what to do, poor thing.

ANNA. Tell you what, Nicholas—ask Mary to come and see me some time. I'll make friends with her and—anyway I shan't try to act as a go-between or anything. We'll see what she's made of and either get rid of her or take her seriously. Let's hope—. [*Pause.*] To me you're just a baby, you're an awful lightweight—that's why I meddle in your affairs. Your move. My advice is—leave her alone or marry her. Marriage or nothing, mind. If you do spring a surprise and choose marriage, look before you leap. Mind you have a real look at her from every angle. Think, consider, weigh it up—then you won't be sorry afterwards, do you hear?

NICHOLAS. Of course, I'm all ears.

ANNA. I know you. You're so impulsive and you'll marry on impulse. A woman can twist you round her finger. Consult your friends, in fact don't trust your own feeble brain. [*Bangs the table.*] That's what your head's made of. [*Whistles.*] The wind whistles through your ears, man—you're all brain and no sense.

NICHOLAS. Whistles like a peasant. Amazing woman! [*Pause.*] Mary won't visit you.

ANNA. Why not?

NICHOLAS. Because Platonov's always hanging round here. She just can't stand him since he started pitching into her. The man decided she was silly—he got that idea in his great shaggy head and it damn well can't be budged. He thinks it's his job to annoy silly girls, I don't know why, and he's always playing tricks on them. Your move. But she's no fool. A fat lot he knows about people!

ANNA. Don't worry, we'll keep him in line. Tell her she has nothing to fear. But why is Platonov so late? It's high time he was here. [*Looks at the clock.*] It's very bad manners, we haven't met for six months.

NICHOLAS. I passed the schoolhouse on my way here, and the shutters were all closed. He must still be asleep. The man's a swine. I haven't seen him for ages myself.

ANNA. Is he well?

NICHOLAS. He always is, there's life in the old dog yet.

[PORFIRY *and* SERGEY *come in.*]

SCENE II

[*The above,* PORFIRY *and* SERGEY.]

PORFIRY [*coming in*]. Yes, my dear Sergey, we old stagers are a bit better at this business—and a bit luckier—than you young hopefuls. Men lost nothing, you see, and women gained. [*They sit down.*] Let's sit down, I'm tired. We loved women chivalrously, believed in them, worshipped them—because we thought they were superior. Woman's a superior being, Sergey.

ANNA. Hey, stop cheating!

NICHOLAS. Cheating?

ANNA. Who put this piece here?

NICHOLAS. *You* did.

ANNA. Oh yes. Sorry.

NICHOLAS. So I should jolly well think.

PORFIRY. Then we also had our friends. Friendship went deeper when I was young—was less of a luxury. We had literary circles and clubs too. By the way, any of us would have gone through hell-fire and high water for our friends.

SERGEY [*yawns*]. Yes, those were the days.

NICHOLAS. In these dreadful times we employ the fire brigade to go through fire for our friends.

ANNA. Don't be silly, Nicholas. [*Pause.*]

PORFIRY. At the Moscow opera last winter I saw a young man reduced to tears by good music. Now wasn't that nice?

SERGEY. Very much so, I should say.

PORFIRY. So should I. But why did women and their escorts, sitting near by, have to smile at him—eh? What was there to grin at? When he realized they could all see him crying, he squirmed in his seat, blushed, produced a ghastly grin of his own, and left the theatre. People weren't ashamed of honest tears in our day, and no one laughed at them.

NICHOLAS [*to* ANNA]. I wish this sentimental old ninny would die of melancholia—I hate such talk, it gets on my nerves.

ANNA. Shush!

PORFIRY. We were luckier than you. Music-lovers didn't have to leave the theatre in our day, they'd stay till the opera was over. You're yawning, Sergey, I must be getting you down——

SERGEY. No, but do wind up, Glagolyev. It's time——

PORFIRY. Ah well, and so on and so forth. To sum up, people loved and hated in our day, that's what it comes to, so they could feel indignation and scorn——

SERGEY. I see, and nowadays they can't, eh?

PORFIRY. That's what I think.

[SERGEY *gets up and goes to the window.*]

PORFIRY. You don't find that sort any more—that's what's wrong with us these days. [*Pause.*]

SERGEY. Bit sweeping, aren't you?

ANNA. Oh, I say—! He stinks of cheap scent, I feel quite sick. [*Coughs.*] Move back a bit, please.

NICHOLAS [*moving away*]. She's losing—so blame the wretched scent. What a woman.

SERGEY. You should be ashamed to bandy accusations based on pure guesswork and a bias in favour of your own long-vanished youth.

PORFIRY. I may be mistaken.

SERGEY. May be. Forget the 'may be'. Your accusation's not particularly funny.

PORFIRY [*laughs*]. But you're getting annoyed, old boy, and that proves you're unsporting and don't know how to respect your opponent's views.

SERGEY. It's enough to prove I can feel indignation, isn't it?

PORFIRY. I'm not condemning everyone out of hand, of course—there are exceptions.

SERGEY. Of course. [*Bows.*] Thank you for those kind words, such admissions are the secret of your charm. But what if you ran across some booby who didn't know you, and who thought you knew what you were talking about? You'd have him believe that all of us —me, Nicholas, Mother and anyone else more or less young—are incapable of indignation or scorn.

PORFIRY. Look here, I didn't say——

ANNA. I want to listen to Mr. Glagolyev. Let's stop, I've had enough.

NICHOLAS. No, no. You can play and listen at the same time.

ANNA. I've had enough. [*Gets up.*] I'm fed up, we can finish the game later.

NICHOLAS. When I'm losing she's glued to her chair, but let me start winning and she wants to hear Glagolyev. [*To* PORFIRY.] Who wants to hear you, you nuisance? [*To* ANNA.] Kindly sit down and get on with the game, or I shall say you've lost.

ANNA. Do, for all I care. [*Sits opposite* PORFIRY.]

SCENE III

[*The above and* ABRAHAM.]

ABRAHAM [*comes in*]. Isn't it hot? It's so hot—reminds me of Palestine, seeing I'm a Jew. [*Sits at the piano and strums.*] I'm told it's very hot there.

NICHOLAS [*stands up*]. I'll note it down. [*Takes a notebook from his pocket.*] I'll make a note of it, dear lady. [*Makes a note.*] Mrs. Anna Voynitsev, the widow of General Voynitsev—three roubles. That makes ten all told. Now when do I see the colour of my money?

PORFIRY. You never saw the old days, ladies and gentlemen, you'd sing a different tune if you had. You'd understand—. [*Sighs.*] But how can you?

SERGEY. I think we could trust literature and history more. We haven't seen the past, but we feel it. That feel often comes from here. [*Hits the back of his neck.*] Now you don't see the present day, you've no feel for that.

NICHOLAS. Shall I chalk it up to your ladyship, or will you pay now?

ANNA. Stop, I can't hear what they're saying.

NICHOLAS. Why listen, they'll be on all afternoon?

ANNA. Sergey, give this lunatic ten roubles.

SERGEY. Ten? [*Takes out his pocket-book, to* PORFIRY.] Let's change the subject.

PORFIRY. All right, if you don't like it.

SERGEY. I like listening to you, but I don't want to hear what sounds like slander. [*Gives* NICHOLAS *ten roubles.*]

NICHOLAS. Thanks. [*Slaps* ABRAHAM *on the shoulder.*] That's how to get on in the world. Sit a defenceless woman at the chess-board and take ten smackers off her without a pang of conscience. Pretty good, eh?

ABRAHAM. I agree. You'd do quite well in Jerusalem, Doctor.

ANNA. Stop it, Triletsky. [*To* PORFIRY.] So you think woman's a superior being, Mr. Glagolyev.

PORFIRY. Yes.

ANNA. I see. You must be a great ladies' man.

PORFIRY. Yes, I adore women, dote on them. One reason is, I see in them everything I like, generosity and——

ANNA. You adore them, but are they worth it?

PORFIRY. Yes.

ANNA. Are you sure? Quite sure, or have you just talked yourself into it?

[NICHOLAS *picks up the violin and bows it.*]

PORFIRY. I'm quite sure, I only need to know you to be so.

ANNA. Really? You're certainly quite a character.

SERGEY. He's a romantic.

PORFIRY. Perhaps. Why not? Is romanticism such a bad thing? You people have thrown it out. A good idea, but perhaps you've got rid of the baby with the bath-water.

ANNA. Well, don't let's quarrel over it, my friend, I'm no debater. We may have got rid of this or that, but we're certainly cleverer, thank God. Aren't we? And that's the main thing. [*Laughs.*] As long as you have clever people getting cleverer, the rest can look after itself. Oh, stop that awful noise, Nicholas. Put that fiddle down.

NICHOLAS [*hanging up the violin*]. A fine instrument.

PORFIRY. Platonov once put it rather well. 'We've learnt sense about women,' he said. 'But that's only meant dragging both ourselves and women through the mud.'

NICHOLAS [*laughs*]. It must have been his birthday, he'd had a drop too much.

ANNA. Did he say that? [*Laughs.*] Yes, he likes to make these utterances sometimes, but he only said it for effect, surely? And talking of friend Platonov, what's he really like, do you think? Is he really such a knight in shining armour?

PORFIRY. Well—I think Platonov's a superb example of modern vagueness. He's the hero of our best modern novel, one that hasn't yet been written, I'm sorry to say. [*Laughs.*] Vagueness seems to me typical of modern society, and your Russian novelist senses it. He's baffled and bewildered, he has nothing to hold on to, he doesn't understand. And these people aren't easy to understand. [*Points to* SERGEY.] Our novels are abominable, affected and trivial and no wonder. Everything's so vague and blurred—it's one great chaotic mess. And it's this vagueness which the sagacious Platonov typifies, I think. Is he well?

ANNA. He's said to be well. [*Pause.*] Such a nice little man.

PORFIRY. Yes, you can't help looking up to him. I went to see him several times last winter and I'll never forget the few hours I was lucky to spend with him.

ANNA [*looks at the clock*]. It's time he was here. Did you send for him, Sergey?

SERGEY. Yes, twice.

ANNA. You're all talking nonsense. Triletsky, quickly—send Jacob for him.

NICHOLAS [*stretches*]. Shall I tell them to lay the table?

ANNA. No, I'll do that.

NICHOLAS [*moves off and knocks into* BUGROV *by the door*]. Our grocer man's puffing like a steam engine. [*Pats him on the stomach and goes out.*]

SCENE IV

[ANNA, PORFIRY, ABRAHAM, SERGEY *and* BUGROV.]

BUGROV [*coming in*]. Gosh! Frightfully hot, isn't it? Must be going to rain.

SERGEY. Did you come through the garden?

BUGROV. Yes.

SERGEY. Is Sonya there?

BUGROV. Which Sonya?

SERGEY. My wife.

ABRAHAM. Back in a minute. [*Goes into the garden.*]

SCENE V

[ANNA, PORFIRY, SERGEY, BUGROV, PLATONOV *and* SASHA, *who wears Russian national dress.*]

PLATONOV [*in the doorway, to* SASHA]. After you, young woman. [*Comes in after* SASHA.] Well, we got away at last. Say hallo to everyone, Sasha. Good morning to your ladyship. [*Goes up to* ANNA, *kisses one hand and then the other.*]

ANNA. You cruel, horrid man. How could you keep us waiting all this time? You know how impatient I am. Dearest Sasha. [*Kisses* SASHA.]

PLATONOV. Well, we got away at last, thank God. We haven't seen a parquet floor for six months—or armchairs, high ceilings or human beings even. We've hibernated in our den like bears. We've only just crawled out into the light. Sergey, my dear fellow. [*Embraces* SERGEY.]

SERGEY. You've grown, you've put on weight and—damn it, how you've filled out, Sasha. [*Shakes her hand.*] Are you well? Plumper and prettier than ever!

PLATONOV [*shakes hands with* PORFIRY]. Glad to meet you.

ANNA. How are things, Sasha, how are you keeping? Please sit down, all of you. Now tell us all about it. Let's sit.

PLATONOV [*laughs*]. Heavens, can that be Sergey? Where's the long hair, the fancy shirt and that nice tenor voice? Come on, speak!

SERGEY. Oh, what an ass I am. [*Laughs.*]

PLATONOV. That's a bass voice—a true bass. Shall we sit down then? Come and sit near me, Mr. Glagolyev. I sit. [*Sits.*] Sit down, everyone. Phew, isn't it hot? Smell anything, Sasha? [*They sit.*]

SASHA. Yes. [*Laughter.*]

PLATONOV. Human flesh—delightful smell! It's as if we hadn't met for ages. Winter seems to drag on for ever, hang it. There's my chair—see, Sasha? I used to sit there day in day out six months ago, seeking the meaning of life with her ladyship and gambling away your shiny ten-copeck pieces. Isn't it hot?

ANNA. I've been dying to see you. Are you well?

PLATONOV. Very much so. Your ladyship, I report that you've put on weight and are looking somewhat prettier. It's hot and stuffy today, I miss the cold weather already.

ANNA. Yes, they've both filled out madly, lucky people. How was life, Michael?

PLATONOV. Rotten as usual. I slept all winter, didn't see the sky for six months. I ate, drank, slept, read Mayne Reid to my wife. Rotten!

SASHA. It was all right, but of course we were bored.

PLATONOV. Not just bored, dear—paralysed. I missed you awfully, you're a sight for sore eyes. To see you, Anna, after seeing no one or only crashing bores all this dreary while—it's the height of luxury.

ANNA. That earns you a cigarette. [*Gives him one.*]

PLATONOV. Thanks. [*They light up.*]

SASHA. Did you get here yesterday?

ANNA. Yes, at ten o'clock.

PLATONOV. I saw your lights on at eleven, but I was afraid to call. I bet you were tired.

ANNA. You should have popped over, we sat up talking till two.

[SASHA *whispers in* PLATONOV's *ear.*]

PLATONOV. Damnation! [*Slaps his forehead.*] What a memory—why didn't you tell me before? Sergey!

SERGEY. Yes?

PLATONOV. He's struck dumb too. Gets married and doesn't breathe a word. [*Gets up.*] I forget and they don't mention it.

SASHA. I forgot too, what with all his talk. [*To* SERGEY.] Congratulations and all the best.

PLATONOV. I have the honour—. [*Bows.*] I wish you every happiness, man. It's marvellous, I never thought you'd take the plunge. What speed off the mark. Who'd have expected anything so odd?

SERGEY. Good for me, eh? Quick off the mark! [*Laughs.*] I never contemplated anything so odd myself—it was fixed in a jiffy, old boy. I fall in love. I marry.

PLATONOV. This love business went on every winter, it's the marrying that's new. You'll have to watch your step now, as our priest says.

A wife's the worst and fussiest kind of busybody. If she's stupid you're done for. Have you got a job?

SERGEY. I was offered one at a school, but I don't know. I don't really want it, the pay's poor, and anyway——

PLATONOV. Will you take it?

SERGEY. I haven't the foggiest yet—probably not.

PLATONOV. I see, so we're going to take things easy. Three years, isn't it, since we left college?

SERGEY. Yes.

PLATONOV. I see. [*Sighs.*] You need a good hiding. I'll have to speak to your wife—wasting three good years!

ANNA. It's too hot for all this palaver, I feel like yawning. Why didn't you come over before, Sasha?

SASHA. We were busy. Michael was mending the bird-cage and I was at church. The cage broke and we couldn't leave our nightingale just like that.

PORFIRY. What's on in church today—saint's day or something?

SASHA. No. I went to ask Father Constantine to hold a requiem. Today was Michael's old father's name-day, and I couldn't very well miss church. I had a mass said for him. [*Pause.*]

PORFIRY. How long since your father died, Platonov?

PLATONOV. Three, four years.

SASHA. Three years eight months.

PORFIRY. Lord, how time flies. Three years eight months. It must be some while since we last met. [*Sighs.*] It was at Ivanovka, we were both on jury service, and something happened utterly typical of the old boy. A surveyor, a wretched boozy little man, was being tried for taking bribes and [*laughs*] we found him not guilty—on your poor father's insistence. He kept on at us for two or three hours, arguing away and getting quite hot under the collar. 'I shan't find against him,' he shouts, 'till you all swear you don't take bribes either.' Illogical, but—we could do nothing with him. Quite wore us out, he did. Old General Voynitsev was with us at the time—your husband, Anna. He too was quite somebody.

ANNA. You wouldn't catch *him* letting anyone off!

PORFIRY. No, he was all set on 'guilty'. I remember them both—red in the face, fair gibbering with rage. The villagers on the jury backed the general, and the rest of us, people of our class, were for old Mr. Platonov. We won, of course. [*Laughs.*] Your father challenged the general to a duel and the general called him—sorry!—a thorough-going swine. What a lark. Later we got them drunk and they made it up—there's nothing easier than reconciling Russians. He was so kind, your father—most kind-hearted.

PLATONOV. Not kind—just feckless.

PORFIRY. A great man in his way. I thought a lot of him, we were on the best of terms.

PLATONOV. That's more than I can claim. We parted company when I was a mere boy and for the last three years we were at daggers drawn. I didn't think much of him and he thought I was no good—and we were both right. I disliked the man, I still do—for dying peacefully. He died like an honest man. To refuse to admit what a swine you are—that's the awful thing about your Russian scoundrel.

PORFIRY. *De mortuis aut bene, aut nihil.*

PLATONOV. No, that's a Latin heresy. My view is—*de omnibus aut nihil, aut veritas.* I prefer the truth to keeping quiet, though—at least you learn more. I don't think the dead need these concessions.

[IVAN *comes in.*]

SCENE VI

[*The above and* IVAN.]

IVAN. Well, well, well—my son-in-law and daughter. Stars from the Constellation Triletsky. Morning, my dears, and a salvo of greetings to you. God, it's hot. Michael, old boy——

PLATONOV [*stands up*]. Morning, Colonel. [*Embraces him.*] Fit?

IVAN. I always am. The Lord's kind and doesn't punish me. Sasha. [*Kisses* SASHA's *head.*] Haven't clapped eyes on you for ages. Are you all right?

SASHA. Yes. And you?

IVAN [*sits down by* SASHA]. I'm always fit, not a day's illness in my life. Haven't seen you for ages. Not a day but I mean to go over, see my grandson and criticize the universe with my son-in-law, but I never manage it, I'm so busy, my dears. I wanted to go over two days ago and show you my new double-barrelled shot-gun, Michael, but I was waylaid by the police inspector who made me play cards. That shot-gun's terrific. English and lethal at five hundred feet. Is baby well?

SASHA. Yes, he sends his regards.

IVAN. Is he old enough for that?

SERGEY. Metaphorically speaking, you know.

IVAN. I see. Metaphorically. Tell him to grow up quickly, Sasha, I'll take him shooting. Got a little gun lined up for him already. I'll make a sportsman of the boy so I've someone I can leave my hunting stuff to when I die.

ANNA. Isn't the colonel a darling? I'm going quail-shooting with him on St. Peter's Day.

IVAN. Oho! We'll mount an anti-snipe campaign, Anna, we'll launch a polar expedition to Satan's Bog.

ANNA. And we'll try out your new gun.

IVAN. That we will, divine Diana. [*Kisses her hand.*] Remember last year, dear? Ha ha! I like your sort, God help me, I don't like softies. This is women's emancipation with a vengeance. Sniff her shoulder and you smell gunpowder, she's a regular Amazon, a fighter, a real warrior chief. Give her a pair of epaulettes and she'd wreck the world. So let's go. And we'll take Sasha along, we'll take everyone. We'll show them what stuff the army's made of, divine Diana, your ladyship, Alexandra of Macedon.

PLATONOV. Been at the bottle, eh, Colonel?

IVAN. Of course, stands to reason.

PLATONOV. Hence all the blah, blah, blah.

IVAN. I got here about eight, old boy, when everyone was still asleep and I had nothing to do but kick my heels. I saw her come out and laugh, so we knocked back a bottle of good old madeira. Diana here drank three glasses and I dealt with the rest.

ANNA. Trust you to shout it from the roof-tops!

[NICHOLAS *runs in.*]

SCENE VII

[*The above and* NICHOLAS.]

NICHOLAS. Hallo, relatives.

PLATONOV. Aha, her ladyship's personal physician grade three. *Argentum nitricum aquae destillatae.* Glad to see you, old man. All healthy glow and shine and scent!

NICHOLAS [*kisses* SASHA'*s head*]. Old Michael's filled out, damn it, he's like a ruddy great ox.

SASHA. What a stink of scent. How are you?

NICHOLAS. Fit as a fiddle. It was a bright idea to come. [*Sits down.*] How's things, Mike?

PLATONOV. Things?

NICHOLAS. With you, of course.

PLATONOV. Oh. Who knows? It's a long story, old man, and a dull one. Where did you get that natty hair cut? Pretty stylish! Cost you a rouble?

NICHOLAS. I won't have barbers do my hair, I use women for that and if I pay them roubles, it's not for hair-dos! [*Eats fruit drops.*] You know, my dear fellow, I——

PLATONOV. Trying to be funny? Well, don't. Don't put yourself out. Spare us, please.

SCENE VIII

[*The above*, PETRIN *and* ABRAHAM. PETRIN *comes in with a news-paper and sits down.* ABRAHAM *sits in a corner.*]

NICHOLAS [*to his father*]. How about a good cry, revered parent?

IVAN. Why should I?

NICHOLAS. For joy—why not? Look at me. I'm your son. [*Points to* SASHA.] Here's your daughter. [*Points to* PLATONOV.] This young fellow's your son-in-law. Your daughter alone is a pearl beyond price, Father. Only you could have fathered such a fascinating daughter. And what about your son-in-law?

IVAN. Why cry, though, my boy? I don't see the need.

NICHOLAS. And your son-in-law? What a man! You might go to the ends of the earth and not find his like. Honest, decent, generous, fair. And take your grandson. He's no end of a lad, the little bounder. Waves his hands, holds his arms out like this. 'Where's grandpa?' he squeals. 'Bring the old pirate here. Let me pull those ruddy great whiskers!'

IVAN [*takes a handkerchief from his pocket*]. But why should I cry? Oh well, thank God. [*Cries.*] No need to cry.

NICHOLAS. Blubbing, Colonel, eh?

IVAN. No, why should I? Ah well, the Lord be praised.

PLATONOV. Stop it, Nicholas.

NICHOLAS [*stands up and sits by* BUGROV]. There's a lot of heat being generated today, Bugrov.

BUGROV. Very true, it's as hot as an oven. Ninety in the shade, I reckon.

NICHOLAS. What does it mean? Why all the heat, Bugrov?

BUGROV. You should know.

NICHOLAS. I don't, I only studied medicine.

BUGROV. I think it's hot because a cold June would strike us both as pretty funny. [*Laughter.*]

NICHOLAS. I see. Which is better for the grass, Bugrov—the climate or the atmosphere?

BUGROV. Everything's good for it, but for crops a spot of rain's more the thing. What use is a climate with no rain? It isn't worth a row of beans.

NICHOLAS. Quite, very true. Words of purest wisdom, I shouldn't wonder. What's your view of things in general, Mr. Grocer?

BUGROV [*laughs*]. I have none.

NICHOLAS. As if that needed proving! You have your head screwed on, sir. Now, how about Anna doing the impossible and giving us some food?

ANNA. Why can't you wait like everyone else?

NICHOLAS. She doesn't know how hungry we are. She doesn't know what a frightful thirst you and I have, especially the former. We'll put away the food and drink all right! To start with—. [*Whispers in* BUGROV'*s ear.*] Not bad, eh? Down the hatch—it's the same in any language. There's everything out there, to be consumed on or off the premises. Caviare, sturgeon, salmon, sardines. Then there's a six- or seven-decker pie, this big—and stuffed with sundry grotesque flora and fauna of the Old World and the New. If we could only get at it! Pretty ravenous, are you, Bugrov? Frankly——

SASHA [*to* NICHOLAS]. You're not all that hungry, you just want to make a scene. You can't bear people sitting quietly.

NICHOLAS. I can't bear people starving to death, you little dumpling.

PLATONOV. If that's meant to be funny, why is no one laughing?

ANNA. What a bore, isn't he? And what awful, ghastly cheek. You wait, you wretch. I'll give you something to eat. [*Goes out.*]

NICHOLAS. And not a moment too soon.

SCENE IX

[*The above except* ANNA.]

PLATONOV. It's not a bad idea, actually. What's the time? I'm starving too.

SERGEY. Where's my wife? Platonov hasn't seen her yet, I must introduce him. [*Gets up.*] I'll go and look for her. She likes the garden so much, you can't get her out of it.

PLATONOV. By the way, Sergey, I'd rather you didn't introduce me to your wife, I'd like to see if she recognizes me. I once knew her slightly and——

SERGEY. You knew Sonya?

PLATONOV. Once upon a time—in my student days, I think. Don't introduce me, please, and don't say anything. Not a word about me.

SERGEY. All right. The man knows everyone. When does he find time to meet them all? [*Goes in the garden.*]

NICHOLAS. What price my piece in the *Russian Courier*! Have you read the great work, everyone? Have you, Mr. Vengerovich?

ABRAHAM. Yes.

NICHOLAS. Splendid, wasn't it? I put you over as a regular vampire, didn't I? The things I wrote—why, all Europe will be shocked.

PETRIN [*guffaws*]. So that's who you meant—the one you call 'V'. But who's 'B', pray?

BUGROV [*laughs*]. That's me. [*Mops his brow.*] Confound him.

ABRAHAM. Never mind, it's all very praiseworthy. If I could write I'd certainly write for the papers. You get paid, for a start, and then in Russia writers are thought to be terribly clever, I don't know why. Only you didn't write that article, Doctor—Mr. Glagolyev did.

PORFIRY. How do you know?

ABRAHAM. I just do.

PORFIRY. That's funny. It's true I wrote it, but how did you know?

ABRAHAM. You can always find things out if you want. You sent it by registered post and—well, our post-office clerk has a good memory, that's all. It's no mystery, my Hebrew cunning has nothing to do with it. [*Laughs.*] Don't worry, I'm not going to try and get my own back.

PORFIRY. I'm not worried, but—it is odd.

[MARY *comes in.*]

SCENE X

[*The above and* MARY.]

NICHOLAS [*jumps up*]. Mary, how nice—this *is* a surprise.

MARY [*shaking hands*]. Hallo, Nicholas. [*Nods to all.*] Good morning, all.

NICHOLAS [*helps her off with her cape*]. Let me take your cape. Fit and keen? Good morning once again. [*Kisses her hand.*] How are you?

MARY. Same as usual. [*Is embarrassed and sits on the first available chair.*] Is Anna in?

NICHOLAS. Yes. [*Sits by her.*]

PORFIRY. Good morning, Mary.

IVAN. This the Grekov girl? Why, I hardly knew you. [*Goes up to* MARY *and kisses her hand.*] Nice to see you.

MARY. How do you do, Colonel? [*Coughs.*] It's terribly hot. Please don't kiss my hand, it embarrasses me—I don't like it.

PLATONOV [*goes up to* MARY]. How do you do? [*Tries to kiss her hand.*] How are you? Hey, give me your hand.

MARY [*snatches her hand away*]. No.

PLATONOV. Why? Not worthy, eh?

MARY. I don't know how worthy you are, but—you were being insincere, weren't you?

PLATONOV. Insincere? How can you tell?

MARY. You wouldn't have tried to kiss my hand if I hadn't said I disliked it. You always do like annoying me.

PLATONOV. Aren't you rather jumping to conclusions?

NICHOLAS [*to* PLATONOV]. Go away.

PLATONOV. In a minute. How's your essence of bed-bugs, Miss Grekov?

MARY. What essence?

PLATONOV. I hear you're distilling something out of bed-bugs—a contribution to science. A good idea.

MARY. You're always joking.

NICHOLAS. Yes, he's quite the funny man. Well, here you are, Mary. How's your mother keeping?

PLATONOV. Now isn't she nice and pink! Must be feeling the heat.

MARY [*stands up*]. Why are you saying all this?

PLATONOV. I want a word with you, it's ages since our last talk. But why so annoyed? Isn't it time you stopped being angry with me?

MARY. I've noticed you're never quite yourself when we meet. I don't know what bothers you about me, but—I humour you by keeping out of your way. If Nicholas hadn't sworn you wouldn't be here I'd have stayed away. [*To* NICHOLAS.] Aren't you ashamed to tell lies?

PLATONOV. Shame on you for lying, Nicholas. [*To* MARY.] You're about to cry. Carry on—tears can be a great relief.

[MARY *hurries towards the door, where she meets* ANNA.]

SCENE XI

[*The above and* ANNA.]

NICHOLAS [*to* PLATONOV]. This is downright stupid, do you hear? Any more of this and you'll answer to me.

PLATONOV. What business is it of yours?

NICHOLAS. This is silly, you don't know what you're doing.

PORFIRY. It's also rather cruel, Platonov.

ANNA. Mary, I'm so glad. [*Shakes* MARY's *hand.*] You come here so seldom, but now you are here I love you for it. Let's sit down. [*They sit down.*] So glad. It's all Nicholas's doing—he managed to get you away from your village.

NICHOLAS [*to* PLATONOV]. What if I love her?

PLATONOV. Then go ahead. Get on with it.

NICHOLAS. You don't know what you're saying.

ANNA. How are you, dear?

MARY. All right, thanks.

ANNA. You're worn out. [*Looks into her face.*] Driving fifteen miles is quite a business when you're not used to it.

MARY. No—. [*Puts her handkerchief to her eyes and cries.*] That's not it——

ANNA. What is it, Mary? [*Pause.*]

MARY. Nothing——

[NICHOLAS *walks up and down the stage.*]

PORFIRY [*to* PLATONOV]. You should apologize, Platonov.

PLATONOV. Whatever for?

PORFIRY. How can you ask? You were most unkind.

SASHA [*goes up to* PLATONOV]. Apologize, or I'm leaving. Say you're sorry.

ANNA. I often cry after a journey myself, one gets so much on edge.

PORFIRY. Now come on, I insist. You've been most unkind, I'm surprised at you.

SASHA. Apologize when you're told. Have you no shame?

ANNA. Oh, I see. [*Looks at* PLATONOV.] He's already managed to—. Sorry, Mary. I forgot to talk to this—this—. It's my fault.

PLATONOV [*goes up to* MARY]. Mary!

MARY [*raises her head*]. What do you want?

PLATONOV. I'm sorry. I apologize publicly, I'm consumed with shame, positively incinerated. Give me your hand. I mean it, I give

you my word. [*Takes her hand.*] Let's be friends and stop snivelling.
Are we friends? [*Kisses her hand.*]

MARY. Yes.

[*Covers her face with her handkerchief and runs out.* NICHOLAS
follows her.]

SCENE XII

[*The above except* MARY *and* NICHOLAS.]

ANNA. I never thought you'd go so far. Really!

PORFIRY. Go easy, Michael, for God's sake.

PLATONOV. That'll do. [*Sits on the sofa.*] Wretched girl. I was silly to
talk to her, but it isn't worth wasting words on silliness.

ANNA. Why did Triletsky go after her? Not all women like to be
seen crying.

PORFIRY. I respect women's sensitivity. You didn't say anything much,
did you? But—. One word, one little hint——

ANNA. It was very wrong of you.

PLATONOV. I've apologized, haven't I?

[*Enter* SERGEY, SONYA *and* ISAAC.]

SCENE XIII

[*The above,* SERGEY, SONYA, ISAAC *and, later,* NICHOLAS.]

SERGEY [*runs in*]. She's coming. [*Sings.*] Here she is.

[ISAAC *stands by the door, his arms folded on his chest.*]

ANNA. The heat's got Sonya down at last. Do come in.

PLATONOV [*aside*]. Sonya! God Almighty, hasn't she changed!

SONYA. I was so interested talking to Mr. Vengerovich, I quite forgot
the heat. [*Sits on the sofa about a yard away from* PLATONOV.] I
love your garden, Sergey.

PORFIRY [*sits down near* SONYA]. Sergey——

SERGEY. Yes?

PORFIRY. Sonya promised you'd all come over to my place on Thursday, old friend.

PLATONOV [*aside*]. She looked at me.

SERGEY. We'll be as good as our word and drive over *en masse*.

NICHOLAS [*comes in*]. 'Oh, women, women,' said Shakespeare. But he was wrong, he should have said 'Oh, wretched women!'

ANNA. Where's Mary?

NICHOLAS. I took her in the garden to walk it off.

PORFIRY. You've never called on me, Sonya, but you'll like my place, I hope. I've a better garden than you, a deep river and some decent horses. [*Pause.*]

ANNA. Silence. One more idiot's been born. [*Laughter.*]

SONYA [*quietly to* PORFIRY, *nodding towards* PLATONOV]. Who's this— the man sitting next to me.

PORFIRY [*laughs*]. Our schoolmaster—don't know his name.

BUGROV [*to* NICHOLAS]. Doctor, can you cure all diseases or only some?

NICHOLAS. All.

BUGROV. Anthrax included?

NICHOLAS. Yes.

BUGROV. If a mad dog bit me, could you cure that?

NICHOLAS. Why, has one bitten you? [*Moves away.*]

BUGROV [*taken aback*]. God, I hope not. Really, Doctor, draw it mild! [*Laughter.*]

ANNA. How do we reach your place, Mr. Glagolyev? Through Yusnovka?

PORFIRY. No, that's the long way round. Go straight to Platonovka. I live quite near, just over a mile away.

SONYA. I know Platonovka. It still exists then?

PORFIRY. But of course.

SONYA. I knew the owner once—name of Platonov. Any idea of his whereabouts, Sergey?

PLATONOV [*aside*]. She might ask me.

SERGEY. I think so. Can you remember his first name? [*Laughs.*]

PLATONOV. I used to know him myself, I think it's Michael. [*Laughter.*]

SONYA. That's right. Michael Platonov. I knew him as a student, almost a boy. You all laugh, but I'm afraid I don't see anything funny about it.

ANNA [*laughs and points at* PLATONOV]. Do recognize him for goodness' sake, the suspense is killing him.

[PLATONOV *gets up.*]

SONYA [*gets up and looks at* PLATONOV]. Yes, it's him. Why don't you speak, Michael? Is it really you?

PLATONOV. Don't you know me. Sonya? No wonder. Four and a half years, in fact nearly five, have passed, and they've made inroads on my face—worse than if the rats had got at it.

SONYA [*gives him her hand*]. I'm just beginning to recognize you. How you have changed.

SERGEY [*takes* SASHA *to* SONYA]. This is his wife Sasha—sister of that great wit Nicholas Triletsky.

SONYA [*shakes hands with* SASHA]. How do you do? [*Sits down.*] So you're married—doesn't time fly? Still, five years is five years.

ANNA. Good for Platonov—never goes anywhere, but knows everyone. I commend him as one of our best friends.

PLATONOV. This flowery introduction entitles me to ask you how things are, Sonya. How are you keeping?

SONYA. Things aren't too bad, but I'm keeping none too well. And you? What are you up to these days?

PLATONOV. Fate's played me a trick I never expected at the time when you thought me a second Byron, and I saw myself as a Christopher Columbus and Cabinet Minister rolled into one. I'm just a schoolmaster.

SONYA. What—you!

PLATONOV. Yes, me. [*Pause.*] I suppose it is a bit funny.

SONYA. It's grotesque. But why—couldn't you have done better?

PLATONOV. I can't answer that in one sentence. [*Pause.*]

SONYA. You at least got your degree, didn't you?

PLATONOV. No, I gave it up.

SONYA. But you're still human aren't you?

PLATONOV. Sorry, I don't quite understand.

SONYA. I put it badly. You're still a man, you can still work, I mean to say, in the field of—freedom, say, or women's emancipation. There's nothing to stop you serving an ideal, is there?

NICHOLAS [*aside*]. The girl's talking through her hat.

PLATONOV [*aside*]. I see. [*To her.*] How can I put it? Perhaps there is nothing to stop me, but then how could there be? [*Laughs.*] How can anything stop me when I'm not in motion anyway? I'm like a great rock—a stumbling block, in fact.

[SHCHERBUK *comes in.*]

SCENE XIV

[*The above and* SHCHERBUK.]

SHCHERBUK [*in the doorway*]. Don't give my horses any oats, they pulled so badly.

ANNA. Oh good, my boy friend's here.

ALL. Paul. Mr. Shcherbuk.

SHCHERBUK [*silently kisses* ANNA's *and* SASHA's *hands, silently bows to the men in turn, then bows to the whole company*]. Friends, will anyone tell an unworthy specimen where the person is that he yearns to see? I strongly suspect that it's she. [*Points at* SONYA. *To* ANNA.] Will you introduce me to the lady—give her some idea what I'm like?

ANNA [*takes his arm and leads him to* SONYA]. Paul Shcherbuk, retired cornet of guards.

SHCHERBUK. Can't you put more feeling in it?

ANNA. Sorry—friend, neighbour, escort, guest and creditor.

SHCHERBUK. Quite right, I was the old general's bosom friend. Used to make conquests under his supervision—lead the ladies a dance, in other words. [*Bows.*] May I kiss your hand?

SONYA [*holds out her hand and snatches it back*]. Very charming, but—no.

SHCHERBUK. I'm hurt. I held your husband in my arms when he was no higher than this table, and he left a mark on me that I'll carry till my dying day. [*Opens his mouth.*] See? Tooth missing, isn't there? [*Laughter.*] I held him in my arms, but he knocked out my tooth with a pistol he happened to be playing with. That put me in my place, ha, ha, ha! Oh, he was quite a handful. You must keep him in hand, ma'am—don't know your name. Your beauty reminds me of some picture, but the nose is different. Can't I kiss your hand?

[PETRIN *sits by* ABRAHAM *and reads him something from the newspaper.*]

SONYA [*holds out her hand*]. If you insist then——

SHCHERBUK [*kisses her hand*]. Thanking you kindly. [*To* PLATONOV.] How are you, Michael? Quite a lad you've grown into! [*Sits down.*] When I knew you, you were still the wide-eyed innocent. But he does keep growing, doesn't he? I won't go on or I'll bring bad luck. You're one hell of a good-looking fellow, though. Why not join the army, boy?

PLATONOV. I've a weak chest.

SHCHERBUK [*points at* NICHOLAS]. Is that what he says? Trust that ass and you'll find yourself minus a head.

NICHOLAS. Don't be rude, Shcherbuk.

SHCHERBUK. He treated me for back trouble. It was 'don't eat this, don't eat that, don't sleep on the floor'. And then he never cured me. 'Why take my money when you didn't cure me?' I ask him. 'It was one thing or the other,' says he—'either cure you or take your money.' Isn't he priceless?

NICHOLAS. Don't talk such nonsense, monster. What did you pay me, may I ask? Six times I visited you, remember, and got one rouble— a torn note too. I offered it to a beggar, but he wouldn't take it, said it was torn and the number was missing.

SHCHERBUK. My illness didn't bring him over six times, it was my tenant's daughter, who's quite something.

NICHOLAS. Platonov, you're sitting near him—bang that hairless pate with my compliments, be a good fellow.

SHCHERBUK. Oh, pack it in, let sleeping dogs lie. Children should be seen and not heard. [*To* PLATONOV.] Your father was a bit of a lad too. We were great friends, the old boy and I. He loved his little joke—you don't find jokers like him and me these days. Those were the days. [*To* PETRIN.] Hey, Petrin, for heaven's sake! Read the paper while we're talking, would you? Where are your manners?

[PETRIN *goes on reading.*]

SASHA [*jogs* IVAN's *shoulder*]. Don't go to sleep here, Father, aren't you ashamed?

[IVAN *wakes up, but falls asleep again a minute later.*]

SHCHERBUK. No, I can't go on. [*Stands up.*] Better listen to him, he's reading.

PETRIN [*stands up and goes over to* PLATONOV]. What did you say, sir?

PLATONOV. Nothing whatever.

PETRIN. Yes, you did, you mentioned me.

PLATONOV. You must have imagined it.

PETRIN. A bit censorious, aren't you?

PLATONOV. I didn't speak. You imagined it, I tell you.

PETRIN. Oh, talk away for all I care. Petrin this, Petrin that. What about Petrin? [*Puts the newspaper in his pocket.*] Perhaps Petrin was at university, perhaps he took a law degree. Or didn't you know? I shall carry my degree to my grave with me. Yes sir. And I'm quite high up in the civil service, I'd have you know. I've been around a bit longer than you—I'll soon be sixty, praise God.

PLATONOV. Very nice too, but where does it get us?

PETRIN. When you're as old as me, boy, you'll know. It's no joke, life isn't, it can turn nasty on you.

PLATONOV [*shrugs*]. I really don't know what you mean, Petrin, can't make you out. First you're on about yourself, then you get on to life. What has being alive to do with you? I don't see any connection.

PETRIN. When life's shaken you up and broken you, you'll start giving young people a wide berth. Life, sir—well, what is it? Man takes one of three roads at birth—there are only three. Turn right and be eaten by wolves. Or turn left and eat them. Or else carry straight on and eat yourself.

PLATONOV. Amazing. I see. Did you reach this conclusion empirically?

PETRIN. I did.

PLATONOV. Oh, did you? [*Laughs.*] Tell that to the marines, my dear Petrin. In fact you'll spare me this high-minded chat if you take my advice. It makes me laugh and I honestly don't believe it. I distrust your senile, home-spun wisdom. You're old friends of my father, but I profoundly distrust—and I mean what I say—your homely talk of complex things and all the various bees in your bonnets.

PETRIN. Oh, indeed. You **can** make anything out of a young sapling,

I suppose—a house, a ship and so on. But an old tree's too tall and wide to be any use, of course.

PLATONOV. I'm not talking about just any old men, I mean my father's old friends.

PORFIRY. I was one too, you know.

PLATONOV. He had any amount of them, sometimes our whole yard was jammed with carriages.

PORFIRY. But—you mean you don't trust me either? [*Laughs.*]

PLATONOV. How can I put it? No, I don't trust you much either.

PORFIRY. Oh? [*Holds out his hand.*] Thanks for being so blunt, boy, it makes me like you more than ever.

PLATONOV. You're a good sort. I think a lot of you actually, but——

PORFIRY. Come on, out with it.

PLATONOV. But—. One would have to be frightfully gullible to believe in these absurd characters from eighteenth-century Russian plays—these respectable fuddy-duddies and smarmy worthies from Fonvizin who've spent their lives hobnobbing with the scum of the earth, not to mention various tyrants who are thought saintly because they do neither good nor harm. Please don't be annoyed.

ANNA. I don't like this kind of talk, especially from Platonov. It always ends badly. Michael, meet our new friend. [*Points to* ISAAC.] Isaac Vengerovich, student.

PLATONOV. Oh. [*Gets up and goes towards* ISAAC.] Delighted indeed. [*Holds out his hand.*] What I'd give to be a student again. [*Pause.*] I'm trying to shake hands, so either take mine or give me yours.

ISAAC. I won't do either.

PLATONOV. What!

ISAAC. I won't shake hands with you.

PLATONOV. This is highly mysterious. And why not?

ANNA [*aside*]. What the blazes——

ISAAC. I know what I'm doing. I despise your sort.

PLATONOV. Loud cheers. [*Looks him over.*] Awfully good, all this. Or so I'd say, but I don't want to tickle your ego—you want to look after that, you may need it later. [*Pause.*] You look down at me from a great height. No doubt you're some kind of giant.

ISAAC. I'm an honest man, not a cheap mediocrity.

PLATONOV. Oh, congratulations. Of course one hardly expects dis-
honesty in a young student, but it happens that your honesty isn't
under discussion. So you won't shake hands, boy?

ISAAC. I don't feel all that charitable.

[NICHOLAS *hisses.*]

PLATONOV. So you won't shake hands? Have it your own way. I
was talking about good manners, not about your views on charity.
Do you despise me very much?

ISAAC. As much as any man who heartily loathes scroungers, phoneys
and mediocrities.

PLATONOV [*sighs*]. I haven't heard this sort of thing for ages, it's quite
like the old days. At one time I was pretty good at dishing it out
myself. Unfortunately it's all just talk—all very nice, but a lot of
hot air. Oh for one grain of sincerity! False notes jar terribly when
one's not used to them.

ISAAC. How about changing the subject?

PLATONOV. Why? The audience is enjoying it and we're not yet
utterly sick of each other. Let's carry on in the same vein.

[VASILY *runs in, followed by* OSIP.]

SCENE XV

[*The above and* OSIP.]

OSIP [*comes in*]. Hurrumph! Honoured and delighted to congratulate
your ladyship on your safe arrival. [*Pause.*] May all your prayers be
granted. [*Laughter.*]

PLATONOV. Who's this I see? The devil's bosom pal? The scourge of
the neighbourhood? The fiend in human shape?

ANNA. Really, this is the last straw! What brought you here?

OSIP. I came to pay my respects.

ANNA. You needn't have bothered. Now go and lose yourself.

PLATONOV. So it's you, the man who strikes terror by day and night.
Haven't seen you for ages, you apocalyptic beast. Aren't you going
to hold forth, my murderous friend? Pray silence for great Osip!

OSIP [*bows*]. Glad to see your ladyship. Best wishes to you, Mr. Voynitsev, on the occasion of your marriage. Best of luck on the family side—all the best of everything.

SERGEY. Thank you. [*To* SONYA.] This is the family bogyman.

ANNA. Don't let him stay, Platonov, he must leave. I'm very annoyed with him. [*To* OSIP.] Tell them to give you a meal in the kitchen. Look at his eyes, like a wild beast. How much of our timber did you steal this winter?

OSIP [*laughs*]. Only three or four trees. [*Laughter.*]

ANNA [*laughs*]. Rubbish, you stole more. Why, he's got a watch chain! I really believe it's gold. May I ask what time it is?

OSIP [*looks at the clock on the wall*]. Twenty-two minutes past one. May I kiss your hand?

ANNA [*lifts her hand to his lips*]. All right then.

OSIP [*kisses her hand*]. Thank you for your kindness, ma'am. [*Bows.*] Why are you holding me, Mr. Platonov?

PLATONOV. I don't want you to go. I like you, old man, you're a hell of a fellow, damn you! But what possessed you to call here, O sage?

OSIP. I was chasing that ass Vasily and took the chance to drop in.

PLATONOV. A wise man chasing a fool—shouldn't it be the other way round? Ladies and gentlemen, I have the honour to present a fascinating specimen. One of the most intriguing carnivores from the contemporary circus. [*Turns* OSIP *in all directions.*] Known to one and all as Osip—horse-thief, parasite, murderer, burglar. Born in Voynitsevka, he's done his murders and burglaries in that village and it's there he's finishing his rake's progress. [*Laughter.*]

OSIP [*laughs*]. You are a funny one, Mr. Platonov.

NICHOLAS [*looks* OSIP *over*]. What's your job, my man?

OSIP. Thieving, sir.

NICHOLAS. I see. A nice sort of job. You're pretty cynical, I must say.

OSIP. What's cynical?

NICHOLAS. Cynic's a Greek word. Translated into your language it means someone who's a filthy swine and doesn't care ho knows it.

PLATONOV. Ye gods, he grins! And what a grin! And look at his face —solid concrete, they don't come any tougher. [*Takes him to a mirror.*] Look, monster. See? Aren't you amazed?

OSIP. I'm no better than the next man. Worse perhaps.

PLATONOV. Think so? But you're a hero, you're quite fabulous. [*Claps him on the shoulder.*] O bold, conquering Russian! You put us all in the shade, us miserable little parasites, with our fidgeting and mooning around. We ought to go into the desert with you and the knights of old. We should have a go at some of those giants with two-ton heads and all their hissing and whistling. I believe you'd take on the devil himself.

OSIP. Don't rightly know, sir.

PLATONOV. You'd soon settle his hash, you're tough enough, with those muscles like steel cables. Why aren't you in prison, by the way?

ANNA. Platonov, stop it, this is a bore.

PLATONOV. Done time, haven't you, Osip?

OSIP. I've been inside—every winter, actually.

PLATONOV. Very right and proper. It's cold in the woods, so go to prison. But why aren't you there now?

OSIP. I don't know. Can I go now, sir?

PLATONOV. A bit out of this world, aren't you? Outside time and space? Above custom and the law?

OSIP. Look, sir. The law says you can only be sent to Siberia if you're caught red-handed or there's proof against you. Everyone knows I'm a thief and a villain, granted [*laughs*], but not everyone can prove it. People are so feeble these days, they're stupid, haven't any sense. They're always afraid, so they're afraid to give evidence. They could get me deported, but they don't know their law. They're afraid of everything. In fact your peasant's an ass, sir. They gang up and do things behind your back, oh, they're a rotten, miserable lot. Shocking ignorant they are. They deserve what they get, that bunch.

PLATONOV. What pompous talk, you swine. Got it all worked out, haven't you? Repulsive animal! All based on theory! [*Sighs.*] What rotten things can still happen in Russia.

OSIP. I'm not the only one, sir, everyone's this way nowadays—take Mr. Vengerovich here——

PLATONOV. Yes, but he's outside the law too. We all know it, no one can prove it.

ABRAHAM. Can't you leave me out of it?

PLATONOV [*to* OSIP]. No point bringing him in, he's the same as you, except for having more sense and being happy as a sandboy. And one can't quite tell him what one thinks of him—unlike you. You're both tarred with the same brush, but—. He owns sixty taverns, man —sixty! You don't own sixty copecks.

ABRAHAM. Sixty-three, actually.

PLATONOV. It'll be seventy-three by next year. He gives to charity, holds dinner parties. People respect him, take their hats off to him, while you—you may be a great man, but you don't know how to live, boy. You haven't the art, you rascal.

ABRAHAM. This is getting a bit fanciful, Platonov. [*Gets up and sits on another chair.*]

PLATONOV. He's better insured against sudden storms. He'll live in peace to twice his present age, if not longer, and he'll die a peaceful death, won't he?

ANNA. Stop it, Platonov.

SERGEY. Take it easy, Michael. Osip, please leave, you only bring out the worst in Platonov.

ABRAHAM. He'd like to get rid of me too, but he won't.

PLATONOV. I will—or else I'll leave myself.

ANNA. Will you stop, Platonov? Don't beat about the bush—will you give over or not?

SASHA. For heaven's sake be quiet. [*Quietly.*] This isn't very nice, you're letting me down.

PLATONOV [*to* OSIP]. Buzz off! I heartily wish you may get lost double quick.

OSIP. A friend of mine called Martha has a parrot that calls everyone 'you fool'—dogs too. But when it sees a hawk or Mr. Vengerovich, it shouts, 'Damn you!' [*Laughs.*] Good-bye. [*Goes.*]

SCENE XVI

[*The above except* OSIP.]

ABRAHAM. Don't lecture me, boy, or adopt that line—you're the last person who should take such a liberty. I'm a citizen and, I can truthfully say, a useful one. I'm a father. But what are you, boy? A popinjay, sir, a bankrupt squire too corrupt to parade as a crusader.

PLATONOV. If you're a citizen, that makes citizen a very dirty word indeed.

ANNA. Won't he stop? Must you wreck our day with your harangues? Why talk so much, what right have you?

NICHOLAS. These paragons of justice and honesty are uncomfortable to live with, they must have a finger in every pie.

PORFIRY. I say, isn't this getting rather out of hand?

ANNA [*to* PLATONOV]. Quarrelsome guests embarrass their hosts, remember?

SERGEY. True, so let's all simmer down this instant. Let's have peace, harmony and silence.

ABRAHAM. He's always badgering me. What have I done to him? The man's a mountebank!

SERGEY. Shush!

NICHOLAS. Let them quarrel, it's more amusing. [*Pause.*]

PLATONOV. When you look around and really think, you feel ready to faint. Anyone at all decent and tolerable holds his tongue and just looks on, that's what's so awful. They all stand in awe of this bloated upstart and kow-tow to him. Everyone's in his clutches. Decency's flown out of the window.

ANNA. Take it easy, Platonov. This is last year's business all over again, and that I can't stand.

PLATONOV [*drinks water*]. All right. [*Sits down.*]

ABRAHAM. All right. [*Pause.*]

SHCHERBUK. I'm in agony, friends—agony.

ANNA. What is it now?

SHCHERBUK. I'm so unhappy, everyone. Better be dead and buried than live with a bad wife. There's been another to-do. Last week she and that blasted, red-haired lover-boy of hers practically murdered me. I'm sleeping out of doors under the apple-tree enjoying my dreams and looking enviously on scenes from my past life. [*Sighs.*] Then all of a sudden there's a great blow on my head. Help! My last hour's come, thinks I. Is it an earthquake? The elements in conflict, a flood, a rain of fire? I open my eyes and there's friend Ginger. Catches me round the middle in a ruddy great bear hug, then hurls me on the ground. Up jumps that evil woman, grips me by my innocent beard. [*Clutches his beard.*] It was no joke. [*Hits his bald head.*] They nearly killed me, I thought my hour had come.

ANNA. You're exaggerating.

SHCHERBUK. She's an old woman. She's as old as they come, all skin and bone, the old hag—and she has to have a lover. Old bitch! That suits Ginger down to the ground, of course. It's my money, not her love, he's after.

[JACOB *comes in and hands* ANNA *a visiting card.*]

SERGEY. Who's that from?

ANNA. Oh, do be quiet, Mr. Shcherbuk. [*Reads.*] 'Le Comte Glagolyev.' Why so much ceremony? Please ask him in. [*To* PORFIRY.] Your son.

PORFIRY. My son? Where's he sprung from? He's abroad.

[CYRIL *comes in.*]

SCENE XVII

[*The above and* CYRIL.]

ANNA. My dear Cyril, this is nice.

PORFIRY [*stands up*]. So you're here? [*Sits down.*]

CYRIL. Morning, ladies, Platonov, Vengerovich, Triletsky. So the eccentric Mr. Platonov's here. Best wishes, all. It's fearfully hot in Russia. I'm straight from Paris, straight from French soil. Phew! You don't believe me? My word of honour. I just took my suitcase home. Well, everyone, Paris is quite a town!

SERGEY. Sit down, Frenchman.

CYRIL. No, no, no. I'm not staying, just dropped in. I only need a word with Father. [*To his father.*] Now look here, what does this mean?

PORFIRY. What does what mean?

CYRIL. Trying to pick a quarrel? Why didn't you send me the money I asked for?

PORFIRY. We can talk about that at home.

CYRIL. Why didn't you send me the money? Laughing, are you, think it's just a joke? Oh, very funny! Ladies and gentlemen, can a man live abroad without money?

ANNA. How did you get on in Paris? Do sit down, Cyril.

CYRIL. Thanks to him I came back with only a toothbrush. Thirty-five telegrams I sent him from Paris. Why didn't you send me money, eh? Red in the face, are you? Feeling ashamed of yourself?

NICHOLAS. Don't shout, your lordship. If you won't stop I'll send your visiting card to the police and prosecute you for passing yourself off as a count. It's not decent.

PORFIRY. Don't make a scene, Cyril. I thought six thousand was enough. Do calm down.

CYRIL. Give me some money so I can go back again. Give it me right away. I'm just leaving, so hurry up. No time to waste.

ANNA. Why the great rush? You've plenty of time. Tell us about your travels instead.

JACOB [*comes in*]. Lunch is served, madam.

ANNA. Oh, in that case let's go and eat.

NICHOLAS. Lunch, eh? Loud cheers! [*Takes* SASHA's *arm with one hand and* CYRIL's *with the other and starts to run off.*]

SASHA. Let me go, you lunatic. I can get there without your help.

CYRIL. Let go, you lout. I don't like jokes. [*Breaks away.*]

[SASHA *and* NICHOLAS *run out.*]

ANNA [*takes* CYRIL's *arm*]. Come, Mr. Parisian, don't get hot under the collar. [*To* ABRAHAM *and* BUGROV.] Lunch, gentlemen. [*Goes out with* CYRIL.]

BUGROV [*stands up and stretches*]. You could starve to death waiting for lunch here. [*Goes out.*]

PLATONOV [*offers* SONYA *his arm*]. May I? Don't look so surprised. This is an unknown world to you—a world [*in a quieter voice*] of idiots, Sonya, complete, utter, hopeless idiots. [*Goes out with* SONYA.]

ABRAHAM [*to his son*]. See what I mean?

ISAAC. A most original scoundrel. [*Goes out with his father.*]

SERGEY [*nudges* IVAN]. Lunch, Colonel.

IVAN [*jumps up*]. Eh? Who's that?

SERGEY. No one. Come and have lunch.

IVAN. Splendid, old boy. [*Goes out with* SERGEY *and* SHCHERBUK.]

SCENE XVIII

[PETRIN *and* PORFIRY.]

PETRIN. Are you game then?

PORFIRY. I don't mind, as I said before.

PETRIN. So you'll really marry her, old man?

PORFIRY. I don't know, old boy. Is she at all keen?

PETRIN. You bet your life she is.

PORFIRY. I don't know, one mustn't take things for granted. You never know what's at the back of people's minds. But where do you come in?

PETRIN. My concern for you, old boy. You're a good man, she's a fine woman. Shall I put in a word?

PORFIRY. No, I'll do that. Keep it to yourself, please try not to fuss, I'm quite capable of marrying without assistance. [*Goes out.*]

PETRIN [*alone*]. If only he were! Holy Moses, put yourselves in my place. If Anna Voynitsev marries him, I'm rich, I'll get back all the money I lent her, by God! The idea's so marvellous, I don't think I can eat my lunch. Dost thou, Anna, take this man Porfiry to be thy wedded husband? Or should it be the other way round?

[ANNA *comes in.*]

SCENE XIX

[PETRIN *and* ANNA.]

ANNA. Why don't you come and have lunch?

PETRIN. Can you take a hint, Anna dear?

ANNA. Yes, but be quick about it, I'm busy.

PETRIN. I see. How about giving me a spot of cash, dear?

ANNA. Hint! I don't call that a hint. How much? One rouble? Two?

PETRIN. Can't you do something about that money you owe me? I'm fed up with IOUs—they're a great fraud, a mirage. The money's yours on paper, but in practice it isn't.

ANNA. You're not still on about that sixty thousand? Aren't you ashamed? I don't know how you have the nerve to bother me about it—scandalous! What can an old bachelor like you want with the wretched stuff?

PETRIN. It just happens to be mine, dear lady.

ANNA. You wangled those IOUs out of my husband when he was drunk and ill, remember?

PETRIN. What do you mean? That's what IOUs are for, so you can present them for payment. Accounts should be settled.

ANNA. All right, that will do. I've no money and never shall have for your sort. Run along and sue me, Mr. Legal Eagle. All this jiggery-pokery when you've already got one foot in the grave! You *are* funny.

PETRIN. May I drop a hint, dear?

ANNA. You may not. [*Moves towards the door.*] Come and have some grub.

PETRIN. One moment, dear lady. Do you like friend Porfiry?

ANNA. Mind your own business and keep your nose out of mine, even if you do have a law degree.

PETRIN. Mind my own business! [*Beats his chest.*] And who, might I ask, was the late Major-General's best friend? Who closed his eyes when he died?

ANNA. You, you, you—and much good may it do you.

PETRIN. I'll go and drink to his memory. [*Sighs.*] And to you too. You're proud and arrogant, madam. Pride's a vice. [*Goes out.*]

[PLATONOV *comes in.*]

SCENE XX

[ANNA *and* PLATONOV.]

PLATONOV. What damned cheek! You tell him to go and he blandly stays put—a self-centred, money-grubbing oaf if ever I saw one. What are you thinking about, madam?

ANNA. Have you calmed down?

PLATONOV. Yes, but don't let's be annoyed. [*Kisses her hand.*] Your guests all deserve to be sent packing, dearest lady.

ANNA. I'd love to throw them out myself, you awful man. You were holding forth about decency and making some digs at me. But it's

easy enough to be decent in theory, the trouble comes when you try
to put it into practice. Neither you nor I have the right to chuck them
out, my eloquent friend. They're our patrons and creditors, you see.
I've only to look at them the wrong way and we'll be put off this
estate tomorrow. It's my honour or my estate, you see. I've chosen
the estate. Make what you like of it, my talkative friend, and unless
you want me to leave this delightful neighbourhood, don't talk to
me about decency and don't interfere. Someone's calling me. Let's
go for a ride this afternoon, and don't you dare go away! [*Claps
him on the shoulder.*] We'll have some fun. Come and eat. [*Goes out.*]

PLATONOV [*after a pause*]. I'll boot him out none the less, I'll have
them all out. Stupid and bad-mannered it may be, but I'll do it. I
swore I'd leave these swine alone, but I can't help it. You can't keep
a good man down—still less a weakling.

[ISAAC *comes in.*]

SCENE XXI

[PLATONOV *and* ISAAC.]

ISAAC. Look here, Mr. Schoolmaster, I'd advise you to leave my father
alone.

PLATONOV. I'm grateful for your advice.

ISAAC. I'm not joking. My father has a lot of friends, so he can easily
get you sacked. I'm warning you.

PLATONOV. Very decent of you, boy. What's your first name?

ISAAC. Isaac.

PLATONOV. So Abraham begat Isaac, did he? Thank you, my noble
young friend. Now, will you in turn kindly give your dear daddy this
message? For all I care he and his many friends can go and boil their
heads. Now get some food, boy, or you'll find it's all gone.

ISAAC [*shrugs his shoulders and moves towards the door*]. This is funny, if
not downright silly. [*Stops.*] Don't think I'm annoyed with you
for bothering my father because I'm not. I'm not annoyed, I'm
simply observing—studying you as a typical modern square peg in a
round hole. I understand you all too well. If you were happy, if you
weren't so bored and idle, you'd leave my father alone, believe me.
You aren't seeking the meaning of life, my dear misfit, you're just
indulging yourself, having a good time. There are no serfs these

C 4534   E

days, so you have to find someone else to take it out of, which is why you pitch into every Tom, Dick and Harry.

PLATONOV [*laughs*]. This is really good, honestly. You know, you actually have some degree of imagination.

ISAAC. You never pick on my father in private—that sticks out a mile, that's what's so disgusting. You stage your little entertainment in the drawing-room where fools can see you in all your glory. Quite the showman, aren't you?

PLATONOV. I'd like a word with you in about ten years, or even five. I wonder how you'll last. Will the tone of voice and flashing eyes still be intact? But I fear you'll go down the drain, boy. How are your studies? Not well, I see from your face. You'll come to no good. Anyway, go and get your lunch. I shan't talk to you any more, I dont like that bad-tempered face.

ISAAC [*laughs*]. You're quite the sensitive plant! [*Goes towards the door.*] I'd rather seem bad-tempered than look as if I wanted a good punch on the jaw.

PLATONOV. No doubt, but run along and eat.

ISAAC. We're not on speaking terms, and don't you forget it. [*Goes out.*]

PLATONOV [*alone*]. That young fool thinks a lot and talks a lot—behind people's backs. [*Looks through the door of the dining-room.*] She's looking round, looking for me with those lovely, soft eyes. How pretty she still is, how beautiful her face is. Her hair's the same, same colour and style. How often I've kissed that hair and what wonderful memories that little head brings back. [*Pause.*] Can I really be so old that I must live on memories? [*Pause.*] Memories are all right in a way, but—is my day really over? God, I hope not, I'd rather be dead. I must live, must go on living. I'm still young.

[SERGEY *comes in.*]

SCENE XXII

[PLATONOV, SERGEY *and, later,* NICHOLAS.]

SERGEY [*comes in and wipes his mouth with a napkin*]. Come and drink Sonya's health, don't hide in here. Well?

PLATONOV. I've been admiring your wife—magnificent woman.

[SERGEY *laughs.*]

PLATONOV. You're a lucky man.

SERGEY. Quite true. Well, actually, er—one can't call me always lucky, but I suppose I usually am.

PLATONOV [*looks through the dining-room door*]. I've known her for ages, Sergey, I know her pretty well in fact. She's very good-looking, but not a patch on what she used to be. Pity you didn't know her then —what a lovely woman!

SERGEY. Yes.

PLATONOV. What eyes.

SERGEY. And what hair.

PLATONOV. She was a splendid girl. [*Laughs.*] But what about my Sasha! There's a real peasant for you. There she is, you can just see her behind the vodka decanter. All hot and bothered about my behaviour. In agony, poor thing, because I'm in bad odour over my slanging match with Vengerovich.

SERGEY. Excuse my asking, but are you happy together?

PLATONOV. She's my wife, man. If I lost her, I think I'd go to seed completely. Good old family life—you'll learn in good time. It's a pity you haven't knocked around enough and don't know what a good thing a family is. I wouldn't take a million roubles for dear old Sasha. She's a fool and I'm a dead loss, so we get on like a house on fire.

[NICHOLAS *comes in.*]

PLATONOV [*to* NICHOLAS]. Been tanking up?

NICHOLAS. Not half. [*Slaps his stomach.*] Good solid stuff. Come on, boys and girls, have a drink! Little welcome-home celebration! Good old pals! [*Embraces both together.*] Come and have a drink. Ah well. [*Stretches.*] Ah well, such is life. Happy the man who doth not visit the congregation of the unrighteous. [*Stretches.*] Good old pals! Lot of dirty scoundrels!

PLATONOV Seen your patients to-day?

NICHOLAS. Tell you later. Look here, Michael, once and for all, will you leave me alone? I'm sick and tired of you and your lectures. Have a heart! You'll get no change out of me, I can tell you that. If you can't help coming out with these things, let me have your stuff in writing—I'll learn it by heart. Or lecture me at some definite time of day. You can have one hour a day, say four to five in the afternoon, eh? I'll even pay you a rouble an hour. [*Stretches.*] The whole day long——

PLATONOV [*to* SERGEY]. I say, what's the idea of that advertisement in the *Gazette*? Has it really come to that?

SERGEY. No, don't worry. [*Laughs.*] It's a little business deal. There'll be an auction and Glagolyev will buy the estate. He'll get the bank off our necks and we'll pay him the interest instead. It's his idea.

PLATONOV. I don't get it. What's in it for him? Or is he just being generous? I don't understand such generosity, and I can't see that you—well, need it.

SERGEY. No. Actually, I don't quite see it either. Better ask Mother, she'll explain. I only know that we'll keep the estate after the sale and we'll pay Glagolyev for it. Mother's giving him a down payment of five thousand straight away. He's easier to deal with than the bank, anyway. God, am I fed up with that bank! I'm even more sick of it than Triletsky is of you. Don't let's talk business. [*Takes* PLATONOV *by the arm.*] Come on, we'll drink and be friends. Nicholas, come on, old man. [*Takes* NICHOLAS *by the arm.*] Let's drink and be friends, friends. I don't care if I lose all I possess, and to hell with these commercial transactions, as long as those I love are alive and well—you, my Sonya and my mother-in-law. You're my whole life. Come on.

PLATONOV. Coming. I'll drink to all that, so I'll probably drink you dry. I haven't been drunk for ages and I feel like really pushing the boat out.

ANNA [*through the door*]. So this is what friendship means. A fine team you three make. [*Sings.*] 'When I harness three fleet horses——'

NICHOLAS. 'Yes, a team of nut-brown horses.' Let's start on the brandy, boys.

ANNA [*through the door*]. Come and eat, you scroungers, it's all cold.

PLATONOV. So this is friendship. I've always been lucky in love but never in friendship. I'm afraid you too may all come to regret my friendship. Let's drink to the happy ending of all friendships, our own included. May it end as quietly and peacefully as its beginning. [*Goes into the dining-room.*]

END OF ACT ONE

ACT TWO

PART ONE

The garden. In the foreground a flowerbed which has a path round it and a statue in the middle with a lampion on top. Benches, chairs, small tables. On the right, the front of the house with porch. Open windows through which comes the sound of laughter, conversation, and of a piano and violin playing quadrilles, waltzes and so on. At the back of the garden, a Chinese summer-house festooned with lanterns, and with the monogram 'S.V.' over the entrance. Beyond that a game of skittles is in progress, the rolling of balls is heard and shouts: 'Five down, four up' and so on. The garden and house are lit up. Guests and servants dart about the garden. VASILY *and* JACOB *(drunk and in tails) hang up lanterns and light lampions.*

SCENE I

[BUGROV *and* NICHOLAS, *who wears a peaked cap with a cockade.*]

NICHOLAS [*comes out of doors arm-in-arm with* BUGROV]. Come on, it's nothing to you—I'm only asking for a loan.

BUGROV. Don't be hard on me, sir, I honestly can't.

NICHOLAS. But you can, Bugrov, you can afford anything. You could buy the universe twice over, but you can't be bothered. I only want a loan, man, don't you see? I swear I'll never pay it back.

BUGROV. You see! Let the cat out of the bag there, didn't you?

NICHOLAS. I see nothing except how callous you are. Come on, great man, hand over. Come on, man. I ask you—beg you then. Are you really so unfeeling? Have a heart.

BUGROV [*sighs*]. Well, Doctor, you may not cure your patients, but you certainly know how to present your bill.

NICHOLAS. Well said. [*Sighs.*] You're right.

BUGROV [*takes out his wallet*]. You're always making fun of people, always ready with your sniggers. You shouldn't, you know, you really shouldn't. I haven't much book-learning, but I am a Christian, same as you brainy fellows. If I say something silly, put me right—

don't just laugh. No sir. We're only peasants, we're a rough, thick-skinned lot, so don't expect too much—make allowances. [*Opens his wallet.*] For the last time. [*Counts.*] One, six, twelve.

NICHOLAS [*looks into the wallet*]. Ye gods! And Russians are always said to be broke! Where did you pick up that lot?

BUGROV. Fifty. [*Gives him the money.*] For the last time.

NICHOLAS. What's that little note? Hand that over too, it's looking at me with tears in its eyes. [*Takes the money.*] Come on, hand over.

BUGROV [*gives it to him*]. Take it. You are greedy, though.

NICHOLAS. What, all in one-rouble notes? Been going round begging or something? Not forgeries, are they?

BUGROV. Give them back if they're forgeries.

NICHOLAS. I would if you needed them. Thanks, and may you put on still more weight and get a medal. But tell me, why do you lead such an odd life? You drink a lot, you talk in that deep voice, you sweat, and you don't sleep at the right times. Why aren't you asleep now, for instance? You're a bilious, bad-tempered little grocer with high blood pressure and you ought to go to bed early. And you have more veins than ordinary people. How can you kill yourself like this?

BUGROV. I say——

NICHOLAS. Oh, you do, do you? Anyway, don't be frightened, I'm only joking. You're not ready to die yet, you'll survive. Pretty well-heeled, aren't you, Bugrov?

BUGROV. I've enough to last my day.

NICHOLAS. You're a nice, clever fellow, but a great rogue. Excuse me, I'm speaking as a friend. We are friends, aren't we? A great rogue. Why are you buying up Voynitsev's debts and lending him money?

BUGROV. That's a bit out of your depth, sir.

NICHOLAS. So you want to get your paws on Anna Voynitsev's mine, you and Vengerovich? She's to take pity on her stepson and give him the mine to save him from going bankrupt, is that the idea? You're a great man, but a rogue—a real shark.

BUGROV. Now I'm going to have a nap somewhere near the summer-house. Will you wake me up when supper's ready?

NICHOLAS. Splendid. Go and have your nap.

BUGROV [*moves off*]. If they don't serve supper, wake me at half past ten. [*Goes off to the summer-house.*]

SCENE II

[NICHOLAS *and, later,* SERGEY.]

NICHOLAS [*examines the money*]. Smells of peasant! The swine's certainly lined his pockets! What shall I do with it? [*To* VASILY *and* JACOB.] Hey, flunkeys! Vasily, tell Jacob to come here. Jacob, tell Vasily to come here. Come on, this way and look slippy.

[JACOB *and* VASILY *come up to* NICHOLAS.]

NICHOLAS. In tails too, damn it! Quite the gentlemen of leisure. [*Gives* JACOB *a rouble.*] One for you. [*To* VASILY.] And one for you. That's for having long noses.

JACOB *and* VASILY [*bow*]. Many thanks, sir.

NICHOLAS. Unsteady on your pins, lads? Drunk, eh? Both feeling a bit ropy? You'll catch it if the mistress finds out, you'll get your ears boxed. [*Gives them another rouble.*] Another rouble for you. That's because you're Jacob and he's Vasily, and not the other way round. Now bow.

[JACOB *and* VASILY *bow.*]

NICHOLAS. Very nice. And here's another rouble because I'm Nicholas and not Ivan. [*Gives them another.*] Bow. That's right. And mind you don't spend it all on drink, or I'll prescribe you something nasty. Quite the gentlemen, aren't you? Now go and light lanterns. Quick march, I've had enough of you.

[JACOB *and* VASILY *go out.* SERGEY *crosses the stage.*]

NICHOLAS [*to* SERGEY]. Here's three roubles for you.

[SERGEY *takes the money, puts it in his pocket automatically and goes to the back of the garden.*]

NICHOLAS. You might say thanks.

[IVAN *and* SASHA *come out of the house.*]

SCENE III

[NICHOLAS, IVAN *and* SASHA.]

SASHA [*coming in*]. Oh, when will all this end? Dear God, why have you punished me so? Here's Father drunk, and so are Nicholas and Michael. Have you no shame? Have you no fear of God, even if you don't care what men think? They're all looking at you. And I— how do you think I feel with them all pointing at you?

IVAN. That's all wrong. Stop, you've got me mixed up. Stop it.

SASHA. You're not fit to be let inside a decent house—hardly through the front door and already drunk. You're quite revolting! And at your age! You should set an example, not join in.

IVAN. Stop it, you've got me mixed up. What was I on about? Oh yes. I'm not lying, girl. Another five years in the army, and I'd have been a general, take it from me. Don't you think so? Faugh! [*Laughs.*] What, not a general—a man of my calibre! With my education? You've precious little sense if that's your idea, precious little.

SASHA. Let's go. Generals don't drink so much.

IVAN. Everyone drinks when he's happy. I'd be a general. And kindly shut up, you're just like your mother—fuss, fuss, fuss, God help us. She kept at it day and night, nothing was ever right. Fuss, fuss, fuss! Now what was I on about? Yes, you're your mother's image, my pet, absolutely. Eyes and hair—. She waddled like a goose too. [*Kisses her.*] Darling, you're just like your dear mother, I loved her terribly.

SASHA. That'll do. Let's go on. Seriously, Father, it's time you gave up drinking and making scenes. Leave it to these hearty types. They're young, and it really doesn't suit an old man like you.

IVAN. Very well, dear, I see what you mean. I'll stop then. All right, I take the point. Now what was I on about?

NICHOLAS [*to* IVAN]. A hundred copecks, Colonel. [*Gives him a rouble.*]

IVAN. Just so. I accept, son. Thanks. I wouldn't take it from just anyone, but from my son—with great pleasure, always. I don't like other people's money, children, God I don't. I'm an honest man, your father's honest. Never robbed my country or my family in my life, though I only had to help myself here and there to be rich and famous.

NICHOLAS. Good for you, Father, but don't boast.

IVAN. I'm not, I'm giving you children a few tips, showing you the ropes. I'll answer for you to the Almighty.

NICHOLAS. Where are you going?

IVAN. Home. I'm taking this little creature home too. She's been on and on about it, really pitched into me—so I'm seeing her home. She's afraid to go alone, so I'll see her there and come back again.

NICHOLAS. Come back, of course. [*To* SASHA.] Would you like some too? Here you are then, three roubles for you.

SASHA. Give me two more while you're about it, so Michael can have some summer trousers—he only has one pair. It's awful only having one pair, he has to wear woollen ones when they're being washed.

NICHOLAS. If I had my way he'd get none, light or heavy. Let him make do. But how can I refuse you? Here's two more. [*Gives her the money.*]

IVAN. What was I on about? Oh yes, it all comes back to me—I was on the general staff once, thinking of ways to kill Turks. I was an armchair warrior—never one for cold steel, no sir. Ah, well.

SASHA. Why are we hanging about? Let's go. Good-bye, Nicholas. Come on, Father.

IVAN. One moment. For God's sake shut up. Chatter, chatter, chatter, like a ruddy bird-cage. Now this is how to live, children—with decency, honesty, integrity. Yes indeed. I got the Order of St. Vladimir, third class.

SASHA. That'll do, Father. Come on.

NICHOLAS. We know you already—no need to make speeches. Now run along and see her home.

IVAN. You're a smart lad, Nicholas, you might turn out like Pirogov— a great doctor.

NICHOLAS. Oh, run along.

IVAN. What was I on about? Oh yes. I once met Pirogov, when he was still in Kiev. Yes indeed—very smart boy, Pirogov, pretty good. All right, I'm off. Come on, Sasha. I'm so weak, I feel as if I'm on my last legs. Lord, forgive us sinners. I have sinned, yea I have sinned.

Yes indeed. I'm a sinner, children, I serve Mammon. Never said my prayers as a boy, always had my eye on the main chance. I've been a real materialist, I have. Yes indeed. You must pray for me not to die, children. Have you gone, Sasha? Where are you? Oh, there you are. Come on.

[ANNA *looks out of the window.*]

NICHOLAS. He still hasn't budged. The old chap's raving. Run along then, and don't go past the mill or the dogs'll get you.

SASHA. You've got his cap on, Nicholas. Give it him or he'll catch cold.

NICHOLAS [*takes the cap and puts it on his father*]. On your way, revered parent. Left turn and quick march!

IVAN. Left incline! Yes indeed. You're quite right, Nicholas, God knows. And so's Michael. He's a free-thinker, but he has the right ideas. All right, I'm going. [*They move off.*] Come on, Sasha. Are you coming or shall I carry you?

SASHA. Don't be silly.

IVAN. Let me carry you. I always used to carry your mother—made me a bit unsteady on my pins, though. Once came a cropper carrying her over a little hill. She just laughed, dear woman—wasn't a bit angry. Let me carry you.

SASHA. Don't make things up. And put your cap on properly. [*Adjusts his cap.*] You're still quite one of the boys, Father.

IVAN. Yes indeed.

[*They go out.* PETRIN *and* SHCHERBUK *come in.*]

SCENE IV

[NICHOLAS, PETRIN *and* SHCHERBUK.]

PETRIN [*comes out of doors arm-in-arm with* SHCHERBUK]. Put fifty thousand in front of me and I'd steal it. On my word of honour. As long as I knew I wouldn't be caught. I'd steal it, and you'd do the same.

SHCHERBUK. No, I would not.

PETRIN. Put down one rouble and I'd steal that. Honesty! You make me sick. Who wants your honesty? Show me an honest man and you show me a fool.

SHCHERBUK. I'm a fool then.

NICHOLAS. Here's a rouble each, reverend sirs. [*Gives them each a rouble.*]

PETRIN [*takes the money*]. Let's have it.

SHCHERBUK [*laughs loudly and takes the money*]. Thanks, Doctor.

NICHOLAS. A bit pickled, eh, gentlemen?

PETRIN. A bit.

NICHOLAS. And here's another rouble to have prayers said for your souls. You're sinful, aren't you? So take it. I should tell you both to go to hell, but as it's a holiday—I'll be generous, damn it.

ANNA [*at the window*]. Triletsky, give me a rouble. [*Disappears.*]

NICHOLAS. What, one rouble for a major-general's widow! You get five. Coming. [*Goes indoors.*]

PETRIN [*looks at the window*]. Has our fairy princess disappeared?

SHCHERBUK [*looks at the window*]. Yes.

PETRIN. I can't stand her. She's a bad woman, too proud. Women should be quiet and respectful. [*Shakes his head.*] Have you seen Glagolyev? What a stuffed shirt. Squats there like a toadstool, doesn't move or speak—just goggles at you. Is that how to win a lady's heart?

SHCHERBUK. He'll marry her.

PETRIN. Yes, but when? In a hundred years? A hundred years is no good to me, thank you.

SHCHERBUK. Why should the old boy marry, Gerasim? If he really must, he should marry some ordinary woman. He's no good for Anna. She's a girl of spirit, a true European, educated——

PETRIN. Oh, I do wish he would—I'm so keen on it, words fail me. You see, they haven't had a bean since the old general died, may he rest in peace. She owns a mine, but Vengerovich has his eye on that, and who am I to cross swords with Vengerovich? And what can I get on their IOUs as things stand? If I present them now, what'll I get?

SHCHERBUK. Not a thing.

PETRIN. But if she marries Glagolyev, I'll know how to get my money. I'll send in my bills at once and put the bailiffs in. She won't let her stepson go bankrupt, she'll pay up. Oh Lord, may all my dreams come true. Sixteen thousand roubles, Paul my boy.

SHCHERBUK. They owe me three thousand. My old woman tells me to get it back, but I don't know how to. We're not dealing with peasants, they're our friends. Just let *her* try and get it out of them! Shall we go over to the lodge, Gerasim?

PETRIN. What for?

SHCHERBUK. We'll whisper sweet ballads while the ladies dance.

PETRIN. Is Dunyasha there?

SHCHERBUK. Yes. [*They move off.*] It's more fun there. [*Sings.*] 'I've been so unhappy since I stopped living there.'

PETRIN. Tick tock, tick tock. [*Shouts.*] Yes indeed. [*Sings.*]
  'We greet the New Year with delight
  Among our very dearest friends.'

[*Goes out.*]

SCENE V

[SERGEY *and* SONYA, *emerging from the back of the garden.*]

SERGEY. What are you thinking about?

SONYA. I really don't know.

SERGEY. Why won't you let me help you—don't you think I can? Why all the mysteries, Sonya—secrets from your husband? [*They sit down.*]

SONYA. What secrets? I don't know what's the matter with me either. Don't torment yourself for no reason, and pay no attention to my bad moods. [*Pause.*] Let's go away from here.

SERGEY. What, leave?

SONYA. Yes.

SERGEY. Why?

SONYA. I want to, I want to go abroad. How about it?

SERGEY. You want to—. But why?

SONYA. This life is good, healthy and lots of fun, but it's all too much for me. Everything in the garden's lovely, only—we must go away. You promised you wouldn't ask questions.

SERGEY. We'll go tomorrow then, get away from here. [*Kisses her hands.*] You're bored here and no wonder, I know how you feel. What a damn awful lot! These Petrins and Shcherbuks——

SONYA. It's not their fault, let's leave them out of it. [*Pause.*]

SERGEY. How do you women manage to get so depressed. Why so downhearted? [*Kisses her cheek.*] That'll do, now cheer up. Make the most of life. Can't you pack up your troubles, as Platonov says? Oh yes—talking of Platonov, why do you avoid him? He's quite a big noise—cultured chap, anything but a bore. Why not have a heart-to-heart with him and unbend a bit? That should chase the cobwebs away. And you should talk to Mother and Triletsky more. [*Laughs.*] Talk to them, don't look down on them, you don't know what they're like yet. I want you to know them better because they're my type, I'm fond of them. You'll like them too when you know them better.

ANNA [*at the window*]. Sergey, Sergey! Who's there? Will someone tell Sergey I want him?

SERGEY. What for?

ANNA. Oh, there you are. Come in for a moment.

SERGEY. Coming. [*To* SONYA.] We'll leave tomorrow then unless you change your mind. [*Goes indoors.*]

SONYA [*after a pause*]. It's really almost tragic. Already I can forget my husband for days on end, I ignore him, don't listen to him—it's all getting me down. What can I do? [*Reflects.*] It's awful, we've been married such a short time, and already—. It's all his—Platonov's—doing. I'm helpless, I've no moral fibre, I can't resist the man. He pursues me morning, noon and night, seeks me out, doesn't give me a moment's peace with his meaning glances. It's dreadful—and so stupid. I can't even answer for myself. He only has to lift a finger and anything could happen.

SCENE VI

[SONYA *and* PLATONOV. PLATONOV *comes out of the house.*]

SONYA. Here he is, looking for someone. Who? I can tell who he wants by his walk. It's a rotten trick to pester me.

PLATONOV. Isn't it hot? I shouldn't have drunk so much. [*Seeing* SONYA.] You here, Sonya? All on your own? [*Laughs.*]

SONYA. Yes.

PLATONOV. Avoiding mere mortals, eh?

SONYA. Why should I? I've nothing against them and they don't bother me.

PLATONOV. Really? [*Sits down by her.*] May I? [*Pause.*] Then if you're not avoiding people, Sonya, why avoid me? Eh? No, let me finish. I'm glad to get a word in at last. You avoid me, keep out of my way, don't look at me. What is it? A joke, or do you mean it?

SONYA. I never meant to avoid you, what gave you that idea?

PLATONOV. You seemed pleased to see me at first and favoured me with your attention, but now you can't stand me. If I go into one room, you go in another. If I go in the garden, you leave it. If I speak to you, you fob me off or give me a dry, stuffy 'yes' and go away. Our relations are in a sort of mess. Is it my fault? Am I so repulsive? [*Stands up.*] I don't feel particularly guilty. Do you mind ending this absurd, childish business here and now? I won't have any more of it.

SONYA. I admit I do, er, avoid you a bit. If I'd known you disliked it so much I'd have managed it differently.

PLATONOV. You avoid me? [*Sits down.*] And admit it? But why, why?

SONYA. Don't shout, I mean don't talk so loud. You don't think you're reprimanding me, I hope. I don't like being shouted at. It's not you, it's your conversation I've been avoiding. You're a good man as far as I know. Everyone here likes you and thinks highly of you, while some people actually worship you, and are flattered to speak to you.

PLATONOV. Oh come, come.

SONYA. When I came here I joined your audience after our first talk, but things turned out badly, I was out of luck. I soon found you almost unbearable—I can't think of a milder word, sorry. You told me nearly every day how you once loved me, how I loved you and so on. The student loved the girl, the girl loved the student— the story's too old and commonplace to waste many words on or to be thought important to us now. Anyway, the point is, when you spoke about the past, you—you spoke as if you wanted something, something that you failed to get in the past and would like to lay your hands on now. Your tone never changed, which was a bore, and every day I felt you were hinting at alleged obligations imposed on us both by a common experience. And I thought you attached too much importance to—that, to put it more clearly, you were reading too much into a relationship which was just that of two good friends. You have this odd way of looking, and there are your outbursts and shouting, and you clutch my hand and follow me about —as if you were spying on me. What's it all in aid of? You won't leave me alone, in fact. But why the supervision? What am I to you? Really, one might think you were up to something and playing a kind of waiting game. [*Pause.*]

PLATONOV. Finished? [*Gets up.*] Thanks for being frank. [*Moves towards the door.*]

SONYA. Annoyed? [*Gets up.*] Don't go, don't be so touchy. I didn't mean——

PLATONOV [*stops*]. Oh, really! [*Pause.*] So you're not bored with me, you're afraid, you're a coward—aren't you, Sonya? [*Goes up to her.*]

SONYA. Stop it, Platonov. That's an absolute lie. I never was afraid and I don't intend to be now.

PLATONOV. Where are your will-power and common sense—if any man in the least bit unusual can seem a danger to your Sergey? I used to come here every day before you arrived and I spoke to you because I thought you an intelligent, sensible woman. What frightful depravity! In fact—. I'm sorry, I was carried away. I had no right to talk to you like that, you must excuse the unseemly outburst.

SONYA. Indeed you have no right to talk like that. People may listen to you, but that doesn't mean you can say the first thing that comes into your head. Go away and leave me alone.

PLATONOV [*laughs*]. Persecuted, are we, much in demand? Our hand is clutched, is it? Poor little girl, does someone want to take her away from her husband? Platonov loves you, does he? The eccentric Mr. Platonov! Oh joy, oh bliss! I've never known such a quantity of humbug outside a sweet shop. What a joke! No educated woman should feed her vanity on that scale! [*Goes indoors.*]

SONYA. You're rude and impertinent, Platonov. You must be crazy. [*Goes after him and stops by the door.*] It's awful, why did he say all that? He wanted to shock me. Well, I'm not having it. I'll go and tell him——

[*Goes indoors,* OSIP *comes out from behind the summer-house.*]

SCENE VII

[OSIP, JACOB *and* VASILY.]

OSIP [*comes in*]. 'Five down, six up.' What the hell do they think they're playing? Cards would suit them better, some card game or other. [*To* JACOB.] Hallo, Jacob. Is what's-his-name, er, Vengerovich here?

JACOB. Yes.

OSIP. Go and call him. Bring him out here quietly, say it's important.

JACOB. All right. [*Goes indoors.*]

OSIP [*tears down a lantern, puts it out and sticks it in his pocket*]. Last year I played cards in town at Darya's place—the one who buys stolen goods and runs the licensed premises complete with young ladies. The lowest stake was three copecks, but the forfeits went up to two roubles. I won eight roubles. [*Tears down another lantern.*] It's fun in town.

VASILY. Those lanterns weren't put up for your benefit. Why take them down?

OSIP. I can't even see you. Hallo, old donkey. How's things? [*Goes up to him.*] How's everything, old horse? [*Pause.*] You swineherd, you! [*Takes* VASILY'*s cap off.*] God, you are funny, you haven't an ounce of sense. [*Throws the cap at a tree.*] Slap my face for being a bad man.

VASILY. Someone else can, I shan't.

OSIP. Then murder me. If you've any sense you'll do it on your own, not in a gang. Spit in my face for being a bad man.

VASILY. No. Leave me alone.

OSIP. Won't spit? Afraid of me, eh? Down on your knees! [*Pause.*] Kneel! Who am I talking to, a live man or thin air? [*Pause.*] Well?

VASILY [*kneels*]. It ain't right, Mr. Osip.

OSIP. Ashamed to kneel, eh? That's good—a gent in tails kneeling to a thief. Now give three cheers at the top of your voice. Come on.

[ABRAHAM *comes in.*]

SCENE VIII

[OSIP *and* ABRAHAM.]

ABRAHAM [*comes out of the house*]. Does someone want me?

OSIP [*quickly takes off his cap*]. Me, sir.

[VASILY *stands up, sits on the bench and cries.*]

ABRAHAM. What is it?

OSIP. You were asking for me at the inn, sir, so I came along.

ABRAHAM. Oh. But couldn't you have picked another place?

OSIP. One place is as good as another for honest men, sir.

ABRAHAM. I need you slightly. Come over to that bench. [*They go to a bench at the back of the stage.*] Stand a bit further away and look as if you weren't talking to me—that's right. Was it the innkeeper Lev Solomonovich who sent you?

OSIP. Yes sir.

ABRAHAM. He shouldn't have, it wasn't you I wanted, but—it can't be helped. You're past praying for, I should have no truck with you. You're a real wrong 'un.

OSIP. Very bad, sir, they don't come no worse.

ABRAHAM. Keep your voice down. You've had lots of cash from me, but you don't seem interested—my money might be so much waste paper. You're rude, you steal. Turning away? Don't like the truth? Hurts a bit, doesn't it?

OSIP. Yes sir, but not coming from you, sir. Is that why you sent for me, to read me a lecture?

ABRAHAM. Not so loud. Do you know—Platonov?

OSIP. The schoolteacher? Of course.

ABRAHAM. Yes, the teacher. A teacher of bad language, more like—that's about all he does teach. What would you take to cripple him?

OSIP. Cripple him?

ABRAHAM. Not kill him—maim him. Murder's wrong, and what's the point of it? It's a thing I, er—. I want him damaged, given a beating he'll remember all his life.

OSIP. That can be arranged.

ABRAHAM. Break him up a bit, spoil his looks. How much do you want? Shush! Someone's coming, let's move off a bit.

[*They go to the back of the stage.* PLATONOV *and* MARY *come out of the house.*]

SCENE IX

[ABRAHAM VENGEROVICH *and* OSIP *at the back of the stage.* PLATONOV *and* MARY.]

PLATONOV [*laughs*]. What did you say? [*Laughs loudly.*] I didn't quite catch——

MARY. Oh. Then I'll say it again—put it even more bluntly. You won't take offence, of course. You're so used to all kinds of rudeness, I doubt if what I say will surprise you at all.

PLATONOV. Come on, out with it, my beauty.

MARY. I'm not beautiful, anyone who thinks that has no taste. I'm ugly, aren't I? Be honest, what do you think?

PLATONOV. I'll tell you later, you speak first.

MARY. Well, listen then. You're either an outstanding man or a scoundrel, one or the other.

[PLATONOV *laughs.*]

MARY. You laugh—actually, it is funny. [*Laughs.*]

PLATONOV [*laughs*]. She actually said it. Good for Miss Stupid. Well, well, well. [*Takes her by the waist.*]

MARY [*sits down*]. But let me——

PLATONOV. So she wants a go at me as well. Holds forth, studies chemistry, issues weighty pronouncements. Get away with you, you awful girl. [*Kisses her.*] You pretty, funny little beast.

MARY. One moment, what is this? I, er, I didn't say anything. [*Gets up and sits down again.*] Why did you kiss me? I'm not that sort of——

PLATONOV. You've quite flabbergasted me. 'I'll come out with something striking,' thinks she. 'Show him how clever I am.' [*Kisses her.*] Baffled, eh? And with that silly stare. Ah me.

MARY. You—do you love me? Do you?

PLATONOV [*shrieks*]. Do you love me?

MARY. If, if—er, yes. [*Cries.*] You do love me, don't you, or you wouldn't have behaved like this. Do you?

PLATONOV. Not at all, darling. I don't like half-wits, I can't help it. I do love one silly creature, but that's only because I've nothing else to do. Aha, we blench, our eyes flash! 'I'll show him who he's dealing with,' thinks she!

MARY [*stands up*]. Are you being funny or something? [*Pause.*]

PLATONOV. We'll be slapping his face any minute.

MARY. I'm too proud, I won't soil my hands, sir. I told you you were an outstanding man or a scoundrel. Now I say you're an outstanding scoundrel. I despise you. [*Moves off towards the house.*] I shan't cry, I'm only glad to have learnt what you're like at last.

[NICHOLAS *comes in.*]

SCENE X

[*The above and* NICHOLAS, *who wears a top hat.*]

NICHOLAS [*coming in*]. The cranes are crying. Where have they sprung from? [*Looks up.*] It's so early.

MARY. Nicholas, if you've any respect for me or yourself, have nothing to do with this person. [*Points to* PLATONOV.]

NICHOLAS [*laughs*]. Have a heart, he's one of my revered relatives.

MARY. A friend too?

NICHOLAS. Yes.

MARY. I can't say I envy you. Or him either, I think. You're not a bad sort, but—you're so jocular. Sometimes your jokes make me sick. I don't want to be unkind, but I've just been insulted, and you're joking. [*Cries.*] I've been insulted. Anyway, I shan't cry, I'm too proud. Go on seeing this person, be fond of him, worship his intellect, fear him. You all think he's like Hamlet. Admire him if you must. I don't care, I want nothing from you. Joke with him to your heart's content, the scoundrel. [*Goes indoors.*]

NICHOLAS [*after a pause*]. Did you take that in, old boy?

PLATONOV. Not really.

NICHOLAS. Can't you have the decency to leave her alone, Michael? Aren't you ashamed? An intelligent, capable man like you going in for this damned hanky-panky! No wonder you've been called a scoundrel. [*Pause.*] I can't very well split in two and respect you with one half, while the other takes the side of the girl who just called you a scoundrel.

PLATONOV. Don't respect me then, and you won't need to tear yourself apart.

NICHOLAS. I can't help respecting you. You don't know what you're saying.

PLATONOV. Then all you can do is not take her side. I don't understand you, Nicholas—how can a clever man like you find good in such a silly girl?

NICHOLAS. Well, Anna Voynitsev's always saying I'm no gentleman. She points to you as a model of the proprieties. But I think her reproach applies just as much to you, the model gentleman. Everyone round here, you more than anyone, is shouting from the rooftops that I'm in love with her. You laugh at me, make fun of me, suspect me, spy on me.

PLATONOV. Be a bit clearer.

NICHOLAS. I'm being quite clear already, I think. You also have the nerve to call her a silly little ninny in front of me. You're no gentleman. Gentlemen know that lovers have their pride. She's no fool, take it from me, she's just a scapegoat. There are times when you're ready to hate someone, aren't there? You want to pitch into them and vent your spite. So why not try her? She fits the bill. She's weak and defenceless, she looks on you with such foolish trustfulness. Oh, it's all very clear. [*Stands up.*] Come and have a drink.

OSIP [*to* ABRAHAM]. If you don't pay me the rest after the job I'll steal my hundred roubles' worth, make no mistake about that!

ABRAHAM [*to* OSIP]. Not so loud. As you beat him, don't forget to say it's with the innkeeper's compliments. Shush! Run along.

[*Goes towards the house.* OSIP *goes out.*]

NICHOLAS. Vengerovich, damn it! [*To* ABRAHAM.] Not ill, are you?

ABRAHAM. Don't worry, I'm all right.

NICHOLAS. A pity, seeing I'm so short of money—honestly, I'm really cut up about it.

ABRAHAM. It sounds more as though you need a few patients to 'cut up', Doctor. [*Laughs.*]

NICHOLAS. Very funny! Brilliant—if a bit on the heavy side. Ha ha ha. I repeat, ha ha ha. Laugh, Platonov. [*To* ABRAHAM.] Hand over, old chap—see what you can do.

ABRAHAM. But you owe me so much already.

NICHOLAS. No need to mention it, it's no secret. How much is it, anyway?

ABRAHAM. About, er, two hundred and forty-five roubles, I think.

NICHOLAS. Come on, big-wig, do me a favour—I'll do as much for you one day. Be kind, generous and brave. The bravest Jew is the one who lends money without receipt, so act accordingly.

ABRAHAM. Jews, Jews—always Jews! I never met a Russian in my life who lent money without an IOU, believe me. And nowhere is the loan of money without security so much in vogue as amongst us dishonest Jews. Lord strike me, I'm not lying. [*Sighs.*] You young men could learn a lot from Jews, especially us older ones, and that's a fact. [*Takes his wallet out of his pocket.*] We're glad to make you a loan, but you will laugh and joke about it. It's not right, though. I'm an old man with children. You may think I'm a low hound, but treat me as human. That's what university education's for.

NICHOLAS. Well put, Abe old man.

ABRAHAM. This won't do. You educated people seem no better than my shop-assistants. Who said you could call me by my first name? How much do you want? It won't do, young sirs. How much?

NICHOLAS. What you like. [*Pause.*]

ABRAHAM. I can let you have, er, fifty. [*Gives him the money.*]

NICHOLAS. Munificent! [*Takes it.*] You're a great man.

ABRAHAM. You've got my hat on, Doctor.

NICHOLAS. Have I? Oh. [*Takes the top hat off.*] Here. Why not send it to the cleaners, they're quite cheap. What's the Yiddish for hat?

ABRAHAM. Whatever you like. [*Puts on the hat.*]

NICHOLAS. A top hat really suits you, you're a regular baron. Why not buy a title?

ABRAHAM. I've no idea, please leave me alone.

NICHOLAS. You're a great man. Why can't people understand you?

ABRAHAM. I'd rather hear why people can't leave me in peace. [*Goes indoors.*]

SCENE XI

[PLATONOV *and* NICHOLAS.]

PLATONOV. Why did you borrow that money?

NICHOLAS. I just did. [*Sits down.*]

PLATONOV. What does that mean?

NICHOLAS. I took it, and that's that. Not sorry for him are you?

PLATONOV. That's not the point, man.

NICHOLAS. Then what is?

PLATONOV. Don't you know?

NICHOLAS. No.

PLATONOV. Rubbish, of course you do. [*Pause.*] I might really take to you, old boy, if you could only live by some sort of code, however pathetic, for one week, even one day. Your type needs rules as much as their daily bread. [*Pause.*]

NICHOLAS. I don't know, we can't change our nature, old boy—can't crush the flesh. I knew that when we both used to get nought out of ten for Latin at school. So let's stop this silly talk before we're struck dumb. [*Pause.*] Two days ago I was visiting a lady friend's house and saw some portraits called Public Figures of Our Day, and read their biographies. And do you know, they hadn't got you and me there! I couldn't find us, however hard I tried. *Lasciate ogni speranza*, as the Italians say. Neither you nor me is a Public Figure and, do you know, I don't care. Now Sonya somehow does care.

PLATONOV. Where does Sonya come in?

NICHOLAS. She's hurt because she's not a Public Figure either. She thinks, if she lifts a finger the earth should gape and men throw their hats in the air. She thinks—there's more tommy-rot in her head than in the most pretentious modern novel. Actually, she's no good, she's an iceberg, a stone, a statue. You long to go and chip a bit of plaster off her nose. Always ready with her hysterics, sighs and lamentations, and so feeble, a sort of clever doll. She looks down on me, thinks I'm

the scum of the earth, but is her Sergey any better than you and me?
Is he? The only good thing about him is, he doesn't drink vodka, has
all sorts of airy ideas and has the nerve to call himself a go-ahead
person. Anyway, judge not that ye be not judged. [*Stands up.*]
Let's go and have a drink.

PLATONOV. No thanks, it's too close in there.

NICHOLAS. Then I'll go. [*Stretches.*] By the way, what's the meaning of
this S and V in the monogram? Sonya Voynitsev or Sergey Voynitsev? Whom did our scholarly friend wish to honour—himself or
his wife?

PLATONOV. I think it stands for 'Salute to Vengerovich'. He's paying
for this orgy.

NICHOLAS. True. What's up with Anna Voynitsev today—laughing,
groaning, kissing people? Not in love, is she?

PLATONOV. Who can she love here? Herself? Don't trust her laughter.
When an intelligent woman never cries you can't take her laughter
as genuine—she laughs when she wants to cry. But our Anna doesn't
want to cry—feels more like shooting herself, you can see it in her
eyes.

NICHOLAS. Women don't shoot themselves, they take poison. But
don't let's generalize, I talk such rot when I do that. Anna's a fine
woman. When I see a woman I usually feel frightfully lecherous, but
my evil designs slide off her like water off a duck's back, and I can't
say that of anyone else. Looking at that matter-of-fact face, I start
believing in platonic love. Coming?

PLATONOV. No.

NICHOLAS. Then I'll go and have a drink with the priest. [*Moves off and
bumps into* CYRIL *near the door.*] Ah, your Lordship, the self-appointed
count! Have three roubles. [*Shoves three roubles in his hand and goes out.*]

SCENE XII

[PLATONOV *and* CYRIL.]

CYRIL. What an odd person, with his 'have three roubles' right out of
the blue. [*Shouts.*] I can afford to give you three roubles. Idiot.
[*To* PLATONOV.] I'm most impressed by his stupidity. [*Laughs.*]
Hideously stupid, he is.

PLATONOV. You dance, don't you? Then why aren't you dancing?

CYRIL. Dance? Here? Who with, pray? [*Sits down next to him.*]

PLATONOV. No lack of partners, is there?

CYRIL. What specimens they all are with their ugly mugs, hooked noses and the airs they put on. And the women! [*Laughs loudly.*] Hell! Give me the bar, in such company, not the dance floor. [*Pause.*] Isn't Russian air stale—so dank and stuffy, somehow. I can't stand Russia, stinking, barbarous place! Ugh! How different in—ever been to Paris?

PLATONOV. No.

CYRIL. Pity. Anyway, you may still get around to it. Let me know when you do, I'll initiate you. I'll give you three hundred letters of introduction and that'll put three hundred of the smartest little fillies in Paris at your disposal.

PLATONOV. No thanks, I've been well catered for in that direction. I say, is it true your father wants to buy my estate?

CYRIL. I don't know, I don't dabble in trade. Have you noticed *mon père* making up to Anna Voynitsev? [*Laughs.*] Another odd specimen! The old stoat wants to get married—more fool him. Your Anna's charming, and not bad looking. [*Pause.*] Delightful, she is —those curves! Quite shocking! [*Claps PLATONOV on the shoulder.*] You lucky man, you. Does she wear corsets, eh? Tight ones?

PLATONOV. I've no idea, I don't watch her dressing.

CYRIL. But from what I heard—. Mean to say you don't——?

PLATONOV. Count, you're an idiot.

CYRIL. I was only joking. Why so annoyed? You are a funny chap. [*Quietly.*] Is it true she—er, a slightly ticklish question, but it need go no further, I hope. Is it true that she goes mad about money every so often?

PLATONOV. Better ask her, I don't know.

CYRIL. What, straight out? [*Laughs.*] What an idea! You don't know what you're saying, Platonov.

PLATONOV [*sits down on another bench*]. You're a prize bore.

CYRIL [*guffaws*]. Perhaps I will ask—why not, anyway?

PLATONOV. Yes, why not? [*Aside.*] Carry on, she'll smack your silly face. [*To CYRIL.*] Go on then.

CYRIL [*jumps up*]. My word, a splendid idea! Hell and damnation! I'll ask her, Platonov, and I swear she'll be mine, I can feel it. I'll ask her at once and I bet you she'll be mine. [*Runs towards the house and meets* ANNA *and* NICHOLAS *in the doorway.*] My humblest apologies, madam.

[*Scrapes his feet and goes off.* PLATONOV *sits down in his previous place.*]

SCENE XIII

[PLATONOV, ANNA *and* NICHOLAS.]

NICHOLAS [*sitting on the front steps*]. There's our great pundit, all agog and eagerly awaiting a victim for one of his bed-time harangues.

ANNA. He's not rising.

NICHOLAS. That's bad. Somehow he's not taking the bait today. Wretched moralizer! I'm sorry for you, Platonov. Still, I'm drunk and—the priest's waiting for me. Good-bye. [*Goes off.*]

ANNA [*goes towards* PLATONOV]. What are you doing out here?

PLATONOV. It's stuffy indoors and this lovely sky's better than your ceiling whitewashed by village women.

ANNA [*sits down*]. What marvellous weather. Cool, clear air, a starry sky and the moon. It's a pity ladies can't sleep out of doors. As a little girl I always slept in the garden in summer. [*Pause.*] Is that a new tie?

PLATONOV. Yes. [*Pause.*]

ANNA. I'm in a funny mood today. I like everything, I'm having a good time. Do say something, Platonov. Why won't you speak? I only came out to hear you talk, you wretch.

PLATONOV. What am I to tell you?

ANNA. Some nice, spicy bit of news. You're such a good, pretty little boy this evening, I think I'm more in love with you than ever. You're a darling—and not so naughty as usual.

PLATONOV. And you're really beautiful this evening—you always are, as a matter of fact.

ANNA. Are we friends, Platonov?

PLATONOV. Probably, I suppose so. What else can you call it?

ANNA. Anyway, we're friends?

PLATONOV. Great friends, I should think. I'm fond of you, devoted. I shan't forget you in a hurry.

ANNA. Great friends?

PLATONOV. Why all the questions? Pack it in, dear. 'Friends, friends.' You're like an old maid.

ANNA. Very well, we're friends, but do you know, sir, that friendship between a man and a woman's only one step removed from love? [*Laughs.*]

PLATONOV. So that's it! [*Laughs.*] What are you leading up to? However far we may get, we're not likely to go the whole hog, are we?

ANNA. Love—whole hog! What a juxtaposition. It's a good job your wife can't hear you, Michael. Sorry, I used your Christian name, I honestly didn't mean to. But why shouldn't we go all the way? We're human, aren't we? Love's a wonderful thing. So why blush?

PLATONOV [*stares at her*]. I see you're either making a nice little joke or want to—come to some arrangement. Let's go and waltz.

ANNA. You can't dance. [*Pause.*] And it's time we had a proper talk. [*Looks round.*] Listen, dear, and please don't make speeches.

PLATONOV. Come and dance.

ANNA. Let's sit a bit further off. Come here. [*Sits on another bench.*] Only I don't know how to start. You're such an awkward, slippery brute.

PLATONOV. Shall I start then?

ANNA. You'll only talk a lot of rot if you do. Good grief, the man's embarrassed. Only I wouldn't be too sure of it! [*Claps* PLATONOV *on the shoulder.*] You like your little joke, don't you? Speak then. But be brief.

PLATONOV. I will. What's the point? That's all I have to say. [*Pause.*] It's honestly not worth it.

ANNA. Why not? Listen. You don't understand me. If you were free I'd marry you without a second thought, and give you the title deeds of this valuable property, but as it is—. Well? No answer—does that mean you agree, eh? [*Pause.*] Look, Platonov, it's not decent to remain silent at a time like this.

PLATONOV [*jumps up*]. Let's forget what's been said, Anna. Let's pretend our talk never took place, for God's sake. It never happened.

ANNA [*shrugs her shoulders*]. But why, you funny man?

PLATONOV. Because I respect you. And my own feelings for you also inspire me with respect—I'd rather die than lose it. I'm free, dear, I don't mind having a good time, I'm not against affairs with women, I don't even object to the odd high-minded intrigue. But to start some back-stairs liaison with *you*, to make *you* the target of my idle designs—you, an intelligent, beautiful, free woman! No! It's asking too much, I'd rather you told me to go and bury myself. To spend a stupid month or two together and part feeling thoroughly ashamed of it!

ANNA. We're talking about love.

PLATONOV. Do you think I don't love you? I do—you're so good, intelligent, gracious. I love you desperately, madly. I'll give my life for you if you want, I love you as a woman and as a person. Don't try and tell me that love must always involve a certain relationship, because my love's a thousand times dearer to me than the sort you have in mind.

ANNA [*stands up*]. Go away, dear, and wake up. Then we'll talk.

PLATONOV. Let's forget what's been said. [*Kisses her hand.*] We'll be friends, but we won't play games together, our friendship deserves a better fate. Another point—I am slightly married, you know. So let's drop the subject and let everything be as it was.

ANNA. Go away, dear, do. A married man—. But you love me, don't you? Why drag in your wife? Quick march! We'll talk again in a couple of hours. At the moment you've got a bad attack of lying.

PLATONOV. I couldn't lie to you. [*Quietly, into her ear.*] If I could, I'd have been your lover long ago.

ANNA [*brusquely*]. Oh, go away!

PLATONOV. Nonsense, you're not really annoyed—you're just pretending——. [*Goes indoors.*]

ANNA. What a funny man. [*Sits down.*] He has no idea what he's saying. 'Love must always involve a certain relationship.' Poppycock! He might be discussing the love of a male and female novelist. [*Pause.*] The wretch! This way we shan't be done chattering till doomsday. Well, if I can't get my way by fair means, I'll use foul. Tonight! It's time we escaped from this absurd state of suspense, I'm fed up with it. I shall use force. Who's there? Porfiry Glagolyev, and looking for me.

[PORFIRY *comes in.*]

SCENE XIV

[ANNA *and* PORFIRY.]

PORFIRY. What a bore, their conversation's a year out of date and they think as I thought as a child, all old, stale stuff. I'll have a word with her and go.

ANNA. What are you muttering, may I ask?

PORFIRY. You here? [*Goes towards her.*] I was blaming myself for being odd man out here.

ANNA. Because you're not like us? Come, come—if people can get used to black-beetles, you can get used to us. Sit down and let's talk.

PORFIRY [*sits by her*]. I was looking for you, I want a word with you.

ANNA. Carry on.

PORFIRY. I want to talk to you, want an answer to my—letter.

ANNA. I see. Why did you pick on me?

PORFIRY. Look, I'll give up my, er, conjugal rights, never mind them. I need a friend, a good housekeeper. I have a paradise, but no angels in it.

ANNA [*aside*]. What a lot of soft soap. [*To* PORFIRY.] Being a woman and no angel, I often wonder what I'd do in paradise if I ever got there.

PORFIRY. How can you know what you'll do in paradise if you don't know what you're doing tomorrow. A sensible woman can always find something to do, both on earth and in heaven.

ANNA. That's all very well, but would it be worth my while to live with you? It's all so odd, Mr. Glagolyev. Sorry, but your proposal does seem so very peculiar. Why should you marry? What do you need with a little bit of skirt? Sorry, it's not my business, but as we've got this far I'll finish. If I was your age and as rich, clever and fair-minded as you, I'd seek nothing on this earth but the common good. I mean I'd look only for the reward of loving my neighbour, if I can put it like that.

PORFIRY. I'm no champion of human welfare, that needs ability and will-power such as God didn't give me. I was born to admire great deeds and do lots of trivial, worthless ones. I'm only an admirer. Won't you come to me?

ANNA. No, and don't mention it again. Don't attach too much significance to my refusal. It's such a waste of time, man. If we all owned everything we admire, we'd have no room for our possessions. So it's not always stupid or unkind to say no. [*Laughs.*] There's a bit of philosophy to get your teeth in. What's that noise? Hear anything? I bet it's Platonov kicking up a row again. What a man!

[MARY *and* NICHOLAS *come in.*]

SCENE XV

[ANNA, PORFIRY, MARY *and* NICHOLAS.]

MARY [*coming in*]. I was never so insulted in my life. [*Cries.*] Never! Only someone thoroughly depraved could keep silent in face of such a thing.

NICHOLAS. All right, I believe you, but where do I come in? I can hardly go and beat him up, can I?

MARY. Yes, you can, if you've no better idea. Go away. I'm only a woman, but I wouldn't keep quiet if I saw you insulted in that rotten, beastly, uncalled-for way.

NICHOLAS. But I, er—. Do be sensible. What have I done wrong?

MARY. You're a coward, that's what you are. Now go and prop up that repulsive bar. Good-bye. And don't bother to come and see me again, we don't need one another. Good-bye.

NICHOLAS. All right, good-bye, if that's the way you want it. I'm sick and tired of the whole thing. Tears, tears, tears. God, now my head's going round— a case of *coenurus cerebralis*. Oh dear. [*Makes a gesture of resignation and goes out.*]

MARY. *Coenurus cerebralis*. [*Moves off.*] What an insult. Why? What have I done?

ANNA [*comes up to her*]. I won't try and stop you, Mary, I'd leave myself in your place. [*Kisses her.*] Don't cry, dear, most women were created just for men to use as door-mats.

MARY. But not me, I'll—have him dismissed. I won't have him as schoolmaster here, he has no right to teach. I'll go and see the education officer tomorrow.

ANNA. That will do. I'll come and see you in a day or two and we'll find fault with Platonov together, but meanwhile you calm down. Stop crying, you shall have satisfaction. And don't be annoyed with Triletsky, dear. He's too kind and gentle, that's why he didn't stick up for you—such people can't stick up for anyone. What did Platonov do?

MARY. Kissed me in public, called me a fool and pushed me into the table. Don't think he'll get away with it! Either he's mad or—. I'll show him a thing or two. [*Goes out.*]

ANNA [*calls after her*]. Good-bye, we'll meet soon. [*To* JACOB.] Have Miss Grekov's carriage brought round, Jacob. Oh, Platonov, Platonov—his quarrelling will get him into hot water one day.

PORFIRY. What a lovely girl. But the worthy Platonov's taken against her—he insulted her.

ANNA. And for no reason at all—insults her today, apologizes tomorrow. Isn't that your upper-class Russian all over?

[CYRIL *comes in.*]

SCENE XVI

[*The above and* CYRIL.]

CYRIL [*aside*]. He's with her again! Hell, what can this mean? [*Glares at his father.*]

PORFIRY [*after a pause*]. What do you want?

CYRIL. While you sit here you're wanted in there. Go in, they're asking for you.

PORFIRY. Who wants me?

CYRIL. Some people.

PORFIRY. So I should think. [*Gets up.*] Say what you like, Anna, I shan't give you up. When you get to know me you may change your tune. I'll be seeing you. [*Goes indoors.*]

SCENE XVII

[ANNA *and* CYRIL.]

CYRIL [*sits by her*]. The old stoat! What an ass! No one's asking for him, I was just pretending.

ANNA. When you grow wiser you'll be sorry you treated your father like that.

CYRIL. You're joking. What I came for was a couple of words. Yes or no?

ANNA. Meaning?

CYRIL [*laughs*]. As if you didn't know! Yes or no?

ANNA. You have me baffled.

CYRIL. You'll soon catch on. A spot of lucre is a great help to understanding. If it's yes, captain of my soul, then please feel in my pocket and pull out my wallet full of Daddy's money. [*Turns his side pocket towards her.*]

ANNA. You're very frank, but don't be too clever or you might get your face slapped.

CYRIL. To have your face slapped by an attractive woman—that's quite an agreeable prospect. She starts by slapping your face, but ends up saying yes a bit later.

ANNA [*gets up*]. Take your hat and clear out this instant.

CYRIL [*gets up*]. Where to?

ANNA. Wherever you like. Get out and don't dare show your face in here again.

CYRIL. But why so angry? I won't go.

ANNA. Then I'll have you thrown out. [*Goes indoors.*]

CYRIL. Aren't you angry! I never said anything, did I? No need to be angry. [*Follows her out.*]

SCENE XVIII

[PLATONOV *and* SONYA *coming out of the house.*]

PLATONOV. I'm still only an ordinary schoolteacher, a thing I'm not really cut out for—that's all that's happened since we met last. [*They sit down.*] Evil pullulates around me, contaminating the earth and swallowing up my countrymen and brothers in Christ, while I sit idle as if I'd just done a job of work. I sit, watch and say nothing. I'm twenty-seven and I'll be no different when I'm thirty, I don't expect to change. I'll be just as fat, lazy, dull and totally indifferent to everything except the flesh. Then there's death to be thought of. My life's ruined. My hair stands on end when I think of dying. [*Pause.*] How can I lift myself up, Sonya? [*Pause.*] You don't speak, you don't know—and how could you? I'm not sorry for myself, but to hell with me, anyway. What's happened to you? Where's your high-mindedness, your sincerity, your sense of fair play, your courage? What's become of your health? What have you done with it? To spend years on end in idleness while others wear their fingers to the bone for you, to watch others' sufferings, and still feel able to look people in the face—that's real depravity, Sonya.

[SONYA *stands up, but* PLATONOV *makes her sit down again.*]

PLATONOV. Just a moment, this is my last word. What turned you into an affected, idle chatterbox? And who taught you to lie? You used to be so different. All right, I'll let you go in a moment, but please may I finish? What a fine, generous woman you were. Perhaps you can still rise again, Sonya dear, it may not be too late. Think, pull yourself together and lift yourself up, for God's sake. [*Clutches her hand.*] Tell me frankly, dear, in the name of all we used to have in common, what made you marry that man? What could that marriage offer?

SONYA. He's a fine person.

PLATONOV. Don't say things you don't believe.

SONYA [*stands up*]. He happens to be my husband, and I must ask you——

PLATONOV. I don't care who he is, I'll still tell the truth. Sit down. [*Helps her to sit down.*] Why didn't you pick a man who could work and suffer? Why not marry someone else, not this little man sunk in debt and sloth?

SONYA. Let me alone. Don't shout, someone's coming.

[*Some guests pass across the stage.*]

PLATONOV. Let them hear, blast them. [*Quietly.*] I'm sorry to be so blunt, but I did love you. I loved you more than anything in the world, so you're still dear to me. How I loved this hair, these hands, this face. Why are you powdering your face, Sonya? Stop it. Oh, if only someone else had come along, you'd soon have been on your feet, but here you'll only sink deeper and deeper, poor thing. If my wretched strength would run to it, I'd get us both out of this dump. [*Pause.*] Such is life, but why can't we live it as we ought?

SONYA [*stands up and covers her face with her hands*]. Leave me alone. [*Noises are heard in the house.*] Go away. [*Moves towards the house.*]

PLATONOV [*follows her*]. Take your hands away, that's right. You're not going away, are you? Let's be friends, Sonya. You won't go, will you? We'll have another talk, eh?

[*More noise comes from the house and there is the sound of people running downstairs.*]

SONYA. Yes.

PLATONOV. Let's be friends, dear—why should we be enemies? Just a moment, I've a couple more things to say.

[SERGEY *runs out of the house, followed by some guests.*]

SCENE XIX

[*The above,* SERGEY *and guests. Later,* ANNA *and* NICHOLAS.]

SERGEY [*running in*]. Ah, here are the people we want. Come and let off some fireworks. [*Shouts.*] Jacob, to the river—quick march! [*To* SONYA.] Not changed your mind, have you?

PLATONOV. She won't go, she'll stay here.

SERGEY. Oh? Good for you in that case. Shake hands, Michael. [*Shakes* PLATONOV's *hand.*] I always believed in your eloquence. Let's go and let off fireworks. [*Moves into the back of the garden with the guests.*]

PLATONOV [*after a pause*]. Yes, that's the way of it, Sonya. Ah well.

SERGEY [*off-stage*]. Where are you, Mother? Platonov? [*Pause.*]

PLATONOV. I'd better go too, damn it. [*Shouts.*] Just a moment, Sergey, don't start without me. I say, old man, will you send Jacob back here for the balloon. [*Runs into the garden.*]

ANNA [*runs out of the house*]. Wait, Sergey, we're not all here yet. Just fire the cannon for the moment. [*To* SONYA.] Come on, Sonya—why so downhearted?

PLATONOV [*off-stage*]. This way, my lady. We'll keep up the old song and not start a new one.

ANNA. Coming, dear. [*Runs off.*]

PLATONOV [*off-stage*]. Who's coming in the boat with me? Come on the river, Sonya?

SONYA. To go or not to go? [*Reflects.*]

NICHOLAS [*comes in*]. Hey, where are you? [*Sings.*] I'm coming, coming! [*Glares at* SONYA.]

SONYA. What do you want?

NICHOLAS. Nothing.

SONYA. Then go away, I'm in no mood to talk or listen this evening.

NICHOLAS. All right, all right. [*Pause.*] Somehow I'm terribly keen to run my finger over your forehead and see what it's made of. Not to insult you, just as a sort of gesture.

SONYA. You clown! [*Turns away.*] You're not a true humorist, you're just a clown, a buffoon.

NICHOLAS. Yes, a buffoon. That's why I get board and lodging here, as a kind of court jester. Pocket money too. When they tire of me I'll be kicked out in disgrace. True, isn't it? Anyway, I'm not the only one who says so. You said the same on a visit to Glagolyev, that up-to-date freemason.

SONYA. All right, all right, I'm glad you were told. Now you know I can tell the difference between clowning and true wit. If you were an actor you'd be a hit with the gallery, but the stalls would give you the bird. I favour the stalls.

NICHOLAS. A most felicitous witticism. Well done. And now I'll take my leave. [*Bows.*] Till our next pleasant meeting. I'd go on talking to you, but I'm scared, struck dumb. [*Goes to the back of the garden.*]

SONYA [*stamps her foot*]. Useless man! He doesn't know what I really think of him, futile little creature!

PLATONOV [*off-stage*]. Who's coming on the river?

SONYA. Oh well, it must be fate. [*Shouts.*] Coming. [*Runs off.*]

SCENE XX

[PORFIRY *and* CYRIL *come out of the house.*]

PORFIRY. You're lying, you loathsome little brat.

CYRIL. Don't be silly, why on earth should I? Ask *her* if you don't believe me. Just after you'd gone I whispered a few words to her on this very bench, put my arms round her and gave her a whacking great kiss. She began by asking three thousand roubles and I, er, did a spot of bargaining and we settled for one. So give me a thousand.

PORFIRY. This concerns a woman's honour, Cyril. Don't defile that, it's holy. Say no more.

CYRIL. But I swear! Don't you believe me? I swear by all I hold most sacred. So give me that thousand roubles, I'll take them along straight away and——

PORFIRY. This is dreadful. You're lying. She was just having you on, stupid.

CYRIL. But I embraced her, I tell you. What's surprising about that? Women are all the same these days, they're not all that innocent— don't you believe it, I know them! And you were actually thinking of marriage! [*Guffaws.*]

PORFIRY. For God's sake, Cyril, don't you know what slander is?

CYRIL. Give me a thousand, I'll hand it to her in your presence. I embraced her on this very bench, kissed her and struck my bargain. I swear it, what more do you want? That's why I got rid of you—so we could discuss terms. He doesn't believe I can dominate women. Offer her two thousand, and she's yours. I know women, man.

PORFIRY [*takes his wallet out of his pocket and throws it on the ground*]. Take it.

[CYRIL *picks it up and counts the money.*]

SERGEY [*off-stage*]. I'm starting. Fire away, Mother. Triletsky, climb on the summer-house. Who trod on that box? You?

NICHOLAS [*off-stage*]. I'm climbing, damn me. [*Laughs.*] Who's that? Someone's squashed Bugrov, I trod on Bugrov's head. Where are the matches?

CYRIL [*aside*]. I am avenged. [*Shouts.*] Hip, hip, hooray! [*Runs off.*]

NICHOLAS. Who's that yelling? Let him have it in the neck.

SERGEY [*off-stage*]. Shall we start?

PORFIRY [*clutches his head*]. God, how depraved. A rotten business. I worshipped her, God forgive her. [*Sits on the bench and buries his face in his hands.*]

SERGEY [*off-stage*]. Who took the string? Aren't you ashamed, Mother? Where's my string that was lying here?

ANNA [*off-stage*]. There it is. You've got eyes, haven't you?

[PORFIRY *falls off the bench.*]

ANNA [*off-stage*]. You! Who are you? Don't hang around here. [*Shouts.*] Give it here, give it to me.

[SONYA *runs in.*]

SCENE XXI

[SONYA, *alone.*]

SONYA [*pale, with ruffled hair*]. This is all much too much for me. [*Clutches her breast.*] Does this mean my ruin? Or my happiness? It's close out here. He'll either ruin me or show me how to lead a new life. I welcome and bless you, my new life. So that's settled.

SERGEY [*off-stage, shouting*]. Look out!

[*Fireworks.*]

PART TWO

A forest clearing. To the left, where the clearing begins, a school-house. Through the clearing, which stretches as far as the eye can see, runs a railway-line, turning right near the school. A row of telegraph poles. Night.

SCENE I

[SASHA *sits by an open window.* OSIP *stands in front of it with a gun slung over his shoulder.*]

OSIP. How did it happen? Quite simply. I'm walking in the woods near here and she's standing in a little gully with her dress tucked up, scooping water from the stream with a burdock leaf—keeps scooping and drinking, and then wetting her head. I climb down, go up and look at her. She pays no attention, as if to say 'Another country bumpkin, so why bother?' 'Wanted a nice drink of cold water, did you, ma'am?' says I. 'None of your business,' says she. 'Run off back where you came from.' She doesn't look at me as she says it, and I get a bit frightened, and ashamed and hurt, being only an ordinary peasant like. 'Why goggle at me, you fool?' she asks. 'Never seen human beings before?' She stares at me. 'Taken a fancy to me?' she asks. 'That I have,' says I. 'You're a fine woman, ma'am—kind-hearted and beautiful too. Never saw anything lovelier.' And I tell her about Manka the policeman's daughter, prettiest girl in our village. 'But put her beside you,' says I, 'and she ain't no more than a horse or camel. You're so delicate like. If I kissed you, I think I'd drop dead.' She bursts out laughing. 'All right,' says she, 'kiss me if you want.' I go hot all over when she says them words, I go up to her, take her gently by the shoulder and give her a whacking great kiss between cheek and neck, right here.

SASHA [*laughs*]. What did she do?

OSIP. 'Now clear out,' says she. 'Wash more often,' says she, 'and mind you clean your finger-nails.' So I go away.

SASHA. Bit forward, isn't she? [*Gives* OSIP *a bowl of soup.*] Eat that. Sit down somewhere.

OSIP. I don't matter, I can stand. Grateful for your kindness, ma'am, I'll pay you back one day.

SASHA. Take your cap off, you shouldn't eat with it on. And say grace first.

OSIP [*takes his cap off*]. I haven't been that pious in years. [*Eats.*] I seem to have gone clean off my head since then—can't eat, can't sleep, can you believe it? I keep thinking I see her. If I close my eyes, there she is. I get so soft-hearted, I'm ready to burst. I was so low I nearly drowned myself, I felt like taking a pot shot at the general. When she was widowed I started doing errands for her. Shot partridges, snared quail, painted her summer-house various colours. I once brought her a live wolf. Did lots of things to please her, whatever she told me. If she'd told me to go away and eat myself, I would have. The tender passion—you can't help it, can you?

SASHA. I know. When I fell in love with Michael—before I knew he loved me—I was terribly miserable too. I sometimes prayed I might die, sinful as it was.

OSIP. There you are, you see—that's what feelings can do. [*Drinks soup straight from the bowl.*] No more soup, is there? [*Gives her his bowl.*]

SASHA [*goes away and appears by the window half a minute later with a saucepan*]. There's no soup, would you like potatoes? Fried in goose fat.

OSIP. Thank you kindly. [*Takes the saucepan and eats.*] I've made a thorough pig of myself. Well, there was I dashing round like a lunatic, to go back to what we were just talking about. Kept visiting her, I did. After last Easter I brought her a hare. 'Here you are, ma'am,' I says. 'I've brought this cross-eyed creature.' She takes it in her hands, strokes it. 'Is it true you're a robber, Osip?' she asks. 'True,' says I. 'Otherwise people wouldn't say so.' So I came out with the whole story. 'Turn over a new leaf,' says she. 'Go on a pilgrimage— walk to Kiev,' she says. 'From Kiev go to Moscow, then to the Monastery of the Trinity and St. Sergius, on to New Jerusalem Monastery and back home. That'll make a new man of you in a year.' So I got myself up as a poor man, put on a knapsack and started for Kiev. But it didn't work out. I did reform, but not all that much. Fine potatoes! Near Kharkov I got in with a fast set, spent all my money on drink, got in a fight and came home. Even lost my identity papers. [*Pause.*] Now she won't take anything from me, she's annoyed.

SASHA. Why don't you go to church?

OSIP. I would, but, er, it would make people laugh. 'Look at him, come to confess his sins!' And I'm scared to go near the church in daytime. There are lots of people about, they might kill me.

SASHA. Well, why do you harm poor people?

OSIP. Why not? You wouldn't understand, ma'am, you can't judge such low things or make sense of them. Doesn't your husband ever hurt people?

SASHA. No. Or if he does, he never means to. He's kind.

OSIP. I look up to him more than anyone, I must say. The general's boy, Mr. Voynitsev, is a fool, hasn't any sense. Your brother has no sense either, even if he is a doctor. But Mr. Platonov's very brainy like. Does he hold any rank in the service?

SASHA. Of course he does.

OSIP. Does he? [*Pause.*] He does, does he? Good for him. Only he is a bit hard like. Calls everyone a fool or a lackey, it's not right. I wouldn't do that, if I was a good man—I'd be nice to all these lackeys, fools and swindlers. They're a wretched lot, you know—they need pity. He's a hard man, he is. True, he's not stuck up and he's matey with everyone, but there ain't no kindness in him. You wouldn't understand. Thanking you most kindly, I could eat potatoes like this till the cows come home. [*Gives her the saucepan.*] Thanks.

SASHA. Don't mention it.

OSIP [*sighs*]. You're a fine woman, ma'am. Why do you always feed me? You've not a drop of feminine malice in you, have you? You're real saintly. [*Laughs.*] I've never seen your like before. Saint Sasha, pray for us sinners. [*Bows.*] Rejoice, Saint Sasha.

SASHA. My husband's coming.

OSIP. You can't fool me. Just now he's discussing the tender passion with the young mistress. Handsome fellow, isn't he? He could have the whole female sex running after him if he liked. Has the gift of the gab too. [*Laughs.*] He's always making up to Mrs. Voynitsev, but she'll settle his hash—won't care how handsome he is. He might be quite keen, but she——

SASHA. That's going too far, I don't like it. You'd better be off.

OSIP. At once. You should have been in bed long ago. Waiting up for your husband, I reckon?

SASHA. Yes.

OSIP. You're a good wife. It must have taken Platonov ten years' hard looking to find you. He managed it, though. [*Bows.*] Good-bye, Mrs. Platonov. Good night.

SASHA [*yawns*]. Do go.

OSIP. All right. [*Moves off.*] I'll go home—to where my floor's the ground, my ceiling the sky. Where walls and roof are, goodness only knows. Such is the home of a man cursed by God—plenty of room, but nowhere to lay your head. One good thing—you pay no rates. [*Stops.*] Good night, ma'am, come and see me in the woods some time. Ask for Osip, the birds and lizards all know the way. See that tree stump glowing? Like a ghost? And that other one? My mother told me that tree-stumps shine like that where a sinner's buried, so people will pray for him. I'll have one shining over my grave, I'm no angel. Look, there's another. There's lots of sinners in this world. [*Goes off and can be heard whistling every minute or two.*]

SCENE II

[SASHA, *alone.*]

SASHA [*comes out of the schoolhouse with a candle and book*]. Michael's a long time. [*Sits.*] I hope he won't ruin his health. That's all these walks do—make you ill—and I want to go to bed. Where did I get to? [*Reads.*] 'Finally, it's time to proclaim anew those great, eternal ideals of humanity, those immortal principles of freedom—our fathers' guiding stars which we have unfortunately betrayed.' What does it mean? [*Reflects.*] I can't understand. Why don't they write so it's clear to anyone? It goes on—. I'll leave out the preface. [*Reads.*] 'Sacher-Masoch', what a funny name—can't be Russian. I'll read on—Michael said I must, so I must. [*Yawns and reads.*] 'One gay winter's evening.' I can skip that, it's only a description. [*Turns the leaves and reads.*] 'It was hard to tell who was playing what instrument. The majestic power of an organ played by a man's iron hand suddenly gave way to a tender flute, seemingly played by a lovely woman's lips. Then the sounds died away.' Shush, someone's coming. [*Pause.*] It's Michael. [*Puts out the candle.*] At last. [*Stands up and shouts.*] Hallo, quick march! Left, right, left, left!

[PLATONOV *comes on.*]

SCENE III

[SASHA *and* PLATONOV.]

PLATONOV [*coming in*]. Right, right, I'm walking out of step just to annoy you. Actually, dear, it's neither left nor right. A drunk man knows no left or right. All he knows is forwards, backwards, sideways and downwards.

SASHA. Come and sit here, you old soak, I'll teach you to walk sideways and downwards. Sit. [*Flings herself on* PLATONOV's *neck.*]

PLATONOV. Let's. [*Sits.*] Why aren't you in bed, microbe?

SASHA. I don't feel like it. [*Sits by him.*] They kept you late.

PLATONOV. True. Has the express gone by?

SASHA. No. The goods train went through about an hour ago.

PLATONOV. So it can't be two yet. Been back long?

SASHA. I reached home at ten. Little Nicholas was yelling his head off when I got in. I left without saying good-bye, I hope they won't mind. Was there dancing after I left?

PLATONOV. Dancing, supper and a few rows. By the way, do you know—did it happen while you were there? Old Glagolyev had a stroke.

SASHA. What!

PLATONOV. Yes. Your brother bled him and generally presided.

SASHA. But why? What was the matter? He looks so well.

PLATONOV. It was only a slight stroke—lucky for him, but bad luck on that little ass he's fool enough to call his son. They've taken him home. Not an evening passes without some scene, we must be fated.

SASHA. How scared Anna and Sonya must have been! What a fine woman Sonya is, I don't often see such pretty women. There's something about her. [*Pause.*]

PLATONOV. Oh, how stupid and nasty.

SASHA. What?

PLATONOV. What have I done! [*Buries his face in his hands.*] How shameful.

SASHA. What is it?

PLATONOV. Well may you ask. Nothing good. When did I ever do anything I wasn't ashamed of later?

SASHA [*aside*]. The poor boy's drunk. [*To* PLATONOV.] Come to bed.

PLATONOV. I've never sunk so low. How can I respect myself after that? There's nothing worse than losing your self-respect. God, there's nothing solid about me, nothing to respect or love. [*Pause.*] You love me, that's what I don't understand. You must have found something lovable in me then? Do you love me?

SASHA. What a question! How can I help it?

PLATONOV. I know, but what makes you love me? What's good about me that you love? Name it.

SASHA. Why do I love you—? You are funny tonight. Why shouldn't I, when you're my husband?

PLATONOV. So you only love me because I'm your husband?

SASHA. I don't understand.

PLATONOV. Oh, don't you? [*Laughs.*] You hopeless idiot, you should have been a housefly. With that brain you'd have been the smartest fly on record. [*Kisses her forehead.*] What would happen if you could understand me and lost that admirable innocence? Would you be such a happy woman if that pure little mind could grasp how unlovable I am? If you want to love me, my pet, don't try and find out about me. [*Kisses her hand.*] My little female! Thanks to your innocence I'm happy too and have a family like anyone else.

SASHA [*laughs*]. You're funny.

PLATONOV. My treasure, my dear, silly little woman—you shouldn't be my wife, I should keep you in a glass case on my desk. How did we contrive to produce young Nicholas? You're of an age to make little pastry soldiers, my dearest better half, not to give birth to baby Nicholases.

SASHA. This is silly talk.

PLATONOV. God grant you don't understand me. And don't try to either. Let the earth continue to rest on whales and those whales on pitchforks. Where should we find faithful wives if it wasn't for the Sashas of this world? [*Tries to kiss her.*]

SASHA [*not giving in*]. Go away. [*Angrily.*] Why marry me if I'm so stupid, why not choose someone cleverer? I didn't force you to.

PLATONOV [*laughs*]. Even get angry, can you? Damn it, that's a discovery in the field of—. In what field? It's quite a discovery, anyway, dear. So you're capable of anger, eh? Not joking, are you?

SASHA [*stands up*]. Go to bed, man. You wouldn't make these discoveries if you didn't drink. You drunkard. Call yourself a schoolmaster? You're no schoolmaster, you're a pig. Go to bed. [*Claps him on the back and goes into the schoolhouse.*]

SCENE IV

[PLATONOV, *alone.*]

PLATONOV. Am I really drunk? I can't be, I didn't have that much. Still I do feel a bit queer in the head. [*Pause.*] When I talked to Sonya—was I drunk then? [*Thinks.*] No, I wasn't, that's just the

trouble, ye gods! I was sober, damn me. [*Jumps up.*] What harm did
her wretched husband do me? Why did I have to drag him through
the mire in front of her? I'll never forgive myself. I spouted away
like some wretched posturing boy, showing off and boasting. [*Mimics
himself.*] 'Why didn't you marry a man who works and suffers?'
What the blazes does she want with a hard-working sufferer?
Why say things you don't mean, you fool? But God, she believed it,
listened to those idiot ravings, dropped her little eyes—felt all
sloppy and sentimental, poor girl. How stupid, sordid and inept!
I'm sick of it all. [*Laughs.*] Opinionated fool! Complacent businessmen are figures of fun, though people don't know whether to
laugh or cry at them. But when will someone laugh at me, that's
what I'd like to know? It's funny enough—he doesn't take bribes
or steal, doesn't beat his wife, his ideas are quite respectable, but he's
no good, that's the funny thing, no damn good at all. [*Pause.*] I must
be off. I'll ask the school inspector for a new job, I'll write to town
today.

[ISAAC *comes in.*]

SCENE V

[PLATONOV *and* ISAAC.]

ISAAC [*coming in*]. Ah, there's the schoolhouse where that half-baked
philosopher does his sleeping. Is he asleep as usual? Or is he quarrelling
—also as usual? [*Seeing* PLATONOV.] There he is, the empty windbag,
neither sleeping nor quarrelling, an abnormal state. [*To* PLATONOV.]
Not in bed yet?

PLATONOV. You've got eyes, haven't you? Why stop here? May I
wish you good night?

ISAAC. I'm going in a moment. Enjoying a little solitude? [*Looks
round.*] Monarch of all you survey, eh? On a lovely night like this.

PLATONOV. Going home?

ISAAC. Yes. Father took the carriage, so I've got to walk. Enjoying
yourself? Nice, isn't it, to drink champagne and observe yourself
under the influence? Can I sit by you?

PLATONOV. Yes.

ISAAC. Thanks. [*Sits.*] I always like saying thanks. It must be nice to
sit on these steps and feel you're a lord of creation. Where's the lady

friend, Platonov? What with nature rustling and grasshoppers chirping, we only need a little amorous chit-chat to turn this place into a paradise. This flirtatious, timid breeze only wants your sweetheart's warm breath to make your cheeks glow with happiness. Mother Nature's whispers need setting off with words of love. I want a woman! You look surprised. Ha ha! Yes, it's not how I usually talk—not my normal lingo. When I'm sober I'll blush at what I've said, but why shouldn't I do some romantic babbling anyway? Who's to stop me?

PLATONOV. No one.

ISAAC. So the language of the Gods doesn't suit my station, perhaps, or my appearance? You think I don't look romantic?

PLATONOV. Exactly.

ISAAC. Unromantic—. I see. I'm glad. Jews don't look romantic. Nature played a joke on us—issued us with unromantic faces. People usually judge by appearances, so they deny us romantic feelings on the strength of our looks. It's said there are no Jewish poets.

PLATONOV. Who says so?

ISAAC. Everyone, and it's a rotten slander.

PLATONOV. Stop quibbling. Who says so?

ISAAC. Everyone. Yet how many true poets we have—not Pushkins or Lermontovs, but real ones—Auerbach, Heine, Goethe.

PLATONOV. Goethe was a German.

ISAAC. He was a Jew!

PLATONOV. He was a German!

ISAAC. He was a Jew! I know what I'm saying.

PLATONOV. I know what I'm saying too, but have it your own way. It's hard to get the better of a half-educated Jew.

ISAAC. Very hard. [*Pause.*] But suppose there were no Jewish poets, what matter? If we have some, fine—but if we haven't, even better. As a sensual man a poet is usually a parasite and egoist. Did Goethe as a poet ever give a crust of bread to one German working man?

PLATONOV. That'll do, boy, it's been said before. He never took a crust of bread off a German working man either, that's what matters. And it's a million times better to be a poet than a nobody. But let's stop this. You haven't the faintest idea what you're talking about, so leave us all alone—the crust of bread, the poets who are beyond your desiccated understanding, and me whom you're for ever pestering.

ISAAC. All right, I won't try to stir your generous heart, you effervescent fellow. I won't try to pull the blanket of illusions off you. Go to sleep. [*Pause.*] Look at the sky. Yes, it's nice and quiet here, with nothing but trees around. There are none of those sleek, self-satisfied faces. No indeed. The trees don't whisper to me, and the moon doesn't look down as favourably on me as it does on this fellow Platonov. It tries to look coldly. 'You're not one of us,' it seems to say. 'So leave paradise. Run along to your dirty Jewish shop.' But what nonsense, I'm raving—I must stop.

PLATONOV. Quite so. Go home, boy. The longer you stay, the more nonsense you'll talk. And, as you said, you'll blush for all this rubbish later. Go.

ISAAC. But I want to talk. [*Laughs.*] Now I'm a poet.

PLATONOV. You can't be a poet if you're ashamed to be young. You are young, so make the most of it—that may be funny and stupid, but it's at least human.

ISAAC. If you say so, but what nonsense it all is. You're a funny fellow, Platonov, like everyone else round here. You should have lived before the flood. Anna Voynitsev's funny too, and so's Sergey. She's not bad-looking actually, anatomically speaking, with those clever eyes and fine fingers. She's not bad in parts. Splendid breast and neck—. [*Pause.*] Why not? Aren't I as good a man as you? It's only once in a lifetime. If thoughts can have such a powerful attraction for, er, the marrow of my spine, what would happen if she appeared among those trees and beckoned me with her ethereal fingers? I'd melt away in sheer ecstasy! Don't look at me like that. All right, so I'm a silly young fool. But who dares tell me I can't be foolish once in my life? Just as a scientific experiment I want to play the fool—or be happy, as you'd call it. And happy I am. What has that to do with anyone else, eh?

PLATONOV. But—. [*Looks at* ISAAC'*s watch-chain.*]

ISAAC. Individual happiness is a form of selfishness, anyway.

PLATONOV. Oh yes! Individual happiness is selfishness, individual misery is virtue—what ghastly poppycock you talk! And what a watch-chain! What wonderful seals. How it shines!

ISAAC. It interests you, eh? [*Laughs.*] Tinsel and glitter fascinate you. [*Shakes his head.*] You preach at me, practically break into verse—yet you can admire gold at the same time! Take the chain. Throw it away. [*Tears off the chain and throws it aside.*]

PLATONOV. What a splendid sound—you can tell it's heavy from the noise it makes.

ISAAC. Gold's a burden in more ways than weight. You're lucky you can sit on these filthy steps where the full weight of filthy lucre isn't felt. Oh, my golden chains—golden fetters, more like.

PLATONOV. Fetters can be broken! Our fathers managed to waste theirs on drink.

ISAAC. There are so many wretched, hungry, drunken people in this world. These millions who sow much, but eat not—when will they starve no more? When? I asked you a question, Platonov—why don't you answer?

PLATONOV. Leave me alone, do you mind? I don't like bells that go on and on ringing to no purpose. You must leave me, sorry, I want to go to bed.

ISAAC. Me a bell? You, more like.

PLATONOV. We're both bells, the difference being that I ring myself and you're rung by others. Good night. [*Gets up.*]

ISAAC. Good night. [*The school clock strikes two.*] Two already. I should be asleep by now, but I can't—what with insomnia, champagne and excitement. It's an unhealthy life, it's ruining my system. [*Gets up.*] I already have a pain in my chest, I think. Good night. I shan't shake hands, I'm proud to say. You've no right to shake hands with me.

PLATONOV. Don't be silly, what do I care?

ISAAC. I hope no one overheard what we said and my, er, chatter, and I hope it won't be passed on. [*Goes to the back of the stage and comes back.*]

PLATONOV. What do you want?

ISAAC. My chain was here somewhere.

PLATONOV. There's your chain. [*Kicks it.*] So you didn't forget it. Look, do me a favour—donate this chain to a friend of mine who's one of those who sow much, but eat not. This chain will keep his family for years. May I give him it?

ISAAC. No. I'd be glad to, but I honestly can't. It's a gift, a souvenir.

PLATONOV. I see. Then get out!

ISAAC [*picks up the chain*]. Leave me alone, please. [*Moves off, wearily sits down on the railway track at the back of the stage and buries his face in his hands.*]

PLATONOV. How vulgar—if you're young you should be an idealist. What frightful depravity. [*Sits down.*] Aren't people disgusting when they remind you of your own murky past? I was a bit like that once. Ah me!

[*The sound of horses' hooves.*]

SCENE VI

[PLATONOV *and* ANNA, *who comes in wearing a riding-habit and carrying a hunting-crop.*]

PLATONOV. It's Anna.

ANNA. How can I see him? Shall I knock? [*Seeing* PLATONOV.] You here? That's lucky. I knew you wouldn't be asleep. How can people sleep at such a time? God gave us the winter to sleep in. Good evening, you great oaf. [*Holds out her hand.*] Well? What are you doing, where's your hand?

[PLATONOV *holds out his hand.*]

ANNA. Not drunk, are you?

PLATONOV. Damned if I know—I'm either sober or completely sozzled. But what are you doing? Going for a walk? Have you nothing better to do, dear sleep-walker?

ANNA [*sits by him*]. Yes. [*Pause.*] Yes, Michael. [*Sings.*] 'Such happiness, such torture.' [*Laughs.*] What huge, astonished eyes! Come on, don't be scared, old friend.

PLATONOV. I'm not—not for myself, anyway. [*Pause.*] I can see you're in a silly mood.

ANNA. In my old age——

PLATONOV. Old women can be excused, they *are* silly. But who says you're old? You're as young as a June morning, your whole life lies ahead of you.

ANNA. I want a bit of life now, not ahead of me. I am young, Platonov, terribly young. I feel it, it seems to blow through me like a wind. I'm hellishly young. It's cold. [*Pause.*]

PLATONOV [*jumps up*]. I refuse to understand or guess or have ideas. I don't want anything! Go away. Tell me what a lout I am and go away, go on! Don't look like that! You just—think what you're doing.

ANNA. I already have.

PLATONOV. Think again, you proud, intelligent, lovely woman. What turned your steps in this direction? Oh——

ANNA. I didn't step, I drove, dear.

PLATONOV. Such a clever, lovely young woman—and comes to me? I can't believe my eyes or ears. She came to conquer, to storm the fortress, only I'm no fortress and you'll make no conquests. I'm so weak, so terribly weak, you must see that.

ANNA [*gets up and goes to him*]. Humility can be worse than pride. What will happen, Michael? This thing must end somehow, you must see that——

PLATONOV. I can't end something I haven't even begun.

ANNA. What a foul way to argue! And aren't you ashamed to lie? On such a night, under such a sky—and telling lies! Lie in autumn if you want, with mud and slush everywhere—but not now, not here. You can be heard, you're being watched. Look up, silly. [*Pause.*] Look, your lies have made the very stars twinkle. You've said quite enough, dear. Now be good—like the sky and the stars. Don't break this harmony with your petty selfishness. Drive your devils away. [*Puts one arm round him.*] We're made for each other. Let's enjoy this love and let others settle all the problems that torment you. [*Kisses him.*] Let's enjoy our love.

PLATONOV. Ulysses deserved the Sirens' song, but I'm no Ulysses, Siren. [*Embraces her.*] If only I could make you happy! You're so lovely. But I shan't make you happy, I'll make you what I've made all the women who've thrown themselves at me—miserable.

ANNA. You've a pretty high opinion of yourself. Are you really such a lady-killer? [*Laughs.*] You do look nice by moonlight—charming.

PLATONOV. I know what I'm like. Love affairs only end happily when I'm not involved.

ANNA. Let's sit. Over here. [*They sit on the railway track.*] Any more to say, O sage?

PLATONOV. If I was an honourable man I'd leave you. I knew this would happen, I had a feeling earlier today. I'm such a cad, why didn't I leave?

ANNA. Chase those devils away, Michael. Don't poison yourself. Your visitor's a woman, isn't she, not a wild beast. What a long face! Tears in his eyes! Really! If you don't want me, I'll go. Well? I'll go and everything will be as it was. All right? [*Laughs.*] Take it, you fool, snatch it, grab it! What more do you want? Smoke me like a cigarette, press me out, smash me, be a man! [*Shakes him.*] You silly boy.

PLATONOV. But are you really meant for me? Really? [*Kisses her hands.*] Run along, dear, and find someone worthy of you.

ANNA. That's enough silly talk. It's all very simple, surely. You love a woman. She loves you. And here she is. It's a fine night. What could be simpler? So why all the clever talk? Trying to show off, or what?

PLATONOV. I see. [*Gets up.*] But what if you only want a bit of hanky-panky, fun and games and all that? Eh? I'm not cut out for anything casual. You shan't trifle with me. You won't get rid of me with just a pat on the back as you have of so many others. I'm too expensive for a cheap affair. [*Clutches his head.*] To respect and love you in the middle of all this pettiness, mediocrity, provincialism and vulgar frivolity——

ANNA [*comes up to him*]. You do love and respect me, so why all the fuss, why bargain with me, why say such nasty things? Why all the ifs? I love you. I've told you so, you know it's true. What else do you want? I need peace. [*Puts her head on his chest.*] Peace and quiet. I need a rest, Platonov, so get that into your head. I want to forget everything, that's all. You just don't know—what a trial my life is. I want some real life for a change.

PLATONOV. You'll get no peace from me.

ANNA. Then at least cut out the clever talk. Live! Everything lives and moves, life's all around us, so let's have some life too. We'll solve our problems tomorrow, but today—tonight—let's live! Live, I tell you. [*Pause.*] Really, why do I carry on like this? [*Laughs.*] Oh, for heaven's sake! I grow lyrical and he can only squirm.

PLATONOV [*grips her arm*]. Listen. For the last time. I speak as an honourable man. Go away. It's my last word. Go!

ANNA. Oh yes? [*Laughs.*] Not trying to be funny, are you? Don't be silly, man. Now I'll never leave you. [*Throws her arms round his neck.*]

Do you hear? For the last time, I won't let you go, come what may. Ruin me, destroy yourself, but I'll have you! Let's live! Whoopee! Don't try and get away, silly. You're mine. *Now* churn out your clever talk!

PLATONOV. Once more, as an honourable man——

ANNA. If I can't get you honourably, I'll take you by force. If you love me—love me, don't fool around. Hurrah, hurrah! 'Ring out, ye peals of victory.' Come, come to me. [*Throws a black kerchief over his head.*] Come to me.

PLATONOV. To you? [*Laughs.*] You're no good. You're asking for trouble, you'll be sorry for this. I shan't be your husband, because you're not my type and I won't let you monkey with me. We'll see who laughs last. You'll be sorry. Shall we go?

ANNA [*laughs*]. Allons! [*Takes his arm.*] Wait, someone's coming, let's hide behind a tree. [*They hide behind a tree.*] It's someone in a frock-coat, not a peasant. Why don't you write leading articles for the papers? You'd do it well, seriously.

[NICHOLAS *comes in.*]

SCENE VII

[*The above and* NICHOLAS.]

NICHOLAS [*goes to the schoolhouse and bangs on a window*]. Sasha! My dear sister!

SASHA [*opens the window*]. Who's there? You, is it, Nicholas? What do you want?

NICHOLAS. Not asleep yet? Let me stay the night, dear.

SASHA. Come on then.

NICHOLAS. Put me in a classroom, but please don't let Michael know I'm staying, or he'll keep me awake talking. I feel terribly dizzy, I'm seeing double. I stand in front of one window, but there seem to be two, so which shall I climb through? What a business! It's a good job I'm not married, I'd think I'd committed bigamy. Everything's double, I see two heads on your two necks. By the way, dear, I blew my nose near that felled oak by the stream—you know the one—and forty roubles must have fallen out of my handkerchief. Pick them up early tomorrow, darling, you can keep them.

SASHA. The carpenters will get them at dawn. You are careless, Nicholas. Oh, I nearly forgot. The shopkeeper's wife called—wants you to go over as soon as possible, she was most urgent. Her husband's been taken ill, a stroke or something. Better be quick.

NICHOLAS. Confound the man, I can't bother. I have a splitting head myself and a belly-ache too. [*Climbs through the window.*] Out of my way.

SASHA. Hurry up, you're treading on my dress. [*Shuts the window.*]

PLATONOV. Hell, there's someone else coming.

ANNA. Stay where you are.

PLATONOV. Let me go, I'll leave if I want. Who's there?

ANNA. Petrin and Shcherbuk.

[PETRIN and SHCHERBUK *come in without their frock-coats, tottering.* PETRIN *wears a black top hat,* SHCHERBUK *a grey one.*]

SCENE VIII

[ISAAC, *at the back of the stage,* PLATONOV, ANNA, PETRIN *and* SHCHERBUK.]

PETRIN. Long live Petrin! Hurrah for our learned lawyer! Which is the way? Where have we got to? What's that? [*Laughs.*] Aha, a branch of the Ministry of Education, Paul, where they teach fools to forget God and swindle man. So that's where we are. Well, well, well. It's where that—what the hell's his name?—Platonov lives, the man of culture. But where's the fellow now? Speak out, don't be ashamed. Is he singing a duet with our general's widow? Thy will be done, O Lord. [*Shouts.*] Glagolyev's a fool. She told him to take a running jump at himself, and he went and had a stroke.

SHCHERBUK. I want to go home—must get to bed. Blast them all.

PETRIN. Where are our coats, Paul? We're staying at the station-master's—and with no coats! [*Laughs.*] Did the girls take them off? You gay dog, you! The girls took our coats. [*Sighs.*] Get any champagne, Paul? I bet you're drunk now? And whose did you drink? Mine. You took my drink and ate my food. Anna Voynitsev's clothes belong to me, and so do Sergey's stockings—it's all mine, I gave them the lot. And my old boots need mending, the heels are crooked. I give them everything, squander it on them, and what do I get, eh? A lot of damn rudeness. Their servant misses me out at table, manages to jog me with his elbow. She treats me like a swine.

PLATONOV. I'm fed up with this.

ANNA. Wait, they'll go in a minute. What an animal Petrin is, what lies he tells! And that old sissy believes him.

PETRIN. They treat that Jew better than us. The Jew's on top and we're at his feet. Why? Because the Jew lends more money.

> 'And on his brow are writ the words:
> "For sale by public auction".'

SHCHERBUK. That's from Nekrasov, they say he's dead.

PETRIN. All right, not a penny more do they get, do you hear? Not one. The old man can turn over in his grave and curse the grave-diggers! I've had enough, I'll sue her. Tomorrow! I'll make her name mud, ungrateful hussy.

SHCHERBUK. She's a real aristocrat, every inch the general's lady, while I'm a complete outsider and must make do with some village wench. What a bumpy road, there should be a highway with telegraph poles and jingling bells.

[*They go out.*]

SCENE IX

[*The above without* PETRIN *and* SHCHERBUK.]

ANNA [*comes out from behind a tree*]. Have they gone?

PLATONOV. Yes.

ANNA [*takes him by the shoulders*]. Shall we proceed?

PLATONOV. All right, I'll come, but if you only knew how unwilling I am. It's not me coming to you, it's the devil who keeps on at me and says I've got to. It's not me you'll get, it's my weak body. I'd have booted you out if I hadn't such a badly behaved body.

ANNA. What a foul thing to say. [*Hits* PLATONOV *with her riding-crop.*] Talk away—but don't talk rot. [*Moves away from* PLATONOV.] You want, you don't want—to hell with that! I'm not going down on my bended knees to you, that's asking too much.

PLATONOV. It's a bit late to take umbrage.

[*Goes after her and takes her hand. She snatches it away.*]

PLATONOV. I'll come anyway, the devil inside me can't be stopped now. Turn away, would you? It's a bit late to take umbrage, as I say. We're both so placed, we can't part however much we insult each other. And get this clear. If I can't accept your love in my heart, it's just that I'm quite sure you're making a fatal mistake.

SASHA [*at the window*]. Michael, where are you?

PLATONOV. Blast!

SASHA [*at the window*]. Ah, there you are. Who are you with? [*Laughs.*] Anna! I hardly recognized you, you look so black. What are you wearing? Hallo there.

ANNA. Hallo, Sasha.

SASHA. Wearing your riding-habit? You're out riding then? That's a good idea, it's such a lovely night. Let's join her, Michael.

ANNA. I've ridden far enough, I'm going home now.

SASHA. Well, in that case, of course—. Come inside, Michael. I really don't know what to do—Nicholas isn't well.

PLATONOV. Which Nicholas?

SASHA. My brother. He must have had too much to drink. Come in, please, and you come too, Anna. I'll just fetch some milk from the cellar. We'll have a glass each, it's nice and cold.

ANNA. No thanks, I'm on my way home. [*To* PLATONOV.] You go in, I'll wait.

SASHA. I'm only going to run down to the cellar. Come in, Michael. [*Disappears.*]

PLATONOV. I'd quite forgotten she existed. She trusts me so. You run along, I'll put her to bed and come after you.

ANNA. Be quick about it.

PLATONOV. We just missed having a flaming row! Good-bye for now. [*Goes into the schoolhouse.*]

SCENE X

[ANNA *and* ISAAC, *followed by* OSIP.]

ANNA. A nice surprise—I'd forgotten she existed myself. [*Pause.*] How cruel. Still, it's not the first time he's deceived the poor child. Ah well, may as well be hung for a sheep as a lamb. Only God will know, and it's happened before. How ghastly—now I have to wait till he's put her to bed, an hour or more.

ISAAC [*goes up to her*]. Mrs. Voynitsev. [*Falls on his knees.*] Mrs. Voynitsev. [*Clutches her hand.*] Anna.

ANNA. Who's this? Who are you? [*Bends down to him.*] Who is it? You, Mr. Vengerovich, is it? What's the matter?

ISAAC. Anna. [*Kisses her hand.*]

ANNA. Go away, this is all wrong. Call yourself a man?

ISAAC. Anna.

ANNA. Take your hands off me. Go away. [*Pushes his shoulder.*]

ISAAC [*falls flat on the ground*]. Oh, how stupid!

OSIP [*comes in*]. Hallo, you funny people. Not you, is it, ma'am? [*Bows.*] What brought you to our sanctum?

ANNA. Is it you, Osip? Hallo! Seeing what you can pick up? Spying out the land? [*Takes him by the chin.*] Did you see it all?

OSIP. Yes.

ANNA. Why so pale, though? [*Laughs.*] Are you in love with me, Osip?

OSIP. As you wish, ma'am.

ANNA. Are you?

OSIP. I can't make you out. [*Weeps.*] I thought you were a saint. If you'd asked me to go through fire, I'd have been glad to.

ANNA. Why didn't you go to Kiev?

OSIP. What do I want in Kiev? I thought you were a saint, I worshipped you.

ANNA. That'll do, you fool. Bring me some more hares, I'll take them again. All right, good-bye. Come and see me tomorrow, I'll give you some money and you can go to Kiev by rail. All right? Good-bye. And don't dare lay your hands on Platonov, do you hear?

OSIP. I'll take no more orders from you.

ANNA. Good grief, he'll tell me to get myself to a nunnery next. What business is it of his? Well, well, well. Crying? Not a child, are you? Stop it. When he comes out, you fire a shot.

OSIP. At him?

ANNA. No, in the air. Good-bye, Osip. Fire a loud shot, all right?

OSIP. Yes.

ANNA. There's a good boy.

OSIP. Only he won't come, he's with his wife now.

ANNA. Oh, won't he? Good-bye, assassin. [*Runs out.*]

SCENE XI

[OSIP *and* ISAAC.]

OSIP [*bangs his hat on the ground and cries*]. It's all over. Everything can go to hell.

ISAAC [*lying on the ground*]. What does he say?

OSIP. I saw and heard the whole business. My eyes were ready to pop and there was a ruddy great banging in my ears. I heard it all. What else can I do but kill him, if I feel ready to tear him up and swallow him alive. [*Sits on the embankment with his back to the school.*] I must kill him.

ISAAC. What's that? Kill who?

SCENE XII

[*The above,* PLATONOV *and* NICHOLAS.]

PLATONOV [*pushes* NICHOLAS *out of the schoolhouse*]. Get out! Off with you to the shopkeeper's this instant—at the double!

NICHOLAS [*stretches*]. Better have hit me with a stick tomorrow than woken me up today.

PLATONOV. You're a real stinker, do you hear?

NICHOLAS. It can't be helped, it must be the way I'm built.

PLATONOV. What if the shopkeeper's already dead?

NICHOLAS. May he rest in peace in that case, and if he's still battling for life, there's no point in putting the wind up me. I'm not going to see any shopkeeper, I want to go to bed.

PLATONOV. You damn well shall go, you hound. [*Shoves him.*] I won't let you sleep. Who do you think you are, I'd like to know? Why do you never do anything? Why are you fooling around here, idling away the best years of your life?

NICHOLAS. Don't be a nuisance. You are a little tick, old man.

PLATONOV. What order of being are you, may one ask? This is ghastly. What do you live for? Why don't you study, continue your education? Why don't you study, animal?

NICHOLAS. Let's discuss this fascinating topic some time when I'm not sleepy. Now let me get back to bed. [*Scratches himself.*] It's a bit steep, all this 'Arise, you stinker' stuff, coming clean out of the blue. Professional ethics? Damn and blast professional ethics.

PLATONOV. What God do you serve, you odd creature? What sort of man are you? We'll never be any good, I can tell you that.

NICHOLAS. Look here, Michael, who gave you the right to lay your ruddy great frozen paws on people's hearts? You're so rude, old boy, it takes one's breath away.

PLATONOV. We'll never be more than the scum of the earth. We're done for, we're no damn good. [*Weeps.*] There's nobody one can bear to contemplate. How dirty, second-rate and second-hand everything is. Clear out, Nicholas, go!

NICHOLAS [*shrugs*]. Crying? [*Pause.*] I'll go and see the shopkeeper. I'm going, do you hear?

PLATONOV. Do what you like.

NICHOLAS. I'm going, look.

PLATONOV [*stamps*]. Buzz off!

NICHOLAS. All right. Go to bed, Michael—no need to get het up. Good-bye! [*Moves off and stops.*] One last word. You can tell all moralizers, yourself included, to practise what they preach. You can't bear to contemplate yourself, but I'm no sight for sore eyes either. Your eyes look very good in the moonlight, by the way, glittering like green glass. Another thing, I shouldn't be talking to you. You need a really good hiding, you should be torn to pieces. I should have nothing more to do with you because of that little girl. Shall I tell you something you've never heard in all your born days? No I can't, I'm no good at duelling, luckily for you. [*Pause.*] Good-bye. [*Goes.*]

SCENE XIII

[PLATONOV, ISAAC *and* OSIP.]

PLATONOV [*clutches his head*]. It's not just me, they're all that way, the whole lot. God, where are there any real people? But who am I to talk? 'Don't visit her, she's not yours, she belongs to someone else, you'll ruin her life, do her permanent harm.' Shall I leave? I shall not. I shall visit her, I shall live here as a drunken scapegrace. Depraved, drunken fools—always drunk, the mother a fool, the father a drunk. Father, mother—. Father—. Rot in your graves for the rotten mess you made of my poor life with your drunken folly. [*Pause.*] No—. What have I said? God forgive me, may they rest in peace. [*Bumps into* ISAAC *who is lying on the ground.*] Who's this?

ISAAC [*gets on his knees*]. What a wild, ugly, disgraceful night.

PLATONOV. Oh, go and write it all down in your stupid diary in the ink of your father's conscience. Clear out!

ISAAC. All right, I'll make a note of it. [*Goes out.*]

PLATONOV. What was he doing here? Eavesdropping? [*To* OSIP.] Who are you? What do you want, pirate? Eavesdropping too? Clear out! No, wait. Run after Vengerovich and take his chain.

OSIP [*gets up*]. What chain?

PLATONOV. He has a large gold chain on his chest. Catch him up and take it. Look slippy. [*Stamps.*] Hurry up or you'll miss him, he's rushing to the village like a maniac.

OSIP. And you to Anna Voynitsev, I suppose?

PLATONOV. Hurry up, you rogue. Don't beat him up, just take his chain. Off with you. Don't stand around. Run!

[OSIP *runs off.*]

PLATONOV [*after a pause*]. To go or not? [*Sighs.*] I'll go, and a long, fundamentally boring and ugly episode will begin. I thought I was proof against this sort of thing, and what happens? A woman says one word and all hell breaks loose inside me. Others have problems of world significance, my problem's a woman. All life's a woman. Caesar had the Rubicon, I have—woman. I'm always chasing a bit of skirt. It would be less pitiful if I didn't fight against it, but I do fight. I'm weak, utterly weak.

SASHA [*at the window*]. You there, Michael?

PLATONOV. Yes, my poor treasure.

SASHA. Come indoors.

PLATONOV. No, Sasha. I want a spell outside. I've got a splitting headache. Go to sleep, angel.

SASHA. Good night. [*Shuts window.*]

PLATONOV. It hurts to deceive someone who trusts you blindly. It made me sweat and blush. Coming!

[*Moves off.* KATYA *and* JACOB *come towards him.*]

SCENE XIV

[PLATONOV, KATYA *and* JACOB.]

KATYA [*to* JACOB]. Wait here, I shan't be long. I'll get a book. Mind you don't go away. [*Goes to meet* PLATONOV.]

PLATONOV [*seeing* KATYA]. You? What do you want?

KATYA [*terrified*]. Oh, it's you, sir. I was looking for you.

PLATONOV. You, Katya? You're all night-birds, from the mistress to the maid. What do you want?

KATYA [*quietly*]. I've a letter for you from my mistress, sir.

PLATONOV. What?

KATYA. A letter from my mistress.

PLATONOV. What's this nonsense? Which mistress?

KATYA [*more quietly*]. Miss Sonya, sir.

PLATONOV. What? Are you mad? You'd better put your head in cold water. Get out.

KATYA [*hands over a letter*]. This is it, sir.

PLATONOV [*snatches the letter off her*]. A letter—a letter. What letter? Couldn't you have brought it in the morning? [*Opens it.*] How can I read in this light.

KATYA. She said please be quick.

PLATONOV [*strikes a match*]. What the hell brought you here? [*Reads.*] 'Am taking first step. Come and take it with me. Am new woman. Come and take me. Am yours.' What the blazes! A sort of telegram. 'Shall wait till four in summer-house near four pillars. Husband drunk, gone hunting with young Glagolyev. All yours, S.' God, this is the giddy limit! [*To* KATYA.] What are you looking at?

KATYA. How can I help looking? I've got eyes, sir.

PLATONOV. Then put them out. Is that letter really for me?

KATYA. Yes.

PLATONOV. Nonsense. Get out!

KATYA. Very good, sir. [*Goes off with* JACOB.]

SCENE XV

[PLATONOV, *alone.*]

PLATONOV [*after a pause*]. So that's how it turned out. You have landed in a mess, old boy, you've ruined a woman, a living creature. What was the point, where was the need? Damn my idle tongue, look where it's got me. What can I do now? Come on, head—think, if you're so clever. Curse yourself, tear your hair. [*Thinks.*] I must go away, go away at once and not dare show my face again here this side of doomsday. I'll make myself scarce double quick and buckle down to a life of poverty and hard work. Better live badly than get entangled like this. [*Pause.*] I'll go away, but—does Sonya really love me? [*Laughs.*] But why? What a dark, strange world it is. [*Pause.*] Strange. That lovely, magnificent woman with her wonderful hair—can she really love a penniless eccentric? I don't believe it. [*Lights a match and scans the letter.*] Yes. Me? Sonya? [*Laughs.*] Love? [*Clutches his chest.*] Happiness—that's what this means! Me—happy! A new life, new people, new scenery! I'm coming. Quick march to the summer-house near the four pillars! Wait for me, Sonya, you have been mine, you shall be again. [*Moves off and stops.*] No, I can't. [*Moves back.*] How can I destroy my family? [*Shouts.*] Sasha, I'm coming in, open up. [*Clutches his head.*] I won't, I shan't, I will not go! [*Pause.*] I will! [*Moves off.*] I'll go, I'll destroy, trample, defile. [*Bumps into* SERGEY *and* CYRIL.]

SCENE XVI

[PLATONOV, SERGEY *and* CYRIL. SERGEY *and* CYRIL *run in with guns slung across their backs.*]

SERGEY. Here he is! [*Embraces* PLATONOV.] Well? Coming shooting?

PLATONOV. No, just a minute.

SERGEY. Trying to shake me off, old man? [*Laughs.*] Drunk. I'm drunk. For the first time in my life. God, I'm so happy, old boy. [*Embraces* PLATONOV.] Shall we go? She sent me—told me to bag some game for her.

CYRIL. Hurry, it's getting light.

SERGEY. Heard of our idea? A stroke of genius, eh? We want to put on *Hamlet*—honestly. It'll be one hell of a performance. [*Laughs.*] You are pale. Drunk too, are you?

PLATONOV. Drunk. Let me go.

SERGEY. Wait. It's my idea. We start painting the scenery tomorrow. I'll take Hamlet, Sonya will be Ophelia, you can be Claudius and Triletsky will be Horatio. I'm so happy, really pleased. Shakespeare, Sonya, you and Mother—what more could a man want? Oh yes, a spot of Glinka, that's all. I'm Hamlet.

> 'O shame! where is thy blush? Rebellious hell,
> If thou canst mutine in a matron's bones,
> To flaming youth let virtue be as wax,
> And melt in her own fire.'

[*Laughs.*] Quite a Hamlet, eh?

PLATONOV [*breaks away and runs off*]. You swine. [*Runs out.*]

SERGEY. I say, he *is* drunk! Oh, who cares? [*Laughs.*] What do you think of our friend?

CYRIL. Pretty well loaded. Come on.

SERGEY. Come on then. You'd be my friend too if—. 'Ophelia, nymph, in thy orisons be all my sins remembered.' [*Goes out. Sound of an approaching train.*]

SCENE XVII

[OSIP, *followed by* SASHA.]

OSIP [*runs in carrying the chain*]. Where is he? [*Looks round.*] Where is he? Gone? Not here? [*Whistles.*] Platonov! Michael! Hallo there!

[*Pause.*] Not here? [*Runs up to the window and knocks.*] Mr. Platonov! [*Smashes the pane.*]

SASHA [*at the window*]. Who's that?

OSIP. Call Platonov. Hurry up.

SASHA. What's happened? He's not in here.

OSIP [*shouts*]. Isn't he? Then he must be with Anna Voynitsev, she was here asking him to come to her. All is lost. He's gone to her, blast him.

SASHA. That's a lie.

OSIP. He's gone to her, so help me God. I heard and saw it all, they were embracing and kissing here.

SASHA. That's a lie.

OSIP. It isn't, or may my father and mother never go to heaven. He's gone to Anna Voynitsev. Left his wife. Go after him, ma'am. No, no, it's too late. Now you're unhappy too. [*Takes the gun off his shoulders.*] She gave me her final order and I'm carrying it out— finally. [*Shoots into the air.*] Just let them meet. [*Flings his gun on the ground.*] I'll cut his throat, ma'am. [*Jumps across the embankment and sits on a tree stump.*] Don't worry, ma'am, I'll cut his throat, never doubt. [*Lights appear.*]

SASHA [*comes out in her nightdress with her hair down*]. He's gone, betrayed me. [*Sobs.*] I'm done for. God, kill me after this! [*A whistle.*] I'll throw myself under the train, I don't want to live. [*Lies on the rails.*] He betrayed me. Kill me, Mother of God! [*Pause.*] Forgive me, Lord, forgive me. [*Shrieks.*] Nicholas! [*Rises to her knees.*] My son! Save me, save me! The train's coming! Save me!

[OSIP *jumps towards* SASHA.]

SASHA [*falls on the rails*]. Oh——

OSIP [*picks her up and carries her into the schoolhouse*]. I'll cut his throat, don't worry.

[*The train passes.*]

END OF ACT TWO

ACT THREE

A room in the schoolhouse. Doors, right and left. A cupboard containing crockery, a chest of drawers, an old upright piano, chairs, a sofa upholstered in oilcloth, a guitar and so on. All very untidy.

SCENE I

[SONYA *and* PLATONOV. PLATONOV *is asleep on the sofa by the window with a straw hat over his face.*]

SONYA [*wakes* PLATONOV *up*]. Platonov! Michael! [*Gives him a shove.*] Wake up. [*Takes the hat off his face.*] Why put this dirty old hat over your face? Ugh, what a slovenly fellow! What a pigsty! He's lost his studs and sleeps with his chest bare, unwashed, in a dirty nightshirt. Michael, I'm talking to you. Get up.

PLATONOV. What?

SONYA. Wake up.

PLATONOV. In a moment. All right.

SONYA. That's enough of that. Get up, will you?

PLATONOV. Who is it? [*Sits up.*] Is it you, Sonya?

SONYA [*holds a watch near his eyes*]. Look.

PLATONOV. All right. [*Lies down again.*]

SONYA. Platonov!

PLATONOV. What do you want? [*Sits up.*] Eh?

SONYA. Look at the time.

PLATONOV. What is this? Another of your tricks, Sonya?

SONYA. Exactly. Kindly look at the watch. What time is it?

PLATONOV. Half past seven.

SONYA. Exactly. Have you forgotten our arrangement?

PLATONOV. What arrangement? Say what you mean, Sonya, I'm in no mood for jokes or nonsensical riddles.

SONYA. 'What arrangement'! Have you forgotten? What's wrong with you? Your eyes are bloodshot and you look an awful mess. Are you ill? [*Pause.*] We arranged to be at the hut at six o'clock this morning. Have you forgotten? It's long past six.

PLATONOV. Anything else?

SONYA [*sits by him*]. Aren't you ashamed? Why didn't you come? You did promise.

PLATONOV. I'd have kept my promise too, if I hadn't fallen asleep. You can see I've been sleeping, can't you? Don't pester me.

SONYA [*shakes her head*]. You are unreliable. Don't look so angry, you're unreliable towards me, anyway. Think. Have you ever been on time at any of our meetings? How often you've broken your promises to me!

PLATONOV. I'm glad to hear it.

SONYA. That's not very clever, Platonov, you should be ashamed. Why have you stopped being decent, intelligent and sincere when I'm with you? Why these vulgar outbursts unworthy of the man I owe my salvation to? You always treat me like an ogre—no kind looks, no tender words, not one word of love. I come and see you and you smell of drink, you're dressed horribly, you haven't done your hair and you answer rudely and at random.

PLATONOV [*jumps up and strides about the stage*]. At it again!

SONYA. Drunk, are you?

PLATONOV. Mind your own business.

SONYA. What a charming remark. [*Weeps.*]

PLATONOV. Women!

SONYA. Don't talk to me about women. You go on about women a thousand times a day and I'm fed up. [*Gets up.*] What are you doing to me? Do you want to kill me? You've made me ill, my chest aches day and night, thanks to you. Can't you see, aren't you interested? You hate me. You wouldn't dare treat me like this if you loved me. I'm not an ordinary village girl without manners or refinement, and I shan't let someone like you—. [*Sits down.*] For God's sake! [*Weeps.*]

PLATONOV. That will do.

SONYA. Why are you killing me? It's not three weeks since that night and I'm already as thin as a rake. Where's the happiness you promised? Where will your antics end? Think, if you're so clever, noble and decent—give thought, Platonov, before it's too late. Think now. Sit on this chair, make your mind a blank and concentrate on what you're doing to me.

PLATONOV. I'm no good at thinking. [*Pause.*] You think. [*Goes up to her.*] Come on. I've taken away your family, your well-being and your future. Why? What for? I've robbed you as if I was your worst enemy. What can I give you? How can I repay your sacrifices? This sordid affair is your misfortune, downfall and ruin. [*Sits down.*]

SONYA. I give myself to him and he has the nerve to call our relationship a sordid affair.

PLATONOV. This is hardly the time to quibble. You have your view of this affair and I have mine. I've ruined you and that's that—you're not the only one either. Wait and see what your husband has to say when he finds out.

SONYA. Are you afraid he may make things unpleasant for you?

PLATONOV. No, I'm not, I'm afraid we may kill him.

SONYA. Then why did you come to me that day, you miserable coward, if you knew we were going to kill him?

PLATONOV. Oh, don't be so emotional. This heart-rending stuff leaves me cold. But why did you—? Anyway—. [*Makes a gesture of resignation.*] Speaking to you means bringing on floods of tears.

SONYA. Yes, I never cried before our affair. It's time you started shivering with fear because he knows already.

PLATONOV. What?

SONYA. He knows already.

PLATONOV [*sits up*]. What!

SONYA. He knows. I told him this morning.

PLATONOV. You're joking.

SONYA. You've turned pale. I should hate you, not love you. I must be mad. I don't know why—why I do love you. Yes, he knows. [*Plucks his sleeve.*] So tremble in your boots. He knows everything, I tell you. Go on, tremble.

PLATONOV. Impossible. I don't believe it. [*Pause.*]

SONYA. He knows. He had to be told some day, didn't he?

PLATONOV. But why are *you* trembling? How did you put it? What did you say?

SONYA. I told him I—I couldn't——

PLATONOV. And he?

SONYA. He was just like you—scared. You look quite insufferable at the moment.

PLATONOV. What did he say?

SONYA. He thought I was joking at first, but when he saw I wasn't he blenched, staggered, burst into tears and crawled on all fours. He looked as disgusting as you do now.

PLATONOV. What have you done, you loathsome woman! [*Clutches his head.*] You've killed him. Can you—dare you—say all this so cold-bloodedly? You've killed him. Did you name me?

SONYA. Yes, what do you think?

PLATONOV. What did he say?

SONYA [*jumps up*]. You really should be ashamed, Platonov, you don't know what you're saying. You think I shouldn't have told him, I suppose?

PLATONOV. You certainly shouldn't. [*Lies on the sofa, face downwards.*]

SONYA. Is that the way for a decent man to talk?

PLATONOV. It would have been more decent to say nothing than to kill him, because that's what we've done. He cried and crawled on all fours. Oh dear! [*Jumps up.*] Poor wretch—if it wasn't for you he'd never have known about us till the day he died.

SONYA. I had to tell him as an honest woman.

PLATONOV. You know what you've done by telling him, I take it? You can never go back to your husband now.

SONYA. Yes, never. What else do you think? You're beginning to talk like a thorough cad, Platonov.

PLATONOV. 'Never—.' But what will happen to you when we part— as we soon shall? You'll be the first to realize the error of your ways and see the light. You'll leave me first. [*Makes a gesture of resignation.*] Anyway, do as you like, Sonya. You're cleverer and more honest than I, so you'd better take charge. This is a fine kettle of fish—you'd better deal with it. Bring me back to life if you can and set me on my feet. Only hurry up, for God's sake, or I'll go mad.

SONYA. We leave here tomorrow.

PLATONOV. Yes, yes, we'll go. But let's hurry.

SONYA. I must get you away. I wrote to Mother about you, we'll go and see her.

PLATONOV. Anywhere you like, do as you wish.

SONYA. This means a new life, dear, can't you see? Do as I say, let me have my way. My head's clearer than yours. Trust me, darling, I'll put you back on your feet. I'll take you to a brighter place with no dust, grime, idleness or dirty nightshirts. I'll make a man of you—I'll make you happy, can't you see? [*Pause.*] I'll make you work. We'll be real people, Michael, we'll eat our own bread, sweat, get blisters. [*Lays her head on his chest.*] I shall work.

PLATONOV. Where will you work? Other women, stronger than you, lie around idle because they've nothing to do. You don't know how to work and what job will you do? The way we're fixed, Sonya, we'd do better to think straight—not take comfort in illusions. But have it your own way.

SONYA. You'll see. I'm stronger than these other women. I'll light the way for you, believe me, Michael. You've brought me back to life and I shall always be grateful. Shall we leave tomorrow then? I'll go and start packing, and you do the same. Come to the hut at ten o'clock and bring your things. All right?

PLATONOV. Yes.

SONYA. Promise?

PLATONOV. Look, I've said I will, haven't I?

SONYA. Promise.

PLATONOV. All right, we'll go. I swear.

SONYA [*laughs*]. I believe you. Come a bit earlier if you like, I'll be ready before ten. We'll drive off tonight. We'll have lots of fun, Michael. You don't know your own luck, silly boy. Why, this is our happiness, our life. Tomorrow you'll be a different man, new and fresh. We'll breathe a new air, new blood will flow through our veins. [*Laughs.*] Farewell, our decrepit old selves. Here's my hand. Hold it tight.

[*Gives him her hand.* PLATONOV *kisses it.*]

SONYA. Mind you're there, you old porpoise. I'll be waiting. Good-bye for the moment and cheer up. I'll be packed in a jiffy. [*Kisses him.*]

PLATONOV. Good-bye. Did you say ten or eleven?

SONYA. Ten. Or come a bit earlier. Good-bye. Put on some decent
clothes for the journey. [*Laughs.*] I have some money, we can get
supper on the way. Good-bye. I'll go and get ready. Cheer up, I
expect you at ten. [*Runs off.*]

SCENE II
[PLATONOV, *alone.*]

PLATONOV [*after a pause*]. Tell me the old, old story—I've heard all
that hundreds of times. [*Pause.*] I'll write to him and Sasha. They
can have a bit of a cry, and forgive and forget. Good-bye, Voynitsevka. Good-bye, Sasha, Anna and all. [*Opens the cupboard.*] I'll be a
new man tomorrow, terribly new. What shall I put my clothes in?
I've no suitcase. [*Pours some wine.*] Good-bye, school. [*Drinks.*] Good-
bye, children, you won't see your Mr. Platonov again—that bad, but
kind teacher. Was I drinking just now? Why? I'm going to give it
up, this is the last time. I'll sit down and write to Sasha. [*Lies on the
sofa.*] Sonya truly believes—and blessed are those who have faith.
Laugh away, Anna, because laugh you will, and pretty loud at that.
Oh yes, I think I had a letter from her. Where is it? [*Gets a letter from
the window-sill.*] It's the hundredth, if not the two hundredth, since
that wild night. [*Reads.*] 'Platonov, you who don't answer my
letters, you tactless, cruel, stupid lout. If you don't answer this one
either and don't come and see me—then I'll come and see *you*,
damn you. I've been waiting all day. It's silly, Platonov—anyone
would think you were ashamed of that night. Oh, forget it then.
Sergey and Sonya are behaving abominably—their wild honey-
moon is over and all because they haven't their talkative idiot with
them, meaning you. Good-bye.' [*Pause.*] What handwriting—neat
and bold, with commas and full stops, and no spelling mistakes. A
literate woman's a pretty rare thing. [MARKO *comes in.*] I must
write her a letter or she may turn up here. [*Seeing* MARKO.] A pretty
rare thing——

SCENE III
[PLATONOV *and* MARKO.]

PLATONOV. Come in. Who do you want? [*Gets up.*]

MARKO. You, sir. [*Takes a document out of his bag.*] A summons for
you, sir.

PLATONOV. Oh. Very nice too. What summons? Who sent you?

MARKO. The magistrate, sir.

PLATONOV. I see. And what does he want? Give it here. [*Takes the summons.*] I don't understand, is he inviting me to a christening? The old so-and-so breeds like a rabbit. [*Reads.*] ' . . . as defendant charged with assault on the person of Mary, daughter of Councillor Grekov.' [*Laughs.*] Oh hell! Loud cheers! Damn it all! Good old distilled bed-bugs! When's the case on? The day after tomorrow? I'll be there. Tell them I'm coming, reverend sir. Good for her, I must say. What a girl, she should have done it long ago.

MARKO. Would you mind signing, sir?

PLATONOV. Signing? All right. You look awfully like a dying duck, old boy.

MARKO. Permission to disagree, sir.

PLATONOV [*sits at the table*]. Then what do you look like?

MARKO. The image and likeness of God, sir.

PLATONOV. An old soldier, eh?

MARKO. Yes sir. Discharged after Sevastopol, sir. Had four years in hospital on top of my service. Sergeant of artillery, sir.

PLATONOV. I see. Were your guns any good?

MARKO. Ordinary ones—with a round barrel, like.

PLATONOV. Pencil all right?

MARKO. Yes sir. To say you duly received this summons. Put your full name, sir.

PLATONOV [*gets up*]. There. I've signed five times. How's the magistrate? Still gambling?

MARKO. Yes sir.

PLATONOV. Round the clock from five in the afternoon?

MARKO. Just so, sir.

PLATONOV. Has he lost his chain of office yet?

MARKO. No sir.

PLATONOV. Tell him—no, don't tell him anything. He doesn't pay his gambling debts, of course. Silly fool gambles, runs up debts and has a horde of children. What a clever little girl, honestly I never expected it. Who are the witnesses then? Who's being subpoenaed?

MARKO [*fingers through the summonses and reads*]. 'To Dr. Nicholas Triletsky', sir——

PLATONOV. Triletsky? [*Laughs.*] That should be quite amusing. Anyone else?

MARKO [*reads*]. 'To Mr. Cyril Glagolyev; to Mr. Alphonse Schrifter; to Mr. Maxim Aleutov, retired cornet of the guards; to Master Ivan Talye, son of Councillor Talye; to Mr. Sergey Voynitsev, graduate of St. Petersburg Nonversity——'

PLATONOV. Is that how it's spelt—'nonversity'?

MARKO. No sir.

PLATONOV. Then why read it out that way?

MARKO. Sheer ignorance, sir. [*Reads.*] 'Uni-uni-nonversity; to his wife, Mrs. Sonya Voynitsev; to Mr. Isaac Vengerovich, student of Kharkov Nonversity.' That's all.

PLATONOV. This is for the day after tomorrow, and I must leave tomorrow. What a pity. It would have been quite a case, I imagine. Well. What a nuisance, I'd have given her a run for her money. [*Walks up and down the stage.*] A great pity.

MARKO. Matter of a tip, sir.

PLATONOV. Eh?

MARKO. A tip. I had to walk four miles.

PLATONOV. A tip? I don't need one. But what am I saying? All right, old man, but I won't give you money, I'll give you tea instead to save my pocket and keep you sober. [*Takes a caddy from the cupboard.*] Come here. It's good strong tea—not seventy degrees proof, but strong. How would you like it?

MARKO [*holds out his pocket*]. In here, sir.

PLATONOV. What, straight in your pocket? Won't it smell?

MARKO. Pour away, sir, do. Don't hesitate.

PLATONOV [*pours tea leaves into his pocket*]. Enough?

MARKO. Thanking you kindly, sir.

PLATONOV. I say, aren't you old! I like old sweats like you—grand chaps. You sometimes meet a really awful one, though.

MARKO. It takes all sorts, sir. Only God's perfect. Good luck, sir.

PLATONOV. Wait a moment. [*Sits down and writes on the summons.*]

'I kissed you because—because I was annoyed and didn't know what I wanted, but I'd kiss you now with the greatest respect. I was rotten to you, I admit, just as I am to everyone. We shan't meet in court, I fear—tomorrow I leave for good. Good luck, and do at least be fair to me by not forgiving me.' [*To* MARKO.] Do you know where Miss Grekov lives?

MARKO. Yes, sir. About eight miles away if you cross by the ford.

PLATONOV. Oh, yes—in Zhilkovo. Take her this letter and you'll earn three roubles. Give it to the young lady in person. No answer's needed, and if she tries to give you one, don't accept it. Take it today, this instant. Take it first, and deliver the summonses later. [*Walks up and down the stage.*]

MARKO. I understand, sir.

PLATONOV. What else? Oh, yes. Tell everyone I apologized to Miss Grekov, but she wouldn't accept my apology.

MARKO. I see. Good luck, sir.

PLATONOV. Good-bye, old boy, and look after yourself.

[MARKO *goes out.*]

SCENE IV

[PLATONOV, *alone.*]

PLATONOV. So the Grekov and I are quits. She'll drag my name through the mud all over the county, and serve me right. It'll be the first time I've been punished by a woman. [*Lies on the sofa.*] Treat them like dirt and they only cling harder. Take Sonya. [*Covers his face with a handkerchief.*] I used to be free as the wind, but now I lie here, dreaming. Love—*amo, amas, amat.* Why did I get involved? I've wrecked her life and a fat lot of good I've done myself! [*Sighs.*] Poor Voynitsevs. And there's Sasha, poor kid—how will she get on without me? She'll pine away and die. She went away, she could sense what was happening and left with the child without a single word. She left after that night. I ought to say good-bye to her.

ANNA [*at the window*]. Can I come in? Hey, anyone there?

PLATONOV. Anna! [*Jumps up.*] Anna Voynitsev! What can I say to her? Why should she come here, anyway, I wonder? [*Straightens his clothes.*]

ANNA [*at the window*]. Can I come in? I'm coming, do you hear?

PLATONOV. She's here! How can I keep her out? [*Does his hair.*] How can I get rid of her? I'll have a drink before she comes in. [*Quickly opens the cupboard.*] What the hell is she after? I've no idea. [*Takes a quick drink.*] I'm all right if she doesn't know anything, but what if she does? I shall look such a fool.

SCENE V

[PLATONOV *and* ANNA. ANNA *comes in.* PLATONOV *slowly closes the cupboard.*]

ANNA. Hallo there. How are you?

PLATONOV. It won't shut. [*Pause.*]

ANNA. I say—hallo there.

PLATONOV. Ah, you, Anna, is it? Sorry, I didn't notice. Wretched door won't shut. Odd. [*Drops the key and picks it up.*]

ANNA. Come a bit nearer and leave that cupboard alone, do.

PLATONOV [*goes up to her*]. Hallo.

ANNA. Why don't you look at me?

PLATONOV. I'm too ashamed. [*Kisses her hand.*]

ANNA. What of?

PLATONOV. Everything.

ANNA. I see. Seduced someone, have you?

PLATONOV. Something of the sort.

ANNA. Same old Platonov! Who's the girl?

PLATONOV. I shan't tell you.

ANNA. Let's sit down. [*Sits on the sofa.*] We'll find out, young man, we'll find out. Why so ashamed? I've long known your sinful nature, haven't I?

PLATONOV. Don't ask questions, Anna. I'm not inclined to participate in an inquisition. Speak if you want, but don't ask questions.

ANNA. All right. Did you get my letters?

PLATONOV. Yes.

ANNA. Then why didn't you come?

PLATONOV. Oh, this is too much.

ANNA. Why is it too much?

PLATONOV. Because it is.

ANNA. Are you sulking?

PLATONOV. No, why should I? For God's sake don't ask questions.

ANNA. Kindly answer me, sir. Sit down properly. Why haven't you been to see us in the last three weeks?

PLATONOV. I've been ill.

ANNA. That's a lie.

PLATONOV. All right, it's a lie. Don't question me, Anna.

ANNA. You smell of booze. What's the meaning of this, Platonov? What's up? You look like nothing on earth—eyes bloodshot, ghastly face. You're filthy, so's your house. Take a good look round, the place is like a pigsty. What's the trouble—been drinking?

PLATONOV. Heavily.

ANNA. It's last year's business all over again. Last year you seduced some girl and went round till autumn looking the most awful drip—just as you look now, great lover and cringing worm all rolled into one. How dare you drink!

PLATONOV. I'll stop.

ANNA. Promise? But why should I bother you with promises? [*Gets up.*] Where's your drink?

[PLATONOV *points to the cupboard.*]

ANNA. Aren't you ashamed to be such a worm? Where's your backbone? [*Opens the cupboard.*] What a mess. Sasha will give you what for when she gets back. Do you want her back?

PLATONOV. Don't ask questions and don't stare at me, that's all I ask.

ANNA. Which bottle has liquor in it?

PLATONOV. All of them.

ANNA. What, all five? You old soak, you. A regular grog-shop in his cupboard! It's high time Sasha came back. You must explain things to her somehow. I'm not a very terrible rival. I'm ready to compromise—it's not my plan to keep you two apart. [*Sips from a bottle.*] Very tasty. Come on, how about a little drink? Eh? We'll just have one and then give it up.

[PLATONOV *goes to the cupboard.*]

ANNA. Hold your glass. [*Pours.*] Down the hatch. That's all you're getting.

[PLATONOV *drinks.*]

ANNA. Now I'll have one. [*Pours.*] To bad men everywhere. [*Drinks.*] You're one of them. Quite decent liquor, you have some taste. [*Hands him the bottles.*] Catch! Bring them here. [*They go to the window.*] Now say good-bye to your nice drinks. [*Looks through the window.*] Pity to pour it away, though—how about another, eh?

PLATONOV. As you like.

ANNA [*pours*]. Drink up, be quick about it.

PLATONOV [*drinks*]. Your health! And good luck.

ANNA [*pours and drinks*]. Have you missed me? Let's sit, and put the bottles down for a moment. [*They sit.*] Miss me?

PLATONOV. Every moment.

ANNA. Then why didn't you come?

PLATONOV. Don't ask. I shan't tell you, not because I have any secrets from you, I just want to spare your ears. I'm going completely to the dogs, darling, what with my pangs of conscience, misery, depressions—it's sheer torture in fact. You came, and that cheered me up.

ANNA. You look thin and ugly. I loathe these romantic heroes. What are you trying to pose as? Someone in a magazine story? Depression, misery, the battleground of passions, love complete with trimmings. Come off it, be a man. Can't you live like ordinary people, you idiot? Who do you think you are—God Almighty? Can't you live, sit and breathe like a mere mortal?

PLATONOV. It's easy to talk. What can I do?

ANNA. A living man—and doesn't know what to do! Most peculiar. What can he do? All right, I'll answer as well as I can, though the question's too idle to need an answer.

PLATONOV. You can't answer.

ANNA. Firstly, live like a human being. Don't drink, don't loll about, wash a bit more often and come and see me. Secondly, be content with what you have. You're being silly, my good sir. Isn't it enough to have gone in for this schoolmastering caper? [*Stands up.*] Come over to my place at once.

PLATONOV. What? [*Stands up.*] Go to your house? Oh dear me no.

ANNA. Come on. You'll meet a few people, talk, listen, argue a bit.

PLATONOV. No, no, no. And don't order me about.

ANNA. Why not?

PLATONOV. I can't go, and that's that.

ANNA. Oh yes you can, put on your hat and come.

PLATONOV. I can't, Anna, nothing would induce me. I won't move one step from this house.

ANNA. Oh yes you can. [*Puts his hat on his head.*] You're just fooling around, my dear man, don't try this funny stuff with me. [*Takes his arm.*] Left, right! Come on, Platonov. Quick march. [*Pause.*] Come along, Michael.

PLATONOV. I can't.

ANNA. He's stubborn as a mule. Put your best foot forward. Come on. Left, right—. Michael, darling, my dearest precious one.

PLATONOV [*breaking away*]. I'm not going, Anna.

ANNA. Then let's stroll round outside the school.

PLATONOV. Why must you pester me? Didn't I say I wasn't coming? I want to stay here, so leave me alone. [*Pause.*] I'm not going.

ANNA. I tell you what, I'll lend you some money and you go away for a month or two.

PLATONOV. Where to?

ANNA. Moscow, St. Petersburg—. How about it? Do go, Michael. You badly need a change. You can go for drives, look at the people, visit the theatres, tune yourself up and give yourself an airing. I'll give you money and letters. Like me to come with you? Eh? We'll drive around, have fun and come back refreshed and radiant.

PLATONOV. A fine idea, but it can't be done, sorry. I leave here tomorrow, but not with you.

ANNA. As you wish. Where are you going?

PLATONOV. Where I'm going. [*Pause.*] I'm leaving here for good.

ANNA. Don't be silly. [*Drinks from the bottle.*] Rubbish!

PLATONOV. It's not rubbish, dear, I'm going for good.

ANNA. But why on earth, you funny man?

PLATONOV. Don't ask me, but I'm not coming back, really. I'm leaving and—. Good-bye, that's all. Don't ask questions, you'll learn nothing from me now.

ANNA. Rubbish.

PLATONOV. This is our last meeting. I shall disappear for good. [*Takes her by the sleeve, then by the shoulder.*] Forget that idiot, ass, scoundrel and blackguard Platonov. He'll be swallowed up into the earth and vanish. We may meet in a few dozen years when we'll both be able to laugh and shed senile tears over these days, but now to hell with it! [*Kisses her hand.*]

ANNA. Come on, have a drink. [*Pours him some.*] A drunk can be excused for drivelling.

PLATONOV [*takes a drink*]. I won't get drunk. I'll remember you, fairy godmother, I'll never forget. All right, laugh, my emancipated blonde! Tomorrow I escape—from this place and from myself. Don't know where I'm going. I'm running away to a new life. I've a fair idea how it'll turn out!

ANNA. This is all very well, but what's come over you?

PLATONOV. What? I—. You'll find out later. My dear, when you shudder at what I'm going to do, don't curse me. I've been pretty well punished already, remember. Isn't it punishment enough to part from you for ever? Why do you smile? Believe me, you must believe me. I feel so beastly rotten and foul, I could strangle myself.

ANNA [*through tears*]. I can't think you could do anything awful. Will you write to me at least?

PLATONOV. I shan't dare to, and you won't want my letters anyway. Once and for all, unconditionally—farewell!

ANNA. You'll go to the dogs without me, Platonov. [*Rubs her forehead.*] I'm a bit drunk. Let's go together.

PLATONOV. No. Tomorrow you'll learn all and——. [*Turns to the window.*]

ANNA. Need money?

PLATONOV. No.

ANNA. Quite sure I can't help?

PLATONOV. I don't know. Send me a picture of yourself today. [*Turns back.*] Go away, Anna, or I don't know what the hell I'll do. I'll burst into tears, beat my breast and—. Go away. I can't stay, I tell you straight. So what are you waiting for? I must go, get that in your head. Why look at me like that and pull such faces?

ANNA. Good-bye. [*Gives him her hand.*] We'll meet again.

PLATONOV. No. [*Kisses her hand.*] That's enough—go away, dear. [*Kisses her hand.*] Good-bye. Leave me. [*Covers his face with her hand.*]

ANNA. He's all sloppy and sentimental, dear boy. Well? Let go my hand. Good-bye. How about a farewell drink? [*Pours.*] Drink up! Happy journey to you and good luck on arrival.

[PLATONOV *drinks.*]

ANNA. Couldn't you stay, though? [*Pours and drinks.*] We could have some fun. That's not a crime, is it? Can such a thing be imagined at Voynitsevka? [*Pause.*] Another one? To drown our sorrows?

PLATONOV. Yes.

ANNA [*pours*]. Drink up, darling. To hell with everything!

PLATONOV [*drinks*]. Good luck. Live here and—. You don't need me.

ANNA. If we're to drink, let's make a good job of it. [*Pours.*] You die if you drink and you die if you don't, so it's better to drink and to die. [*Drinks.*] I'm a drunkard, eh, Platonov? Want some more? I suppose we shouldn't. We'll get tongue-tied and then what shall we talk with? [*Sits down.*] There's nothing worse than being an educated woman, one with nothing to do. What's the point of me? Why do I live? [*Pause.*] I can't help being immoral. I'm an immoral woman, Platonov. [*Laughs.*] Eh? Perhaps that's why I love you, because I'm immoral. [*Rubs her forehead.*] I'll come to a bad end, my sort always do. I should be a professor, a headmistress or something. If I'd been a diplomat I'd have given the world a pretty thorough shake-up. An educated woman with nothing to do. I'm not needed, you see. Horses, cows and dogs are needed but not me—I'm just no use. Well? Why don't you speak?

PLATONOV. We're both in a bad way.

ANNA. If only I had children. Do you like children? [*Gets up.*] Stay behind, darling. Will you? We'd have lots of fun together. What will happen to me if you leave? I want a holiday, need a good rest. I want to be—a wife and mother. [*Pause.*] Say something. Speak. Won't you stay? You do love me, don't you, silly?

PLATONOV [*looks out of the window*]. I'll kill myself if I stay here.

ANNA. You love me, don't you?

PLATONOV. Who doesn't?

ANNA. You love me, I love you—what more do you want? You must be going crazy. What more do you want? Why didn't you come and see me that night? [*Pause.*] Are you staying?

PLATONOV. For God's sake go. You're torturing me.

ANNA [*gives him her hand*]. Well, in that case—good luck.

PLATONOV. Go away, or I shall tell everything and if I do I'll kill myself.

ANNA. I'm giving you my hand, can't you see? I'll pop over for a minute this evening.

PLATONOV. Don't, I'll come over and say good-bye myself. I'll come over—no, I will not! We've seen the last of each other. You won't want to see me, you won't want any more to do with me. A new life—. [*Embraces and kisses her.*] For the last time. [*Pushes her through the door.*] Good-bye. Run along, and good luck to you. [*Bolts the door.*]

ANNA [*behind the door*]. I swear we'll meet again.

PLATONOV. Never! Good-bye! [*Stuffs his fingers in his ears.*] I can't hear. Shut up and go away, I've blocked my ears.

ANNA. I'm going. I'll send Sergey over, and I guarantee you won't leave, unless it's with me. Good-bye. [*Pause.*]

SCENE VI

[PLATONOV, *alone.*]

PLATONOV. Has she gone? [*Goes to the door and listens.*] Yes. Perhaps not. [*Opens the door.*] She is rather a handful, isn't she? [*Looks out through the door.*] Gone. [*Lies on the sofa.*] Good-bye, my dear. [*Sighs.*] That's the last I'll see of you. Gone. She might have stayed five minutes longer. [*Pause.*] It wouldn't have been a bad idea. I'll ask Sonya to put off our departure by a couple of weeks, and go off with Anna. Only two weeks. Sonya will agree, she can stay with her mother for the time being. Shall I ask her, eh? While I'm away with Anna, Sonya can have a rest—pull herself together in fact. I shan't be away for ever, after all. [*A knock on the door.*] I'm leaving, it's settled. Excellent. [*Another knock.*] Who's knocking? Is it Anna? Who's there? [*Another knock.*] Is that you? [*Stands up.*] I won't let you in. [*Goes to the door.*] Is it her? [*Another knock.*] I think she's giggling. [*Laughs.*] It's her, I must let her in. [*Opens the door.*] Oh!

[*Enter* OSIP.]

SCENE VII

[PLATONOV *and* OSIP.]

PLATONOV. What on earth? You, damn you? What brings you here?

OSIP. Good evening, Mr. Platonov.

PLATONOV. What have you to say for yourself? To what and to whom do I owe the honour of so important a visit? Say your piece quickly and get to hell out of here.

OSIP. I'll sit. [*Sits.*]

PLATONOV. Oh, carry on. [*Pause.*] Is this you, Osip? What's wrong? You look as if you'd suffered all ten plagues of Egypt. What's wrong with you—pale, thin, worn? Are you ill?

OSIP. You've a pretty plaguy look yourself. What's happened to you? I'm in the hell of a state—how about you?

PLATONOV. Me? I'm not in touch with hell, I provide my own. [*Touches* OSIP'*s shoulder.*] All skin and bones.

OSIP. You're not so plump yourself? Not ill, are you, sir? Been behaving too well, is that it?

PLATONOV [*sits down by him*]. What are you doing here?

OSIP. I want to say good-bye.

PLATONOV. Oh? Going somewhere?

OSIP. I'm not—*you* are.

PLATONOV. Oh, I see. How do you know?

OSIP. It's pretty obvious.

PLATONOV. You needn't have bothered, because I'm not going.

OSIP. Oh yes you are, sir.

PLATONOV. You seem to be quite a know-all and busybody. You're a magician, Osip. I am going, my dear fellow, you're quite right.

OSIP. So I did know, you see. I even know where you're going.

PLATONOV. Oh? What a man! I don't know that myself. You must be a real pundit—all right, where am I going?

OSIP. Want to know?

PLATONOV. Please, I'm interested. Where?

OSIP. To the next world, sir.

PLATONOV. That's a long way. [*Pause.*] Most mysterious—you wouldn't be going to dispatch me, would you?

OSIP. Just so, sir. I've brought you your ticket.

PLATONOV. Very nice of you. Well, well. So you've come to murder me?

OSIP. Yes sir.

PLATONOV [*imitating him*]. 'Yes sir.' What damned cheek! He's come to dispatch me to the next world. Is this your idea, or are you someone's agent?

OSIP [*shows him a twenty-five rouble note*]. Vengerovich gave me this to break your lordship's bones. [*Tears up the note.*]

PLATONOV. Old Vengerovich, eh?

OSIP. Yes.

PLATONOV. Then why tear it up? To show how noble you are, or what?

OSIP. That's a bit beyond me. I tore it up so you won't think I killed you for money when you get to the next world.

[PLATONOV *stands up and walks up and down the stage.*]

OSIP. Afraid, sir? Scared? [*Laughs.*] Run, shout if you want. I'm not standing by the door or holding it—you can get away. Go and call someone, tell them Osip came to kill you. Because I did. Don't you believe me? [*Pause.*]

PLATONOV [*goes up to* OSIP *and looks at him*]. Remarkable. [*Pause.*] What are you grinning at, idiot? [*Hits his arm.*] Stop grinning when I'm talking to you. And shut up. I'll hang you. I'll knock you into a cocked hat, you crook. [*Goes quickly away from him.*] Anyway—don't annoy me, I'm not supposed to get angry. I don't feel well.

OSIP. I'm a bad man, sir, so slap my face.

PLATONOV. By all means. [*Goes up to* OSIP *and slaps his face.*] Staggered you a bit? You wait, you'll stagger a sight more than that when hundreds of sticks smash in your empty skull. Remember how pock-marked Filka died?

OSIP. He lived like a dog and died like a dog.

PLATONOV. Ugh, you vile rat! I've a good mind to break a few bones, you blackguard. Why do you hurt people, you mean wretch, like some plague or conflagration? What have they done to you? Ugh, you horror! [*Slaps his face.*] Filthy swine. I'll show you, I'll—. [*Quickly goes away from* OSIP.] Now get out.

OSIP. Spit in my eyes, sir, for being such a bad man.

PLATONOV. I wouldn't waste good saliva.

OSIP [*stands up*]. How dare you talk like that?

PLATONOV. Get out of here before I really sort you out.

OSIP. You wouldn't dare, you're a bad man too.

PLATONOV. Bandy words with me, would you? [*Goes up to him.*] You came to kill me, I think? Well then, carry on. Here I am, go ahead.

OSIP. I used to think a lot of you, sir, used to think you were quite somebody. But now—. I'm sorry to kill you, but I must, you do too much damage. Why did the young lady come to see you today?

PLATONOV [*ruffles* OSIP's *chest*]. Go on, kill me.

OSIP. Why did Mrs. Voynitsev come here after her? You're deceiving her too, are you? And where's your wife? Which of the three do you really care for? Still think you're not a bad man? [*Swiftly trips* PLATONOV *and falls on the floor with him.*]

PLATONOV. Get out. I'll do the killing, not you. I'm stronger. [*They struggle.*] Less noise!

OSIP. Now on to your stomach. And keep your arm still—it hasn't done anything wrong, so why twist it? There you go again! My regards to General Voynitsev in the next world.

PLATONOV. Let go.

OSIP [*takes a knife from his belt*]. Less noise, I shall kill you anyway. Oh, aren't we big and strong, sir? Don't want to die, eh? Then keep your hands off what ain't yours.

PLATONOV [*shouts*]. My arm! Wait, wait! My arm!

OSIP. Don't feel up to dying, sir? You'll be in paradise in two ticks.

PLATONOV. Don't stab me in the back, monster. Stab me in the chest. My arm! Let go, Osip! I have a wife and son. Is that your knife shining, you vicious brute?

[SASHA *runs in.*]

SCENE VIII

[*The above and* SASHA.]

SASHA [*runs in*]. What's the matter? [*Shrieks.*] Michael! [*Runs towards the struggling pair and falls on them.*] What are you doing?

OSIP. Who's this? You, ma'am? [*Jumps up.*] I'll let him off. [*To* SASHA.] Here—my knife. [*Gives her the knife.*] I won't cut his throat while you're here, I'll let him off and do it later—he won't get away. [*Jumps out of the window.*]

PLATONOV [*after a pause*]. Blast the man. Hallo, Sasha—it's you, is it? [*Groans.*]

SASHA. Did he hurt you? Can you stand up? Quick.

PLATONOV. I don't know, he's a pretty tough customer. Give me your hand. [*Gets up.*] Don't worry, dear, I'm right as rain—he only roughed me up a bit.

SASHA. Vile creature! I told you to keep clear of him.

PLATONOV. Where's the sofa? What are you staring at? Your faithless husband's alive, can't you see? [*Lies on the sofa.*] Thank goodness you came, or I'd be dead and you a widow.

SASHA. Put your head on this pillow. [*Puts a pillow under his head.*] That's right. [*Sits on his leg.*] Feel any pain? [*Pause.*] Why have you closed your eyes?

PLATONOV. Oh, it's nothing. So you're here, Sasha? Back home, eh, precious? [*Kisses her hand.*]

SASHA. Little Nicholas is ill.

PLATONOV. Why, what's the matter?

SASHA. A sort of cough, a rash, and his temperature's up. He hasn't slept for two nights and he keeps crying. He won't eat or drink. [*Weeps.*] He's seriously ill, Michael, I'm so afraid. I had a bad dream too.

PLATONOV. What's your dear brother playing at? He's a doctor, isn't he?

SASHA. Well may you ask—you get no sympathy from him. He did look in three or four days ago, kicked his heels a bit and left. I tell him about Nicholas's illness and he just pinches himself and yawns. He said I was being silly.

PLATONOV. He can't talk, the fathead! He'll forget his own name next. He'd run away from his own sickbed, let alone anyone else's.

SASHA. What can we do?

PLATONOV. Hope for the best. Are you living at your father's?

SASHA. Yes.

PLATONOV. How is he?

SASHA. All right. He walks up and down his room, smokes his pipe and means to come and see you. I went to him in a bit of a state and, well, he guessed that I, er, that you and I—. What can we do about Nicholas?

PLATONOV. Don't worry, dear.

SASHA. I can't help it. If he dies, God forbid, what will happen to us?

PLATONOV. God won't take our little boy from you—why punish you? Not for having a no-good husband, surely? [*Pause.*] Look after the little chap, Sasha. Take care of him for me and I swear I'll make a man of him. Everything he does will please you. He is a Platonov after all, poor boy. But he should change his name. I don't add up to much as a man, but I'll make a great father. He'll be all right, don't worry. Oh, my poor arm! [*Groans.*] It aches, that bandit really hurt it. What's the matter with it? [*Examines his arm.*] It's red. Oh, to hell with it! Yes, Sasha—you'll be happy in your son. You laugh. Laugh away, darling. Crying now, eh? Why? Don't cry. [*Embraces her head.*] You came here—but why did you ever leave? Don't cry, my pet. Why all the tears? I do love you, child—very, very much. It's all my fault, but that can't be helped. You must forgive me. There, there.

SASHA. Is that affair over then?

PLATONOV. 'Affair?' What a word, my little suburban housewife.

SASHA. You mean it's still going on?

PLATONOV. How can I put it? There is no 'affair', only a frightful mix-up. Don't let it upset you too much—if it's not over yet it soon will be.

SASHA. But when?

PLATONOV. Quite soon, I should think. We'll go back to our old ways and to hell with everything new. I'm utterly fed up and worn out. The thing won't last, don't you believe it—I don't, it's all pretty casual. She'll cool off first, and be the first to laugh at it and regret it. Sonya's not my type. She's going through a phase I've been through already, and she's all starry-eyed about things that just make me laugh. Not my type at all. [*Pause.*] She won't be your rival much longer, take it from me. What's the matter, Sasha? [SASHA *stands up and stumbles.*]

PLATONOV [*gets up*]. Sasha!

SASHA. So it's—Sonya is it? Not Anna?

PLATONOV. Don't tell me that's news to you.

SASHA. Sonya? What a dirty, rotten business.

PLATONOV. What's the matter? You're pale, you're unsteady on your feet. [*Groans.*] Must you torture me as well? I've got a bad arm, isn't that enough? This isn't the first you've heard of it, surely? Why did you go away then? Not because of Sonya?

SASHA. Anna didn't matter so much. But another man's wife! What a rotten, dirty business. I never thought you could sink so low. God will punish you, you heartless man. [*Goes to the door.*]

PLATONOV [*after a pause*]. Bit shocked, eh? But where are you going?

SASHA [*stops by the door*]. The best of luck——

PLATONOV. Who to?

SASHA. You and Sonya.

PLATONOV. You've read too many trashy novels, Sasha. We're still very close to each other. We have a son, and I'm your husband after all. And I don't need happiness anyway. Don't go, Sasha. You're leaving—for good, I suppose?

SASHA. I can't cope. Oh God, God!

PLATONOV. Can't you?

SASHA. God, can it be true? [*Clutches her temples and sits down.*] I—I don't know what to do.

PLATONOV. Don't you? [*Goes up to her.*] Have it your own way. I'd rather you stayed, though. Don't cry, silly. [*Pause.*] I've done wrong, Sasha, but you can forgive me, surely?

SASHA. Have you forgiven yourself?

PLATONOV. A very questionable question. [*Kisses her head.*] Oh, do stay. Look, I'm sorry. Apart from you there's nothing but vodka, squalor, Osips. I'm fed up. Stay on as a nurse, if not as a wife. Women are queer cattle. You're so funny. If you don't mind feeding that rogue Osip, mollycoddling cats and dogs and staying up half the night to pray for various supposed enemies—can't you toss a crust to your guilty, repentant husband? Why must you hound me too? Don't go away, dear. [*Embraces her.*] I need a nanny. I'm a swine, I've run off with a friend's wife, I'm Sonya's lover, Anna's too perhaps, and I'm promiscuous. Haven't played the game by the family at all. So be as shocked and outraged as you like. But who'll love you, who'll appreciate the little woman as much as me? Who will you cook for? Whose soup will you put too much salt in? You're entitled to go, it's only fair you should, but—. [*Lifts her to her feet.*] Who will set you on your feet like this? Can you do without me, darling?

SASHA. Oh, this is too much—let me go. I'm done for. My life's in ruins—and you make jokes! [*Tears herself away.*] It's not funny, you know. Good-bye, I can't live with you. Now everybody will think you're a rotten swine. How do you think I'll feel? [*Sobs.*]

PLATONOV. All right, go. [*Kisses her head and lies on the sofa.*] I understand.

SASHA. You've wrecked our family. We were happy and contented. I was the happiest woman in the world. [*Sits down.*] How could you, Michael? [*Stands up.*] How could you? We can't put the clock back now. I'm done for. [*Sobs.*]

PLATONOV. All right then, go.

SASHA. Good-bye. You won't see me again. Don't come and see us. Father will bring Nicholas over. May God forgive you as I forgive you. You've wrecked our lives.

PLATONOV. Still here?

SASHA. No. Oh, all right! [*Looks at* PLATONOV *for some time and goes out.*]

SCENE IX

[PLATONOV *alone, followed by* SERGEY.]

PLATONOV. Look who's starting a new life now. That hurts! I'm losing everything, going crazy! God, that Sasha, that insect—that microbe!—should *dare*, and think she's so saintly that she can sling mud at me, damn it all!

[*Lies on the sofa.* SERGEY *comes in and stands by the door.*]

PLATONOV [*after a pause*]. Is this the epilogue or is the farce still going on? [*Seeing* SERGEY, *closes his eyes and snores gently.*]

SERGEY [*goes up to* PLATONOV]. Platonov! [*Pause.*] You're not asleep, I can tell from your face. [*Sits near him.*] I shouldn't have thought this was the time for sleep——

[PLATONOV *sits up.*]

SERGEY [*stands up and looks through the window*]. You've killed me, do you know that? [*Pause.*] Thank you very much. Oh, what do I care, confound you? Let it go, it must be fate.

[*Weeps.* PLATONOV *stands up and walks slowly to the opposite corner of the room.*]

SERGEY. I once had a stroke of luck, but I had to lose even that. He's clever, good-looking, great-hearted. But that wasn't enough—he had to have my happiness as well. He took it and I—. What of me? I don't count, it's all right. I'm ill, I'm not quite all there, I'm a sentimental, godforsaken weakling with leanings towards idleness, mysticism and superstition. And a friend gave me the *coup de grâce*.

PLATONOV. Get out!

SERGEY. In a moment. I came to challenge you to a duel, but now I'm here I'm in tears. I'll go. [*Pause.*] Have I lost her for ever?

PLATONOV. Yes.

SERGEY [*whistles*]. I see. Of course——

PLATONOV. Get out, please! Go!

SERGEY. In a moment. What can I do here? [*Goes towards the door.*] Nothing. [*Pause.*] Give her back, Platonov, be decent. She is mine, isn't she? Platonov! You can be happy without her. Save me, old boy, eh? Give her back. [*Sobs.*] She is mine. Mine, is that clear?

PLATONOV [*goes towards the sofa*]. Do go, or I swear I'll shoot myself.

SERGEY. Don't do that, damn you. [*Makes a gesture of despair and goes out.*]

PLATONOV [*clutches his head*]. Miserable wretch. Oh God, a curse upon my godforsaken head! [*Sobs.*] Leave people alone, you snake! I've made others unhappy, and they've done the same to me. So keep away from them. They're always doing me harm, but they can't quite do me in. Under every chair and piece of wood squats an assassin, staring at me, wanting to kill me. Then strike! [*Beats his chest.*] Strike before I kill myself. [*Runs to the door.*] But don't strike my breast, that's already torn to shreds! [*Shouts.*] Sasha! Sasha, for God's sake!

[*Opens the door.* PORFIRY *comes in.*]

SCENE X

[PLATONOV *and* PORFIRY, *followed by* CYRIL.]

PORFIRY [*comes in well wrapped up and carrying a crutch*]. You in, Platonov? Delighted. I'm intruding, but I won't keep you, I'll leave directly. I just want to ask one thing and I'll go away when I get an answer. What's the matter? You're pale, unsteady on your feet, shuddering. What's up?

PLATONOV. What, me? Eh? I must be drunk, or—I'm going mad. I'm drunk, drunk. My head's spinning.

PORFIRY [*aside*]. I'll ask my question. The sober hide what drunks confide. [*To* PLATONOV.] It's an odd—perhaps even stupid— question, but for God's sake answer, the matter's vital to me. I'll believe you, knowing you're a decent sort. If you think the question odd, absurd, silly—insulting, even—never mind. Just answer, for God's sake. I'm in an awful spot. Someone we both know—you know her well—. I thought she was beyond reproach. I mean Anna Voynitsev. [*Supports* PLATONOV.] Don't fall down, for God's sake.

PLATONOV. Go away, Porfiry—Mr. Glagolyev, I mean. I always thought you were a stupid old man.

PORFIRY. You're a friend of hers, you know her pretty well. She's either been misrepresented to me or—my eyes have been opened. She's a virtuous woman, isn't she? She—she—. Has she the right to be the wife of an honourable man? [*Pause.*] I don't know how to put my question. Try to understand, for God's sake. I've been told she——

PLATONOV. Everything in this world is rotten, vile and dirty. Everything—. Rotten, filthy—. [*Faints on* GLAGOLYEV *and collapses on the ground.*]

CYRIL [*comes in*]. Why hang round here? I'm not waiting any longer.

PORFIRY. 'Everything is rotten, vile and dirty.' Everything—that must include her.

CYRIL [*looks at* PLATONOV]. Father, what's wrong with Platonov?

PORFIRY. He's disgustingly drunk. Yes, rotten and filthy. The full, cruel, bitter truth. [*Pause.*] We're off to Paris.

CYRIL. What? Pa—Paris? What do you want to do in Paris? [*Laughs.*]

PORFIRY. Wallow, like that swine. [*Points to* PLATONOV.]

CYRIL. Wallow? In Paris?

PORFIRY. We'll try our luck in new surroundings. I've had enough. I'm tired of acting a farce for my own benefit and worrying my head with ideals. There's no more trust, no love, no decent people. Let's go.

CYRIL. To Paris?

PORFIRY. Yes. If sin we must, let's sin abroad, not in Russia. Let's have a good time before we rot. You can show me the ropes, Cyril. Paris, here we come!

CYRIL. This *is* nice, Father. You taught me to read, I'll teach you to live. Let's go.

[*They go.*]

END OF ACT THREE

ACT FOUR

The study of the late General Voynitsev. Two doors. Antique furniture, Persian rugs, flowers. The walls are hung with guns, pistols, Caucasian daggers and so on. Family portraits. Busts of Krylov, Pushkin and Gogol. A cabinet with stuffed birds in it. A bookcase. On it are cigarette-holders, boxes, sticks, gun-barrels and so on. A desk piled with papers, portraits, statuettes and firearms. Morning.

SCENE I

[SONYA *and* KATYA *come in.*]

SONYA. Don't be upset. Tell me what you mean.

KATYA. Something awful's going on, ma'am. The doors and windows are all wide open. Everything indoors has been turned upside down and broken. The door's been pulled off its hinges. Something awful's happened, ma'am. No wonder our hen started crowing like a cock.

SONYA. What do you think happened?

KATYA. I don't know, ma'am—what can I think? I only know it must be something. Either Mr. Platonov's left or he's done away with himself. He's very hot-tempered, he is. I've known him these two years.

SONYA. I don't believe it. Have you been down to the village?

KATYA. Yes, but he's not about. I was looking for three or four hours.

SONYA [*sits down*]. What, oh what can I do? [*Pause.*] Quite sure he's nowhere round here, are you?

KATYA. I don't know, ma'am. Something awful must have happened —no wonder I've got this pain in my heart. Give it up, ma'am, it's a sin. [*Cries.*] I'm so sorry for the master. Such a handsome man he was, and now look at him. Two days, and he's turned into a proper wreck, poor fellow. Goes round in a daze. That's the end of a kind gentleman. I'm sorry for Mr. Platonov too. A most cheerful gentleman, he was—he was a proper scream, but now he looks like death. Give it up, ma'am.

SONYA. Give what up?

KATYA. Love. What good is it? It only brings disgrace. I'm sorry for you too, you look like nothing on earth. You've grown thin, you don't eat, drink or sleep—all you do is cough.

SONYA. Katya, would you mind trying the schoolhouse again—he may be back.

KATYA. All right, ma'am. [*Pause.*] You ought to go to bed.

SONYA. Go over again, Katya. Not gone yet?

KATYA [*aside*]. It's all very well for you, you're not a servant. [*Brusquely and tearfully.*] Where am I to go then, ma'am?

SONYA. I want to go to bed, I got no sleep all night. Don't shout so, and be off with you.

KATYA. Very well, ma'am, but you shouldn't torture yourself like this. You should go to your room and lie down. [*Goes out.*]

SCENE II

[SONYA, *followed by* SERGEY.]

SONYA. This is terrible. He promised me yesterday to be at the hut by ten, but he didn't turn up. I waited till daybreak. So much for his promises. And so much for our love and going away together. He doesn't love me.

SERGEY [*comes in*]. I'll go to bed, might get a bit of sleep. [*Seeing* SONYA.] You—here? In my study?

SONYA. Me—here? [*Looks round.*] Yes, I just happened to come in without noticing. [*Goes towards the door.*]

SERGEY. One moment.

SONYA [*stops*]. Yes?

SERGEY. Can you give me a few minutes? Are you capable of staying here for two or three minutes?

SONYA. If you've something to say, say it.

SERGEY. Yes. [*Pause.*] There was a time when we could meet in here not as strangers.

SONYA. There was.

SERGEY. Sorry, I don't know what I'm talking about. Are you going away?

SONYA. Yes.

SERGEY. I see. Soon?

SONYA. Today.

SERGEY. With him?

SONYA. Yes.

SERGEY. I hope you'll both be happy. [*Pause.*] You've a solid base to build on—rampant lust, plus a third party's unhappiness! One man's meat is another man's poison. That's been said before, anyway. And it's nicer to hear a new lie than an old truth. Do what you like, confound you both.

SONYA. You had something to say.

SERGEY. I'm not exactly silent, am I? All right then, this is it. I want to do the right thing by you and not be in your debt, so I'd like to apologize for the way I behaved last night. I was nasty to you, I was rude and spiteful. Please forgive me, will you?

SONYA. Yes. [*Makes to go out.*]

SERGEY. Wait, wait, I've something else to say. [*Sighs.*] I'm crazy, Sonya. I simply can't bear this terrible blow. I'm mad, but I can still understand. In the vast fog of my brain—a sort of grey, leaden, heavy cloud—there's a gleam of light by which I see everything. If I lose that, it means I'm lost—completely. But I see all this clearly enough. [*Pause.*] Here am I in my own study, once used by my father, Major-General Voynitsev of His Majesty's suite, who held the Order of St. George—a great and famous man. People saw only his bad side. They saw him hitting out and trampling on people, but when he was beaten and trampled himself, no one cared. [*Points to* SONYA.] May I introduce my ex-wife?

[SONYA *makes to go out.*]

SERGEY. Wait, let me finish. I may be talking stupidly, but please hear me out—it's the last time, isn't it?

SONYA. You've said it all before. What can you add? We must separate—what else is there to say? Do you want to prove it's my fault? Don't bother, I know what to think of myself.

SERGEY. What can I say? Oh, Sonya, you don't know anything, or you wouldn't look at me so arrogantly. Something ghastly's happening to me. [*Kneels before her.*] What are you doing, where are you pushing us both? For God's sake have pity. I'm dying, I'm going off my head. Don't leave me. I'll forget—I already have forgiven. I'll be your slave, I'll love you, love you more than ever. I'll make you happy as the day is long, which is more than he'll do. You'll only wreck your life and his, you'll destroy Platonov. I know I can't make you love me, but don't leave me. You'll be happy again, you won't be so deathly pale and wretched. I'll be a man again, and Platonov can come and see us. This may be a mere pipe-dream, but don't go. Let's put back the clock while there's still time. Platonov will agree, I know him. He doesn't love you, it's just that—you gave yourself to him and he took you. [*Gets up.*] Are you crying?

SONYA [*gets up*]. Don't think I'm crying on your account. Platonov may agree, I don't care. [*Harshly.*] You're a rotten lot. Where is Platonov?

SERGEY. I don't know.

SONYA. Don't pester me, leave me alone—I hate you. Clear out! Where's Platonov? You're all rotten! Where is he? I hate you.

SERGEY. Why?

SONYA. Where is he?

SERGEY. I paid him some money and he promised to leave. If he's kept his word he must have gone by now.

SONYA. You bribed him? Why do you lie?

SERGEY. I gave him a thousand roubles and he said he'd give you up. I'm lying, actually—it's all a lie. For God's sake don't believe me. Friend Platonov's still alive and kicking, blast him. Go and get him, slobber over him, I didn't bribe him. But will you—will he—really be happy? Is this my wife, my Sonya? What does it all mean, though? I still can't believe it. The whole thing's platonic, isn't it? You haven't gone, er, the whole way?

SONYA. I'm his wife, his mistress—call it what you like. [*Makes to go out.*] Why keep me here? I haven't time to listen to all sorts of——

SERGEY. Wait, Sonya. You—his mistress! How could you? And brazen it out like this! [*Clutches her hand.*] How could you, oh, how could you?

[ANNA *comes in.*]

SONYA. Leave me alone. [*Goes out.*]

SCENE III

[SERGEY *and* ANNA.]

[ANNA *comes in and looks out of the window.*]

SERGEY [*with a gesture of despair*]. This is the absolute end! [*Pause.*] What's going on out there?

ANNA. Osip's been lynched by the villagers.

SERGEY. Already?

ANNA. Yes, near the well. Do you see? There he is.

SERGEY [*looks out of the window*]. Well, it serves him right. [*Pause.*]

ANNA. Heard the news, dear? They say Platonov's made himself scarce and—. Have you read his letter?

SERGEY. Yes.

ANNA. What price our estate! How do you like that? Gone with the wind! The Lord gave and the Lord taketh away. So much for our famous deal! It was all because we believed Glagolyev—he said he'd buy it, but didn't show up at the auction. The servants say he's gone to Paris. He's turned funny in his old age, the swine. But for him we'd have quietly paid off the interest and stayed on here. [*Sighs.*] Never trust your enemies in this world—or your friends either!

SERGEY. Yes, never trust your friends.

ANNA. Well, what will you do now, Squire? Where will you go? What the Lord gave your ancestors, he took from you—you've nothing left.

SERGEY. I don't care.

ANNA. Oh yes you do. How will you eat? Let's sit. [*They sit.*] Don't be so gloomy, it can't be helped. It hurts to say good-bye to your nice little home, but what can you do, dear? You can't put the clock back now. So that's the way of things. Be a good boy, Sergey, and the great thing is, do keep cool.

SERGEY. Don't bother about me, Mother, leave me out of it. You're not exactly calm either, so comfort yourself first and attend to me later.

ANNA. Well—. This isn't women's business, we must always stay in the background. The great thing is, keep cool. You've lost what you had, but it's the future that matters, not the past. You have your whole life ahead, a man's life with lots of good hard work in it, so why mope? Get a job in some school and start work. You're no end of a fellow—a scholar, a solid citizen. You never dabble in anything shady, you have your principles and you're a staid married man. You can go far if you want to, you're a very good little boy. Only don't quarrel with your wife—hardly married and already quarrelling! Why don't you speak, dear? You're upset, but you won't say why. What's happening between you two?

SERGEY. It's not happening, it *has* happened.

ANNA. What has? Or is it a secret?

SERGEY [*sighs*]. A ghastly calamity has struck our house, Mother. I don't know why I didn't tell you before—I kept hoping, and besides, I was ashamed to talk of it. And I myself only found out about it yesterday morning. As for the estate, I don't give a damn.

ANNA [*laughs*]. I'm quaking in my shoes! I suppose she's a bit annoyed with you or something.

SERGEY. Well may you laugh—you wait, you'll find yourself laughing on the other side of your face. [*Pause.*] She's been unfaithful to me. May I introduce myself—the well-known cuckold!

ANNA. Oh, don't be so silly. Whatever next! This is quite outrageous— you should think before you speak. You're fantastic, you do come out with the most shocking remarks. Cuckold my foot! You can't know the meaning of the word.

SERGEY. Oh yes I do, and not in theory either—I've found out the hard way.

ANNA. You are funny, you shouldn't insult your wife. Oh——

SERGEY. I swear it's true. [*Pause.*]

ANNA. How odd. What you say is quite impossible. It's slander too, and it can't be true. What—here in our village!

SERGEY. Yes, here in your blasted village.

ANNA. I see. But who in our blasted village can have had the grotesque idea of planting a pair of horns on your patrician brow? There just isn't anyone. You can't mean Cyril Glagolyev? Hardly—he's stopped coming here. There's no one here to interest your Sonya, it's just stupid jealousy, dear.

SERGEY. It's Platonov.

ANNA. What's Platonov?

SERGEY. He's the one.

ANNA [*jumps up*]. You can talk nonsense, but the sort of nonsense you're talking now—. Look, it's sheer poppycock. There are limits. You're being unforgivably stupid.

SERGEY. Then ask her. Or go and ask him if you don't believe me. I didn't want to believe it myself, I still don't, but she's leaving today—deserting me—so I have no choice. He's going with her. Look—I'm about as full of life as a dead cat, can't you see? I'm done for.

ANNA. It can't be true, Sergey—it's a figment of your childish imagination, I tell you. There's nothing in it.

SERGEY. She is leaving today, I tell you. I can also tell you that she's been on about being his mistress for the last couple of days. She told me herself. Incredible as it may seem, and however much it goes against the grain, one's just got to believe it.

ANNA. I remember, it's all clear to me now. Give me a chair, Sergey. No, don't bother. So that's it! I see. Wait, let me remember properly.

[*Pause.* BUGROV *comes in.*]

SCENE IV

[ANNA, SERGEY *and* BUGROV.]

BUGROV [*comes in*]. Hallo there. A happy Sunday morning to you. Alive and kicking, eh?

ANNA. Yes, yes, yes. This is awful.

BUGROV. There's a spot of rain, but it's hot. [*Mops his brow.*] Phew! Drive or walk, it's like an oven. Are you well? [*Pause.*] I really called because, as you know, the auction was held yesterday. Now the point is, er, and [*laughs*] a bit of a sore point it is to you, of course, a mite painful. So I, er—. Don't hold it against me, please. I didn't buy your estate. Abraham Vengerovich bought it, only in my name.

SERGEY [*rings the bell violently*]. To hell with them!

BUGROV. Precisely. Now don't think I—. It wasn't me—. So you see, it was only in my name.

[*Sits down.* JACOB *comes in.*]

SERGEY [*to* JACOB]. How many times have I asked you rotten filthy [*coughs*] swine not to let anyone in unannounced. You all deserve a

x

good thrashing. Brutes! [*Throws the bell under the table.*] Get out, you swine.

[*Walks up and down the stage.* JACOB *shrugs his shoulders and goes out.*]

BUGROV [*coughs*]. It's only in my name. Mr. Vengerovich told me to say you can live here as long as you like—till Christmas, even. There will be one or two changes round here, but they won't bother you. Or if they do you can move into the lodge, where there's lots of room and it's warm. He also told me to ask if you'll sell me the mine—I mean sell it to him in my name. It's your mine, ma'am, so how about it? We'll pay a good price.

ANNA. No, I'm not damn well selling. What are you offering? Chicken-feed, I suppose? You can put that where the monkey put the nuts.

BUGROV. Vengerovich told me to say that if you don't agree to sell him the mine, ma'am, deducting what Mr. Voynitsev and the late general owe him—he's going to sue. And so shall I, ma'am, te he he! We're all friends here, but business is business. A little matter of commerce. Trouble is, damn it, I, er, bought your IOUs from Petrin.

SERGEY. I won't let anyone trade on my stepmother's estate paying my debts. The estate's hers, not mine.

BUGROV. Perhaps the lady will have pity on us.

SERGEY. I won't bandy words with you. Oh, really! [*Makes a gesture of despair.*] Do what you like.

ANNA. Please leave us, Mr. Bugrov. Sorry, but please go.

BUGROV. Very well. [*Gets up.*] Now don't worry, you can stay on, till Christmas even. I'll drop in tomorrow or the next day. The very best to you. [*Goes out.*]

ANNA. We'll leave tomorrow. Yes, now I remember—Platonov! So that's why he's skedaddling.

SERGEY. Let them do what they like, let them take the lot. I've lost my wife, so nothing else matters. My wife's left me, Mother.

ANNA. Yes, so she has. But what on earth did he see in that ninny Sonya, what did he—what *could* he—find in the girl? How blind men are, how stupid, swept off their feet by any—. But what were you playing at? Call yourself a husband? Where were your eyes, you awful drip? Snivelling while someone whips his wife from under his very nose! Call yourself a man! You're just a baby. Fancy marrying a brat like you, a silly little donkey—what a farce! You're both no good—you and your precious Platonov. This is quite ghastly.

SERGEY. Nothing will help now, and it's no use blaming me either. I've lost her and you've lost him, there's no more to be said. Leave me alone, Mother. You can't bear my stupid face, can you?

ANNA. What am I to do? Something must be done, we must save them.

SERGEY. Save who? I'm the one who needs saving. They're happy for the moment. [*Sighs.*]

ANNA. Oh, you and your reasoning! They need saving, not you. Platonov doesn't love her, you know. He seduced her, as you once seduced that silly German girl. He doesn't love her, I tell you. What did she say? Why don't you speak?

SERGEY. She said she was his mistress.

ANNA. She's more of a fool than a mistress. Now shut up! Perhaps it's not too late to mend things. Platonov's capable of making a great song and dance if a girl so much as kisses him or holds his hand. It hasn't gone all that far yet, I'll be bound.

SERGEY. Oh yes it has.

ANNA. You're a bit out of your depth.

[MARY *comes in.*]

SCENE V

[SERGEY, ANNA *and* MARY.]

MARY [*comes in*]. So there you are. Good morning. [*Shakes hands with* ANNA.] Good morning, Sergey. Sorry, I seem to be in the way. An uninvited visitor's worse than, worse than—what's the saying— worse than the plague, that's it. I've only looked in for a moment. You'll never believe this! [*Laughs.*] I must show it you, Anna. I'm sorry, Sergey, we must keep this between the two of us. [*Takes* ANNA *to one side.*] Just read that. [*Gives her a note.*] It came yesterday. Read it.

ANNA [*scans the note*]. Oh.

MARY. I'm having him prosecuted, you know. [*Puts her head on* ANNA'*s breast.*] Will you send for him, please? He must come here.

ANNA. What's all this in aid of?

MARY. I want to see the look on his face now. Send for him, please, I've a word or two to say to him. You don't know what I've been up to. Don't listen, Sergey. [*In a whisper.*] I went to see the school inspector, and Platonov's being given a job somewhere else at my request. Oh, what have I done! [*Weeps.*] Send for him. Who'd have thought he would write a letter like this. Oh, if only I'd known! God, it's agony.

ANNA. Go to the library, dear, I'll join you in a minute and we can discuss it. I must talk to Sergey in private.

MARY. The library? All right. But you will send for him, won't you? What he must look like now after this letter! You did read it? Let me put it away. [*Puts the letter away.*] My dear, my darling—please! I'll go—but you send for him. Don't listen, Sergey. We'll talk German, Anna. *Schicken Sie, meine Liebe!*

ANNA. All right. Now run along.

MARY. Very well. [*Quickly kisses her.*] Don't be angry, dear, you just can't think what agony this is. I'm going, Sergey, you can carry on your talk. [*Goes out.*]

ANNA. I'm going to get at the truth. Now don't you go off the deep end, perhaps your marriage can still be patched up. What a frightful business—who'd have thought it? I'll have a word with Sonya at once, I'll really put her through it. You're making a silly mistake. Perhaps I'm wrong, though. [*Buries her face in her hands.*] No, no, no.

SERGEY. No, I'm not mistaken.

ANNA. Still, I'll have a word with her. And with him too.

SERGEY. Oh, go and have your words! But you might as well save your breath. [*Sits at the table.*] Let's get out of here. There's no hope, not even a straw to clutch at.

ANNA. I'm going to get at the facts. You can stay here and cry. Go to bed, you great baby. Where's Sonya?

SERGEY. She must be in her room.

[ANNA *goes out.*]

SCENE VI

[SERGEY, *followed by* PLATONOV.]

SERGEY. What a ghastly business. How long will it drag on—a day or two, a week, a month, a year? There's no end to this anguish. I ought to shoot myself.

PLATONOV [*comes in with his arm in a sling*]. There he is—I think he's crying. [*Pause.*] Peace be on you, my poor friend. [*Goes up to* SERGEY.] For God's sake, listen. I haven't come to make excuses. I'm not to be judged by you—or by myself. I've come to ask a favour for your sake, not my own, and I ask it as a good friend. Hate me, despise me, think what you like of me—but don't kill yourself. I'm not thinking of bullets, but of your all-round situation. You're not all that strong and unhappiness will finish you. My life will end, so let me be the suicide—not you. Do you want me to die? Do you? [*Pause.*]

SERGEY. I don't want anything.

[ANNA *comes in.*]

SCENE VII

[SERGEY, PLATONOV *and* ANNA.]

ANNA. Is he here? [*Goes slowly up to* PLATONOV.] Platonov, is it true?

PLATONOV. Yes.

ANNA. And he dares, dares to speak so casually. So it's true. You low swine, you knew you were playing a dirty game, didn't you?

PLATONOV. Low swine—can't we be a bit more civil? I knew nothing. All I knew or know about this business is that I've never wished him a thousandth part of his present sufferings.

ANNA. You might also note that one friend's wife shouldn't be another's plaything. [*Shouts.*] You don't love her, you were just bored.

SERGEY. Ask him what he came for, Mother.

ANNA. What a rotten thing to do—to toy with people. They're flesh and blood like you. Think you're awfully clever, don't you?

SERGEY [*jumps up*]. And he has the nerve to come here! What for? I know what you're after, but you won't surprise or shock us with a lot of hot air.

PLATONOV. Who's 'us'?

SERGEY. Now I know what your pompous talk's worth. You leave me alone. If you came here to atone by speechifying, your fine phrases won't work, believe you me.

PLATONOV. Angry screams don't prove a man's guilt, any more than fine phrases condone it. I think I did mention that I mean to shoot myself?

SERGEY. That's not the way to atone—in words I no longer trust. I despise your words. That's how a Russian atones. [*Points at the window.*]

PLATONOV. What is it?

SERGEY. Out there by the well lies a man who's atoned for his misdeeds.

PLATONOV. I saw him. But why all the eloquence, Sergey? You're unhappy, I believe, overwhelmed with grief—so why show off? What's the reason—insincerity or stupidity?

SERGEY [*sits down*]. Ask him why he came, Mother.

ANNA. What do you want here, Platonov?

PLATONOV. Ask your own questions—why trouble your stepmother? The game's up, your wife's left you and you're done for, you've nothing left. Sonya's as lovely as a spring morning—she's perfection itself. A man without a woman's like a steam-engine with no steam. You've lost your steam and your life's ruined. All is lost—your honour, your human dignity and your aristocratic pretensions—the whole thing! It's all over.

SERGEY. I'm not listening, you may as well leave me alone.

PLATONOV. Oh, naturally! Don't try and insult me, Voynitsev—I didn't come here to be insulted. Your unhappiness doesn't give you the right to ride roughshod over me. I'm a human being, so treat me as one. You're unhappy, but you and your unhappiness are nothing to the anguish I've felt since you left. That was a terrible night after you left, Voynitsev. I can tell you lovers of humanity that your unhappiness is nothing to my agony.

ANNA. Very possibly, but who cares about your agony or what happened that night?

PLATONOV. Don't you care either?

ANNA. I'm quite sure I don't.

PLATONOV. Oh? Don't lie, Anna. [*Sighs.*] Perhaps you're right in your way. Perhaps. But where can I find decent people, where can I turn? [*Buries his face in his hands.*] Where are there such people? They don't understand me, so who will? They're stupid, cruel, heartless.

SERGEY. I understand you all right, I've taken your measure. This grovelling doesn't suit you, my dear sir and ex-friend. I know what you are—you're a slippery customer, that's what.

PLATONOV. I'll overlook that remark, you fool, but you watch your step—don't say it again. [*To* ANNA.] Why are you hanging around? You like a good scene, don't you? Interesting, isn't it? This is none of your business, we don't need witnesses.

ANNA. It's none of your business either. And you can clear off. Damn cheek! Behaves like a filthy rotten cad, then comes here feeling sorry for himself. That's what I call being tactful! Anyway—sorry, but you'd please better go or you'll learn a few more home truths.

SERGEY [*jumps up*]. What more does he want from me? What do you want, what do you expect? That's what I don't see.

PLATONOV. I can see you don't. The thing is to drown your sorrows when you're unhappy, not go looking for company—that's been proved thousands of times. [*Goes to the door.*] I'm sorry I lowered myself by talking to you, I was foolish enough to think you were decent. But you're all the same—a lot of wild, uncouth provincial clod-hoppers. [*Goes out and slams the door.*]

ANNA [*wrings her hands*]. How revolting. Run after him at once and say—. Tell him——

SERGEY. What can I say?

ANNA. You'll find something to say. Anything. Hurry, please. He meant well, as you should have seen, but you were so cruel. Hurry, darling.

SERGEY. I can't, leave me alone.

ANNA. He's not the only one to blame, you know, we all are—we all have passions, we're all weak. So run along and say something nice. Show you're human, for goodness' sake. Go on—run!

SERGEY. I'm going mad.

ANNA. Then go mad, but don't dare insult people. Run, for God's sake. [*Cries.*] Sergey!

SERGEY. Leave me alone, Mother.

ANNA. I'll go myself. Why don't I go? I'll——

PLATONOV [*comes in*]. Oh!

[*Sits on the sofa.* SERGEY *gets up.*]

ANNA [*aside*]. What's the matter with him? [*Pause.*]

PLATONOV. My arm aches, I'm nearly starved to death. I'm cold, feverish, in pain. I'm suffering, can't you see? My life's over. What do you want from me, what more do you need? Wasn't that blasted night enough?

SERGEY [*goes up to* PLATONOV]. Let's forgive each other, Michael. I—. You can understand my feelings. Let's part friends. [*Pause.*] I forgive you—honestly, I do. If I could forget too, I'd be happier than I ever was. Let's leave each other in peace.

PLATONOV. Let's. [*Pause.*] But I've really come unstuck, the machine's broken. I'm terribly sleepy and my eyes won't stay open, but I can't sleep. I prostrate myself, I apologize, I'm sorry, I'm silent. Do and think what you like.

[SERGEY *goes away from* PLATONOV *and sits at the table.*]

PLATONOV. I'm not quitting this house if you set fire to it. If I'm annoying anyone they can leave the room. [*Makes to lie down.*] Give me something warm—not to eat, to put over myself. I'm not going home, it's raining. I'll lie here.

ANNA [*goes up to* PLATONOV]. Go home, Michael, I'll send over what you need or bring it. [*Touches his shoulder.*] Go on, go home.

PLATONOV. If anyone doesn't want me in here they can leave. Give me a drink of water, I'm thirsty.

[ANNA *hands him a carafe.*]

PLATONOV [*drinks from the carafe*]. I'm ill, really ill, dear.

ANNA. Go home. [*Puts her hand on his brow.*] Your head's hot. Go home and I'll send for Triletsky.

PLATONOV [*quietly*]. I'm in a bad way, madam, a very bad way.

ANNA. Well, how do you think I feel? You go. Please, you *must* go, do you hear?

[SONYA *comes in.*]

SCENE VIII

[The above and SONYA.*]*

SONYA *[comes in]*. Will you kindly take your money back? Very generous! I think I've told you once—. [*Seeing* PLATONOV.] You—here! Why? [*Pause.*] Odd. What are you doing here?

PLATONOV. Me?

SONYA. Yes, you.

ANNA. Let's go out, Sergey. [*Goes out and comes in on tiptoe a minute later and sits in the corner.*]

PLATONOV. It's all over, Sonya.

SONYA. Meaning what?

PLATONOV. What it means. We'll talk later.

SONYA. What do you mean by 'all', Michael?

PLATONOV. I need nothing, neither love nor hate—just a bit of peace. Please. I don't even want to talk. What's happened is good enough for me. So please——

SONYA. What's he saying?

PLATONOV. I'm saying I've had enough. I don't want any new life. I don't know what to do with the old one, I don't want anything.

SONYA *[shrugs]*. This makes no sense.

PLATONOV. Oh? The affair's finished, that's all.

SONYA. You mean you're not coming away with me?

PLATONOV. There's no point in going pale, Sonya—Mrs. Voynitsev, rather.

SONYA. Is this some caddish trick?

PLATONOV. Probably.

SONYA. You rotten swine! [*Weeps.*]

PLATONOV. I know, I've been told hundreds of times. We should have talked later, without witnesses.

[SONYA *sobs.*]

PLATONOV. You'd better go to your room, there's nothing more useless than tears when you're unhappy. It had to happen and it has. There are laws in nature and there's a logic in our lives. It's all been logical. [*Pause.*]

SONYA [*sobs*]. What has this to do with me or with my life which you took over till you were tired of it? Where do I come in? Don't you love me any more?

PLATONOV. You'll console yourself somehow, if only by letting this scene be a lesson to you in future.

SONYA. It won't be a lesson, it'll finish me off. How dare you talk like this? What a rotten thing to do.

PLATONOV. Why cry? I'm so sick of all this. [*Shouts.*] I'm ill.

SONYA. He swore oaths, begged me, he began it—and now he comes here! I make you sick, do I? You wanted me, but only for a couple of weeks. I loathe you. I can't stand the sight of him. Clear out! [*Sobs more violently.*]

ANNA. Platonov.

PLATONOV. Yes?

ANNA. Go away.

[PLATONOV *gets up and slowly goes towards the door.*]

SONYA. Wait, don't go. You—is this true? Are you sure you're quite sober? Sit down and think. [*Clutches his shoulder.*]

PLATONOV. I have sat down and thought. Get free of me, Sonya, I'm not meant for you. I rotted and fossilized so long ago, there's no reviving me now. Better to bury me a good way off, so I shan't pollute the air. For the last time, will you believe me?

SONYA [*wrings her hands*]. Tell me, what shall I—what *can* I—do? I shall die, I can't put up with this rotten behaviour. I shan't live five minutes, I'll kill myself. [*Sits in an armchair in the corner.*] What are you doing to me? [*Becomes hysterical.*]

SERGEY [*goes up to* SONYA]. Sonya!

ANNA. Oh good heavens, do calm down, Sonya. Give her some water, Sergey.

SERGEY. Sonya! Don't take on so, stop it. [*To* PLATONOV.] What are you hanging round for? For God's sake, go.

ANNA. That'll do, Sonya. Stop it.

PLATONOV [*goes up to* SONYA]. Well, what is it? Eh? [*Quickly moves away.*] This is idiotic.

SONYA. Leave me, all of you, I don't need your help. [*To* ANNA.] Go away, I hate you. I know who I have to thank for all this. You won't get away with it.

ANNA. Shush! We mustn't quarrel.

SONYA. He wouldn't have ruined me if it hadn't been for your corrupting influence. [*Sobs.*] Go away. [*To* SERGEY.] You go too.

[SERGEY *moves away, sits at the table and puts his head in his hands.*]

ANNA [*to* PLATONOV]. Clear out, I tell you. You're a complete nit-wit today. What more do you want?

PLATONOV [*stops his ears*]. Where can I go? I'm chilled to the bone. [*Goes to the door.*] Let me go to hell, the sooner the better.

[NICHOLAS *comes in.*]

SCENE IX

[*The above and* NICHOLAS.]

NICHOLAS [*in the doorway*]. If you say any more about 'announcing' me, you won't know what's hit you.

JACOB [*off-stage*]. Master's orders.

NICHOLAS. To hell with you and your master, he's as big a fool as you are. [*Comes in.*] He must surely be here. [*Falls on the sofa.*] Oh this is terrible, this, this, this—. [*Jumps up.*] Oh! [*To* PLATONOV.] The tragedy's reached its last act, Mr. Play-actor, it's nearly over now.

PLATONOV. What do you want?

NICHOLAS. Why waste your time hanging round here, you wretch? Aren't you ashamed, don't you feel guilty? Been laying down the law, eh? Preaching sermons?

PLATONOV. Talk sense, Nicholas. What do you want?

NICHOLAS. It's disgusting. [*Sits down and covers his face with his hands.*] It's an utter disaster—and so unexpected.

PLATONOV. What is?

NICHOLAS. 'What is?' Don't you know? Or care? Too busy, I suppose!

ANNA. Nicholas!

PLATONOV. It's about Sasha, is it? Tell me, Nicholas. Oh, this is the limit! What's happened to her?

NICHOLAS. She's poisoned herself by eating matches.

PLATONOV. What!

NICHOLAS [*shouts*]. Poisoned herself with matches. [*Jumps up.*] Here, read this. [*Holds a note before his eyes.*] Read it, my philosophical friend.

PLATONOV [*reads*]. 'It's sinful to commemorate suicides, but pray for me. I'm taking my life because I'm ill. Michael, love little Nicholas and my brother as I love you. Don't abandon Father. Live a good life. Nicholas, my son, may God bless you, even as I bless you with a mother's blessing. Forgive a sinful woman. The key to Michael's chest-of-drawers is in my woollen dress.' My darling! Sinful! Sasha— sinful? This is more than I can take. [*Clutches his head.*] She's poisoned herself. [*Pause.*] Sasha's poisoned herself. Where is she? Look—I must go to her. [*Tears the bandage off his arm.*] I—I'll bring her back to life.

NICHOLAS [*lies on the sofa face downwards*]. Bring her back to life! You shouldn't have killed her in the first place.

PLATONOV. Killed? How can you say such a thing, you lunatic? You can't think I killed her. Did I—did I want her to die? [*Weeps.*] She poisoned herself. That's all I needed to crush me like a squashed worm. If it was done to punish me, then—. [*Shakes his fist.*] It's a cruel, immoral punishment. Oh, it's more than I can bear. How could she? All right, I'm in the wrong, granted, I'm rotten—but I'm still alive, aren't I? [*Pause.*] Look at me, all of you, look at me—. Isn't it a pretty sight?

NICHOLAS [*jumps up*]. Yes, yes, yes. Now we're going to cry—we've always been one for turning on the waterworks, haven't we? You want a good hiding! Put on your cap and come. Call yourself a husband! A fine husband—ruining a woman's life for no reason. Look what you drove her to. And these people want to keep him here, they like him. He's an original type, an interesting case—his fading good looks etched with tragic lines! Come and see what you've done, you original and interesting case.

PLATONOV. Talk less, there's nothing to be said.

NICHOLAS. You're lucky I called in at home at dawn today, you hound. What if I hadn't, if I hadn't caught her? She'd have died. Get that into your head, since you're so good at seeing everything except what's under your nose. And I'd have made you pay, for all your tragic looks. Less goddam blethering from you, a bit more readiness to listen—and this disaster needn't have happened. She's worth ten of you clever people. Let's go.

SERGEY. Don't shout. Oh, I'm so fed up with all of them.

NICHOLAS. Come on.

PLATONOV. Wait. She—isn't dead, you say?

NICHOLAS. You mean you wish she were?

PLATONOV [*shrieks*]. She didn't die! I'll never understand it. She's not dead then? [*Embraces* NICHOLAS.] She's alive! [*Laughs.*] Alive!

ANNA. This makes no sense to me. Do explain, Triletsky. They all seem so stupid today. What does this letter mean?

NICHOLAS. She wrote it. But for me she'd have died, and she's still terribly ill—I don't know that she'll get over it. Just let her die and—. [*To* PLATONOV.] Would you mind keeping away from me?

PLATONOV. You gave me such a scare. God, still alive! So you didn't let her die, you splendid fellow. [*Kisses* NICHOLAS.] My dear fellow! [*Laughs.*] I never believed in medicine, but now I even believe in you. How is she—weak, unwell? We'll have her up and about again.

NICHOLAS. But will she recover?

PLATONOV. She will, I'll make sure of that. Why didn't you say she was alive in the first place? Anna dear, give me a glass of cold water and I'll be happy. Forgive me, all of you. I'm going mad, Anna. [*Kisses* ANNA's *hand.*] Sasha's alive. Water, dear.

[ANNA *goes out with an empty carafe and comes back a minute later with some water.*]

PLATONOV [*to* NICHOLAS]. Let's go and see her, we'll soon have her up and about. We'll turn the whole of medicine upside down from Hippocrates to Triletsky, we'll stir things up a bit! Who has more right to life than Sasha? Come on then. No, wait, my head's swimming, I'm terribly ill. One moment. [*Sits on the sofa.*] I'll rest a bit first. Is she very weak?

NICHOLAS. He's very pleased, but what he's got to be pleased at, I can't see.

ANNA. You gave me a fright too, you should take care what you say. Drink. [*Gives* PLATONOV *some water.*]

PLATONOV [*drinks greedily*]. Thank you, dear. I'm such a frightful hound. [*To* NICHOLAS.] Sit by me. [NICHOLAS *sits down.*] You're dead beat too. Thank you, my friend. Did she take much?

NICHOLAS. Enough to finish her off.

PLATONOV. Sasha of all people! Thank God it's all right. My arm hurts. More water, please. I'm terribly ill myself, Nicholas. Can hardly keep going, I'm on the point of collapse. Must be getting a chill. I keep seeing toy soldiers in cotton uniforms with pointed caps. The background's green and yellow. I want some quinine.

NICHOLAS. You want a damn good hiding.

PLATONOV [*laughs*]. Oh, very funny. You see, I do laugh at some of your jokes. Are you my brother-in-law? God, I'm so ill, you'd never believe it.

[NICHOLAS *feels his pulse.*]

ANNA [*quietly, to* NICHOLAS]. Take him along, Nicholas. I'll come over this evening and see Sasha. What made her give us such a fright? She's not still in danger, is she?

NICHOLAS. I can't say yet. She didn't kill herself, but she's in a pretty bad way.

PLATONOV. What did you give her?

NICHOLAS. What she needed. [*Gets up.*] Come on.

PLATONOV. And what have you just given Anna?

NICHOLAS. You're seeing things. Come on.

PLATONOV. All right. [*Gets up.*] Do give over, Sergey. [*Sits down.*] Pack it in. Why are you so cut up? As if someone had stolen the sun and left us in darkness—and you a former philosophy student! Be a Socrates, go on. [*Quietly.*] I don't know what I'm talking about, actually.

NICHOLAS [*puts his hand on* PLATONOV'*s head*]. Now you have to fall ill! It might do you good, though—clear your conscience.

ANNA. Off with you, Platonov. Send for another doctor in town— a consultation might help. I'll send for one, though, don't bother. And do set Sasha's mind at rest.

PLATONOV. There's a tiny piano crawling over your breast, Anna. What a scream! [*Laughs.*] Very funny. Sit down and play us something, Nicholas. [*Laughs.*] How priceless. I'm ill, Nicholas. I'm quite serious, it's no joke. Come on.

[IVAN *comes in.*]

SCENE X

[*The above and* IVAN.]

IVAN [*dishevelled, in his dressing-gown*]. My poor Sasha! [*Weeps.*]

NICHOLAS. This is the limit—you and your tears. Clear out. What brought you here anyway?

IVAN. She's dying, she's asking for a priest. I'm so frightened. [*Goes up to* PLATONOV.] In God's name, Michael, you dear, clever, fine, honourable fellow—go and tell her you love her. Please! Give up your sordid love affairs, I beg you on my knees. She's dying, you see. She's all I have, if she dies it will finish me—I'll be dead before you can get me a priest. Tell her you love her, that she's still your wife— put her mind at rest, for Christ's sake. A lie can be the means to salvation. You're an upright man, God knows, but tell a lie to save a life. Come on, please. Do me this kindness for Christ's sake, for an old man, and God will reward you a hundredfold. I'm shaking with fear.

PLATONOV. Been at the bottle already, Colonel? [*Laughs.*] We'll cure Sasha and have a drink together. I'm so thirsty.

IVAN. Come on, it really is most awfully decent of you. Just say a couple of words and she's saved. Medicine won't save her if her trouble's in the psychology department.

NICHOLAS. Please leave us for a moment, Father. [*Takes his father by the sleeve.*] Who says she's dying, what gave you that idea? She's not in danger. You wait in that room and we'll go over and see her at once with Platonov. Aren't you ashamed, bursting into a strange house in that condition?

IVAN [*to* ANNA]. You should be ashamed, Diana, God won't forgive you. He's a young man, inexperienced.

NICHOLAS [*pushes him into another room*]. Wait there. [*To* PLATONOV.] Ready to go?

PLATONOV. I'm terribly ill.

NICHOLAS. Will you come or won't you?

PLATONOV [*gets up*]. Don't talk so much. What's the cure for a dry mouth? Let's go. I don't think I brought my cap in here. [*Sits down.*] Would you mind looking for my cap?

SONYA. He should have known this would happen. I gave myself to him without hesitation, knowing I was killing my husband, but I—I stopped at nothing for his sake. [*Gets up and goes over to* PLATONOV.] What have you done to me? [*Sobs.*]

NICHOLAS [*clutches his head*]. What a business! [*Walks up and down the stage.*]

ANNA. Calm down, Sonya, this isn't the time. He's ill.

SONYA. How can you be so inhuman—treat someone else's life as a plaything? [*Sits down by* PLATONOV.] My life's ruined, I'm not really alive any more. Save me, Platonov, it's not too late. [*Pause.*]

ANNA [*cries*]. What do you want, Sonya? There's time for this later— what can he say now? Haven't you heard? Weren't you listening?

SONYA. Platonov, I ask you again. [*Sobs.*] Is it no?

[PLATONOV *moves away from her.*]

SONYA. You don't want me? All right then. [*Falls on her knees.*] Platonov!

ANNA. That's rather overdoing it, Sonya. How dare you? No one's worth grovelling to—. [*Picks her up and helps her to sit down.*] Remember you're a woman.

SONYA [*sobs*]. Tell him—. Persuade him——

ANNA. Pull yourself together. Be firm, you're not a child. Oh, come off it. Go to your room. [*Pause.*] Go and lie down. [*To* NICHOLAS.] What can we do with her?

NICHOLAS. Better ask friend Platonov about that. [*Walks up and down the stage.*]

ANNA. Let's put her to bed. Sergey, Nicholas—well, make yourselves useful!

[SERGEY *gets up and goes over to* SONYA.]

NICHOLAS. Come on then, I must give her a sedative.

ANNA. I wouldn't mind a spot of chloroform myself. [*To* SERGEY.] Be a man, Sergey. You at least must keep your head. I feel no better than you do, but I'm standing on my two feet. Come on,

Sonya. What a ghastly day! [*They lead* SONYA *off.*] Buck up, Sergey. Let's be sensible.

SERGEY. I'll try, Mother, I'm doing my best.

NICHOLAS. Don't mope, Sergey old horse. You'll pull through, don't worry. You're not the first it's happened to and you won't be the last.

SERGEY. I'll do my best, I'll try. [*They go out.*]

SCENE XI

[PLATONOV, *followed by* MARY.]

PLATONOV [*alone*]. A cigarette, Nicholas, and some water. [*Looks round.*] Have they gone? I must leave too. [*Pause.*] I've hounded and ruined weak, innocent women. If I'd destroyed them in some other way—in a fantastic gust of passion, Spanish style—I wouldn't mind. But I just destroyed them so—stupidly. Murder *à la russe* or something. [*Whips his hand in front of his eyes.*] Keep seeing things. Little clouds. It looks as if I'm in for a bout of delirium. I feel a complete and utter wreck. And not so long ago I seemed on top of the world. [*Buries his face in his hands.*] I'm so bitterly, painfully ashamed. [*Gets up.*] I was hungry, cold, worn out. I was going to the dogs, I'd become a complete charlatan and I turned up here, where they took me in, warmed me, clothed me, and cherished me as the apple of their eye. A fine way I've paid them out! But I'm ill. Feel awful. Must kill myself. [*Goes to the table.*] Take your choice, there's a regular arsenal. [*Takes a revolver.*] Hamlet feared dreams, I fear life. What would happen if I went on living? I'd die of shame. [*Puts the revolver to his temple.*] The farce is over. This means one intelligent ape the less. Christ, forgive me. [*Pause.*] Well? So now I can die, and my arm can ache as much as it likes. [*Pause.*] I can't do it! [*Puts the revolver on the table.*] I want to live. [*Sits on the sofa.*] I want to live. [MARY *comes in.*] I'd like some water. Where's Triletsky? [*Seeing* MARY.] Who's that? Aha! [*Laughs.*] My worst enemy. Do we meet in court tomorrow? [*Pause.*]

MARY. Of course we can't be enemies after your letter.

PLATONOV. I don't care. Isn't there any water?

MARY. Water? What's wrong with you?

PLATONOV. I'm ill, I'm going to run a temperature. Yes, I liked that letter, it was rather clever. What would be even cleverer would be if people had nothing to do with me. I wanted to shoot myself. [*Laughs.*] Didn't bring it off, couldn't do it—mind and instinct pulling different ways. You've a smart look about you, are you a clever little girl? [*Kisses her hand.*] Your hand's cold. Listen. Shall I go on?

MARY. Yes, yes, yes.

PLATONOV. Then take me home with you. I'm ill, thirsty. I'm in frightful agony. I want to sleep, but I've nowhere to lie down. Let me sleep in a barn or somewhere, give me some water and a bit of quinine. Please! [*Holds out his hand.*]

MARY. Come on then, I'll be delighted. You can stay as long as you like. You still don't know what I've been up to. Come on.

PLATONOV. Thanks, clever little girl. A cigarette, some water and a bed. Is it raining?

MARY. Yes.

PLATONOV. We'll have to drive in the rain. We won't go to court, we're friends now. [*Looks at her.*] Am I raving?

MARY. Not at all. Let's go. I've a covered carriage.

PLATONOV. You're a pretty little thing. Why are you blushing? I shan't touch you, I'll just kiss your cold little hand. [*Kisses her hand and draws her to him.*]

MARY [*sits on his lap*]. No, this won't do. [*Gets up.*] Come on. You look a bit odd. Let go of my hand.

PLATONOV. I'm ill. [*Gets up.*] Come on. I'll kiss your cheek. [*Kisses her cheek.*] No ulterior motive! This is all beyond me anyway, it's all silly. Come on, Mary, and let's be quick about it. I was going to shoot myself with this revolver. In the cheek. [*Kisses her cheek.*] I'm raving, but I see your face. I love everyone—yes, you too. I've always treasured people. Never wanted to hurt anyone, but I did. I hurt them all. [*Kisses her hand.*]

MARY. Now I see it all, I understand your position. You mean Sonya, don't you?

PLATONOV. Sonya, Zizi, Mimi, Masha—there are enough of you. I love you all. When I was at the university I used to say a few kind words to the street-walkers in Theatre Square. Everyone was in the theatre, but I was out on the square. I bought out one called Raisa. Then I collected three hundred roubles with some other students and we bought another one her freedom. Want to see her letters?

MARY. What's wrong with you?

PLATONOV. Think I'm mad, eh? No, it's just fever and delirium—ask Triletsky. [*Takes her by the shoulders.*] They all love me, all. You insult them—but they still love you. For instance, I insulted the Grekov girl and banged her against the table, but still she loves me. You are the Grekov girl, actually, aren't you? Sorry.

MARY. Where does it hurt?

PLATONOV. Being Platonov hurts. You love me, don't you? Be frank. I don't want anything, just say if you love me.

MARY. Yes. [*Puts her head on his chest.*] Yes.

PLATONOV [*kisses her head*]. They all love me. When I get better I'll seduce you. I used to help prostitutes, now I help to recruit them.

MARY. I don't care. I don't want anything else, you're the only man I care for. I don't want to know anyone else. Do what you like with me, you're the only man for me. [*Weeps.*]

PLATONOV. Now I understand Oedipus putting out his eyes. How low I've fallen and how well I know it. Leave me alone, it's not worth it. I'm ill. [*Frees himself.*] I'm leaving now. Sorry, Mary, I'm going mad. Where's Triletsky?

[SONYA *comes in.*]

SCENE XII

[*The above and* SONYA. SONYA *goes up to the table and rummages on it.*]

MARY [*clutches* PLATONOV's *hand*]. Shush!

[*Pause.* SONYA *takes the revolver, fires at* PLATONOV *and misses.*]

MARY [*stands between* PLATONOV *and* SONYA]. What are you doing? [*Shouts.*] Help! In here, quick!

SONYA. Out of my way! [*Runs round* MARY *and shoots* PLATONOV *point-blank in the chest.*]

PLATONOV. Wait, just a moment—. What is this?

[*Falls.* ANNA, IVAN, NICHOLAS *and* SERGEY *run in.*]

SCENE XIII

[*The above,* ANNA, IVAN, NICHOLAS *and* SERGEY, *followed by servants and* MARKO.]

ANNA [*snatches the revolver off* SONYA *and hurls her on the sofa*]. Platonov!

[*Bends over* PLATONOV. SERGEY *covers his face and turns to the door.*]

NICHOLAS [*bends over* PLATONOV *and quickly unbuttons his frock-coat. Pause.*] Michael, can you hear me? [*Pause.*]

ANNA. For God's sake, Platonov! Michael, Michael! Hurry up, Triletsky.

NICHOLAS [*shouts*]. Water!

MARY [*gives him a carafe*]. Save him, you'll save him, won't you?

[*Walks up and down the stage.* NICHOLAS *drinks the water and throws the carafe to one side.*]

IVAN [*clutches his head*]. Didn't he say I was done for. Well, I am. [*Kneels.*] God Almighty, I'm done for, finished.

[JACOB, VASILY, KATYA *and the* CHEF *run in.*]

MARKO [*comes in*]. A message from the magistrate, sir. [*Pause.*]

ANNA. Platonov!

[PLATONOV *raises himself a little and looks round at everyone.*]

ANNA. Platonov, it's all right—drink some water.

PLATONOV [*points to* MARKO]. Give him three roubles. [*Falls and dies.*]

ANNA. Buck up, Sergey. This will soon be over, Nicholas, it won't last for ever. So pull yourselves together.

KATYA [*bows low to* ANNA]. It's my fault, I delivered the note. It was the money tempted me. I'm sorry, it was unforgivable, ma'am.

ANNA. Pull yourselves together, don't go off the deep end. He's only just—. He'll be all right.

NICHOLAS [*shouts*]. He's dead!

ANNA. No, no.

[MARY *sits at the table, looks at the note and weeps bitterly.*]

IVAN. May he rest in peace. He's gone, done for.

NICHOLAS. Life's only worth a copeck. Good-bye, Michael, you've lost your copeck. What are you all goggling at? He shot himself. The party's over. [*Weeps.*] Who can I celebrate your funeral with? Fools! You couldn't look after Platonov. [*Stands up.*] Father, go and tell Sasha she may as well die. [*Swaying, goes up to* SERGEY.] What about you, eh? [*Embraces* SERGEY.] Poor old Platonov's dead. [*Sobs.*]

SERGEY. What are we to do, Nicholas?

NICHOLAS. Bury the dead and do our best for the living.

ANNA [*slowly gets up and walks towards* SONYA]. Calm yourself, Sonya. [*Sobs.*] What have you done! But, but—calm yourself. [*To* NICHOLAS.] Don't say anything to Sasha, I'll tell her myself. [*Goes to* PLATONOV *and kneels before him.*] Platonov! My darling! I can't believe it. You can't be dead. [*Takes his hand.*] My life!

NICHOLAS. There's work to do, Sergey. We must help your wife, and then——

SERGEY. Yes, yes, yes. [*Goes to* SONYA.]

IVAN. God has forsaken me for my sins. Why did you sin, you silly old clown? I killed God's creatures, got drunk, swore and condemned people. The Lord could put up with no more, and struck me.

END OF ACT FOUR

IVANOV

[Иванов]

A PLAY IN FOUR ACTS

(1887–1889)

CHARACTERS

NICHOLAS IVANOV, a local government official concerned with peasant affairs

ANNA, his wife, *née* Sarah Abramson

COUNT MATTHEW SHABELSKY, his uncle on his mother's side

PAUL LEBEDEV, chairman of the rural district council

ZINAIDA, his wife

SASHA, their daughter, aged 20

EUGENE LVOV, a young doctor on the council's panel

MARTHA BABAKIN, a young widow, estate-owner and daughter of a rich businessman

DMITRY KOSYKH, excise officer

MICHAEL BORKIN, a distant relative of Ivanov and manager of his estate

AVDOTYA, an old woman with no definite means of support

YEGORUSHKA, a dependant of the Lebedevs

FIRST GUEST

SECOND GUEST

THIRD GUEST

FOURTH GUEST

PETER, Ivanov's manservant

GABRIEL, a servant of the Lebedevs

Guests of both sexes, servants

The action takes place in the central Russian countryside

ACT ONE

The garden on IVANOV's *estate. Left, the front of the house, with terrace. One window is open. In front of the terrace is a broad semicircular area, with paths leading into the garden directly in front of the house and to its right. Garden seats, right, also tables, with a lighted lamp on one of them. Evening is drawing in. As the curtain rises there is the sound of a duet for piano and 'cello being practised indoors.*

SCENE I

[IVANOV *and* BORKIN. IVANOV *sits at a table reading a book.* BORKIN *is seen at the back of the garden carrying a shot-gun and wearing high boots. He is rather drunk. Seeing* IVANOV, *he tip-toes up to him and aims the gun at his face from close quarters.*]

IVANOV [*seeing* BORKIN, *starts and jumps up*]. Michael, what on earth—? You gave me a start. I've enough trouble already without your silly games. [*Sits down.*] Great fun, isn't it, frightening people?

BORKIN [*guffaws*]. All right, all right, I'm sorry. [*Sits beside him.*] All right, I won't do it again. [*Takes off his peaked cap.*] It's hot. You know, old boy, I've done over ten miles in about three hours and I'm dead beat. You feel my heart.

IVANOV [*reading*]. Very well, in a minute.

BORKIN. No, do it now. [*Takes* IVANOV's *hand and puts it to his chest.*] Well? Tick tock tick tock tick tock—something wrong with the old ticker, I might drop dead any moment. I say, would you care if I did?

IVANOV. I'm reading. Won't it keep?

BORKIN. But seriously, will you care if I drop dead? Nicholas, do you care if I die?

IVANOV. Leave me alone.

BORKIN. Just tell me if you'd mind, old boy.

IVANOV. What I mind is that smell of vodka. It's disgusting, Michael.

BORKIN [*laughs*]. Smell? That's funny. Actually, though, it isn't—I ran into the magistrate at Plesniki, and we did put away quite a few glasses. Drinking's really very bad for you. Bad for you, I say. Eh? Isn't it?

IVANOV. Look, this is altogether too much. You're behaving outrageously, my dear man.

BORKIN. All right, I'm sorry. Never mind, you take it easy. [*Gets up and moves off.*] Some people are funny, you can't even talk to them. [*Comes back.*] Oh yes, it nearly slipped my mind—I want eighty-two roubles from you.

IVANOV. Eighty-two roubles? What for?

BORKIN. To pay the men tomorrow.

IVANOV. I haven't got it.

BORKIN. Much obliged, I'm sure. [*Mimicking him.*] 'Haven't got it.' But the men have got to be paid. Or don't you think so?

IVANOV. I don't know. I've no money today. Wait till the first of the month when I get my salary.

BORKIN. What good is it bandying words with people like you? The men come for their wages tomorrow morning—not on the first of the month.

IVANOV. Well, what can I do now? Oh, go on, pester me—make my life a misery. But why you have to plague me so abominably just when I'm reading or writing or——

BORKIN. Do the men get paid or not? Yes or no. Oh, what's the good of talking to you? [*Makes a gesture of despair.*] Call yourself a farmer, a goddam landed proprietor? You and your scientific farming! Three thousand acres, and not a penny in his pocket! Owns a wine-cellar, but no corkscrew! I've a good mind to sell your carriage and horses tomorrow. Oh yes I will. I sold the oats before we cut them and tomorrow I'll damn well sell the rye. [*Strides about the stage.*] I'll make no bones about it either. What do you take me for?

SCENE II

[*The above,* SHABELSKY—*off-stage—and* ANNA.]

SHABELSKY [*off-stage, his voice heard through the window*]. It's no use us playing together. You've no more ear for music than a stuffed trout and you have an appalling touch.

ANNA [*seen through the open window*]. Who's talking out here? You, Michael? Why all the marching about?

BORKIN. Friend Nicholas is enough to make anyone's boots itch.

ANNA. I say, will you have some hay put on the croquet lawn?

BORKIN [*with a gesture of despair*]. Leave me alone, please.

ANNA. Really, what a way to talk, it doesn't suit you a bit. If you want women to like you, never let them see you being annoyed or stuffy. [*To her husband.*] Shall we have a romp in the hay, Nicholas?

IVANOV. Standing by an open window, Anna? It's bad for you, please move away. [*Shouts.*] Shut the window, Uncle.

[*The window is shut.*]

BORKIN. Lebedev's interest falls due in two days, don't forget.

IVANOV. I haven't. I'm going over this evening, I'll ask him to wait. [*Looks at his watch.*]

BORKIN. When are you leaving?

IVANOV. At once.

BORKIN [*eagerly*]. Hang on a minute, I do believe today's Sasha's birthday, eh? Tut, tut, tut. And I forgot. What a memory! [*Jumps up and down.*] I'm coming with you. [*Sings.*] Coming, coming. I'll have a bathe, chew some paper, and with three drops of ammonia I'll be a new man. Nicholas, old man, you're a bundle of nerves, dear boy, besides snivelling and being so depressed all the time. Look, we two—hell knows what we couldn't pull off together! I'd do anything for you. Shall I marry Martha Babakin? And split the dowry with you? But no—you can have it all, take the lot.

IVANOV. Don't talk such rot.

BORKIN. No, seriously. Shall I marry Martha and give you half her dowry? But what am I saying? As if you could understand. [*Imitates him.*] 'Don't talk such rot.' You're a nice, clever fellow, but you lack flair, you know—a certain flamboyancy. You should let yourself go and to hell with the consequences. Why, you whining neurotic—if you were a normal man you could be a millionaire in a year. For instance, if I had twenty-three hundred roubles now, I could be twenty thousand in pocket inside a couple of weeks. You don't believe me? Think I'm still 'talking rot'? Not a bit. Give me twenty-three hundred roubles, and I'll get you twenty thousand in a week. Ovsyanov's asking two thousand three hundred for a strip of land just across the river from us. If we buy it, we'll own both banks. Now, with both banks in our hands, we're entitled to dam the river, aren't we? We'll start building a mill, and as soon as we let it be known that we mean to make a dam, everyone down-stream will raise hell. We'll tell them straight—if they don't want a dam, let them come along here and cough up. See what I mean? The Zarevsky factory will pay five thousand, Korolkov three thousand, and the monastery will give five.

IVANOV. This is all very shady, Michael. Keep such things to yourself if you don't want us to quarrel.

BORKIN [*sits down at the table*]. Of course, I knew it! Won't lift a finger himself, and won't let me either.

SCENE III

[*The above,* SHABELSKY *and* LVOV.]

SHABELSKY [*coming out of the house with* LVOV]. Doctors are like lawyers, only lawyers just rob you, while doctors rob you and murder you as well. I'm not talking about present company. [*Sits down on the garden seat.*] They're so bogus, just out for what they can get. There may be some Utopia where there are exceptions to the rule, but—well, I've paid out twenty thousand odd in doctors' bills in my time and never met a doctor yet who didn't strike me as a licensed swindler.

BORKIN [*to* IVANOV]. Yes, won't lift a finger yourself, and won't let me either, which is why we've no money——

SHABELSKY. As I say, I'm not talking about present company. There may be exceptions, though actually—. [*Yawns.*]

IVANOV [*closing his book*]. Well, Doctor?

LVOV [*looking round at the window*]. As I said this morning, she must go to the Crimea straight away. [*Walks up and down the stage.*]

SHABELSKY [*gives a snort of laughter*]. The Crimea! Why don't you and I set up as doctors, Michael? It's so easy. If Mrs. So-and-so, or Miss Whatever-it-is, has a tickle in her throat and starts coughing out of boredom, just pick up a form and make out a proper medical prescription. Take one young doctor. Follow up with one trip to the Crimea, where some picturesque local lad may——

IVANOV [*to the* COUNT]. Oh, don't be such a bore. [*To* LVOV.] Trips to the Crimea cost money. All right, I might lay my hands on some, but you do know she's turned the idea down flat, don't you?

LVOV. Yes, I know. [*Pause.*]

BORKIN. Look, Doctor, can Anna really be so ill that she has to go to the Crimea?

LVOV [*looks round at the window*]. Yes, it's tuberculosis.

BORKIN. Phew! That's bad. She certainly looks as if she wouldn't last long, I've thought that for some time.

LVOV. But—keep your voice down. You can be heard indoors. [*Pause.*]

BORKIN [*sighing*]. Our life—. Man's life is like a bright flower blooming in a meadow. A goat comes along and eats it up. No more flower.

SHABELSKY. Nonsense, nonsense, nonsense. [*Yawns.*] Stuff and nonsense. [*Pause.*]

BORKIN. I say, everyone, I've been trying to show Nicholas how to make money. I gave him a gem of an idea, but the seed fell on stony ground as usual. You can't make him see sense. Look at the man— all that gloom, bad temper, wretchedness, moodiness, general misery——

SHABELSKY [*stands up and stretches*]. You're a great one for ingenious brain-waves and you're always giving advice. You might spare me a bit. Give me a lesson, if you're so clever. Show me some way out.

BORKIN [*stands up*]. I'm going for a swim. Good-bye, all. [*To the* COUNT.] There are at least twenty things you could do. If I were you I'd have twenty thousand in a week. [*Moves off.*]

SHABELSKY [*follows him*]. How? Come on, tell me.

BORKIN. There's nothing to tell, it's dead easy. [*Comes back.*] Lend me a rouble, Nicholas.

[IVANOV *gives him the money without speaking.*]

BORKIN. Thanks. [*To the* COUNT.] You've still a lot of cards up your sleeve.

SHABELSKY [*going after him*]. But what?

BORKIN. If I were you I'd have thirty thousand in a week. If not more. [*Goes out with the* COUNT.]

IVANOV [*after a pause*]. Futile people, futile words and silly questions to answer. Doctor, I'm so fed up with it all. I'm quite ill. I'm irritable, bad-tempered and rude these days, and so touchy, I hardly know myself. I have headaches for days on end, I can't sleep, and my ears buzz. But what can I do? Not a thing.

LVOV. I've a bone to pick with you, Ivanov.

IVANOV. Then pick it.

LVOV. It's your wife. [*Sits down.*] She refuses to go to the Crimea, but she'd go if you went.

IVANOV [*after some thought*]. The trip would cost quite a bit for two. Besides, I can't get much time off, I've already had one holiday this year.

LVOV. All right, I won't argue. Now then, the main cure for tuberculosis is absolute rest. But your wife never has a moment's peace, she's always worried about how you treat her. I'm rather excited, sorry, but I shan't mince my words. What you're doing is killing her. [*Pause.*] Let me think better of you, Ivanov.

IVANOV. It's only too true. I suppose I'm very much to blame, but I'm so mixed up, I feel paralysed, half dead or something. I don't know what I'm doing. I can't understand others, or myself either. [*Looks up at the window.*] We might be overheard, let's go for a stroll. [*They stand up.*] I'd start at the beginning and tell you the whole story, my dear fellow, but it's so long and involved, it would take all night. [*They move off.*] Anna's a splendid, wonderful woman. She gave up her religion for me—left her mother, father and wealthy home. If I'd asked her to give up a hundred more things, she'd have done it without thinking. Now I'm not in the least wonderful, and I've given up nothing. Anyway, it's a long story, but what it boils down to, my dear Doctor [*squirms*] is that—to put it briefly—I married because I was so much in love. I swore to love her for ever, but—well, that was five years ago, and she still loves me, while I—. [*Throws up his hands.*] Now you tell me she'll soon die, and I don't feel love or pity, just a sort of emptiness and exhaustion. I suppose anyone would think I'm behaving terribly, but I don't know myself what's going on inside me.

[*They go out down the garden path.*]

SCENE IV

[SHABELSKY *and, later,* ANNA.]

SHABELSKY [*comes in, laughing heartily*]. He's more than a petty crook, honestly—he's a virtuoso, a genius. We should put up a statue to him. He's every kind of modern rottenness mixed up together—lawyer, doctor, banker, gangster. [*Sits down on the bottom step of the terrace.*] And, you know, I don't think he's ever studied anywhere, that's what's so fantastic. What a master criminal he'd have made if he'd gone in for education and culture. 'You can have twenty thousand in a week,' says he. 'And you also hold the ace of trumps—being a count.' [*Laughs loudly.*] 'Any girl with a dowry would marry you.'

[ANNA *opens the window and looks down.*]

SHABELSKY. 'Shall I marry you to Martha?' he asks. 'Who's Martha?' 'Oh, the Balabalkin woman. Martha Balabalkin, the one like a washerwoman.'

ANNA. That you, Count?

SHABELSKY. What is it?

[ANNA *laughs.*]

SHABELSKY [*with a Jewish accent*]. Vy you are laughing, eh?

ANNA. I thought of something you said. Remember what you said at dinner? 'Pardon a thief—.' Something about a horse——

SHABELSKY.   'Convert a Jew to Christian ways,
                Pardon a thief his life of crime,
                Or take a lame horse to the vet
                —these things are all a waste of time.'

ANNA [*laughs*]. You can't make an ordinary joke without being nasty. You're a bad man. [*Seriously.*] Joking apart, Count, you're very spiteful. It's dull and rather unnerving living in the same house as you. You're always moaning and groaning, and to listen to you everyone's a frightful cad. Tell me frankly, have you ever said something nice about anyone?

SHABELSKY. Why the cross-examination?

ANNA. We've lived under one roof for five years and never once have I heard you talk about people calmly, without sneering and being spiteful. What harm have they done you? And do you really think you're better than everyone else?

SHABELSKY. I don't think so at all. I'm just as much a rotten swine on two legs as the next man. I'm in rotten bad taste, fit only for the rubbish dump. I'm always running myself down. Who am I? What am I? I was rich, free, quite happy—but now I'm a parasite, a scrounger, a degraded buffoon. If I express indignation or contempt, I only get laughed at. And when I laugh they shake their heads sadly and say the old man's a bit cracked. More often than not they don't hear or notice me.

ANNA [*calmly*]. He's hooting again.

SHABELSKY. Who is?

ANNA. The owl. It hoots every evening.

SHABELSKY. Then let it hoot. Things couldn't be worse. [*Stretches himself.*] Ah, my dear Sarah, if I won a few hundred thousand roubles, I'd show you a thing or two. I'd be out of here in no time, I'd leave this dump and my free meals—wouldn't set foot here again till the crack of doom.

ANNA. What would you do if you won that money?

SHABELSKY [*after some thought*]. First thing, I'd go to Moscow to hear the gypsies. And then—then I'd be off to Paris. I'd take lodgings there and go to the Russian church.

ANNA. What else?

SHABELSKY. I'd sit by my wife's grave and think for days on end. I'd just sit there till I died. She's buried in Paris. [*Pause.*]

ANNA. It's terribly boring. Shall we play another duet?

SHABELSKY. All right, get the music out.

SCENE V

[SHABELSKY, IVANOV *and* LVOV.]

IVANOV [*appears on a path with* LVOV]. You only left college last year, my dear Lvov, and you're still young and full of life, but I'm thirty-five, I have the right to advise you. Don't you go marrying Jewesses, neurotics or blue-stockings, but choose something nice and drab and ordinary. Don't go in for bright colours or unnecessary fuss and bother. In fact run your life on conventional lines. The greyer and more monotonous your background the better. Don't take on thousands of people single-handed, boy, don't fight windmills or batter your head against brick walls. And may God save you from things like scientific farming, cranky schools and wild speeches. Crawl into your little shell, get on with what little job God gave you to do. It's cosier, healthier and more decent that way. But the life I've lived—what a trying business, oh, how exhausting. So many mistakes, so much unfairness and silliness. [*Spotting the* COUNT, *irritatedly.*] Uncle, you're always popping up, one can never talk in peace.

SHABELSKY [*tearfully*]. Damnation, you can't relax anywhere. [*Jumps up and goes indoors.*]

IVANOV [*shouts after him*]. All right, I'm sorry. [*To* LVOV.] Why was I rude to him? Oh, I really must be a bit unhinged, I must do something about myself, I must——

LVOV [*agitated*]. I've heard you out, Ivanov, and—I'm sorry, but I'm going to be blunt and call a spade a spade. Your voice and tone, let alone your actual words, are so insensitive, selfish, cold and heartless that—. Someone who loves you is dying just because she does love you. She hasn't long to live, while you—you can be so callous and walk about giving advice and striking attitudes. I can't put it properly, I'm not much of a speaker, but—but I do most thoroughly dislike you.

IVANOV. You may well be right, you can judge so much better, not being involved. Very likely your idea of me is quite right, and I daresay I'm very very much to blame. [*Listens.*] I think they've brought the carriage round, I'll go and change. [*Moves towards the house and stops.*] You dislike me, Doctor, and you don't mind saying so. That does credit to your feelings. [*Goes indoors.*]

LVOV [*alone*]. Damn my feebleness! Again I missed a chance to give him a piece of my mind. I can't speak to him calmly. Hardly have I opened my mouth and uttered one word when I start choking [*points to his chest*] and heaving and I'm tongue-tied. I do most heartily loathe that hypocrite, that pretentious fraud! Now he's going out. His wretched wife's only happy when he's around, she dotes on him, begs him to spend one evening with her, but he—he can't do it, because home cramps his style, don't you see? If he spent an evening at home he'd get so bored he'd blow his brains out.

Poor man—he needs to branch out in some new line of skulduggery. Oh, I know why you go to those Lebedevs every evening, I'm under no illusions.

SCENE VI

[LVOV, IVANOV, *wearing hat and overcoat*, SHABELSKY *and* ANNA.]

SHABELSKY [*coming out of the house with* IVANOV *and* ANNA]. Nicholas, you are a monster, I must say. Every night you go out and leave us on our own, and we get so bored we go to bed at eight. You can't call this living, it's monstrous. If you can go, why can't we, eh?

ANNA. Leave him alone. Let him go, let him——

IVANOV [*to his wife*]. But how could you go when you're not well? You're ill and you're not allowed out after dark—ask the doctor here. You're not a child, Anna, you must be sensible. [*To the* COUNT.] And why do you want to go?

SHABELSKY. I'd rather fry in hell or be eaten by crocodiles than stay here. I'm bored, bored stiff. Everyone's sick of me. You leave me here to keep her company, but she's sick and tired of me and my nagging.

ANNA. Leave him alone, Count, let him go if he enjoys it.

IVANOV. Don't be like that about it, Anna. You know I'm not going there to enjoy myself, I have to talk about the money I owe them.

ANNA. I can't see why you make excuses. Just go, no one's keeping you.

IVANOV. Can't we all stop annoying each other? There's surely no need.

SHABELSKY [*tearfully*]. Nicholas, my boy—take me with you. Please. It might be rather amusing just to have a look at that lot of frauds and nit-wits. I haven't been anywhere since Easter.

IVANOV [*irritatedly*]. All right, come then. I'm fed up with the lot of you.

SHABELSKY. Yes? Oh, many, many thanks. [*Grasps him gaily by the arm and takes him on one side.*] Can I wear your straw hat?

IVANOV. Yes, but do hurry.

[*The* COUNT *runs indoors.*]

IVANOV. I'm fed up with you all. But—God, what am I saying? I've no right to talk to you like this, Anna. I never used to be this way. Ah well, good-bye, I'll be back by one.

ANNA. Nicholas, do stay at home, dear.

IVANOV [*agitated*]. My poor, precious darling, don't try and stop me going out at night, please. I'm cruel and unfair, but let me be unfair. It's such agony to stay in. At sunset things start to get me down, it's sheer hell. Don't ask me why, I don't know myself. I don't know, I tell you. You get fed up here, then you go on to the Lebedevs' where it's even worse. You come back, which means getting even more fed up and it goes on all night. I'm absolutely desperate.

ANNA. Then why not stay at home, dear? We'll talk as we used to. We'll have supper together and read. The old boy and I've learnt a lot of duets for you. [*Puts her arms round him.*] Do stay. [*Pause.*] I simply don't understand you, this has been going on a whole year. Why have you changed?

IVANOV. I don't know, I don't know.

ANNA. Why don't you want me to go out with you at night?

IVANOV. If you must know, I'd better tell you. It's rather a cruel thing to say, but it's better said. When I'm so depressed, I—I begin not to love you. I try to get away, even from you, at these times. In fact I just have to get out of the house.

ANNA. You're depressed, you say. That I understand. Look, Nicholas, why not try singing, laughing and losing your temper, as in the old days. You stay in. We'll laugh, drink home-made wine and cheer you up in no time. Shall I sing? Or shall we go and sit in your study in the dark as we used to, and you can tell me all about how depressed you are. Your eyes are so full of suffering. I'll look into them and cry, and we'll both feel better. [*Laughs and cries.*] What is it, Nicholas? Flowers come round every spring, but happiness doesn't—is that it? All right, go then.

IVANOV. Pray for me, Anna. [*Moves off, stops and thinks.*] No, it's too much! [*Goes out.*]

ANNA. Be off with you. [*Sits down near the table.*]

LVOV [*paces up and down the stage*]. Mrs. Ivanov, you must always come indoors on the stroke of six and stay in till morning. These damp nights are bad for you.

ANNA. Yes sir.

LVOV. 'Yes sir'? I'm perfectly serious.

ANNA. But I don't want to be perfectly serious. [*Coughs.*]

LVOV. There, you see, you're coughing already.

SCENE VII
[LVOV, ANNA *and* SHABELSKY.]

SHABELSKY [*comes out of the house wearing hat and overcoat*]. Where's
   Nicholas? Is the carriage there? [*Quickly comes and kisses* ANNA'*s
   hand.*] Good night, precious. [*Pulls a funny face.*] Vot can I do?
   Excuse, plis. [*Goes out quickly.*]

LVOV. Very funny.
                [*Pause. The sound of an accordion far away.*]

ANNA. How boring. The coachmen and cooks are holding a dance and
   I—I feel forsaken. Doctor, why are you striding about there? Come
   and sit down here.

LVOV. I can't sit still. [*Pause.*]

ANNA. They're playing *Greenfinch* in the kitchen. [*Sings.*]
         'Greenfinch, greenfinch, where have you been?
         Drinking vodka on the green.'

[*Pause.*] Are your mother and father alive, Doctor?

LVOV. My father's dead, but my mother's still alive.

ANNA. Do you miss her?

LVOV. I'm too busy to miss anyone.

ANNA [*laughs*]. Flowers come round every spring, but happiness
   doesn't. Who told me that? Now let me see, I think Nicholas himself said it. [*Pricks up her ears.*] The owl's hooting again.

LVOV. Let it.

ANNA. I'm beginning to think I've been unlucky, Doctor. There are
   lots of people, no better than me perhaps, who are happy and whose
   happiness costs them nothing. But I've paid for everything, every
   single thing. And so dearly. Why charge me such a shocking rate of
   interest? My dear, you're all so careful with me, so very tactful,
   you're afraid to tell me the truth, but do you think I don't know
   what's the matter with me? I know all right. Anyway, it's a boring

subject. [*With a Jewish accent.*] Excuse, plis, can you tell funny chokes?

LVOV. No.

ANNA. Nicholas can. I've also started wondering why people are so unfair. Why can't they love those who love them? Why do they have to lie when they're told the truth? Tell me, when will my mother and father stop hating me? They live nearly forty miles away, but I feel their hatred all day and night, even in my sleep. And what am I to make of Nicholas being so depressed? He says it's only when he's bored stiff in the evenings that he doesn't love me. I understand that, I can accept it. But what if he stops loving me altogether? Of course that can't happen, but—what if it does? No, I mustn't even think of it. [*Sings.*] 'Greenfinch, greenfinch, where have you been?' [*Shudders.*] What horrible thoughts I have. You're not married, Doctor, so there's a lot you can't understand.

LVOV. You're surprised—. [*Sits by her.*] No, it's I—I'm surprised at you. All right, tell me—make me see how you, a decent, intelligent woman, with a nature almost angelic, have let yourself be taken in so blatantly and hauled off to this haunt of owls? Why are you here? What have you in common with that callous, insensitive—but leave your husband out of it. Where do you fit into this whole futile, second-rate set-up? Ye gods! That fossilized maniac count with his non-stop grousing, and that twister Borkin—that frightful crook with his loathsome snout. Go on, tell me why you're here? How did you get here?

ANNA [*laughs*]. That's just how he used to speak, just like that. But his eyes are bigger and when he got excited about something they just blazed! Go on talking.

LVOV [*stands up and makes a gesture of despair*]. What can I say? Please go indoors.

ANNA. You say Nicholas is this and that and the other. What do you know about him? Can you get to know someone in six months? He's a wonderful man, Doctor, and I'm only sorry you didn't know him a year or two ago. Now he's rather under the weather and doesn't speak or do anything. But in the old days—oh, he was so charming, I fell in love at first sight. [*Laughs.*] I took one look and snap went the mousetrap! He said we should go away. I cut off everything, you know, like snipping off dead leaves with some scissors, and followed him. [*Pause.*] But now things are different. He visits the Lebedevs to enjoy other women's company now, while I—sit in the garden and listen to the owl hooting.

[*A watchman is heard tapping.*]

ANNA. Have you any brothers, Doctor?

LVOV. No.

[ANNA *sobs.*]

LVOV. What now? What's the matter?

ANNA [*stands up*]. I can't bear it, Doctor, I'm going over there.

LVOV. Where?

ANNA. Where he is. I'm going, tell them to harness the horses. [*Runs indoors.*]

LVOV. I flatly refuse to treat a patient in these conditions. It's bad enough not paying me, but they play hell with my feelings as well. Yes, I refuse, I've had enough. [*Goes indoors.*]

CURTAIN

ACT TWO

The ballroom in the LEBEDEVS' *house. Access to the garden, centre. Doors, right and left. Expensive antique furniture. A chandelier, candelabras and pictures, all under dust-covers.*

SCENE I

[ZINAIDA, KOSYKH, AVDOTYA, YEGORUSHKA, GABRIEL, *a* MAID, *elderly women guests, young ladies and* MRS. BABAKIN.

ZINAIDA *is sitting on the sofa, with old ladies in armchairs on each side. The young people are sitting on upright chairs. At the back of the stage near the door into the garden a game of cards is in progress, the players including* KOSYKH, AVDOTYA *and* YEGORUSHKA. GABRIEL *stands by the door, right. The* MAID *is handing round snacks on a tray. Throughout the act guests circulate from the garden through the door, right, and back.* MRS. BABAKIN *comes in through the door, right, and goes towards* ZINAIDA.]

ZINAIDA [*gaily*]. Martha, darling!

MRS. BABAKIN. Good evening, Zinaida. Best wishes for Sasha's birthday. [*They kiss.*] May God grant——

ZINAIDA. Thank you, darling, I'm so glad. Now how are you?

MRS. BABAKIN. Well, thanks. [*Sits beside her on the sofa.*] Good evening, young people.

[*The guests stand up and bow.*]

FIRST GUEST [*laughs*]. 'Young people'! You don't call yourself old, do you?

MRS. BABAKIN [*sighing*]. I can't pretend to be all that young.

FIRST GUEST [*laughing respectfully*]. Oh, come, come. You don't look like a widow—you put all the young girls in the shade.

[GABRIEL *brings* MRS. BABAKIN *tea.*]

ZINAIDA [*to* GABRIEL]. Hey, don't serve it like that. Get some jam, gooseberry or something.

MRS. BABAKIN. Don't bother, thanks. [*Pause.*]

FIRST GUEST. Did you come through Mushkino, Mrs. Babakin?

MRS. BABAKIN. No, on the Zaymishche road—it's a better one.

FIRST GUEST. Just so.

KOSYKH. Two spades.

YEGORUSHKA. Pass.

AVDOTYA. Pass.

SECOND GUEST. Pass.

MRS. BABAKIN. Lottery tickets are simply soaring again, darling. It's fantastic—they're up to two hundred and seventy roubles for the first draw and they're practically at two-fifty for the second. It's unheard of.

ZINAIDA [*sighs*]. Very nice for those who have lots of them.

MRS. BABAKIN. I'm not sure, darling. They may be worth a bit, but it doesn't pay to put money in them. They cost the earth to insure.

ZINAIDA. That's as may be, but one lives in hope, dear. [*Sighs.*] God is merciful.

THIRD GUEST. It's no use having capital these days, ladies, if you ask me. That's my view. Investments bring such small dividends, and lending money's a pretty risky business. The way I see it, ladies, a man with capital is in a worse fix these days than one who——

MRS. BABAKIN [*sighs*]. That's true.

[FIRST GUEST *yawns.*]

MRS. BABAKIN. One doesn't yawn in front of ladies, surely.

FIRST GUEST. Sorry, ladies, I didn't mean to.

[ZINAIDA *gets up and goes out of the door, right. A long silence.*]

YEGORUSHKA. Two diamonds.

AVDOTYA. Pass.

SECOND GUEST. Pass.

KOSYKH. Pass.

MRS. BABAKIN [*aside*]. Lord, I'm bored stiff.

SCENE II

[*The above,* ZINAIDA *and* LEBEDEV.]

ZINAIDA [*coming through door, right, with* LEBEDEV, *quietly*]. Why were you skulking in there? Who do you think you are? You sit with your guests. [*Sits in her former seat.*]

LEBEDEV [*yawns*]. Oh dear. [*Seeing* MRS. BABAKIN.] Heavens, there's sugar and spice and all things nice. [*Shakes hands.*] How are we feeling?

MRS. BABAKIN. Very well, thanks.

LEBEDEV. Thank God for that. [*Sits in an armchair.*] Ah well. Gabriel!

[GABRIEL *brings him a glass of vodka and a tumbler of water. He drinks the vodka and chases it down with water.*]

FIRST GUEST. Your health.

LEBEDEV. My health, indeed! I'm only lucky I'm not pushing up the daisies. [*To his wife.*] Where's our birthday girl, Zizi?

KOSYKH [*tearfully*]. Hey, why didn't we win anything? [*Jumps up.*] Why did we lose, damn and blast it?

AVDOTYA [*jumps up, angrily*]. Why? If you don't know the game, don't play, man. What do you mean by leading one of their suits? Can you wonder you were left with the ace?

[*Both run forward from the table.*]

KOSYKH [*tearfully*]. Look here, everyone. I held a run—the ace, king, queen and seven small diamonds, the ace of spades and one small heart, see? And she couldn't declare a little slam, damn it! I bid no trumps.

AVDOTYA [*interrupting*]. It was I started bidding no trumps, you went two no trumps——

KOSYKH. This is infuriating. Look here—you had—. I had—you had—. [*To* LEBEDEV.] Judge for yourself, Lebedev. I had the ace, king, queen and seven more diamonds——

LEBEDEV [*plugs his ears*]. Leave me alone, can't you?

AVDOTYA [*shouts*]. It was I bid no trumps.

KOSYKH [*furiously*]. Damn and blast me if I ever play cards with that old trout again!

[*Hurries out into the garden. The* SECOND GUEST *follows him out, leaving* YEGORUSHKA *at the table.*]

AVDOTYA. Phew, he's made me hot all over. Old trout! Trout yourself!

MRS. BABAKIN. But you lost your temper too, old thing.

AVDOTYA [*seeing* MRS. BABAKIN, *throws up her hands*]. My lovely darling. She's here and I don't even notice her, I must be half blind. Darling! [*Kisses her shoulder and sits by her.*] How delightful. Let me look at you, you beautiful creature. But I mustn't say too many nice things or it'll bring bad luck.

LEBEDEV. Why all the gush? Better find her a husband.

AVDOTYA. I will, I will. I won't lay my sinful old bones to rest before I've found a husband for her and Sasha, that I won't. [*Sighs.*] Only where do you find husbands these days? Look at all our young men —there they sit preening their feathers like a lot of wet hens.

THIRD GUEST. A most unhappy comparison. What I say, ladies, is— if young men would rather stay single these days, that's society's fault.

LEBEDEV. Oh, spare us the generalizations, I don't like them.

SCENE III

[*The above and* SASHA.]

SASHA [*comes in and goes to her father*]. It's such glorious weather and you all sit stewing indoors.

ZINAIDA. Sasha, can't you see Mrs. Babakin's here?

SASHA. Oh, sorry. [*Goes up to* MRS. BABAKIN *and shakes hands.*]

MRS. BABAKIN. You're getting much too high and mighty, Sasha. You might come and see me once in a while. [*They kiss.*] Happy returns, darling.

SASHA. Thank you. [*Sits down by her father.*]

LEBEDEV. Yes, Avdotya, husbands are hard to find these days. You can't lay your hands on a decent best man, let alone an eligible groom. No offence meant, but young men are a pretty spineless, wishy-washy crew nowadays, God help them. Can't dance, can't talk, can't drink properly.

AVDOTYA. Can't drink? Oh yes they can, given the chance——

LEBEDEV. Drinking? There's nothing to it, even a horse can drink. No, the thing is to drink properly. Now, in our time you'd sweat away at your lectures all day long, then you'd make for the bright lights in the evening and buzz around till crack of dawn. You'd dance and amuse the girls and there'd be a bit of this business. [*Pretends to drink.*] Sometimes you'd jabber away nineteen to the dozen. But young men these days—. [*Makes a gesture of dismissal.*] I can't make them out, they're no use to man or beast. There's only one decent young fellow in the whole county, and he's married. [*Sighs.*] And I think he's going a bit off his head.

MRS. BABAKIN. Who's that?

LEBEDEV. Nicholas Ivanov.

MRS. BABAKIN. Yes, he's a nice man [*pulls a face*], only he's so unhappy.

ZINAIDA. Can you wonder, darling? [*Sighs.*] The poor man made a ghastly mistake—marrying that wretched Jewess and thinking her parents would cough up a whacking great dowry. It didn't come off. When she changed her religion they cut her off and cursed her, so not a penny did he get. He's sorry now it's too late.

SASHA. That's not true, Mother.

MRS. BABAKIN [*heatedly*]. Not true, Sasha? But it's an open secret. Why marry a Jewess if there wasn't anything in it for him? Aren't there enough Russian girls to go round? He made a big mistake, darling. [*Eagerly.*] And now he gives her a terrible time, God knows —it's enough to make a cat laugh. The moment he gets home, he's on at her. 'Your father and mother cheated me. Get out of my house!' But where can she go? Her parents won't take her back. She might get a job as a maid, but she's not trained. So he keeps on nagging till the count sticks up for her. If it wasn't for the count, he'd have been the end of her ages ago.

AVDOTYA. Or he locks her in the cellar. 'Eat garlic, you so-and-so,' he says. Eat and eat she does, till the stuff starts coming out of her ears.
[*Laughter.*]

SASHA. That's a lie, Father.

LEBEDEV. Well, what of it? Let them jabber away. [*Shouts.*] Gabriel!
[GABRIEL *gives him vodka and water.*]

ZINAIDA. That's why the poor man's ruined. He's in a bad way, darling. If Borkin didn't run the farm, he and his Jewess would have nothing to eat. [*Sighs.*] And what a fearful nuisance he's been, dear. God alone knows what we've had to put up with. My dear, do you know, he's owed us nine thousand roubles for the last three years?

MRS. BABAKIN [*horrified*]. Nine thousand!

ZINAIDA. Yes, my precious husband arranged to lend it him—he doesn't know who to lend money to and who not. I'm not talking about the loan itself—never mind that—but he might at least pay the interest on time.

SASHA [*heatedly*]. You've said all this thousands of times, Mother.

ZINAIDA. Why should you care? Why do you take his side?

SASHA [*stands up*]. How dare you talk like this about someone who never did you any harm? What harm did he ever do you?

THIRD GUEST. May I say a word, Miss Lebedev? I've a high opinion of Ivanov and have always been honoured to—. But between you and me I think the man's a rogue.

SASHA. Then I can only congratulate you on your insight.

THIRD GUEST. May I quote in evidence a communication made to me by his aide or general guide and philosopher, Borkin? During the cattle epidemic two years ago he bought a lot of cows, insured them——

ZINAIDA. Yes, yes, yes, I remember that business, I heard about it too.

THIRD GUEST. Insured them, mark my words—then infected them with cattle-disease and pocketed the insurance.

SASHA. Oh, that's all nonsense. Nonsense! No one bought cows or infected them, it was all Borkin's idea that he went round boasting about. When Ivanov heard of it he had Borkin going round for a couple of weeks apologizing. Ivanov's only fault is being weak and not having enough go in him to chuck out friend Borkin, and he's wrong to trust people too much. He's been robbed and fleeced left, right and centre—anyone who liked has made a packet out of Ivanov's idealistic plans.

LEBEDEV. Shut up, you little spitfire.

SASHA. Why must they talk such nonsense? Oh, how boring, boring, boring. Ivanov, Ivanov, Ivanov—is there nothing else to talk about?

[*Goes towards the door and returns.*] I'm surprised. [*To the young men.*] I'm really surprised how long-suffering you all are. Don't you ever get tired of sitting round like this? The very air's stiff with boredom. Can't you say something, amuse the girls or move around a bit? All right, if you've nothing to talk about but Ivanov, then laugh or sing or dance or something.

LEBEDEV [*laughs*]. Yes, you jolly well pitch into them.

SASHA. Would you mind listening for a moment? If you don't want to dance or laugh or sing, if you're bored with that, then please, please, just for once in your lives, if only for the novelty or surprise or fun of the thing—join forces and think up something brilliantly witty between you. Let it be rude or vulgar if you like, but funny and original. Or else do some small thing together which may not add up to all that much, but does at least look vaguely enterprising and might make the girls sit up and take notice for once in their lives. Look, you all want to be liked, don't you? Then why not try to be likeable? There's something wrong with you all, and no mistake. The sight of you's enough to kill the flies or start the lamps smoking. Yes, there's something wrong—I've told you thousands of times and I'll go on telling you—something wrong with you all, wrong, wrong, wrong!

SCENE IV

[*The above,* IVANOV *and* SHABELSKY.]

SHABELSKY [*coming in with* IVANOV *through the door, right*]. Who's making the speeches round here? You, Sasha? [*Laughs loudly and shakes hands with her.*] Happy returns, dear. May you live to a ripe old age and not be born a second time.

ZINAIDA [*gaily*]. Mr. Ivanov, Count Shabelsky.

LEBEDEV. Hey, who's this I see? The count. [*Goes to meet them.*]

SHABELSKY [*spotting* ZINAIDA *and* MRS. BABAKIN, *stretches out his arms towards them*]. Two money-boxes on one sofa. What a lovely sight. [*Shakes hands. To* ZINAIDA.] Hallo there, Zizi. [*To* MRS. BABAKIN.] Hallo, my little bit of fluff.

ZINAIDA. I'm so glad. You're such a rare visitor, Count. [*Shouts.*] Tea, Gabriel! Won't you sit down?

[*Stands up, goes out of door, right, and returns immediately, looking extremely worried.* SASHA *sits in her former seat.* IVANOV *greets everyone without speaking.*]

LEBEDEV [*to* SHABELSKY]. Where did you spring from? What brought you here? This is a surprise. [*Kisses him.*] What a way to behave, you old pirate. [*Leads him by the hand towards the footlights.*] Why do you never come and see us, are you angry or something?

SHABELSKY. How am I to get here? Ride on my walking-stick? I've no horses and Nicholas won't bring me—tells me to stay with Sarah and keep her company. Send me your horses and then I'll come.

LEBEDEV [*makes a gesture of resignation*]. That's a point—Zizi'd burst rather than send the horses. Dear old boy, you are my best friend, you know. You and I are the only two left over from the old days.
    'In you I love my former sufferings,
    In you I love my wasted youth.'
Joking apart, I'm nearly crying. [*Kisses the* COUNT.]

SHABELSKY. Let me go, please, you smell like a distillery.

LEBEDEV. My dear man, you can't imagine how I miss my friends— I get bored to death. [*Quietly.*] Zizi's driven off all the nicer people by setting up as a moneylender, and as you see there are only monsters left—these Dudkins and Budkins. Anyway, have some tea.

[GABRIEL *brings the* COUNT *tea.*]

ZINAIDA [*to* GABRIEL, *worried*]. Hey, what a way to serve! Fetch some jam, gooseberry or something.

SHABELSKY [*laughs loudly, to* IVANOV]. There, what did I say? [*To* LEBEDEV.] We had a bet on the way over that Zizi would treat us to gooseberry jam the moment we got here.

ZINAIDA. You still like your little joke. [*Sits down.*]

LEBEDEV. Twenty barrels they've made and she doesn't know what to do with it.

SHABELSKY [*sitting near the table*]. Still hoarding money, Zizi? Run up your first million yet?

ZINAIDA [*with a sigh*]. Oh, we may look as if we're rolling in money, but where do you think it comes from? It's nothing but talk.

SHABELSKY. Quite, quite, we know all about that, we know what a poor hand you are at that game. [*To* LEBEDEV.] Tell me honestly, Paul—have you saved a million yet?

LEBEDEV. I don't know, better ask Zizi about that.

SHABELSKY [*to* MRS. BABAKIN]. And our plump little bit of fluff will soon have her million too. She gets prettier and plumper every hour of the day—that's what it means to be well-heeled.

MRS. BABAKIN. I'm most grateful, my Lord, but I don't particularly like being sneered at.

SHABELSKY. Call that sneering, my little pot of gold? It's just a cry from the heart—the fullness of my heart hath unsealed my lips. I just adore you and Zizi. [*Gaily.*] You're two visions of delight, I can't look at you unmoved.

ZINAIDA. You haven't changed a bit. [*To* YEGORUSHKA.] Put out the candles, Yegorushka. Why waste them if you're not playing? [YEGORUSHKA *starts, puts out the candles and sits down. To* IVANOV.] How's the wife, Nicholas?

IVANOV. Bad. The doctor told us today quite definitely that it's tuberculosis.

ZINAIDA. Oh, no! How awful. [*Sighs.*] And we're all so fond of her.

SHABELSKY. Stuff and nonsense. She hasn't got tuberculosis, that's just so much quackery and hocus-pocus. Our medical genius wants an excuse to hang about—so he makes out it's tuberculosis. It's lucky the husband's not jealous. [IVANOV *makes an impatient gesture.*] As for Sarah herself, I don't believe a thing she says or does. I've never trusted doctors, lawyers or women in my life, it's all stuff and nonsense, quackery and jiggery-pokery.

LEBEDEV [*to* SHABELSKY]. You're a pretty queer fish, Matthew, with this misanthropic pose you make such a parade of. You're no different from anyone else, but when you talk, you sound as if you were fed up to the back teeth.

SHABELSKY. You don't expect me to hobnob with all these rotten swine, do you?

LEBEDEV. What rotten swine? Where are they?

SHABELSKY. Not present company of course. But——

LEBEDEV. But me no buts, this is just a pose.

SHABELSKY. Oh, is it? It's a good job you've no principles.

LEBEDEV. What principles can I have? I sit here waiting to peg out, that's my principle. You and I've no time to think about our principles, old boy. No, indeed. [*Shouts.*] Gabriel!

SHABELSKY. There's been a sight too much of this 'Gabriel' stuff, your nose is like a ruddy great beetroot.

LEBEDEV [*drinks*]. Never mind, old boy, it's not my wedding day.

ZINAIDA. It's ages since Dr. Lvov was here, he's quite forsaken us.

SASHA. My pet aversion. Oh, he's virtue incarnate, can't ask for a glass of water or light a cigarette without displaying his remarkable integrity. Walking or talking, he has 'Honest Joe' written all over him. What a bore.

SHABELSKY. That shallow, narrow-minded medico. [*As if imitating him.*] 'Make way for an honest, hard-working man!' Can't move an inch without squawking parrot-cries. Puts himself on a high moral pedestal and abuses everyone who doesn't squawk like him. His views are remarkably profound. Any peasant who's well-off and lives decently must be a scoundrel on the make. I wear a velvet coat and have a valet, so I'm a scoundrel and slave-driver. Oh, he's very honest, in fact he's bursting with it. And he can never relax. I'm actually afraid of him, I really am. You feel he'll punch you on the jaw any moment or call you a filthy swine—all from a sense of duty.

IVANOV. I find him terribly trying, but I do quite like him—he's so sincere.

SHABELSKY. A nice kind of sincerity. Last night he comes up to me completely out of the blue and says: 'I thoroughly dislike you, Count.' Thank you very much, I must say. And none of this is straightforward, there's always some twist to it. His voice shakes, his eyes flash, he's all of a dither. To hell with his phoney sincerity. Oh, he loathes me, finds me nauseating. It's only natural, I can see that, but why tell me so to my face? I may be no good, but my hair is going white, after all. It's a pretty cheap and uncharitable kind of honesty, his is.

LEBEDEV. Oh come, you've been young yourself, I imagine, and you can make allowances.

SHABELSKY. Yes, I've been young and foolish. I've been quite outspoken in my day and shown up all sorts of blackguards and bounders. But never in my life have I called anyone a thief to his face, nor have I ever plumbed the depths of sheer blatant tactlessness. I was properly brought up. But this dull quack would be tickled pink—he'd feel he'd attained his life's ambition—if he got the chance to bash my face in in public or hit me below the belt in the name of principles and humane ideals.

LEBEDEV. Young men always do have some bee in their bonnet. My uncle was a follower of Hegel. Used to collect a houseful of guests, have a drink and stand on a chair like this and start off. 'You're ignorant! You're the forces of darkness! The dawn of a new life!' Blah blah blah blah. Yes, he let them have it all right.

SASHA. And what about his guests?

LEBEDEV. Oh, they didn't mind, they listened and carried on drinking. Actually, I once challenged him to a duel—my own uncle. It was about Bacon. Now let me think, I remember sitting just where Matthew is now, and Uncle and poor old Gerasim Nilovich were standing here, about where dear old Nicholas is. Then Gerasim Nilovich asks a question, old boy——

[BORKIN *comes in.*]

SCENE V

[*The above and* BORKIN *who comes in through door, right, in his best clothes, carrying a parcel, bobbing up and down and humming. A buzz of approval.*]

GIRLS. Michael!

LEBEDEV. Dear old Mike! Or do my ears deceive me?

SHABELSKY. The life and soul of the party.

BORKIN. Here I am. [*Runs up to* SASHA.] Noble signorina, I make bold to congratulate the universe on the birth of such a wondrous blossom. As a tribute to my joy, I venture to offer [*hands over the parcel*] some fireworks and bengal lights of my own manufacture. May they light up the night just as you make bright the shades in our realm of darkness. [*Gives a theatrical bow.*]

SASHA. Thank you.

LEBEDEV [*laughs loudly, to* IVANOV]. Why don't you get rid of that swine?

BORKIN [*to* LEBEDEV]. My dear Lebedev. [*To* IVANOV.] Respected patron. [*Sings.*] Nicholas *voilà*, ho-hi-ho! [*Goes round to all of them.*] Most revered Zinaida. Divine Martha. Most venerable Avdotya. Your Lordship.

SHABELSKY [*laughs loudly*]. The life and soul of the party. The moment he came in the tension lifted, did you notice?

BORKIN. I say, I am tired. I think I've said hallo to everyone. Well, what's the news, all of you? Is there some special item to shake us up a bit? [*To* ZINAIDA, *eagerly*.] Listen to this, old thing. On my way here just now—. [*To* GABRIEL.] Tea, please, Gabriel, but no gooseberry jam. [*To* ZINAIDA.] On my way here just now I saw some villagers stripping bark off the willows by your river. Why don't you let a dealer handle that?

LEBEDEV [*to* IVANOV]. Why don't you get rid of the swine?

ZINAIDA [*terrified*]. Do you know, I never even thought of it?

BORKIN [*does some arm exercises*]. I can't keep still. I say, couldn't we do something different, old thing? I'm on top of my form, Martha, I feel exalted. [*Sings*.] 'Once more before you——'

ZINAIDA. Yes, do something, because we're all bored.

BORKIN. Really, why so downhearted anyway, all of you, sitting there like a lot of stuffed dummies? Let's play a game or something. What would you like? Forfeits, skipping, tag, dancing, fireworks?

GIRLS [*clapping their hands*]. Fireworks, fireworks. [*They run into the garden.*]

SASHA [*to* IVANOV]. Why so depressed tonight?

IVANOV. My head aches, Sasha, and I'm bored.

SASHA. Come in the drawing-room. [*They go through the door, right. Everyone goes into the garden except* ZINAIDA *and* LEBEDEV.]

ZINAIDA. Now, that's a bit more like it, that young fellow—wasn't in here a minute before he'd cheered us all up. [*Turns down the large lamp.*] No point in wasting candles when everyone's in the garden. [*Puts out the candles.*]

LEBEDEV [*following her*]. We ought to give the guests some food, Zizi.

ZINAIDA. Lord, what a lot of candles—no wonder people think we're rich. [*Puts them out.*]

LEBEDEV [*following her*]. You might give them some food, Zizi. They're young folk, they must be starved, poor things. Zizi——

ZINAIDA. The count hasn't finished his tea. What a waste of sugar. [*Goes through door, left.*]

LEBEDEV. Ugh! [*Goes into the garden.*]

SCENE VI

[IVANOV *and* SASHA.]

SASHA [*coming in with* IVANOV *through door, right*]. They've all gone in the garden.

IVANOV. That's how things are, Sasha. I used to work hard and think hard, I never got tired. Now I do nothing and think of nothing, but I'm tired, body and soul. I feel so conscience-stricken all the time. I feel terribly guilty, but just where I went wrong I can't see. Now there's my wife's illness, my money troubles, this non-stop back-biting, gossip and idle chit-chat—and that ass Borkin. I'm sick and tired of my home, and living there's sheer hell. Frankly, Sasha, I can't even stand having my loving wife about. You're an old friend and won't be annoyed if I speak my mind. I came here to enjoy myself, but I'm bored here too, and feel like going back. Excuse me, I'll just slip away.

SASHA. I understand you, Nicholas. You're unhappy because you're lonely. You need someone near you that you love and who'll appreciate you. Only love can make a new man of you.

IVANOV. Now really, Sasha. For a bedraggled old wreck like me to start a new love affair, that would be the last straw. God save me from any such disaster. No, it's not love affairs I need, dear girl. God knows, I can stand all this—depression, neurosis, ruin, the loss of my wife, premature old age, being lonely. But despising myself— that's what I can't put up with. That a strong, healthy man like me should have turned into a sort of Hamlet, Manfred, odd-man-out or hell knows what—I could die of shame. Some wretched people are flattered to be called Hamlets or outsiders, but to me that's con-temptible, it offends my pride, I'm overwhelmed with shame and I suffer agonies.

SASHA [*joking, through tears*]. Let's run away to America, Nicholas.

IVANOV. I'm too lazy to go as far as that door and you want to go to America. [*They go towards the exit to the garden.*] It's not much of a life for you here, Sasha, I must say. When I look at the people round you, it frightens me. Who can you marry here? The only hope is, some young subaltern or student may pass this way and run off with you.

SCENE VII

[ZINAIDA *comes through door, left, with a jar of jam.*]

IVANOV. Excuse me, Sasha, I'll catch you up.

[SASHA *goes into the garden.*]

IVANOV. Mrs. Lebedev, may I ask you a favour?

ZINAIDA. What is it, Mr. Ivanov?

IVANOV [*hesitates*]. Well, the thing is, you see, the interest on your loan falls due in two days' time. I'd be most obliged if you'd give me a bit longer or let me add the interest to the loan. At the moment I'm out of money.

ZINAIDA [*horrorstruck*]. Mr. Ivanov, what a shocking suggestion! Put it right out of your mind. And for God's sake don't bother me, I've troubles enough.

IVANOV. Sorry, sorry. [*Goes into the garden.*]

ZINAIDA. Heavens, how he upset me, I'm all of a tremble. [*Goes out of the door, right.*]

SCENE VIII

KOSYKH [*comes through door, left, and crosses the stage*]. I had the ace, king, queen and seven small diamonds, the ace of spades and one—one tiny heart, but she couldn't declare a little slam, damn her! [*Goes out of door, right.*]

SCENE IX

[AVDOTYA *and* FIRST GUEST.]

AVDOTYA [*coming out of the garden with the* FIRST GUEST]. Oh, I could tear her in pieces, the old skinflint—that I could. It's no joke. I've been here since five, and not one stale herring have we had to eat. What a house, and what a way to run it.

FIRST GUEST. This is all such a crashing bore, I feel like taking a running dive into a brick wall. God, what people! You get so bored and ravenous, like a howling, man-eating tiger.

AVDOTYA. I could tear her in pieces, God help me.

FIRST GUEST. I'll have a drink, old girl, and be off home. And I'm not interested in any of your marriageable young women. How the hell can a man think of love when he doesn't get a drink after dinner?

AVDOTYA. Let's go and find some, eh?

FIRST GUEST. Shush! There's some schnapps in the dining-room, I think, in the sideboard. We'll get hold of Yegorushka. Shush! [*They go out by door, left.*]

SCENE X

[ANNA *and* LVOV *come through the door, right.*]

ANNA. It's all right, they'll be pleased to see us. There's no one here, they must be in the garden.

LVOV. Why bring me to this vampires' lair, I wonder. This is no place for you and me, honest men shouldn't breathe this air.

ANNA. Listen to me, my honest friend. When you take a lady out, it's not very nice to keep on and on about how honest you are. Honest you may be, but you're also, to put it mildly, a bore. Never talk to a woman about your good points, let her see those for herself. At your age Nicholas only sang and told stories in ladies' company, but everyone could see what he was really like.

LVOV. Don't talk about friend Nicholas, I know his sort!

ANNA. You're a good man, but you don't understand anything. Let's go in the garden. He never said things like: 'I'm honest, this air chokes me, vampires, owl's nest, crocodiles.' He left out the zoology, and all I heard from him when he got annoyed was: 'I was so unfair today,' or 'I'm sorry for that man, Anna'. That's how he was, but you—. [*They go out.*]

SCENE XI

[AVDOTYA *and* FIRST GUEST.]

FIRST GUEST [*coming through door, left*]. It's not in the dining-room, so it must be in the larder somewhere. We must try Yegorushka. Let's go through the drawing-room.

AVDOTYA. I could tear her in pieces. [*They go out through door, right.*]

SCENE XII

[MRS. BABAKIN, BORKIN *and* SHABELSKY. MRS. BABAKIN *and* BORKIN *run in from the garden, laughing.* SHABELSKY *comes tripping after them, laughing and rubbing his hands.*]

MRS. BABAKIN. What a bore. [*Laughs loudly.*] Oh, what a bore, everyone walking about or sitting around like a lot of stuffed dummies. I'm so bored, I feel quite ossified. [*Jumps about.*] Must stretch my legs. [BORKIN *puts his arm round her waist and kisses her cheek.*]

SHABELSKY [*laughs loudly and snaps his fingers*]. Dash it all! [*Clears his throat.*] To some extent——

MRS. BABAKIN. Let me go, let go of my arms, you naughty man—or goodness knows what the count will think. Let me alone.

BORKIN. My angel, my heart's own little carbuncle. [*Kisses her.*] Lend me twenty-three hundred roubles.

MRS. BABAKIN. No, no. I'm sorry, but where money's concerned, the answer's no thank you—. No, no, no. Do let go of my arms.

SHABELSKY [*prances around*]. My little bit of fluff, delightful creature——

BORKIN [*seriously*]. Stop it. Let's come to the point, get down to brass tacks like businessmen. Tell me straight without beating about the bush—yes or no? Listen. [*Points to the* COUNT.] He needs money, three thousand a year at least. You need a husband. Want to be a countess?

SHABELSKY [*laughs loudly*]. How remarkably cynical.

BORKIN. Want to be a countess? Yes or no?

MRS. BABAKIN [*upset*]. Do think what you're saying, Michael. These things aren't managed in that slapdash way. The count can speak for himself if he wants, and—this is all so sudden, I don't know——

BORKIN. Cut out the funny stuff, it's a business deal. Yes or no?

SHABELSKY [*laughing and rubbing his hands*]. Well, I don't know. How about it? A damn shabby trick—but why not play it? My little bit of fluff. [*Kisses* MRS. BABAKIN *on the cheek.*] Tasty morsel!

MRS. BABAKIN. One moment, you've quite upset me. Go away, please. No, come back.

BORKIN. Hurry up. Yes or no? There's no time to waste.

MRS. BABAKIN. I tell you what, Count. Come and stay with me for a few days—you'll find it rather fun, not like this place. Come to-morrow. [*To* BORKIN.] You're joking, aren't you?

BORKIN [*angrily*]. What—joke about something so serious?

MRS. BABAKIN. One moment, please. I do feel awful, I feel faint. A countess—I'm fainting, I shall fall.

[BORKIN *and the* COUNT *laughingly take her by the arms and, kissing her cheeks, lead her off through the door, right.*]

SCENE XIII

[IVANOV *and* SASHA, *followed by* ANNA. IVANOV *and* SASHA *run in from the garden.*]

IVANOV [*clutching his head, in despair*]. That's impossible. Stop it, Sasha, you must stop.

SASHA [*carried away*]. I'm crazy about you—life has no meaning, no happiness, no joy without you. You're everything to me.

IVANOV. Oh, what's the use? God, nothing makes sense. Stop it, Sasha.

SASHA. When I was a little girl you were my only joy. I loved you and everything about you as I love myself, and now—I love you, Nicholas. I'll follow you to the ends of the earth, I'll go wherever you like, I'll die if need be, only for God's sake let it be soon, or I shall choke.

IVANOV [*with a peal of happy laughter*]. What does this all mean? Can I start a new life then, Sasha? My happiness! [*Draws her to him.*] My youth, my innocence!

[ANNA *comes in from the garden, sees her husband and* SASHA, *and stands rooted to the spot.*]

IVANOV. So I'm to live, then, am I? And start work again?

[*They kiss. After the kiss* IVANOV *and* SASHA *look round and see* ANNA.]

IVANOV [*in horror*]. Sarah!

CURTAIN

ACT THREE

IVANOV'*s study. A desk on which papers, books, official packages, knick-knacks and revolvers are strewn around untidily. By the papers are a lamp, a decanter of vodka, a plate of herring, hunks of bread and cucumbers. On the walls hang maps, pictures, guns, pistols, sickles, whips and so on.*

Noon.

SCENE I

[SHABELSKY, LEBEDEV, BORKIN *and* PETER. SHABELSKY *and* LEBEDEV *sit, one on each side of the desk.* BORKIN *is astride a chair in the centre of the stage.* PETER *stands by the door.*]

LEBEDEV. France has a clear-cut, definite policy—the French know what they want. They only want to make mincemeat of Brother Fritz, but Germany's another cup of tea, old boy. Germany has other fish to fry besides France.

SHABELSKY. Nonsense. The Germans are cowards, if you ask me, and the French are no better. They're only bluffing each other, and that's as far as it'll go, believe you me. They won't fight.

BORKIN. Why should they, say I? Why all the armaments, congresses and expenses? Know what I'd do? I'd collect dogs from all over the country, give them a good dose of rabies and let them loose on enemy territory. I'd have the enemy all foaming at the mouth within a month.

LEBEDEV [*laughs*]. His head's quite small, isn't it, but it's fairly swarming with brain-waves, shoals of them.

SHABELSKY. The man's a genius.

LEBEDEV. God knows, you do entertain us, old man. [*Stops laughing.*] I say, we've fought quite a few armchair battles, but no one's mentioned vodka. Another dose. [*Pours out three glasses.*] Our very good health! [*They drink and eat.*] There's nothing to touch a spot of herring, old boy.

SHABELSKY. I don't know, cucumber's better. Wise men have cogitated since the dawn of history without hitting on anything smarter than salted cucumber. [*To* PETER.] Peter, go and get more cucumber, and tell them to cook four onion pasties in the kitchen. Make sure they're hot.

[PETER *goes out.*]

LEBEDEV. Caviare isn't bad with vodka, but the thing is to serve it properly. You need a quarter of a pound of pressed caviare, two spring onions and some olive oil. Mix the lot together, and then, you know—add the odd drop of lemon. Hell's bells, the mere smell will make you swoon!

BORKIN. Fried gudgeon also helps the vodka down—but fried properly. First clean. Then dip in toasted bread-crumbs and fry them so crisp, they crunch in your teeth. Crunch, crunch, crunch.

SHABELSKY. There was something good at Martha Babakin's yesterday—mushrooms.

LEBEDEV. Not half they were.

SHABELSKY. Cooked in some special way—with onion, you know, bay-leaves and spices. When they took the saucepan lid off and that steamy whiff came out—sheer ecstasy, it was.

LEBEDEV. What do you say? Another dose, everyone. [*They drink.*] Our good health! [*Looks at his watch.*] It looks as if I'll be gone before Nicholas gets back. Time I was off. You had mushrooms at Martha Babakin's, you say, but we haven't so much as smelt a mushroom round here yet. Will you please tell me why the blazes you're always popping over to Martha's place?

SHABELSKY [*nods at* BORKIN]. It's him—he wants to get me married.

LEBEDEV. Married? How old are you?

SHABELSKY. Sixty-two.

LEBEDEV. Just the age to marry. And Martha's just the wife for you.

BORKIN. Not Martha, Martha's money.

LEBEDEV. Martha's money—you're not asking for much! How about crying for the moon?

BORKIN. You wait till he's married and has his pockets nicely lined. You'll be all over him.

SHABELSKY. He's in earnest, you know. Our brainy friend's sure I'll do what he says and marry her.

BORKIN. Of course! Aren't you sure yourself?

SHABELSKY. What do you mean? When have I been sure of anything? Really!

BORKIN. Thank you, thank you very much. Let me down, would you? Now I'll marry, now I won't—what the hell does that mean? And after I gave my word of honour. You won't marry then?

SHABELSKY [*shrugs his shoulders*]. He's in real earnest. Extraordinary man.

BORKIN [*infuriated*]. In that case why upset a respectable woman? She's crazy to be a countess, can't sleep or eat—it's beyond a joke! Is this what you call honourable?

SHABELSKY [*snaps his fingers*]. It is a pretty foul trick, but how about it, eh? Just for the hell of it. I'll go ahead, honestly I will. What a lark.

[LVOV *comes in.*]

SCENE II

LEBEDEV. Our respects to the medical genius. [*Shakes hands with* LVOV *and sings.*]

'Doctor, save me, save me, save me,
    I'm scared to death of being dead——'

LVOV. Ivanov not here yet?

LEBEDEV. No, he isn't, I've been waiting for over an hour.

[LVOV *paces impatiently up and down the stage.*]

LEBEDEV. How is Anna, old man?

LVOV. In a bad way.

LEBEDEV [*sighs*]. May one pay one's respects?

LVOV. Please don't, I think she's asleep. [*Pause.*]

LEBEDEV. Such a nice, charming woman. [*Sighs.*] When she fainted in our house on Sasha's birthday, I saw from her face that she hadn't long to live, poor thing. I don't know what gave her that turn. When I ran in and looked at her she was lying on the floor as white as a sheet with Nicholas kneeling by her, as white as she was, and Sasha in tears. Sasha and I felt quite shaken for a week after.

SHABELSKY [*to* LVOV]. Tell me, reverend high priest of science, what sage first discovered that ladies' chest complaints yield to frequent visits from a young doctor? A great discovery, great! Would you put it under the heading of homoeopathy or allopathy?

[LVOV *makes to answer, but gives a contemptuous gesture and goes out.*]

SHABELSKY. If looks could kill!

LEBEDEV. Why the blazes did you say that? Why insult him?

SHABELSKY [*irritably*]. Why must he talk such nonsense? 'Tuberculosis, no hope, going to die.' That's a lot of hot air, I hate that stuff.

LEBEDEV. What makes you think he doesn't mean it?

SHABELSKY [*stands up and walks about*]. I can't concede that a living person may suddenly drop dead for no reason. Let's change the subject.

SCENE III

KOSYKH [*runs in out of breath*]. Ivanov in? Good morning. [*Quickly shakes hands with everybody.*] Is he in?

BORKIN. No.

KOSYKH [*sits down and jumps up again*]. In that case good-bye. [*Drinks a glass of vodka and takes a quick bite of food.*] I must go on. So much to do. Worn out. Can hardly stand.

LEBEDEV. Where did you blow in from?

KOSYKH. From Barabanov's. We played bridge all night and we've only just finished. I've been cleaned out. That Barabanov's no good at cards. [*Tearfully.*] Listen, I was playing hearts all the time. [*Turns to* BORKIN, *who jumps away from him.*] He leads a diamond, I play another heart, he plays a diamond. I didn't make a trick. [*To* LEBEDEV.] We were trying to make four clubs. I held the ace, queen and five more clubs and the ace, ten and two more spades——

LEBEDEV [*shuts his ears*]. Spare us, for Christ's sake.

KOSYKH [*to the* COUNT]. See? The ace, queen and five more clubs and the ace, ten and two more spades.

SHABELSKY [*pushes him off*]. Go away, I won't listen.

KOSYKH. Then disaster struck. The ace of spades was the first to get it in the neck——

SHABELSKY [*picks up a revolver from the table*]. Go away or I shoot.

KOSYKH [*with a sweep of the arm*]. Can't one talk to anyone, dash it all? It's like Australia—no common interests or solidarity, each going his own way. Time I was off, though—high time. [*Picks up his peaked cap.*] Time's money. [*Shakes hand with* LEBEDEV.] I pass.

[*Laughter.* KOSYKH *goes out and bumps into* AVDOTYA *in the doorway.*]

SCENE IV

AVDOTYA [*shrieks*]. You nearly knocked me over, damn you.

ALL. Aha! She's everywhere at once.

AVDOTYA. So this is where they are, and me searching all over the house. Good morning, boys, and the best of jolly good appetites. [*Shakes hands.*]

LEBEDEV. What are you doing here?

AVDOTYA. Business, sir. [*To the* COUNT.] It concerns your Lordship. [*Bows.*] I was told to give you warmest regards and ask how you were. And the little darling says, if you don't come and see her this afternoon she'll cry her eyes out. 'Take him aside, dear,' says she, 'and whisper it in his ear secretly.' But why the mystery? We're all friends here, we're not planning to rob the hen-roost, it's all above board, a matter of love and mutual consent. I never touch a drop, God knows, but I'll have a glass to celebrate this.

LEBEDEV. So will I. [*Pours out.*] You look none the worse for wear, you old windbag. I remember you as an old woman thirty years ago.

AVDOTYA. I've lost count of the years. I've buried two husbands and I'd marry a third, but no one'll take me without a dowry. Eight children I've had. [*Takes a glass.*] Now we've made a good start, please God, and God grant we finish the job. They'll have their bit of fun and we'll enjoy watching them. May they live happily ever after. [*Drinks.*] A vodka to be reckoned with!

SHABELSKY [*laughing loudly, to* LEBEDEV]. The funny thing is, they seriously think I—. Fantastic! [*Stands up.*] It's a pretty shabby thing to do, but how about it, Paul? Just for the hell of it—the old dog up to his tricks again, eh?

LEBEDEV. You're raving, Count. We should both think of pushing up the daisies, old boy. Martha and her money aren't for us, our day's over.

SHABELSKY. Yes, I'll do it, honestly I will.

[IVANOV *and* LVOV *come in.*]

SCENE V

LVOV. Can you spare me just five minutes?

LEBEDEV. Nicholas! [*Goes up to* IVANOV *and kisses him.*] Good morning, old boy, I've been waiting a whole hour for you.

AVDOTYA [*bows*]. Good morning, sir.

IVANOV [*sadly*]. Oh, you've made a complete mess of my study again. I've asked you all not to thousands of times. [*Goes up to the desk.*] Look, you've spilt vodka on my papers, there are crumbs and cucumbers. It's disgusting.

LEBEDEV. I'm sorry, Nicholas, do forgive us. I've something important to discuss with you, old boy.

BORKIN. And so have I.

LVOV. I want a word with you, Ivanov.

IVANOV [*points to* LEBEDEV]. He wants a word as well. Please wait, I'll speak to you later. [*To* LEBEDEV.] What is it?

LEBEDEV. Gentlemen, I want this to be private. Please——

[*The* COUNT *goes out with* AVDOTYA, *followed by* BORKIN *and then by* LVOV.]

IVANOV. You drink as much as you like since you're that way afflicted, Paul, but please don't make my uncle drink. He never used to, and it's bad for him.

LEBEDEV [*alarmed*]. I didn't know, my dear chap, never even noticed.

IVANOV. If the old boy dies, which God forbid, it'll be me that suffers, not you. What do you want? [*Pause.*]

LEBEDEV. Look, old man, I don't know how to start—I don't want it to sound too outrageous. I'm so ashamed, Nicholas, I'm tongue-tied, I blush to speak, but put yourself in my shoes, old boy. I'm not free, you must see that, I'm more like a slave or something the cat brought in. I'm sorry——

IVANOV. What is this?

LEBEDEV. My wife sent me. Be a good chap and pay her that interest, please. She's nagged and pestered the life out of me, so for God's sake get out of her clutches.

IVANOV. You know I've no money just now, Paul.

LEBEDEV. I know, I know, but what can I do? She won't wait. If she takes you to court, how can Sasha and I ever face you again?

IVANOV. I'm sorry too, I could kick myself—but where am I to get it? Tell me, where? I can only wait till I sell the crops this autumn.

LEBEDEV [*shouts*]. She won't wait. [*Pause.*]

IVANOV. You're in a nasty, awkward spot—but I'm even worse off. [*Walks up and down, thinking.*] I'm clean out of ideas. There's nothing to sell——

LEBEDEV. Go and ask Milbakh—he does owe you sixteen thousand, you know.

[IVANOV *makes a hopeless gesture of despair.*]

LEBEDEV. I tell you what, Nicholas. I know you'll object, but—do the old soak a favour, between friends. Look on me as your friend. We've both been students, liberals—had the same ideals and interests, both went to Moscow University, the dear old *alma mater*. [*Takes out his pocket-book.*] This is my secret hoard, no one knows anything about it at home. Let me lend you it. [*Takes out money and puts it on the desk.*] Forget your pride, look on this as between friends. I'd take it from you, on my honour. [*Pause.*] Here it is on the table, eleven hundred roubles. Drive over today and hand it to her yourself. 'There you are, Zinaida', say 'and I hope it chokes you.' But for God's sake don't let on you got it from me, or I'll be in hot water with old Gooseberry Jam. [*Stares at* IVANOV's *face.*] All right, never mind. [*Quickly takes the money from the desk and puts it in his pocket.*] Never mind, I was joking. Forgive me, for God's sake. [*Pause.*] Are you awfully fed up?

[IVANOV *makes a gesture of despair.*]

LEBEDEV. What a business. [*Sighs.*] Your trials and tribulations are just beginning. A man's like a samovar, old boy. He doesn't always stand on a cold shelf, there are times when he gets stoked up and starts fairly seething. The comparison's no damn good, but I can't think of anything better. [*Sighs.*] Troubles fortify the spirit. I'm not sorry for you, Nicholas, you'll get out of this mess, it'll come all right. But I'm fed up, old man—irritated with people. I'd like to know what started all the gossip. So many rumours are going round the county about you—you'll have the police in any moment. They call you murderer, vampire, robber.

IVANOV. That doesn't matter. I've a headache.

LEBEDEV. It comes from thinking too much.

IVANOV. I don't think at all.

LEBEDEV. Let it all go to hell, Nicholas, and move over to our place. Sasha likes you—she appreciates and values you. She's an honest, decent girl, I can't think who she takes after—not her father or mother. Sometimes I look at her, and I can't believe a bulbous-nosed old soak like me has such a treasure. Go and have some intelligent conversation with her, it'll make a change for you. She's a devoted, sincere girl. [*Pause.*]

IVANOV. Leave me alone, Paul, please.

LEBEDEV. All right, I understand. [*Quickly looks at his watch.*] I understand. [*Kisses* IVANOV.] Good-bye. I have to attend the opening of a new school. [*Moves towards the door and stops.*] Sasha's a bright girl. We were talking about gossip yesterday. [*Laughs.*] She came out with quite a saying. 'Father,' she says, 'glow-worms shine at night to make it easier for night birds to see them and eat them. And good people are here to give slander and gossip something to bite on.' What price that? A genius, eh? Regular George Sand.

IVANOV. Paul. [*Stops him.*] What's the matter with me?

LEBEDEV. I wanted to ask that myself, but I frankly didn't like to. I don't know, old man. It did look to me as though your various troubles had got you down, but then I know you're not one to— it's not like you to knuckle under. It's something else, but just what— I've no idea.

IVANOV. I don't know either. I think, or rather—never mind. [*Pause.*] Look, this is what I meant. I had a man working here called Simon, remember? When we were threshing once, he wanted to show the girls how strong he was, so he heaved two sacks of rye on his back and broke under the strain—he died soon after. I feel as if I'd broken my spine too. There was school and university, and then farming, village education, other plans—. I believed in different things from other people, married a different sort of wife, got excited, took risks, squandered money left right and centre, as you know, and was happier and unhappier than anyone else in the county. Those things were my sacks, I heaved a load on my back and it cracked. At twenty we're all heroes, tackle anything, nothing's too much for us, but by thirty we're tired and useless. How, how can you explain this fatigue? Anyway, that's probably not the point, not at all the point. Now off you go, Paul, and good luck to you. I'm boring you.

LEBEDEV [*eagerly*]. You know what? Your environment's got you down.

IVANOV. That's silly, and it's been said before. Off with you.

LEBEDEV. Yes, it really was silly, now I see how silly it was. I'm off, I'm off. [*Goes.*]

SCENE VI

IVANOV [*alone*]. I'm just a nasty, miserable nobody. Only another pathetic, bedraggled wreck like Paul could go on liking and respecting me. God, how I despise myself. How I loathe my own voice, footsteps, hands—these clothes, my thoughts. Pretty ridiculous, isn't it? And pretty mortifying. Less than a year ago I was strong and well, I was cheerful, tireless and dynamic. I worked with my hands. My eloquence moved even ignorant louts to tears, I could weep when I saw unhappiness and protest when I met evil. I knew what inspiration meant, I knew the charm and magic of quiet nights when you sit at your desk from dusk to dawn or indulge in flights of fancy. I had faith, I looked at the future as a child looks into its mother's eyes. But now, oh God! I'm worn out, I've no faith, I spend days and nights doing nothing. My brain doesn't obey me, nor do my arms and legs. The estate's going to rack and ruin, the woods fall before the axe. [*Weeps.*] My land seems to look at me like a lost child. There's nothing I hope or care about, and my spirit quails in fear of the morrow. Then there's Sarah. I swore to love her for ever, told her how happy we'd be, offered her a future beyond her wildest dreams. She believed me. These five years I've watched her giving way beneath the weight of her own sacrifices and wilting in the struggle with her conscience, but God knows she's never looked askance at me or uttered one reproach. What then? I stopped loving her. How? Why? What for? I can't understand. Now she's unhappy and her days are numbered. And I'm low and cowardly enough to run away from her pale face, sunken chest and pleading eyes. How shameful. [*Pause.*] Little Sasha's touched by my misfortunes and tells me, at my age, that she loves me. It goes to my head, so I can't think of anything else. I'm spellbound, it's music in my ears. So I start shouting about being born again and being happy. But next day I believe in this new life and happiness about as much as I do in fairies. What's the matter with me? What depths have I sunk to? Where does my weakness come from? What's happened to my nerves? If my sick wife touches me on the raw, or a servant does something wrong, or my gun misfires—then I'm rude, bad-tempered and quite beside myself. [*Pause.*] I just don't understand. I might as well shoot myself and be done with it.

LVOV [*comes in*]. I want a word with you, Ivanov.

IVANOV. If you and I are to have words every day, Doctor, it'll be more than flesh and blood can stand.

LVOV. Do you mind if I have my say?

IVANOV. You have your say every day, but I still don't know what you're driving at.

LVOV. I speak clearly and precisely. Only a very callous person could miss the point.

IVANOV. That my wife's dying, I know. That I'm hopelessly to blame in my dealings with her, I also know. And that you're a blunt, honest man I am also aware. What more do you want?

LVOV. People are so cruel, that's what maddens me. A woman's dying. She has a father and mother that she loves and wants to see before her death. They know full well that she hasn't long to live, that she still loves them, but—damn them for being so cruel! Are they trying to show people how frightfully pious they are, or what? They still curse her. You, for whom she gave it all up—her home, her peace of mind—you drive off to see those Lebedevs every day quite blatantly and with your reasons for going there written all over you.

IVANOV. Look, I haven't been there for two weeks——

LVOV [*not listening*]. With your sort one has to go straight to the point and not mess around. If you don't choose to listen, don't. I call a spade a spade. You need her to die so you can move on to new escapades. All right, but couldn't you wait a bit? If you'd let her die naturally, and hadn't kept bullying her with such barefaced cynicism, would you really have lost the Lebedev girl and her dowry? You'd have had time to turn the girl's head a year or two later, you monstrous hypocrite, and pocket the dowry then. Why does it have to be now? Where's the great hurry? Why must your wife die now, and not in a month or a year?

IVANOV. This is agony. You're not much of a doctor if you think a man can hold himself in for ever. It's quite a strain to me to leave your insults unanswered.

LVOV. Really, who do you think you're fooling? Come off it.

IVANOV. Think a little, my clever friend. You think I'm an open book, don't you? I married Anna for her fortune. I didn't get it, and having slipped up then, I'm now getting rid of her so I can marry someone else and get *her* money. Right? How simple and straightforward. Man's such a simple, uncomplicated mechanism. No, Doctor, we all have too many wheels, screws and valves to judge each other on first impressions or one or two pointers. I don't understand you, you don't understand me and we don't understand ourselves. A man can be a very good doctor without having any idea what people are really like. So don't be too cocksure, but try and see what I mean.

LVOV. You can't really think you're so hard to see through, or that I'm too feeble-minded to tell good from evil.

IVANOV. You and I'll never agree, that's very clear. For the last time, I ask you—and please answer without a lot of mumbo jumbo—exactly what do you want from me? What are you driving at? [*Irritably.*] And to whom am I privileged to speak—a policeman or my wife's doctor?

LVOV. I'm a doctor. And as a doctor I insist you mend your ways—you're killing your wife.

IVANOV. But what can I do about it? What? If you know me better than I do myself, tell me exactly what to do.

LVOV. You might at least keep up appearances.

IVANOV. God, do you know what you're saying? [*Drinks some water.*] Leave me alone. I'm to blame a thousand times over, and I'll answer to God for it. But no one gave you the right to torment me every day.

LVOV. And who gave you the right to insult my sense of fair play? You've tortured me, poisoned me! Before I came to this part of the world I knew there were stupid, crazy people about, but I never believed there were people so criminal that they deliberately, consciously, wilfully chose evil. I respected and loved people, but when I saw you——

IVANOV. I've heard all this before.

LVOV. Oh, have you? [*Sees* SASHA *come in. She wears a riding habit.*] Anyway, I hope we understand each other now. [*Shrugs his shoulders and goes out.*]

SCENE VII

IVANOV [*frightened*]. Is it you, Sasha?

SASHA. Yes. Hallo. Surprised? Why haven't you been to see us for so long?

IVANOV. For God's sake, Sasha—this is most indiscreet. Your visit may have a very bad effect on my wife.

SASHA. She won't see me, I came round the back. I'm just going. I'm worried about how you are. Why haven't you been over for so long?

IVANOV. My wife's distressed as it is, she's almost dying—and you come here. It's a stupid, cruel thing to do, Sasha.

SASHA. I couldn't help it. You haven't been over for two weeks, or answered any letters. I was worried to death. I imagined you might be in a terrible way here—ill or dying. I haven't had one proper night's sleep. I'm just going. At least tell me if you're well.

IVANOV. Really, I've worn myself out and people never stop bothering me. I'm at the end of my tether. And now you turn up. What a morbid, neurotic thing to do! I'm so much to blame, Sasha, so very much.

SASHA. How you love these awful, tragic speeches. You're to blame, you say, very much to blame? Then tell me what you've done.

IVANOV. I don't know, really.

SASHA. That's no answer. If you've done wrong you must know what you've done. Not forging bank-notes, I suppose?

IVANOV. That's not funny.

SASHA. Is it your fault you fell out of love with your wife? Perhaps, but one can't help one's feelings, and you didn't want your feelings to change. Is it your fault she saw me telling you I loved you? No, you didn't want her to.

IVANOV [*interrupting*]. And so on and so forth. In love, out of love, can't help one's feelings—that talk's so cheap and vulgar, it's no help.

SASHA. You are tiring to talk to. [*Looks at a picture.*] Isn't that dog drawn well? Was it done from life?

IVANOV. Yes. And this whole love affair of ours is cheap and vulgar. He loses heart, feels he has nothing to live for. Along comes She, strong and confident, and holds out a helping hand. All very romantic and convincing in a magazine story, but in real life——

SASHA. Life's no different.

IVANOV. You're a fine judge of life, I can see. My whining fills you with awe and you think you've found a second Hamlet, but to me my whole neurosis with all its trimmings is just plain farcical, and that's that. You should laugh yourself silly at my antics, not sound the alarm-bell! All this rescuing and crusading zeal! Oh, I'm so angry with myself today, I'm so tense, I feel something's bound to snap. I'll either smash something or——

SASHA. That's right—it's just what you need. Break something, smash things or start shouting. You're angry with me and it was silly of me to come here. All right, let off steam then, shout at me, stamp your feet. Come on, work up a rage. [*Pause.*] Come on then.

IVANOV. You're funny.

SASHA. Very well. We appear to be smiling. Kindly condescend to smile again.

IVANOV [*laughs*]. I've noticed that when you start rescuing me and giving me good advice, a look of sheer innocence comes over you, and your eyes grow huge, as if you were looking at a comet. Just a moment, there's dust on your shoulder. [*Brushes the dust off her shoulder.*] A naïve man's a fool, but you women have the art of being naïve and carrying it off with such charm, good sense and warm-heartedness—so it isn't as silly as it seems. But why must you all ignore a man so long as he's strong and well and happy—while the moment he starts sliding downhill and being sorry for himself, you throw yourselves round his neck? Is it really worse to be wife to a strong, brave man than nursemaid to a whining failure?

SASHA. Yes.

IVANOV. Why? [*Laughs loudly.*] It's a good job Darwin doesn't know, or he'd give you what for. You're ruining the race. All new babies will be snivelling neurotics, thanks to you.

SASHA. There's a great deal men don't understand. Any girl prefers a failure to a success because we're all fascinated by the idea of love in action. Active love, don't you see? Men are busy with their work, and love's very much in the background for them. You talk to your wife, stroll round the garden with her, pass the time of day nicely and have a little cry on her grave—and that's that. But love is our whole existence! I love you, and that means I long to cure your unhappiness and go with you to the ends of the earth. If you go up in the world, I'll be with you, and if you fall by the wayside, I'll fall too. For instance, I'd love to spend all night copying your papers or watching to see that no one woke you up. Or I'd walk a hundred miles with you. I remember once about three years ago, at threshing time. You came to see us covered with dust, sunburnt, tired out— and asked for a drink. By the time I brought you a glass, you were lying on the sofa, dead to the world. You slept about twelve hours in our house and I stood guard at the door all the time to stop anyone going in. And I felt so marvellous. The more effort you put into love, the better it is—I mean the more strongly it's felt, do you see?

IVANOV. Active love. I see. Is that a perversion of some kind? Or just a young girl's idea of things? Or is it perhaps the way things ought to be? [*Shrugs his shoulders.*] Who the hell knows? [*Gaily.*] Honestly, I'm not such a bad man, Sasha. Judge for yourself—I always liked generalizing, but I've never gone round saying things about our women being demoralized or 'on the wrong track'. I've just been grateful, that's all, there's no more to it. Dear child, how amusing you are. And I—what a silly ass I am, spreading general despondency and feeling sorry for myself for days on end. [*Laughs and quickly moves off.*] But you'd better go, Sasha, we're forgetting ourselves.

SASHA. Yes, it's time I went. Good-bye. I'm afraid our honest doctor might feel in duty bound to report my presence to Anna. Now listen. Go straight to your wife and stay with her, just stay put. If you have to stay a year, stay a year. If it has to be ten years, make it ten. Do your duty. Grieve for her, beg her forgiveness, weep—all as it should be. And above all, don't neglect your affairs.

IVANOV. I seem to have that horrible taste in my mouth again. Again!

SASHA. Well, may God preserve you. You can forget me completely. Just drop me a line every couple of weeks, and I'll think I'm lucky to get that. And I'll be writing to you.

[BORKIN *looks through the door.*]

SCENE VIII

BORKIN. Can I come in, Nicholas? [*Seeing* SASHA.] Sorry, I didn't see. [*Comes in.*] Bong jour. [*Bows.*]

SASHA [*embarrassed*]. Good morning.

BORKIN. You look plumper and prettier.

SASHA [*to* IVANOV]. Well, I'm leaving, Nicholas. I'm off. [*Goes.*]

BORKIN. What a vision of delight! I come looking for prose and walk slap into poetry. [*Sings.*] 'Thou camest like a bird towards the light.'

[IVANOV *walks up and down the stage, greatly upset.*]

BORKIN [*sits down*]. There's something about her, Nicholas, she has got something, eh? Something special, quite out of this world. [*Sighs.*] She's the richest marriageable girl in the county, actually, but her mother's such an old cow, no one'll go near her. It'll all come to Sasha when the old girl dies, but before that she'll give her a miserable ten thousand, a flat-iron and some curling-tongs or something, and expect one to get down on one's knees for that. [*Rummages in his pockets.*] Cigars. Like one? [*Holds out his cigar-case.*] Quite smokable.

IVANOV [*goes up to* BORKIN, *choking with rage*]. Out of my house this instant and don't set foot in it again! Do you hear?

[BORKIN *raises himself slightly and drops his cigar.*]

IVANOV. Get out this instant.

BORKIN. What does this mean, Nicholas? Why so angry?

IVANOV. Why? Where did you get those cigars? Think I don't know where you take the old man every day, and what you're after?

BORKIN [*shrugs his shoulders*]. What has that to do with you?

IVANOV. You low hound! The swindles you plot all over the county, they've made my name mud. We've nothing in common and I must ask you to leave my house this instant. [*Walks quickly up and down.*]

BORKIN. You say that because you're annoyed, I know, so I'm not angry. Insult away. [*Picks up his cigar.*] But it's time to snap out of these depressions, you're not a schoolboy.

IVANOV. What did I say? [*Trembling.*] Trifle with me, would you?

[ANNA *comes in.*]

SCENE IX

BORKIN. Look, Anna's here. I'll go.

[*Goes.* IVANOV *stops near the table and stands with bowed head.*]

ANNA [*after a pause*]. Why did she come here? [*Pause.*] I ask you—why did she come?

IVANOV. Don't ask me, Anna. [*Pause.*] I'm very much to blame. I'll suffer any punishment you like, but—don't question me, I don't feel up to speaking.

ANNA [*angrily*]. What was she doing here? [*Pause.*] So this is what you're like! Now I understand—at last I see the kind of man you are, you rotten cad. Remember coming and telling me lies, saying how you loved me? I believed you, gave up my parents and my religion and married you. You lied about truth and goodness and your noble plans, and I believed every word.

IVANOV. I've never lied to you, Anna.

ANNA. I've lived with you five years, I've been depressed and ill, but I loved you and never left your side. I idolized you. And then what? All that time you were blatantly deceiving me.

IVANOV. Anna, don't tell untruths. I've made mistakes, it's true, but I never told a lie in my life. How dare you call me a liar?

ANNA. Now it all makes sense. You married me, thinking my parents would forgive me and give me money. That's what you thought.

IVANOV. God, to try one's patience like this, Anna—. [*Weeps.*]

ANNA. Shut up! Seeing there was no money in the offing, you started another little game. Now it all comes back, now I see. [*Weeps.*] You never loved me, were never faithful to me. Never!

IVANOV. Sarah, that's a lie. Say what you like, but don't insult me by lying.

ANNA. You rotten, contemptible creature. You're in debt to Lebedev, and now you try to wriggle out of paying by turning his daughter's head and deceiving her as you did me. Well, aren't you?

IVANOV [*choking*]. Hold your tongue, for God's sake, I won't answer for myself. I'm choking with rage and I—I might say something awful.

ANNA. You've always been a barefaced swindler, I'm not the only victim. You pretended all these frauds were Borkin's doing, but I know now who was behind them.

IVANOV. Sarah, stop this and go away or I'll say something I shouldn't. I feel driven to say something horribly insulting. [*Shouts.*] Shut up, you Jewish bitch!

ANNA. I will not shut up, you've made a fool of me too long, I won't be quiet any more.

IVANOV. Oh, won't you? [*Struggles with himself.*] For God's sake——

ANNA. Now go and make a fool of Sasha Lebedev.

IVANOV. Then you may as well know it—you'll soon be dead. The doctor told me you can't last long.

ANNA [*sits down, in a sinking voice*]. When did he say that? [*Pause.*]

IVANOV [*clutching his head*]. What a thing to do! God, I am a brute. [*Sobs.*]

CURTAIN

About a year passes between Act Three and Act Four

ACT FOUR

SCENE I

A drawing-room in LEBEDEV's *house. In the foreground an arch separating the drawing-room from the ballroom. Doors, right and left. Bronze antiques, family portraits, festive decorations. An upright piano with a violin on it, and a 'cello standing near by.*
   Throughout the act guests in evening dress move about the ballroom.

LVOV [*comes in, looks at his watch*]. Gone four. They must be going to bless the bride, and after that they'll take her to church. Thus virtue and justice triumph! He didn't get Sarah's money, so he worried her into her grave. Now he has another victim, he'll play the same little game for her benefit till he gets his hands on the cash, when he'll dispatch her as he did poor Sarah. It's an old story—some people will do anything for money. [*Pause.*] He's in the seventh heaven now, he'll live happily to a ripe old age and die with a clear conscience. No, I'll show you up. I'll tear that damned mask off you so everyone sees what kind of customer you are, and then I'll pitch you out of your seventh heaven into a hell so deep, the devil himself won't get you out of it. As an honest man I'm bound to interfere and open people's eyes. I'll do my duty and leave this blasted neighbourhood tomorrow. [*Meditates.*] But what can I do? It's no use talking to the Lebedevs. Challenge him to a duel? Make a scene? God, I'm nervous as a kitten, I can't think any more. What can I do? A duel?

SCENE II

KOSYKH [*comes in, gaily to* LVOV]. Yesterday I declared a little slam in clubs and got a grand slam. But once again friend Barabanov cooked my goose. We sit down to play and I bid one no trump. He passes. I bid two clubs. He passes. I go on to two diamonds, three clubs and—it's beyond the bounds of credence! I declare a slam and he doesn't show his ace. If the swine had shown his ace I'd have declared a grand slam in no trumps.

LVOV. I'm sorry, I don't play cards and can't share your triumph. Will they bless the bride soon?

KOSYKH. I think so. They're trying to get some sense into Zizi. She's yelling her head off—can't bear to part with the dowry.

LVOV. What about parting with her daughter?

KOSYKH. The dowry, I said. And it is bad luck. Once married, he won't pay what he owes her, and you can't very well take your own son-in-law to court.

SCENE III

[MRS. BABAKIN, *dressed to kill, struts across the stage past* LVOV *and* KOSYKH. *The latter guffaws into his hand. She looks round.*]

MRS. BABAKIN. Don't be silly.

[KOSYKH *touches her waist with his finger and gives a loud laugh.*]

MRS. BABAKIN. Clumsy lout! [*Goes out.*]

KOSYKH [*laughs loudly*]. The woman's off her rocker. Before she set her sights on a title she wasn't a bad sort of female, but now you can't get near her. [*Imitates her.*] 'Clumsy lout!'

LVOV [*upset*]. Look here, tell me frankly—what's your view of Ivanov?

KOSYKH. No good. Plays a rotten game of bridge. Take what happened just before last Easter. We sit down to play—me, the count, Borkin and Ivanov. I'm dealing——

LVOV [*interrupting*]. Is he a good man?

KOSYKH. Ivanov? Quite a snake in the grass, pretty slippery customer. He's been around a bit! He and the count are a precious pair, they've a pretty good eye for the main chance. He slipped up over his Jewess and found himself in queer street, so now he's after Zizi's moneybags. I bet you anything—and I'm damn sure I'm right—he'll turn Zizi out of house and home within the year. He'll handle Zizi and the count will deal with Martha Babakin. They'll pocket the takings and live off the fat of the land. Why so pale today, Doctor? You look ghastly.

LVOV. It's all right, I drank a bit too much yesterday.

SCENE IV

LEBEDEV [*coming in with* SASHA]. We can talk in here. [*To* LVOV *and* KOSYKH.] Clear out, monsters, and join the girls in the ballroom. We want a private talk.

KOSYKH [*passing* SASHA, *snaps his fingers triumphantly*]. Pretty as a picture, the queen of trumps.

LEBEDEV. Move along, caveman, move along.

[LVOV *and* KOSYKH *go out.*]

LEBEDEV. Sit down, Sasha, that's right. [*Sits down and looks round.*] Listen carefully and with due reverence. The fact is, your mother told me to give you a message. Do you see? It's not my idea, it's what your mother told me to say.

SASHA. Do cut it short, Father.

LEBEDEV. Your dowry's to be fifteen thousand roubles. Now look, we don't want arguments afterwards. No, don't speak, this is only the half of it, there are more treats in store. Your dowry's to be fifteen thousand, but as Nicholas owes your mother nine thousand, that's being deducted from the dowry. Now besides that——

SASHA. Why tell me this?

LEBEDEV. Your mother told me to.

SASHA. Can't you leave me alone? If you had any respect for either of us, you wouldn't let yourself talk like this. I don't want your dowry, I never asked for one and I'm not asking now.

LEBEDEV. Why pitch into me? Gogol's two rats had a sniff at each other and then left each other alone, but you're so much the emancipated woman, you lash out without even a sniff.

SASHA. Leave me alone, and don't insult my ears with your cheap calculations.

LEBEDEV [*flaring up*]. Really, you'll all have me stabbing myself or cutting someone's throat. One of you's for ever yelling blue murder, nagging, fussing and counting pennies, while this one's so intelligent, humane and goddam emancipated, she can't understand her own father. I insult her ears. Why—before coming here and insulting your ears I was being torn limb from limb out there. [*Points to the door.*] She can't understand! Oh, I don't know whether I'm on my head or my heels. Confound you all. [*Moves towards the door and stops.*] I don't like you, I don't like anything about any of you.

SASHA. What is it you dislike?

LEBEDEV. Everything, everything.

SASHA. Meaning what?

LEBEDEV. Well, I'm not going to sit back and spout about it. I hate the whole thing, I can't stand the idea of your wedding. [*Goes up to* SASHA *and speaks kindly.*] I'm sorry, Sasha, your marriage may be all very clever, noble, starry-eyed and high-principled, but there's something wrong with it, there really is. It's not like other marriages. You're young, pure, fresh as a spring morning, you're beautiful—and he's a shabby, frowsty widower. And I can't make sense of him, confound him. [*Kisses her.*] Sasha, I'm sorry, there's something not quite nice about it. There's a lot of talk about the way Sarah died and the way he was suddenly all set on marrying you because of this that and the other. [*Briskly.*] I'm an old woman, anyway, I really am, a regular old grandmother. Don't listen to me, don't listen to anyone—listen only to yourself.

SASHA. I don't feel it's right myself, Father. It's wrong, all wrong. If you only knew how depressed I feel. I can't stand it. I feel awkward and afraid to admit it. Do cheer me up for God's sake, Father dear, and tell me what to do.

LEBEDEV. What do you mean, 'what'?

SASHA. I was never so scared in my life. [*Looks round.*] I feel I don't understand him and never will. Not once has he smiled or looked me in the eye since we got engaged. What with his never-ending complaints, vague remorse, hints at some wrong he's done, his shudderings—I'm worn out. Sometimes I even fancy I, er, don't love him as I should. And when he comes here or talks to me it gets so boring. What does it all mean, Father? I'm scared.

LEBEDEV. My darling, my only child, be guided by your old father and call the thing off.

SASHA [*frightened*]. No, no, don't say that.

LEBEDEV. Yes, really, Sasha. There will be an awful scene and it'll be the talk of the county, but better face a scandal than ruin your life.

SASHA. Don't say that, Father, I won't listen to you. I mustn't give way to such gloomy thoughts. He's a good, unhappy, misunderstood man. I shall love and appreciate him and put him on his feet. I'll do my job. That's settled.

LEBEDEV. It's no job, it's just plain hysteria.

SASHA. That'll do. I've told you things I wouldn't even admit to myself. Don't tell anyone. Let's forget it.

LEBEDEV. I can't make sense of it. Either I'm old and dotty, or else you've all grown far too clever. Anyway, I'm hanged if I can make it out.

SCENE V

SHABELSKY [*coming in*]. To hell with everyone, myself included. It's infuriating.

LEBEDEV. What's up?

SHABELSKY. No, seriously, whatever happens, I must do something rotten and foul enough to make everyone else feel as sick as I do. And I will too, honestly. I've told Borkin to announce my engagement today. [*Laughs.*] They're all swine, so let me be one too.

LEBEDEV. I'm fed up with you. Look here, Matthew, if you go on like this you'll be carted off to the madhouse, if you don't mind my saying so.

SHABELSKY. Is the madhouse worse than any other house? Carry on, take me there now if you want, I don't care. Rotten, trivial, worthless second-rate people! I'm disgusted with myself too, and I don't believe one word I say.

LEBEDEV. I tell you what, old man—you put some old rags in your mouth, light them and blow fire on people. Or better still, get your hat and go home. This is a wedding, everyone's enjoying themselves, but you go on like a dying duck in a thunderstorm. I must say——

[SHABELSKY *bends over the piano and sobs.*]

LEBEDEV. Good Lord above! Matthew! Count! What's up? Matthew, my dear good friend, have I offended you? Forgive a silly old man, forgive an old soak. Have some water.

SHABELSKY. I don't want it. [*Raises his head.*]

LEBEDEV. Why are you crying?

SHABELSKY. It's nothing really.

LEBEDEV. Come on, old man, don't tell lies. What's the reason?

SHABELSKY. I happened to look at that 'cello and—and I remembered poor little Sarah.

LEBEDEV. Hey, what a time for reminiscences! May she rest in peace, poor woman, but this is hardly the time to talk about her.

SHABELSKY. We used to play duets together. She was a wonderful, marvellous woman.

[SASHA *sobs.*]

LEBEDEV. What do you think you're doing? Give over. Good grief, they're both howling and I, er, I—. At least go somewhere else, the guests will see you.

SHABELSKY. Paul, you can be happy in a graveyard if the sun shines, and even old age is all right if you have hope. But I've no hope at all.

LEBEDEV. Yes, you really are in a rather bad way—no children, no money, nothing to do. Well, it can't be helped. [*To* SASHA.] What set you off?

SHABELSKY. Lend me some money, Paul. We'll settle up in the next world. I'll go to Paris and visit my wife's grave. I've given a lot away in my time—I gave away half my property, so I've the right to ask. What's more I ask as a friend.

LEBEDEV [*at a loss*]. I haven't a penny, old boy. All right then. I can't promise, that is, but you know—very well then. [*Aside.*] They worry me to death.

SCENE VI

MRS. BABAKIN [*comes in*]. Where's my gentleman friend? How dare you leave me on my own, Count? Oh, you horrid man. [*Hits the* COUNT *on the arm with her fan.*]

SHABELSKY [*with loathing*]. Can't you leave me alone? I hate you.

MRS. BABAKIN [*taken aback*]. What? What was that?

SHABELSKY. Go away.

MRS. BABAKIN [*falls into an armchair*]. Oh dear. [*Cries.*]

ZINAIDA [*comes in crying*]. Someone's just come—the best man, I think. Time to bless the bride. [*Sobs.*]

SASHA [*imploringly*]. Mother!

LEBEDEV. Now they're all howling—quite a quartet. Do turn off the waterworks. Matthew, Martha, this way you'll have me—me crying too. [*Cries.*] Oh, Lord!

ZINAIDA. If you've no use for your mother and won't obey her—oh well, I'll do as you wish and give you my blessing.

[IVANOV *comes in, wearing a tail-coat and gloves.*]

SCENE VII

LEBEDEV. This is the utter limit! What's going on?

SASHA. What are you doing here?

IVANOV. I'm sorry, but please can I talk to Sasha in private?

LEBEDEV. You shouldn't visit the bride before the wedding, you should be on your way to church.

IVANOV. Please, Paul.

[LEBEDEV *shrugs his shoulders. He,* ZINAIDA, *the* COUNT *and* MRS. BABAKIN *go out.*]

SCENE VIII

SASHA [*sternly*]. What do you want?

IVANOV. I'm in a rotten bad temper, but I can speak calmly. Listen. I was dressing for the wedding just now. I looked in the glass and saw grey hairs on my temples. It's all wrong, Sasha. We must end this senseless farce before it's too late. You're young and unspoilt, with your whole life before you, while I——

SASHA. That's not news, I've heard it thousands of times before and I'm sick of it. Go to church and don't keep people waiting.

IVANOV. I'm going straight home. Tell your family the wedding's off, give them some explanation. It's time we came to our senses. I've been acting like Hamlet, you've been the starry-eyed young heroine —and it's gone far enough.

SASHA [*flaring up*]. What a way to speak! I won't listen.

IVANOV. Well, I'm speaking and I shall go on speaking.

SASHA. Why did you come here? Your complaints sound more and more like sneers.

IVANOV. No, I'm not complaining this time. Sneers, you say? Oh yes, I'm sneering. If I could sneer at myself a thousand times harder and set the whole world laughing, then sneer I would. I looked at myself in the glass and something seemed to snap inside me. I laughed at myself and nearly went out of my mind with shame. [*Laughs.*] What price melancholia, noble grief, mysterious misery! The only thing left is for me to write poetry. Moaning and groaning, whining, making people's lives a misery and knowing that my vitality's gone beyond recall, that I've gone to seed, had my day, become weak-minded and am up to the neck in these sickening depressions—to feel all this in bright sunshine, when even an ant carries its load and is content! No, thank you very much! To see that some people think you're a fraud, others feel sorry for you, yet others hold out a helping hand, while a fourth lot—worst of all—listen to your sighs with reverence, looking on you as a great prophet and expecting you to preach a new religion! No, I still have some pride and conscience, thank God. I laughed at myself on my way here, and I felt as though the very birds were laughing at me, and the trees.

SASHA. This isn't anger, it's madness.

IVANOV. Think so? No, I'm not mad. I see things in their true light now, and my thoughts are as innocent as your own. We love each other, but our marriage is not to be. I can rant and fret to my heart's content, but I've no right to destroy anyone else. I poisoned the last year of my wife's life with my snivelling. Since we've been engaged you've forgotten how to laugh, and you look five years older. And your father, who once had a pretty sane outlook, can't make sense of people any more, thanks to me. When I attend meetings, go visiting or shooting—I carry boredom, gloom and despondency everywhere. No, don't interrupt. I'm being brutally frank, but I'm in a rotten temper, sorry, and this is the only way I can speak. I never used to lie or talk about how awful life is, but once I'd taken to grousing I started finding fault with things without meaning to or knowing what I was doing—started complaining and cursing fate, so that everyone who hears me gets infected with the same disgust for life and fault-finding. And what a way to speak—as if I was doing Nature a favour by being alive. To hell with me!

SASHA. Stop. What you've just said makes it clear that you're sick of complaining and it's time you started a new life. A good thing too.

IVANOV. I see nothing good about it. What is this 'new life'? I'm absolutely done for—it's time we were both clear about that. New life indeed!

SASHA. Come off it, Nicholas—who says you're done for? Why all the cynicism? No, I won't talk or listen to you. Go to church.

IVANOV. I'm done for!

SASHA. Don't shout like that or the guests will hear.

IVANOV. Once an intelligent, educated, healthy man begins feeling sorry for himself for no obvious reason and starts rolling down the slippery slope, he rolls on and on without stopping and nothing can save him. Well, where is there hope for me? What could it be? I can't drink, spirits make my head ache. I can't write bad verse, nor can I worship my own mental laziness and put it on a pedestal. Laziness is laziness, weakness is weakness—I can't find other names for them. I'm done for, I tell you, there's no more to be said. [*Looks round.*] We might be interrupted. Listen. If you love me, help me. You must break off the marriage without delay—this very instant. Hurry up——

SASHA. Nicholas, if you did but know how you've tired me out—you've really got me down. You're a kind, intelligent man, so judge for yourself—how can you tell people to do things like that? Every day you set some new task, each one harder than the last. I wanted active love, but our love's sheer martyrdom.

IVANOV. As my wife you'd find these tasks still more involved. So break it off. And get this clear—it's not love that makes you talk like this, it's a stubbornness that comes from your own integrity. You set yourself to rescue me at all costs and make a new man of me, and you liked to think you were being heroic. Now you're ready to back out, but sentimentality stands in your way, don't you see?

SASHA. What strange, mad logic! How can I break it off, how can I? You've no mother, sister or friends. You're ruined, your property's been ransacked, everyone says awful things about you——

IVANOV. I was a fool to come here, I should have done as I intended.

[LEBEDEV *comes in.*]

SCENE IX

SASHA [*runs to her father*]. For God's sake, Father—he rushed in here like a lunatic and he's been torturing me—insists I call it off, doesn't want to spoil my life. Tell him I don't need his generosity, I know what I'm doing.

LEBEDEV. This makes no sense to me. What generosity?

IVANOV. There won't be any wedding.

SASHA. There will be! Father, tell him the wedding's on.

LEBEDEV. Hey, just a moment—why won't you marry her?

IVANOV. I've told her why, but she refuses to see.

LEBEDEV. Don't tell her, tell me. And make it make sense. Nicholas, you've wrought such havoc in our lives, God forgive you—I feel I'm living in a chamber of horrors. I look round, but I can make nothing of it. It's more than flesh and blood can stand. What do you want an old man to do—challenge you to a duel, I suppose?

IVANOV. We don't need duels, we just need to keep our heads and understand plain language.

SASHA [*walks up and down the stage in agitation*]. This is awful, awful, he's just like a child.

LEBEDEV. One can only throw up one's hands in amazement. Listen, Nicholas. To you this is all very clever and subtle and follows the laws of psychology, but to me it's a fiasco, a disaster. Listen to an old man for the last time. What I want to say is—relax! Take the simple view of things like everyone else. Everything in the world's simple. The ceiling's white, boots are black, sugar's sweet. You love Sasha, she loves you. If you love her, stay with her. If you don't love her, go away and we won't hold it against you. What could be simpler? You're both healthy, intelligent, decent people. You have enough to eat, thank God, and you've clothes on your back. What more do you want? You may be hard up, but what matter? Money doesn't bring happiness. Of course, I know your estate's mortgaged and you can't afford to pay the interest, but I'm a father, I understand. Her mother can do what she likes, confound her. If she won't give you any money, never mind. Sasha says she doesn't need a dowry—something about principles, Schopenhauer and all that. Now that's a lot of nonsense. I've ten thousand roubles stowed away in the bank. [*Looks around.*] Not a soul knows about it at home—it was your grandmother's. It's for the two of you. Take it, only you must promise to let Matthew have a couple of thousand.

[*Guests gather in the ballroom.*]

IVANOV. There's nothing to be said, Paul. I'm doing as my conscience tells me.

SASHA. So am I doing as my conscience tells me. Say what you like, I won't let you go. I'm going to call Mother. [*Goes out.*]

SCENE X

LEBEDEV. I can't make sense of anything.

IVANOV. Listen, my poor man. I won't try and explain myself—whether I'm decent or rotten, sane or mad. You wouldn't understand. I used to be young, eager, sincere, intelligent. I loved, hated and believed differently from other people, I worked hard enough—I had hope enough—for ten men. I tilted at windmills and banged my head against brick walls. Without measuring my own strength, taking thought or knowing anything about life, I heaved a load on my back which promptly tore the muscles and cracked my spine. I was in a hurry to expend all my youthful energy, drank too much, got over-excited, worked, never did things by halves. But tell me, what else could you expect? We're so few, after all, and there's such a lot to be done, God knows. And now look how cruelly life, the life I challenged, is taking its revenge. I broke under the strain. I woke up to myself at the age of thirty, I'm like an old man in his dressing-gown and slippers. Heavy-headed, dull-witted, worn out, broken, shattered, without faith or love, with no aim in life, I moon around, more dead than alive, and don't know who I am, what I'm living for or what I want. Love's a fraud, or so I think, and any show of affection's just sloppy sentimentality, there's no point in working, songs and fiery speeches are cheap and stale. Wherever I go I carry misery, indifference, boredom, discontent and disgust with life. I'm absolutely done for. You see a man exhausted at the age of thirty-five, disillusioned, crushed by his own pathetic efforts, bitterly ashamed of himself, sneering at his own feebleness. How my pride rebels, I'm choking with fury. [*Staggering.*] God, I'm on my last legs—I'm so weak I can hardly stand. Where's Matthew? I want him to take me home.

VOICES IN THE BALLROOM. The best man's here.

SCENE XI

SHABELSKY [*coming in*]. I borrowed these shabby tails, and haven't any gloves, so of course I get all these sneering looks, silly jokes and vulgar grins. Loathsome creatures.

BORKIN [*comes in quickly with a bunch of flowers, wearing tails and the best man's buttonhole*]. Phew! Where is he? [*To* IVANOV.] They've been waiting for you at church for ages, and here you are making speeches. You are a scream, honestly. Look, you mustn't go with your bride, but separately with me and I'll come back from church and fetch the bride. Can't you even get that into your head? You really are funny.

LVOV [*comes in. To* IVANOV]. So you're here, are you? [*Loudly.*] Nicholas Ivanov, I want everyone to hear this. *You are the most unmitigated swine!*

IVANOV [*coldly*]. I'm very much obliged to you.

[*General confusion.*]

BORKIN [*to* LVOV]. That was a foul thing to say, sir. I challenge you to a duel.

LVOV. Mr. Borkin, I consider it degrading even to exchange words with you, let alone fight a duel. As for Mr. Ivanov, he may receive satisfaction when he wishes.

SHABELSKY. I shall fight you, sir.

SASHA [*to* LVOV]. What is this? Why did you insult him? Just a moment, everyone, let him tell me—why?

LVOV. I didn't insult him without good reason, Miss Lebedev. I came here as an honest man to open your eyes. Please listen to me.

SASHA. What can you say? That you're an honest man? That's hardly a secret! You'd better tell me frankly whether you know what you're doing or not. You come in here with honest man written all over you, terribly insult him and nearly kill me. Before that you've dogged his footsteps and made his life a misery, quite convinced you were doing your duty as an honest man. You've meddled in his private life, made his name dirt and set yourself up to judge him. You took every chance to bombard me and all his friends with anonymous letters—thinking all the time what a very honest man you were. In the name of honesty you, a doctor, didn't spare even his sick wife, you pestered her with your suspicions. There's no outrageous, rotten, cruel trick you couldn't play while still thinking yourself an unusually honest and progressive man.

IVANOV [*laughing*]. This isn't a wedding, it's a public debate. Loud cheers!

SASHA [*to* LVOV]. Now think for a moment. Do you know what you're doing or don't you? Stupid, callous people. [*Takes* IVANOV *by the hand.*] Come away, Nicholas. Come on, Father!

IVANOV. What do you mean, come on? I'll put an end to all this here and now. I feel like a young man again, it's my old self that's speaking. [*Takes out his revolver.*]

SASHA [*shrieks*]. I know what he wants to do. Nicholas, for God's sake!

IVANOV. I've rolled downhill long enough, it's time to call a halt. I've outstayed my welcome. Go away. Thank you, Sasha.

SASHA [*shouts*]. Nicholas, for God's sake! Stop him!

IVANOV. Leave me alone! [*Runs to one side and shoots himself.*]

CURTAIN

THE SEAGULL

[*Чайка*]

A COMEDY IN FOUR ACTS

(1896)

CHARACTERS

IRINA ARKADIN (MRS. TREPLEV), an actress

CONSTANTINE TREPLEV, her son, a young man

PETER SORIN, her brother

NINA ZARECHNY, a young girl, daughter of a rich land-owner

ILYA SHAMRAYEV, a retired army lieutenant, Sorin's manager

POLINA, his wife

MASHA, his daughter

BORIS TRIGORIN, a writer

EUGENE DORN, a doctor

SIMON MEDVEDENKO, a schoolmaster

JACOB, a labourer

A chef

A housemaid

The action takes place in Sorin's house and garden
There is an interval of two years between Acts Three and Four

ACT ONE

The park on SORIN's *estate. A wide path, leading away from the audience to a lake in the background, is blocked by a rough stage, put up for an amateur dramatic performance. It hides the lake from view. To left and right of this stage, bushes. A few chairs and a small table.*

The sun has just set. JACOB *and other workmen can be heard hammering and coughing on the stage behind the drawn curtain.* MASHA *and* MEDVEDENKO *come in, left, on their way back from a walk.*

MEDVEDENKO. Why do you wear black all the time?

MASHA. I'm in mourning for my life, I'm unhappy.

MEDVEDENKO. Why? [*Reflects.*] I don't understand. You're healthy and your father's quite well off, even if he's not rich. I'm much worse off than you—I'm only paid twenty-three roubles a month, and what with pension deductions I don't even get that. But I don't go round like someone at a funeral. [*They sit down.*]

MASHA. Money doesn't matter, even a poor man can be happy.

MEDVEDENKO. Yes—in theory. But look how it works out. There's me, my mother, my two sisters and my young brother. But I only earn twenty-three roubles and we need food and drink, don't we? Tea and sugar? And tobacco? We can hardly make ends meet.

MASHA [*looking back at the stage*]. The play will be on soon.

MEDVEDENKO. Yes. Nina Zarechny will act in it and Constantine Treplev wrote it. They're in love and this evening they'll be spiritually united in the effort to present a unified work of art. But you and I aren't soul-mates at all. I love you. I'm too wretched to stay at home and I walk over here every day, four miles each way, and it just doesn't mean a thing to you. And that's understandable. I've no money, there are a lot of us at home, and anyway why marry a man who doesn't get enough to eat?

MASHA. What rubbish. [*Takes snuff.*] Your loving me is all very touching, but I can't love you back and that's that. [*Offers him her snuff-box.*] Have some.

MEDVEDENKO. I don't feel like it. [*Pause.*]

MASHA. It's so close, it's sure to thunder tonight. You're always holding forth about something or talking about money. You think there's nothing worse than being poor, but if you ask me it's a thousand times better to be a beggar and wear rags than—. Oh, you can't understand.

[*Enter* SORIN *and* TREPLEV, *right.*]

SORIN [*leaning on a stick*]. Country life doesn't really suit me, boy, and I shall never get used to this place, you can see for yourself. I went to bed at ten o'clock last night and woke at nine this morning, feeling as if all that sleep had glued my brain to my skull or something. [*Laughs.*] Then I happened to drop off again this afternoon, and now I feel more dead than alive. It's a nightmare, that's what it comes to.

TREPLEV. Yes, you should really live in town. [*Seeing* MASHA *and* MEDVEDENKO.] Look here, you'll be told when the show begins, so don't hang round now. Go away, please.

SORIN [*to* MASHA]. Masha, would you mind asking your father to have that dog let off its chain? It's always howling. My sister couldn't sleep again last night.

MASHA. Speak to my father yourself, I shan't. Kindly leave me out of this. [*To* MEDVEDENKO.] Come on.

MEDVEDENKO [*to* TREPLEV]. Let us know when it starts, will you? [*Both go out.*]

SORIN. So that dog will howl again all night. Isn't it typical? I've never done what I liked in the country. At one time I'd take a month off and come down here for a break and so on, but there'd be so much fuss and bother when you got here—you felt like pushing off the moment you arrived. [*Laughs.*] I was always glad to get away. Anyway, now I'm retired I've nowhere else to go, that's what it comes to. I have to live here, like it or not.

JACOB [*to* TREPLEV]. We're going for a swim, Mr. Treplev.

TREPLEV. All right, but mind you're in your places in ten minutes. [*Looks at his watch.*] It won't be long now.

JACOB. Very good, sir. [*Goes out.*]

TREPLEV [*looking round the stage*]. Well, this is our theatre. Just a curtain with the two wings and an empty space beyond. No scenery.

There's an open view of the lake and horizon. We shall put up the curtain at exactly half past eight when the moon rises.

SORIN. Splendid.

TREPLEV. Of course the whole thing will fall flat if Nina Zarechny's late. It's time she was here. Her father and stepmother keep a sharp eye on her and she can't easily get away, she's pretty well a prisoner. [*Puts his uncle's tie straight.*] Your hair and beard *are* a mess. Shouldn't you get a trim?

SORIN [*combing his beard*]. It's the bane of my life. As a young man I always looked as if I had a hangover and so on. Women never liked me. [*Sitting down.*] Why is your mother in a bad mood?

TREPLEV. Well may you ask. She's bored. [*Sitting down beside* SORIN.] And jealous. She has it in for me—and for this performance and the play—because Nina's in it and she isn't. She knows nothing about the play, but she already loathes it.

SORIN [*laughs*]. What an idea——

TREPLEV. She's put out because Nina will be applauded on this little stage and she won't. [*Looks at his watch.*] She's a psychological freak, is Mother. Oh, she's brilliant enough. And clever. She can cry her eyes out over a book, reel off all Nekrasov's poems by heart, and when it comes to nursing the sick she's quite the ministering angel. But you try putting in a word for another actress—Duse, say. I wouldn't advise it, not while she's around. No one else must have a word of praise. The idea is that we write about her, make a great to-do and rave about her marvellous acting in *The Lady with the Camellias* or *It's a Mad Life*. But out here in the country that drug isn't to be had, which is why she's so fed up and bad-tempered. That's why she thinks we're against her and that we're all to blame. What's more, she's superstitious, she thinks thirteen's an unlucky number and that sort of thing. She's stingy too. She has seventy thousand roubles in the bank in Odessa, I know that for a fact. But you ask her to lend you some and you'll have her in tears.

SORIN. You've got it in your head that your mother doesn't like your play and now you're upset and so on. Don't worry, your mother adores you.

TREPLEV [*pulling the petals off a flower*]. She loves me, she loves me not. She loves me, she loves me not. She loves me, she loves me not. [*Laughs.*] You see, Mother doesn't love me—to put it rather mildly.

She likes excitement, romantic affairs, gay clothes—but I'm twenty-five years old and a constant reminder that she's not so young as she was. She's only thirty-two when I'm not around, but when I'm with her she's forty-three, and that's what she can't stand about me. Besides, she knows I've no use for the theatre. She adores the stage. Serving humanity in the sacred cause of art, that's how she thinks of it. But the theatre's in a rut nowadays, if you ask me—it's so one-sided. The curtain goes up and you see a room with three walls. It's evening, so the lights are on. And in the room you have these geniuses, these high priests of art, to show you how people eat, drink, love, walk about and wear their jackets. Out of mediocre scenes and lines they try to drag a moral, some commonplace that doesn't tax the brain and might come in useful about the house. When I'm offered a thousand different variations on the same old theme, I have to escape—run for it, as Maupassant ran from the Eiffel Tower because it was so vulgar he felt it was driving him crazy.

SORIN. But we must have a theatre.

TREPLEV. What we need's a new kind of theatre. New forms are what we need, and if we haven't got them we'd be a sight better off with nothing at all. [*Looks at his watch.*] I'm terribly fond of Mother. But she does lead such an idiotic life, for ever taken up with this author of hers, and her name's always being bandied about in the press—which is all very trying. Then sometimes I can't help being a bit selfish, as anyone would in my position, and I'm sorry to have a famous actress for my mother—feel I'd be better off if she was just an ordinary woman. Can you imagine anything more outrageous and idiotic, Uncle? Sometimes she'll have guests in the house—celebrities, every one of them, actors and writers. Only one non-entity in the whole bunch. Me. They only put up with me because I'm her son. Who am I? What am I? I left the university in my third year, 'for reasons outside our control', as editors sometimes say. I'm no good at anything, I haven't a penny to my name and my pass-port description is 'provincial shopkeeper, resident of Kiev'. That, you see, was my father's official status, though he was well known on the stage himself. So when all these musicians, actors and writers deigned to notice me in her drawing-room, they looked as if they were wondering how anyone could be quite such a worm. I could tell what they thought—I suffered agonies of humiliation.

SORIN. By the way, tell me about this writer—this friend of your mother's. What's he like? He's a bit of a puzzle, he hardly speaks.

TREPLEV. He's intelligent and unassuming—a bit on the melancholy side, you know. Very decent sort. He's nowhere near forty yet, but he's already famous and thoroughly spoilt. As for his works, well, what shall I say? It's charming, clever stuff, but after Tolstoy or Zola you'd hardly care for Trigorin.

SORIN. You know, I'm rather fond of writers, my boy. I once wanted to get married and write books, those were my two great ambitions, but neither of them came off. Ah yes. Even being an obscure writer must be quite nice, come to think of it.

TREPLEV [*listens*]. I hear someone coming. [*Embraces his uncle.*] I can't live without her. The very sound of her footsteps is so beautiful. I'm wildly happy. [*Hurries towards* NINA ZARECHNY, *who now comes in.*] Entrancing creature, my vision of delight——

NINA [*upset*]. I'm not late am I? I can't be.

TREPLEV [*kissing her hands*]. No, no, of course not.

NINA. I've been worried all day, scared out of my wits. I was afraid Father wouldn't let me come, but he's just gone out with my step-mother. The sky was red, the moon was already rising and I rode over as fast as I could. [*Laughs.*] Oh, I'm so pleased. [*Shakes* SORIN *firmly by the hand.*]

SORIN [*laughs*]. You look as though you've been crying. Now that won't do, it really won't.

NINA. It's all right. I'm so out of breath, can't you see? I have to leave in half an hour, so we must be quick. No, no, don't try and keep me, for God's sake. My father doesn't know I'm here.

TREPLEV. It's time we started, anyway. We must go and call the others.

SORIN. I'll see to it and so on. At your service. [*Moves towards the right, singing.*] 'There were once two French Grenadiers.' [*Looks round.*] I once burst into song like that and a fellow in our legal department spoke up. 'You've a mighty powerful voice, sir.' Then he thought a bit and added, 'And a pretty nasty one too.' [*Laughs and goes out.*]

NINA. My father and stepmother won't let me come here. This place is wildly Bohemian according to them, and they're afraid of me going on the stage. But something seems to lure me to this lake like a seagull. My heart's full of my feelings for you. [*Looks round.*]

TREPLEV. We're alone.

NINA. I think there's someone over there.

TREPLEV. No, there isn't. [*They kiss.*]

NINA. What sort of tree is that?

TREPLEV. An elm.

NINA. Why is it so dark?

TREPLEV. Night's falling and everything's getting dark. Don't go home too early. Please.

NINA. I must.

TREPLEV. Then how about me coming over to your place, Nina? I'll stand in the garden all night gazing at your window.

NINA. You can't, the watchman would see you. Our dog doesn't know you yet and he'd bark.

TREPLEV. I love you.

NINA. Shush!

TREPLEV [*hearing footsteps*]. Who's there? Is it you, Jacob?

JACOB [*behind the stage*]. Yes sir.

TREPLEV. Get into position, it's time to start. Is the moon coming up?

JACOB. Yes sir.

TREPLEV. Have you the methylated spirits? And the sulphur? There must be a smell of sulphur when the red eyes appear. [*To* NINA.] Run along then—you'll find everything ready. Nervous?

NINA. Yes, terribly. I don't mind your mother, I'm not afraid of her, but Trigorin's here. To have him in the audience—I'm just a bundle of nerves. A famous writer! Is he young?

TREPLEV. Yes.

NINA. His stories are marvellous, aren't they?

TREPLEV [*coldly*]. I don't know, I've never read them.

NINA. Your play's hard to act, there are no living people in it.

TREPLEV. Living people! We should show life neither as it is nor as it ought to be, but as we see it in our dreams.

NINA. There's not much action, it's just a lot of speeches. I think a play really needs a love interest.

[*Both go behind the stage. Enter* POLINA *and* DORN.]

POLINA. It's getting damp. Go and put your galoshes on.

DORN. I'm hot.

POLINA. You don't take care of yourself, it's sheer pigheadedness. As a doctor you know very well that damp air's bad for you, but you want to make me suffer. And you spent the whole of yesterday evening out on the terrace to spite me.

DORN [*sings quietly*]. 'Oh, tell me not your young life's ruined.'

POLINA. You were so busy talking to Irina, you didn't notice the cold. You think she's attractive, don't you?

DORN. I'm fifty-five years old.

POLINA. Don't be silly, that's not old for a man. You're young for your age and still attractive to women.

DORN. Well, what do you want me to do about it?

POLINA. You men are all the same. When you see an actress you're ready to fall down and worship her.

DORN [*sings quietly*]. 'Once more in thy presence—.' That society makes a fuss of artists and doesn't treat them like tradesmen, say— it's only natural. It's a form of idealism.

POLINA. Women have always fallen in love with you and thrown themselves at you. That's idealism too, I suppose?

DORN [*shrugs his shoulders*]. What's wrong with it? There's a lot to be said for the way women have treated me. I'm a first-rate doctor, that's what they really liked about me. Ten or fifteen years ago, you remember, I was the only decent obstetrician in the county. And then I've always treated people fairly.

POLINA [*clutches his hand*]. My darling!

DORN. Take it easy, someone's coming.

[*Enter* IRINA *on* SORIN's *arm*, TRIGORIN, SHAMRAYEV, MED-VEDENKO *and* MASHA.]

SHAMRAYEV. I remember her acting superbly at the Poltava Trade Fair in 'seventy-three. Terrific, wonderful stuff! Then there was Paul Chadin, the comedian. You don't happen to know what became of him, I suppose? No one could touch his Rasplyuyev, it was better than Sadovsky's, believe me, dearest lady. Where is he now?

IRINA. You always want to hear about these old fossils. How on earth should I know? [*Sits down.*]

SHAMRAYEV [*with a sigh*]. Paul Chadin—you don't find his sort any more. The stage has gone downhill, Irina. Once we had giants, now we've only dwarfs.

DORN. There aren't many real stars these days, I grant you, but the average actor's come on a lot.

SHAMRAYEV. I can't agree, it's a matter of taste anyway. *De gustibus aut bene, aut nihil.*

[TREPLEV *appears from behind the stage.*]

IRINA [*to her son*]. When does the thing start, dear boy?

TREPLEV. In a minute, please be patient.

IRINA [*declaims from* Hamlet].
       'O Hamlet, speak no more:
       Thou turn'st mine eyes into my very soul;
       And there I see such black and grained spots
       As will not leave their tinct.'

TREPLEV [*from* Hamlet].
             'Nay, but to live
       In the rank sweat of an enseamed bed,
       Stew'd in corruption, honeying and making love
       Over the nasty sty——'

[*A horn is sounded behind the stage.*]

TREPLEV. Ladies and gentlemen, we're starting. Attention, please. [*Pause.*] I'm starting now. [*Bangs his stick on the ground and speaks loudly.*] O ye ancient, hallowed shades that float above this lake at night, lull us to sleep, and may we dream of life in two hundred thousand years.

SORIN. In two hundred thousand years there won't be anything left.

TREPLEV. All right then, let them show us that.

IRINA. Let them, we're fast asleep anyway.

[*The curtain rises, opening on to the lake. The moon has risen above the horizon and is reflected in the water.* NINA ZARECHNY, *dressed in white, is sitting on a boulder.*]

NINA. Men, lions, eagles and partridges, horned deer, geese, spiders and silent fishes, denizens of the deep, starfishes and creatures invisible—that is, all life, all life, all life—has completed its melancholy cycle and died. For thousands of centuries Earth has not borne one living creature, and in vain does that poor moon light her lamp. No longer do cranes awake and call in the meadows and no may-beetles can be heard in the lime-groves. It is cold, cold, cold. Empty, empty, empty. Terrible, terrible, terrible. [*Pause.*] The bodies of living creatures have turned to dust, and eternal matter has converted them into stones, water, clouds. But their souls have all been fused into a single whole. That World Spirit am I. I. Within me is the soul of Alexander the Great, of Caesar, Shakespeare and Napoleon—and of the most miserable leech. In me the thoughts of men are mingled with the instincts of animals. I remember all, all, all, and I relive anew in my own being every other life.

[*Will-o'-the-wisps are seen.*]

IRINA [*quietly*]. This is something terribly modern.

TREPLEV [*imploringly and reproachfully*]. Mother!

NINA. I am lonely. Once in a hundred years I open my lips to speak and in this void with none to hear me my voice echoes mournfully. You too, pale lights, you hear me not. The foul marsh brings you forth before sunrise and you drift till daybreak, without thought, without will, without any quiver of life. The Devil, Father of Eternal Matter, fearing that you might bring forth new life, causes your atoms, and those of the stones and water, to change every second, and you are in a state of continual flux. Alone in the whole universe the Spirit remains one and the same. [*Pause.*] Like a prisoner flung into a deep, empty well, I know not where I am or what awaits me. All is hidden from me except that in the cruel, unrelenting struggle with the Devil, the principle of Material Force, I am destined to triumph. Then shall Spirit and Matter unite in wondrous harmony, then shall the reign of Cosmic Will commence. But that will only come about after a long, long succession of millennia, when Moon, bright Sirius and Earth shall gradually have turned to dust. Until then there shall be horror upon horror.

[*Pause. Two red spots appear over the lake.*]

NINA. But see—my mighty antagonist the Devil approaches. I see his awful blood-red eyes——

IRINA. There's a smell of sulphur. Was that really necessary?

TREPLEV. Yes.

IRINA [*laughs*]. Oh, a stage effect.

TREPLEV. Mother!

NINA. He is miserable without human beings——

POLINA [*to* DORN]. You've taken your hat off. Put it on before you catch cold.

IRINA. The doctor took his hat off to the Devil, Father of Eternal Matter.

TREPLEV [*losing his temper, in a loud voice*]. The play's over. Enough! Curtain!

IRINA. But why so annoyed?

TREPLEV. Enough! Curtain! Bring down that curtain! [*Stamping.*] Curtain! [*The curtain falls.*] I'm extremely sorry, I forgot that writing plays and acting are only for the chosen few, I'm poaching on other people's preserves, I—I—. [*Tries to add something, but makes a gesture of resignation and goes off, left.*]

IRINA. What's up with him?

SORIN. My dear Irina, that's hardly how to treat a touchy young man.

IRINA. Why, what did I do?

SORIN. You hurt his feelings.

IRINA. But he told us his play was a joke, and that's just how I treated it.

SORIN. All the same——

IRINA. Now he turns out to have written a masterpiece. Oh, for heaven's sake! I suppose he put on this performance, and choked us with sulphur, not as a joke, but to prove a point. He wanted to show us how to write and act. I've really had about enough of this! These constant outbursts and digs against me—well, say what you like, but they'd try anyone's patience. He's a selfish, spoilt little boy.

SORIN. He only wanted to give you pleasure.

IRINA. Oh, did he? But of course he couldn't choose an ordinary play, we have to sit through this experimental rubbish. Now, I don't mind listening to rubbish for a laugh, but doesn't this stuff claim to be a new art form, something epoch-making? Well, I don't see any new art form here, just a display of bad manners.

TRIGORIN. Everyone writes what he likes as best he can.

IRINA. Then let him write what he likes as best he can, but leave me out of it.

DORN. Jupiter, thou art angry——

IRINA. I'm not Jupiter, I'm a woman. [*Lights a cigarette.*] I'm not annoyed, I'm only sorry to see a young man spend his time so tediously. I didn't mean to hurt his feelings.

MEDVEDENKO. No one has the right to separate Spirit from Matter, since Spirit itself may well be a combination of material atoms. [*To* TRIGORIN, *eagerly.*] But you know, how about writing and staging a play based on the life of us schoolmasters? We have a pretty thin time.

IRINA. Quite right, but no more talk about plays or atoms. It's such a heavenly evening. I say, can you hear someone singing? [*Listens.*] Now isn't that nice?

POLINA. It's on the other side of the lake. [*Pause.*]

IRINA [*to* TRIGORIN]. Sit by me. Ten or fifteen years ago there was music and singing by this lake almost every night. There are six estates on the shore. There was so much laughter, fun and shooting, I remember, and so many, many love affairs. But who was the darling and idol of all six estates? I present [*nods towards* DORN] our doctor, Eugene Dorn. He's still charming, but in those days he was irresistible. Still, I'm beginning to feel rather guilty. Why did I hurt my poor boy's feelings? I'm worried. [*Loudly.*] Constantine, my dear! Constantine!

MASHA. I'll go and look for him.

IRINA. Please do, darling.

MASHA [*moving off, left*]. Hallo there! Constantine! Hallo there! [*Goes out.*]

NINA [*coming out from behind the stage*]. We obviously aren't going on, so I can come out. Good evening. [*Kisses* IRINA *and* POLINA.]

SORIN. Bravo, bravo!

IRINA. Bravo, bravo! We were quite fascinated. With those looks and that perfectly lovely voice you mustn't bury yourself in the country, it would be such a shame. I'm sure you have a real gift, do you hear me? Your duty is to go on the stage.

NINA. Oh, that's what I always dream of. [*With a sigh.*] But it can never be.

IRINA. Who knows? Now let me introduce—Boris Trigorin.

NINA. Oh, pleased to meet you—. [*With embarrassment.*] I always read what you——

IRINA [*giving* NINA *a seat next to her*]. Now don't be shy, darling. He's a famous man, but he's not at all stuffy. And he's a bit shy himself, you see.

DORN. I think we might raise the curtain now, it's a bit spooky like this.

SHAMRAYEV [*loudly*]. Jacob, be a good fellow and pull up the curtain.

[*The curtain goes up.*]

NINA [*to* TRIGORIN]. It's an odd play, isn't it?

TRIGORIN. I couldn't make sense of it. I enjoyed it, though. Your acting was so genuine, and the scenery was superb. [*Pause.*] There must be a lot of fish in that lake.

NINA. Yes.

TRIGORIN. I love angling. There's nothing I enjoy more than sitting on the water's edge in the late afternoon, watching my float.

NINA. After the joy of creative work I should have thought no other enjoyment would mean anything.

IRINA [*laughing*]. Oh, don't say that. Compliments always floor him completely.

SHAMRAYEV. I remember one evening at the Moscow Opera Theatre hearing the great Silva take a lower C. There was a bass from our parish choir sitting in the gallery, as it happened. Suddenly—we were quite flabbergasted, as you can imagine—we hear a voice from the gallery. 'Bravo, Silva!' A whole octave lower. Like this. [*In a deep bass.*] 'Bravo Silva!' You could have heard a pin drop in that theatre. [*Pause.*]

DORN. No one seems to have anything to say.

NINA. Well, I must be going. Good-bye.

IRINA. What! Where are you off to at this hour? We won't let you.

NINA. Father's expecting me.

IRINA. Well, I must say, he is a—. [*They kiss.*] Ah well, that's that, but I do so wish you could stay.

NINA. How I hate leaving, if you only knew.

IRINA. Someone ought to see you home, my pet.

NINA [*terrified*]. Oh, no, no!

SORIN [*to* NINA, *imploringly*]. Do stay.

NINA. I can't, Mr. Sorin.

SORIN. Just one hour and so on. Surely you can——

NINA [*after some thought, through tears*]. I can't. [*Shakes hands and hurries out.*]

IRINA. It really is bad luck on the girl. They say her mother left all her enormous fortune to her father when she died—every last bit of it—and now the child has nothing because the father's going to leave everything to his second wife. It's outrageous.

DORN. Yes, that dear father of hers is a pretty thoroughgoing swine, give him his due.

SORIN [*rubbing his cold hands*]. I think we might go in too, it's getting damp out here. My legs ache.

IRINA. They're so stiff, you can hardly walk. Well, come on, poor old thing. [*Takes his arm.*]

SHAMRAYEV [*offering his arm to his wife*]. Madam?

SORIN. I can hear that dog howling again. [*To* SHAMRAYEV.] Be a good fellow, Shamrayev, and have it let off its chain.

SHAMRAYEV. I can't, my dear sir. Thieves might get in the barn— I've millet in there. [*To* MEDVEDENKO, *who is walking beside him.*] Yes, a whole octave lower. 'Bravo, Silva!' And no concert artist, mind you, just someone from the church choir.

MEDVEDENKO. What do they pay you in a church choir? [*All go out except* DORN.]

DORN [*alone*]. Well, I don't know. Perhaps it's all rather beyond me, perhaps I've gone mad, but I liked the play. It has something. When that child spoke about loneliness, and then afterwards when the Devil's red eyes appeared, my hands shook with excitement. It was all so fresh and innocent. Look, I think he's coming. I want to be as nice about it as I can.

TREPLEV [*coming in*]. They've all gone.

DORN. I'm here.

TREPLEV. Masha's looking for me all over the park. What a ghastly creature.

DORN. I liked your play enormously, Constantine. It's a bit odd in a way, and I haven't heard the end. Still, it made a great impression. You have a real bent that way and you mustn't give up.

[TREPLEV *shakes him firmly by the hand and embraces him impulsively.*]

DORN. Hey—a bit excitable, aren't you? Tears in your eyes—. Now, my point is this. You took your plot from the realm of abstract ideas, and quite right too, because a work of art simply must express some great idea. Nothing can be beautiful unless it's also serious. I say, you are pale.

TREPLEV. So you don't think I should give up?

DORN. No. But you must describe only the significant and the eternal. As you know, I've lived a varied life and enjoyed myself, I'm satisfied. But if I'd ever experienced the uplift that an artist feels when he's creating, I think I'd have scorned my material environment and all that goes with it, and I'd have taken wing and soared away into the sky.

TREPLEV. I'm sorry, where's Nina?

DORN. And then a work of art must express a clear, precise idea. You must know why you write, or else—if you take this picturesque path without knowing where you're going you'll lose your way and your gifts will destroy you.

TREPLEV [*impatiently*]. Where's Nina?

DORN. She's gone home.

TREPLEV [*in despair*]. What can I do? I want to see her, I *must* see her. I'm going over there.

[MASHA *comes in.*]

DORN [*to* TREPLEV]. Take it easy, my boy.

TREPLEV. But I'm going all the same. I must go.

MASHA. Come indoors, Constantine. Your mother wants you, she's worried.

TREPLEV. Tell her I've gone. And look here, can't you all leave me alone? Leave me alone, don't follow me around.

DORN. Come, come, dear boy, you can't go on like this. It's not right.

TREPLEV [*through tears*]. Good-bye, Doctor. Many thanks. [*Goes out.*]

DORN [*with a sigh*]. Ah, to be young!

MASHA. When people can't think what to say they always hold forth about the young. [*Takes some snuff.*]

DORN [*takes the snuff-box off her and hurls it into the bushes*]. That's disgusting. [*Pause.*] I think someone's playing the piano indoors. I must go in.

MASHA. Just a moment.

DORN. What is it?

MASHA. I must tell you again, I must speak. [*Excitedly.*] I don't care for my father, but I have a soft spot for you. Somehow we have so much in common, I feel it with all my heart. So help me. Help me, or else I'll do something silly and make a mess of my life, ruin it. I can't go on.

DORN. Meaning what? How can I help you?

MASHA. I'm so unhappy. No one, no one knows how I suffer. [*Lays her head on his breast, softly.*] I love Constantine.

DORN. What a state they're all in. And what a lot of loving. Oh, magic lake! [*Tenderly.*] But what can I do, my child? What can I do?

CURTAIN

ACT TWO

The croquet lawn. In the background, right, the house, with a large terrace. To the left, a view of the lake with sunlight sparkling on it. Flower beds. It is midday and hot. IRINA, DORN *and* MASHA *are sitting on a bench near the lawn in the shade of an old lime-tree.* DORN *has an open book on his lap.*

IRINA [*to* MASHA]. Let's stand up. [*Both stand up.*] Side by side. You're twenty-two and I'm nearly twice as old. Now, Dr. Dorn, which of us looks younger?

DORN. You, of course.

IRINA. Exactly. And why? Because I work, I feel, I'm always on the go, while you just stay put—you're only half alive. And I make it a rule not to look into the future, I never think of growing old or dying. What is to be will be.

MASHA. I feel about a thousand years old. My life seems to drag on and on endlessly, and I often think I'd rather be dead. [*Sits down.*] That's silly, of course. I must pull myself together and snap out of it.

DORN [*singing quietly*]. 'Oh, speak to her, you flowers——'

IRINA. Then again I'm most particular, dear, like an Englishman. I keep myself in trim and my clothes and hair are always just right. Do I ever go out, even in the garden, with my housecoat on, without doing my hair? No, I don't. That's why I've lasted so well, because I've never been slovenly and let myself go like some I could mention. [*Strolls up and down the lawn, arms akimbo.*] See what I mean? Just like a dear little robin. I could play a girl of fifteen.

DORN. Well, I'll carry on reading anyway. [*Picks up his book.*] We stopped at the corn-dealer and the rats.

IRINA. 'And the rats.' You read. [*Sits down.*] Or rather let me have it, I'll read, it's my turn. [*Takes the book and looks for the place.*] 'And the rats.' Here we are. [*Reads.*] 'For society people to encourage novelists and make a fuss of them is as obviously dangerous as for a corn-dealer to let rats breed in his storerooms. But you see, writers are very popular. So when a woman's marked one down for capture, she keeps on at him, flattering him, being nice to him and spoiling him.' Well, the French may be like that, but we're different, we don't have things so cut and dried. Before a Russian woman tries to ensnare a writer she's usually head over heels in love with him, believe me. No need to look far—take me and Trigorin.

[*Enter* SORIN *leaning on a stick, with* NINA *at his side. Behind them* MEDVEDENKO *pushes an empty bath-chair.*]

SORIN [*kindly, as if to a child*]. Oh yes? Something nice has happened, has it? We're happy today, is that what it comes to? [*To his sister.*] Something nice has happened. Our father and stepmother have gone off to Tver, so we're free for three whole days.

NINA [*sits down beside* IRINA *and embraces her*]. I'm so happy, I belong to you now.

SORIN [*sits down in his bath-chair*]. And doesn't she look pretty this morning?

IRINA. Yes, and so nicely dressed and attractive—what a good little girl. [*Kisses* NINA.] But we mustn't be too nice, we'll bring her bad luck. Where's Boris Trigorin?

NINA. Down at the bathing place, fishing.

IRINA. I wonder he doesn't get bored. [*Is about to go on reading.*]

NINA. What's that?

IRINA. Maupassant's *On the Water*, darling. [*Reads a few lines to herself.*] Oh well, the rest's dull and unconvincing. [*Shuts the book.*] I'm rather worried. Tell me, what's wrong with my son? Why is he so terribly bored and depressed? He spends whole days out by the lake and I hardly ever see him.

MASHA. He's in rather a bad mood. [*To* NINA, *timidly.*] Please recite something from his play.

NINA [*shrugging her shoulders*]. Do you mean it? It's so boring.

MASHA [*restraining her enthusiasm*]. When he recites, his eyes blaze and he turns pale. He has a beautiful, sad voice, and he looks like a poet.

[SORIN *is heard snoring.*]

DORN. Happy dreams.

IRINA. Peter.

SORIN. Eh?

IRINA. Are you asleep?

SORIN. Not at all. [*Pause.*]

IRINA. You won't consult a doctor, dear, and that's very naughty of you.

SORIN. I wouldn't mind—it's the doctor here doesn't want me to.

DORN. What, dose yourself at the age of sixty!

SORIN. One wants to live, even at sixty.

DORN [*annoyed*]. Eh? Then take valerian drops.

IRINA. It would be good for him to go to a spa, I think.

DORN. Why not? Let him go. Or let him stay.

IRINA. What's that supposed to mean?

DORN. Nothing special. It's quite clear. [*Pause.*]

MEDVEDENKO. Mr. Sorin should give up smoking.

SORIN. Oh, rubbish.

DORN. No, it isn't. Drinking and smoking ruin your personality. After a cigar or glass of vodka you're not Peter Sorin any more, you're Peter Sorin plus something. Your ego dissolves and you start thinking of yourself as 'him', in the third person.

SORIN [*laughs*]. It's all right for you to talk, you've enjoyed yourself. But what about me? Twenty-eight years I've worked for the Department of Justice, but I haven't lived yet, haven't experienced anything—that's what it comes to. So I want a bit of fun, it stands to reason. You've always had your own way and you don't care, which is why you're so given to idle chatter. But I want a bit of life, so I drink sherry at dinner and smoke cigars and so on. That's all there is to it.

DORN. One should take life seriously, but to go to your doctor when you're sixty and complain that you didn't enjoy yourself as a young man—well, I'm sorry, but that's just silly.

MASHA [*stands up*]. It must be lunch time. [*Walks in a lazy, drooping fashion.*] My foot's gone to sleep. [*Goes out.*]

DORN. She's off for a couple of quick ones before lunch.

SORIN. The poor child's unhappy.

DORN. Nonsense, sir.

SORIN. You've always had all you want, that's why you talk like this.

IRINA. Oh, could anything be duller than this charming country boredom—so hot and still, with you all lolling round airing your views? You're good company, my dears, and I like listening to you, but—I'd much rather sit in my hotel room learning a part.

NINA [*delightedly*]. Well said, I know what you mean.

SORIN. It's better in town, of course. You sit in your study, with a servant to stop anyone coming in unannounced, and there's a telephone. Then there are cabs in the street and so on.

DORN [*sings softly*]. 'Oh, speak to her, you flowers——'

[SHAMRAYEV *comes in, followed by* POLINA.]

SHAMRAYEV. Here they are. Good morning. [*Kisses* IRINA's *hand, then* NINA's.] Nice to see you looking so well. [*To* IRINA.] My wife says you propose going to town together this afternoon. Is that so?

IRINA. Yes, that is the idea.

SHAMRAYEV. I see. Splendid. And how do you propose travelling, dearest lady? We're carting rye this afternoon and the men are all busy. So which horses are you taking? If you don't mind my asking.

IRINA. Horses? How on earth should I know?

SORIN. We do have some carriage horses.

SHAMRAYEV [*agitatedly*]. Carriage horses? And where am I to get collars? Yes, where am I to get collars? This baffles me, it passes the bounds of credence! Look, dear lady, I worship your genius and I'd give you ten years of my life, but horses I cannot provide.

IRINA. And what if I have to leave? This is most odd.

SHAMRAYEV. You've no idea what running a farm means, dear lady·

IRINA [*losing her temper*]. This is what we're always being told! Well, in that case I leave for Moscow this very afternoon. Hire me horses in the village, or I shall walk to the station.

SHAMRAYEV [*losing his temper*]. Then I resign, you can get yourself another manager. [*Goes out.*]

IRINA. This happens every summer. Every summer I come here to be insulted, I shan't set foot in this place again. [*Goes out, left, in the supposed direction of the bathing place off-stage. A minute later she can be seen going indoors, followed by* TRIGORIN *with fishing-lines and a pail.*]

SORIN [*flaring up*]. What insolence. What the hell *is* all this? I'm fed up, that's what it comes to. Bring all the horses here this instant.

NINA [*to* POLINA]. Fancy saying no to a famous actress like Miss Arkadin. Her slightest wish, her merest whim—surely they're more important than your entire farm. This is beyond belief.

POLINA [*in despair*]. What can I do? Put yourself in my place. What can I do?

SORIN [*to* NINA]. Let's go and find my sister. We'll all beg her to stay, how about it? [*Looking in the direction in which* SHAMRAYEV *disappeared.*] What an awful man. Tyrant!

NINA [*prevents him rising*]. Don't move, stay where you are. We'll wheel you. [*She and* MEDVEDENKO *push the bath-chair.*] Oh, isn't this awful!

SORIN. Yes, it certainly is. But he won't resign, I'll speak to him at once.

[*They go out. Only* DORN *and* POLINA *remain on stage.*]

DORN. Aren't people a bore? Your husband really deserves to be kicked out, but it'll end with that old woman Sorin and his sister apologizing to him, you'll see.

POLINA. He sent the carriage horses out on farm work. We have these mix-ups every day. If you only knew how it upsets me, it makes me ill—see how I'm shaking? I can't stand his rudeness. [*Imploringly.*] Eugene dear, let me come and live with you, darling. Our time's passing, we're not so young as we were. Can't we give up all the lying and pretence now we're getting on in life? [*Pause.*]

DORN. I'm fifty-five, it's too late for me to change my life.

POLINA. You say no because there are other women in your life besides me, I know that. You can't give them all a home, I see that. Sorry, I've been a nuisance.

[NINA *appears near the house, picking flowers.*]

DORN. It's all right.

POLINA. It's agony to me, being jealous. Of course, being a doctor you can't avoid women, I see that.

DORN [*to* NINA, *who comes up to them*]. What's happening?

NINA. Miss Arkadin's crying and Mr. Sorin has a touch of his asthma.

DORN [*stands up*]. I'd better go and give them both valerian drops.

NINA [*gives him some flowers*]. Please take these.

DORN. Thank you so much. [*Goes towards the house.*]

POLINA [*going with him*]. Aren't they nice? [*In a low voice, near the house.*] Give me those flowers, just you give me those flowers! [*Tears them up and throws them away. Both go indoors.*]

NINA [*alone*]. Isn't it funny to see a famous actress cry, and for such a silly reason? Another funny thing—a well-known writer, a celebrity with his name in all the papers, his picture on sale and translations coming out in foreign languages, but he spends all day fishing and is overjoyed when he catches a couple of chub. I thought famous people were proud and standoffish, I thought they despised the common herd, I thought they sort of used their glamour and brilliance to take revenge on people for making so much fuss over birth and wealth. But here they are crying, fishing, playing cards, laughing and losing their tempers like anyone else.

TREPLEV [*comes in without his hat on, carrying a sporting gun and a dead seagull*]. Are you alone?

NINA. Yes.

[TREPLEV *lays the seagull at her feet.*]

NINA. What does that signify?

TREPLEV. I meanly killed that seagull this morning. I lay it at your feet.

NINA. What's wrong with you? [*Picks up the seagull and looks at it.*]

TREPLEV [*after a pause*]. I shall soon kill myself in the same way.

NINA. You've changed so much.

TREPLEV. Yes, but who changed first? You did. You're so different to me now, you look at me coldly and you find me in the way.

NINA. You're touchy lately and you always talk so mysteriously, in symbols or something. This seagull's a symbol too, I suppose, but it makes no sense to me, sorry. [*Lays the seagull on the bench.*] I'm too simple to understand you.

TREPLEV. It all started that evening when my play was such a stupid flop. Women can't forgive failure. I've burnt the thing, every scrap of it. If you only knew how wretched I am. Your coldness terrifies me, I can't believe it, it's as if I'd woken up and found this lake had suddenly dried up or soaked into the ground. You say you're too simple to understand me, but what is there to understand? My play failed, and you despise my inspiration and think me a dreary non-entity like so many others. [*Stamping.*] All this is only too clear.

It's as if someone had banged a nail into my brain, damn it—and damn the selfishness that seems to suck my blood like a vampire. [*Spotting* TRIGORIN, *who walks in reading a book.*] There's genius for you. Struts about like Hamlet. Carries a book too. [*Sarcastically.*] 'Words, words, words.' The great luminary hasn't come near you yet, but you're smiling already, your whole expression has melted in his rays. I won't stand in your way. [*Goes out quickly.*]

TRIGORIN [*making a note in his book*]. Takes snuff. Drinks vodka. Always wears black. Loved by schoolmaster.

NINA. Good morning, Mr. Trigorin.

TRIGORIN. Good morning. Things took an unexpected turn and I think we're leaving today. I don't suppose we'll meet again. I'm sorry, I don't often run across young, attractive girls, and I've forgotten how one feels at eighteen or nineteen—can't picture it. That's why the girls in my stories don't usually come off. I'd love to be in your shoes for an hour to find out how you think and what you're like.

NINA. And I'd like to be in your shoes.

TRIGORIN. Why?

NINA. To see how it feels to be a famous, gifted writer. How *does* it feel? What's the sensation, being a celebrity?

TRIGORIN. Eh? I don't think there is a sensation, I never thought of that. [*After reflection.*] Which means one of two things—either I'm not so famous as you think, or else being famous produces no sensation at all.

NINA. What about seeing your name in the papers?

TRIGORIN. That's all right when they're nice about you. When they're not nice you go about in a bad temper for a day or two.

NINA. What a wonderful world. If you knew how I envy you. People's lives work out so differently. Some barely drag out their days in drab obscurity. They're all alike and all miserable. But others, you for instance—you're one in a million—have fascinating, brilliant lives full of meaning. You're lucky.

TRIGORIN. What, me? [*Shrugging his shoulders.*] Well—. You speak of fame and happiness, and my fascinating, brilliant life. Sorry, but this nice talk only reminds me of boiled sweets—something I never eat. You're very young and kind.

NINA. Your life's marvellous.

TRIGORIN. What's so nice about it? [*Looks at his watch.*] I must go and write now. Sorry, I'm busy. [*Laughs.*] You've done what's called treading on my favourite corn and now I'm getting excited and a bit annoyed. Anyway, let me have my say. Let's talk about my wonderful, brilliant life. Right, where can we start? [*After a little thought.*] Some people have obsessions and can't help thinking day and night about something like the moon. Well, I'm a bit moonstruck too, haunted day and night by this writing obsession. I must write, I must—. Hardly have I ended one story when I somehow have to tackle another, then a third and fourth on top of that. I'm always writing, never stop, can't help it. What's wonderful and brilliant about that, eh? It's such a barbarous life. Here am I talking to you and getting quite excited, yet can't forget for a second that I've an unfinished novel waiting for me. Or I see a cloud over there like a grand piano. So I think it must go in a story. 'A cloud like a grand piano sailed past.' Or I smell heliotrope, and make a quick mental note. 'Sickly scent. Flower. Sombre hue. Mention in description of summer evening.' I try to catch every sentence, every word you and I say and quickly lock all these sentences and words away in my literary storehouse because they might come in handy. When I finish work, I rush off to the theatre or go fishing. That would be the time to relax and forget, but not a bit of it. I already have another great weight on my mind: a new plot. I feel I must go to my desk— hurry up and start writing, writing, writing all over again. This sort of thing goes on all the time, I can never relax, and I feel I'm wasting my life. I feel I'm taking pollen from my best flowers, tearing them up and stamping on the roots—all to make honey that goes to some vague, distant destination. I'm mad, I must be. Well, my friends and acquaintances don't exactly treat me as sane, do they? 'What are you writing now? What have you got in store for us?' They keep on and on and on, and to me it's all so bogus—my friends' attention, praise and admiration. They deceive me, the way one does an invalid, and I'm sometimes afraid they're just waiting to creep up, grab me and cart me off to an asylum like the lunatic in Gogol. And in my young days, in my best years, when I was just beginning, this writing business was sheer agony. An obscure author feels clumsy, awkward, out of place—especially when things aren't going well. He's all on edge with nervous strain. He can't help hanging round literary and artistic people, unrecognized, unnoticed, afraid to look anyone in the face. He's like a gambling addict who has no money. I never saw any of my readers, but I somehow thought of them as hostile and sceptical. I was afraid of the public, scared stiff. When I put on a new play, I always felt the dark-haired people in the audience were against me, while the fair-haired ones didn't care either way. Isn't it awful? What agony it was.

NINA. Yes, but look—there is inspiration, the creative process. Doesn't that give you moments of ecstasy?

TRIGORIN. Yes. Writing's pleasant enough. I like reading proofs too, but as soon as the stuff's in print I can't stand it—I now see it was all wrong, all a mistake, and shouldn't have been written at all, and I feel annoyed and fed up. [*Laughing.*] The public reads it and says: 'Yes. Oh, how nice. Oh, how clever. Very nice, but not a patch on Tolstoy.' Or: 'Marvellous stuff, but Turgenev's *Fathers and Children* is better.' This way my work will go on being nice and clever, nice and clever till my dying day, that's all, and when I'm dead my friends will pass my grave and say: 'Here lies Trigorin, a fine writer. But not as good as Turgenev.'

NINA. Sorry, I don't understand. You're simply spoilt by success.

TRIGORIN. What success? I've never satisfied myself. I dislike my own work. I drift round in a trance and often can't make sense of what I write, that's what's so awful. I love this lake here, the trees and the sky, I've a feeling for nature—it inspires me, gives me a violent urge to write. But then I'm more than an artist, aren't I? I'm a citizen too. I love my country and its people. As a writer, I feel I must discuss ordinary people, their sufferings, their future—science, human rights, all that stuff. So I do discuss it, all in great haste, with everyone furiously hounding me in all directions, while I scurry about like a fox with the pack snapping at his heels. I seem to see life and learning vanishing into the distance, while I lag more and more behind, feeling like the village boy who missed the train, and end up believing that I can only do nature descriptions and that everything else I write is bogus through and through.

NINA. You've been overworking. You're too busy—and too unwilling —to see how important you are. You're not satisfied with yourself. Very well, but to others you're a great man, you're wonderful. If I was a great writer like you, I'd give my whole life to the people, knowing that their only happiness was to rise to my level, and they'd harness themselves to my chariot.

TRIGORIN. A chariot, eh? Who do you take me for—Agamemnon? [*Both smile.*]

NINA. If I was lucky enough to be a writer or actress, I wouldn't mind my family and friends disliking me, or being poor and disappointed. I'd live in a garret on black bread. I'd suffer, being dissatisfied with myself and knowing how imperfect I was. But I should insist on being a real celebrity, with all the tumult and the shouting that go with it. [*Covers her face with her hands.*] My head's swimming. Oh dear!

IRINA [*off-stage, speaking from inside the house*]. Boris!

TRIGORIN. I'm wanted. This means I have to pack. But I don't feel like leaving. [*Looks round at the lake.*] I say, isn't it superb! Wonderful!

NINA. You see the house and garden on the other side?

TRIGORIN. Yes.

NINA. That was poor Mother's place. I was born there, I've spent my whole life near this lake and I know every little island on it.

TRIGORIN. It's a wonderful spot. [*Looking at the seagull.*] What's that?

NINA. A seagull. Constantine shot it.

TRIGORIN. A beautiful bird. I really don't feel like leaving. Can't you persuade Irina to stay? [*Makes a note in his book.*]

NINA. What are you writing?

TRIGORIN. Nothing, just a note. An idea for a plot. [*Putting his book away.*] A plot for a short story. A young girl like you has lived all her life by a lake. Like a seagull, she loves the lake, and she's happy and free like a seagull. But a man happens to come along and wrecks her life for want of anything better to do. As happened to this seagull.

[*Pause.* IRINA *appears at a window.*]

IRINA. Boris, where are you?

TRIGORIN. Coming. [*Moves off and looks back at* NINA. *Near the window, to* IRINA.] What is it?

IRINA. We're staying.

[TRIGORIN *goes indoors.*]

NINA [*comes to the front of the stage, after some reflection*]. It's all a dream.

CURTAIN

ACT THREE

The dining-room in SORIN's *house. Doors, right and left. A side-board and medicine cupboard. A table in the middle of the room. A suitcase, cardboard boxes and other signs of an impending departure.* TRIGORIN *is having lunch and* MASHA *stands by the table.*

MASHA. I'm telling you all this because you're a writer and can use it. Quite honestly, if he'd wounded himself seriously I couldn't have gone on living one minute. I'm quite brave, though, so I simply decided to wrench this love out of my heart and uproot it.

TRIGORIN. But how?

MASHA. By getting married. To Medvedenko.

TRIGORIN. That schoolmaster?

MASHA. Yes.

TRIGORIN. I don't see the need.

MASHA. To be hopelessly in love, just waiting, waiting for years on end—. But when I'm married I shan't bother about love, new worries will drive out old, and anyway it'll make a change, won't it? Shall we have another?

TRIGORIN. Aren't you overdoing it a bit?

MASHA. Oh, come on. [*Fills two glasses.*] Don't look at me like that, women drink a lot more than you think. A few do it openly like me, but most keep quiet about it. Oh yes they do. And it's always vodka or brandy. [*Clinks glasses.*] All the best. You're a decent sort, I'm sorry we shan't see each other again. [*They drink.*]

TRIGORIN. I don't want to go, actually.

MASHA. Then ask her to stay.

TRIGORIN. No, she won't stay now. Her son's being very tactless. First he tries to shoot himself, and now they say he means to challenge me to a duel. Why? He frets, fusses, crusades about new artistic forms—but there's plenty of room for both new and old, isn't there? Must we get in each other's way?

MASHA. He's just jealous. No business of mine, anyway.

[*Pause.* JACOB *crosses the stage from left to right, carrying a suitcase.* NINA *comes in and stands by the window.*]

MASHA. My schoolmaster's not all that bright, but he is kind. He's poor and very much in love with me. I'm sorry for him, and for his old mother too. Ah well, let me wish you all the best. Remember me kindly. [*Shakes him firmly by the hand.*] Thanks for being so nice. Send me your books, and mind you write something in them, not 'with respects'. Just put: 'To Masha, who doesn't know where she comes from or what she's doing on this earth'. Good-bye. [*Goes out.*]

NINA [*stretching one arm towards* TRIGORIN *with the fist clenched*]. Odd or even?

TRIGORIN. Even.

NINA [*with a sigh*]. Wrong, it's odd. I was trying to decide whether to go on the stage or not, I wish someone would advise me.

TRIGORIN. You can't give advice about that sort of thing. [*Pause.*]

NINA. We're parting, perhaps we'll never meet again. Please accept this little medallion to remember me by. I had your initials engraved on it, and there's the title of your book *Days and Nights* on the other side.

TRIGORIN. How charming. [*Kisses the medallion.*] A delightful present.

NINA. Think of me sometimes.

TRIGORIN. I shall indeed, I'll think of you as you were on that sunny day—remember?—a week ago, when you wore your light dress. We were talking and there was that white bird lying on the bench.

NINA [*thoughtfully*]. Yes, the seagull. [*Pause.*] We can't talk any more, someone's coming. Give me two minutes before you go—please. [*Goes out, left. At the same time* IRINA *comes in, right, with* SORIN, *who wears a tail-coat with the star of some decoration. He is followed by* JACOB, *who attends to the luggage.*]

IRINA. Stay at home, old boy. You shouldn't go gadding about, not with your rheumatism. [*To* TRIGORIN.] Who went out just then? Nina?

TRIGORIN. Yes.

IRINA. I'm sorry, we're intruding. [*Sits down.*] I think I've packed everything. I'm worn out.

TRIGORIN [*reads the inscription on the medallion*]. 'Days and Nights, page 121, lines 11 and 12.'

JACOB [*clearing the table*]. Shall I pack your fishing-rods too, sir?

TRIGORIN. Yes, I'll be needing them, but you can give away the books.

JACOB. Yes sir.

TRIGORIN [*to himself*]. 'Page 121, lines 11 and 12.' I wonder what those lines are. [*To* IRINA.] Are there any of my books in the house?

IRINA. Yes, in the corner bookcase in my brother's study.

TRIGORIN. 'Page 121.' [*Goes out.*]

IRINA. You really should stay indoors, Peter.

SORIN. You're leaving and I'll be miserable here without you.

IRINA. But what can you do in town?

SORIN. Nothing much, but still—. [*Laughs.*] They're laying the foundation stone of the new council building and so on. I just want to get out of this backwater for a couple of hours, I feel as stale as someone's old cigarette-holder. I've ordered my carriage for one o'clock, so we can leave together.

IRINA [*after a pause*]. Well, enjoy yourself here, don't get bored or catch cold. And do look after Constantine—take care of him and keep him in order. [*Pause.*] When I leave I still shan't know why Constantine tried to shoot himself. Jealousy was the main reason, I fancy, and the sooner I get Trigorin out of here the better.

SORIN. How can I put it? There was more to it than that. A clever young man, buried in the country, with no money, position or future, with nothing to do either—well, it stands to reason. He's afraid and ashamed to be so idle. I'm very fond of him, and he's devoted to me. Still, he feels he doesn't really belong here, that's what it comes to—feels like a hanger-on or poor relation. It's just a matter of pride, stands to reason.

IRINA. Oh, isn't he a nuisance! [*Thoughtfully.*] Why can't he get a job or something?

SORIN [*whistles, then speaks hesitantly*]. I think it would be best if you—well, let him have a bit of cash. He ought to dress decently for a start and so on. Well, look, he's been going round in that wretched jacket for the last three years and he has no overcoat. [*Laughs.*] It wouldn't hurt the boy to have a bit of fun, go abroad or something— it doesn't cost all that much, you know.

IRINA. Yes, but still—. I might run to a suit, but as for going abroad—.

No, the way things are I can't afford even a suit. [*Decisively.*] I haven't any money.

[SORIN *laughs.*]

IRINA. I haven't!

SORIN [*whistles*]. Very well then. I'm sorry, dear, don't be angry. I believe you. You're a fine, generous woman.

IRINA [*through tears*]. I haven't any money.

SORIN. If I had some I'd give it him myself, stands to reason. But I haven't, I'm broke. [*Laughs.*] My manager takes all my pension and spends it on raising crops, cattle and bees, and my money's all wasted. The bees die, the cows die, and they won't let me use the horses.

IRINA. Well, I do have some money, but I am an actress, you know. My dresses alone have ruined me.

SORIN. You're a nice, kind woman. I think highly of you, indeed I do. But there's something wrong with me again. [*Staggers.*] I feel dizzy. [*Grips the table.*] I feel unwell and so on.

IRINA [*terrified*]. Peter! [*Trying to support him.*] Peter, darling! [*Shouts.*] Help me! Help!

[*Enter* TREPLEV, *with a bandage round his head, and* MEDVEDENKO.]

IRINA. He feels faint.

SORIN. Never mind, it's all right. [*Smiles and drinks some water.*] It's over now and so on.

TREPLEV [*to his mother*]. Don't be frightened, Mother, it's nothing serious. Uncle's been taken like this quite often lately. [*To his uncle.*] You should lie down, Uncle.

SORIN. For a bit, all right. But I'm still going to town. I'll lie down a bit and then go, stands to reason. [*Moves off, leaning on a stick.*]

MEDVEDENKO [*takes his arm*]. Do you know this riddle? 'What walks on four legs in the morning, on two legs at noon and on three legs in the evening?'

SORIN [*laughs*]. Yes, I know. 'And spends the night on its back.' I can manage by myself, thanks very much.

MEDVEDENKO. Come, don't stand on ceremony. [*He and* SORIN *go out.*]

IRINA. How he did scare me.

TREPLEV. Country life's bad for him, it gets him down. Now, Mother, if you suddenly felt generous and lent him a thousand or two, he could spend a whole year in town.

IRINA. I haven't any money. I'm an actress, not a banker. [*Pause.*]

TREPLEV. Will you change my bandage, Mother? You do it so well.

IRINA [*gets some iodine and a box of bandages out of the medicine cupboard*]. The doctor's late.

TREPLEV. He said he'd be here by ten, and it's midday already.

IRINA. Sit down. [*Takes the bandage off his head.*] It looks like a turban. Yesterday there was some visitor in the kitchen asking what nationality you were. Well, it's almost healed up, there's not much wrong now. [*Kisses his head.*] You won't do anything naughty again after I've left, will you?

TREPLEV. No, Mother. That was an instant of wild despair when I couldn't control myself, it won't happen again. [*Kisses her hand.*] You have such wonderful hands. I remember long ago when you were still appearing in the State Theatres and I was a little boy—there was a fight in our yard and one of the tenants, a washerwoman, got hurt badly. She was picked up unconscious, remember? You used to visit her, take her medicine and bath her children in a tub. Don't you remember?

IRINA. No. [*Puts on a fresh bandage.*]

TREPLEV. There were two girls, ballet-dancers, living in the same house. They used to come and have coffee with you.

IRINA. That I do remember.

TREPLEV. They were frightfully pious. [*Pause.*] Just lately, these last few days, I find I love you as tenderly and devotedly as when I was a little boy. I've no one left but you now. But why, why do you give in to that man?

IRINA. You don't understand him, Constantine. He's a fine character.

TREPLEV. Still, when he heard I meant to challenge him to a duel, his fine character didn't save him from an attack of cold feet. He's leaving, running away with his tail between his legs.

IRINA. Don't be silly, I asked him to leave myself.

TREPLEV. A fine character! You and I nearly quarrel over him, while he's in the drawing-room or garden or somewhere, laughing at us, and—drawing Nina out, trying to make her see what a genius he is.

IRINA. You do so enjoy being disagreeable to me. I respect Trigorin, so please don't be nasty about him when I'm around.

TREPLEV. Well, I don't respect him. You want me to think he's a genius too, but I'm no good at lying, sorry, and his books just make me sick.

IRINA. You're envious. Pretentious nobodies always run down really brilliant people, that's all they're good for. I only hope it makes you feel better.

TREPLEV [*ironically*]. Really brilliant people! [*Angrily.*] I'm more talented than all you lot put together, if it comes to that. [*Tears the bandage off his head.*] You hacks have a stranglehold on the arts. You don't recognize or put up with anything except what you do yourselves, everything else you sit on and crush. But I don't accept you! I don't accept either you or him.

IRINA. Miserable decadent!

TREPLEV. Run along to your precious theatre and act in your rotten feeble plays!

IRINA. I've never acted in such plays. Leave me alone! You couldn't even write a tenth-rate farce. Provincial shopkeeper! Scrounger!

TREPLEV. Miser!

IRINA. Tramp!

[TREPLEV *sits down and quietly cries.*]

IRINA. You nobody! [*Walking up and down excitedly.*] Don't cry. Stop crying. [*Cries.*] Do stop. [*Kisses his forehead, cheeks and head.*] My darling boy, I'm sorry. Forgive your wicked mother. Forgive me, I'm so unhappy.

TREPLEV [*puts his arms round her*]. Oh, if you did but know! I've nothing left. She doesn't love me and I can't write any more. My hopes have all come to nothing.

IRINA. Don't give up, it'll all come right. He's going away now and she'll love you again. [*Wipes away his tears.*] Don't cry. We're friends again.

TREPLEV [*kisses her hands*]. Yes, Mother.

IRINA [*tenderly*]. And you make it up with him too. We can't have a duel, can we?

TREPLEV. All right. But I don't want to meet him, Mother, do you mind? This business depresses me, I can't cope.

[TRIGORIN *comes in.*]

TREPLEV. Oh—I'll go. [*Quickly clears the first-aid material into the cupboard.*] The doctor can put my bandage on later.

TRIGORIN [*looking in a book*]. Page 121, lines 11 and 12. Ah. [*Reads.*] 'If you should ever need my life, then come and take it.'

[TREPLEV *picks the bandage off the floor and goes out.*]

IRINA [*glancing at her watch*]. The carriage will be here soon.

TRIGORIN [*to himself*]. 'If you should ever need my life, then come and take it.'

IRINA. I hope all your things are packed?

TRIGORIN [*impatiently*]. Yes, yes. [*Thoughtfully.*] This appeal from a pure, innocent girl—why does it sound so sad? Why does it wring my heart so painfully? 'If you should ever need my life, then come and take it.' [*To* IRINA.] Let's stay another day.

[IRINA *shakes her head.*]

TRIGORIN. Let's stay.

IRINA. I know why you want to stay, dear, but you must pull yourself together. You're a little intoxicated, so sober down.

TRIGORIN. Then you sober down as well—be reasonable and sensible, please. You must look on all this as a true friend. [*Presses her hand.*] You're capable of sacrifice. So be a friend and set me free.

IRINA [*greatly upset*]. Are you so infatuated?

TRIGORIN. She attracts me. Perhaps this is just what I need.

IRINA. The love of a little provincial miss? How little you know yourself.

TRIGORIN. You know how people sometimes sleep-walk? Talking to you now, I feel as if I was asleep, dreaming of her. I'm possessed by visions of delight. Do set me free.

IRINA [*trembling*]. No, no, no. You can't talk to me like that, I'm only an ordinary woman. Don't torture me, Boris. I'm terrified.

TRIGORIN. You can be extraordinary if you want. Young love, enchanting and magical love that sweeps you off your feet into a make-believe world—can anything else on this earth give one happiness? I've never known such love before—never had time for it as a young man because I was for ever hanging round editors' offices and trying to make ends meet. But now, you see, this love has come at last, it calls me on. Why should I run away from it?

IRINA [*angrily*]. You must be mad.

TRIGORIN. Perhaps I am.

IRINA. You're all conspiring to torment me today. [*Cries.*]

TRIGORIN [*clutches his head*]. She doesn't understand, she won't understand.

IRINA. Am I really so old and ugly that you don't mind talking to me about other women? [*Embraces and kisses him.*] Oh, you're mad. My marvellous, splendid man. You're the last page in my life. [*Kneels down.*] My delight, my pride, my joy! [*Embraces his knees.*] If you leave me for one hour I shan't survive, I shall go mad, my wonderful, splendid one. My master.

TRIGORIN. Someone might come in. [*Helps her to her feet.*]

IRINA. Let them, I'm not ashamed of loving you. [*Kisses his hands.*] My dear, reckless boy, you want to do something crazy, but I won't have it, I won't let you. [*Laughs.*] You're mine, mine. This forehead's mine, these eyes are mine, this lovely silky hair's mine too. You're mine, all of you. You're so brilliant, so clever, you're the best writer of our day—Russia's only hope, so sincere and natural, with your spontaneity and healthy humour. You can put over the essence of a person or landscape with one stroke of the pen. Your characters are so alive, one can't read you without being moved. Too much hero-worship, you think? Think I'm flattering you? Then look in my eyes, come on. Do I look like a liar? There, you see, I'm the only one who appreciates you, I'm the only one who tells you the truth, my wonderful darling. You will come, won't you? You won't desert me, will you?

TRIGORIN. I've no will of my own, never have had. I'm a flabby, spineless creature that always does what it's told—surely that's not what women like. Take me then, carry me off, but don't ever let me move one step from your side.

IRINA [*to herself*]. Now he's mine. [*Off-handedly and casually.*] Actually, you can stay on if you want. I'll leave on my own and you can come later, in a week's time. What's the hurry, after all?

TRIGORIN. No, we may as well go together.

IRINA. As you like. We'll go together if you say so.

[*Pause.* TRIGORIN *makes a note in his book.*]

IRINA. What's that?

TRIGORIN. I heard a good phrase this morning—'a virgin pine-wood'. It might come in. [*Stretches.*] So we're going, are we? More railway carriages, stations, refreshment-rooms, mutton-chops and talk.

SHAMRAYEV [*comes in*]. I have the honour to announce with great regret that your carriage is ready. It's time to leave for the station, dearest lady, the train's due in at five past two. Now, would you do me a favour—remember to ask where the actor Suzdaltsev is these days? Is he alive and kicking? We're old drinking companions. He used to steal the show in *The Mail-Coach Robbery*. In those days, I remember, Izmaylov—another remarkable personality who played in tragedies—belonged to the same company in Yelizavetgrad. There's no hurry, dearest lady, you've another five minutes. They were playing the villains in a melodrama once, when they were suddenly caught and Izmaylov was supposed to say: 'We're caught in a trap'. But he said: 'We're trapped in a court'. [*Laughs loudly.*] Trapped in a court!

[*While he is speaking,* JACOB *is busy with the suitcases. The* MAID *brings* IRINA *her hat, cloak, umbrella and gloves. All help* IRINA *into her clothes. The* CHEF *looks in through the door, left, and comes in after some hesitation.* POLINA *comes in, followed by* SORIN *and* MEDVEDENKO.]

POLINA [*with a basket*]. Here are some plums for the journey—very sweet, you might feel like a bite.

IRINA. You're most kind, Polina.

POLINA. Good-bye, my dear. I'm sorry if there's been anything amiss. [*Cries.*]

IRINA [*embraces her*]. Everything's been wonderful, just wonderful—there's no need to cry.

POLINA. Our time is nearly over.

IRINA. That can't be helped.

SORIN [*comes in through the door, left, wearing a hooded coat and a hat, and carrying a stick. Passes through the room*]. It's time we left, Irina, or we may miss the train, that's what it comes to. I'll get in the carriage. [*Goes out.*]

MEDVEDENKO. I'll walk to the station and see them off. It won't take long. [*Goes out.*]

IRINA. Good-bye, darlings. We'll meet again next summer if we're alive and well. [*The* MAID, JACOB *and the* CHEF *kiss her hand.*] Now, don't forget me. [*Gives the* CHEF *a rouble.*] Here's a rouble for you three.

CHEF. Thank you kindly, madam. Have a good journey. Thank you for your kindness.

JACOB. God speed.

SHAMRAYEV. Do drop us a line. Good-bye, Trigorin.

IRINA. Where's Constantine? Will you tell him I'm leaving? I must say good-bye. Ah well, don't think too badly of me. [*To* JACOB.] I gave the cook a rouble. That's for the three of you.

[*All go out, right. The stage is empty. The sound of leave-taking off-stage. The* MAID *comes back to fetch the basket of plums from the table and goes out again.*]

TRIGORIN [*coming back*]. I forgot my stick, I think it's on the terrace there. [*Moves off and meets* NINA *as she comes in through the door, left.*] Ah, it's you. We're just off.

NINA. I was sure we'd meet again. [*Excitedly.*] Mr. Trigorin, I've made up my mind once and for all, I've burnt my boats and I'm going on the stage. I shan't be here tomorrow, I'm leaving Father and throwing everything up to start a new life. I'm going away, same as you—to Moscow. We'll meet there.

TRIGORIN [*looking round*]. Put up at the *Slav Fair*. Let me know at once, I'll be in Molchanov Street—Grokholsky House. I must hurry. [*Pause.*]

NINA. Just a moment——

TRIGORIN [*in an undertone*]. You're so lovely. What happiness to think we'll soon meet again! [*She leans her head on his chest.*] Once more I'll see your wonderful eyes, your tender smile, lovely beyond description. Your soft features, your look of angelic purity. My darling—. [*A lengthy kiss.*]

CURTAIN

There is an interval of two years between Acts Three and Four.

ACT FOUR

A drawing-room in SORIN's *house, which* TREPLEV *has turned into a study. Doors, right and left, leading into inner rooms. Facing the audience, a french window opening on a terrace. Besides the usual drawing-room furniture there is a desk in the corner, right. Near the door, left, an ottoman. A bookcase. Books on window-ledges and chairs.*

Evening. One shaded lamp is alight. It is rather dark. Sound of trees rustling and of wind howling in the chimneys. A watchman is banging. MEDVEDENKO *and* MASHA *come in.*

MASHA [*calling out*]. Constantine, Constantine! [*Looking round.*] No one about. The old man keeps asking for Constantine every minute of the day. He must have him around.

MEDVEDENKO. He's afraid of being lonely. [*Listening.*] What horrible weather, this is the second day of it.

MASHA [*turning up the lamp*]. The lake's very rough, there are huge waves.

MEDVEDENKO. It's dark in the garden. That stage out there—they should have had it knocked down. There it stands, bare and ugly as a skeleton, with the curtain banging in the wind. Going past last night I thought I heard someone crying there.

MASHA. Ah well. [*Pause.*]

MEDVEDENKO. Come home, Masha.

MASHA [*shakes her head*]. I'm staying here tonight.

MEDVEDENKO [*imploringly*]. Come on, Masha, baby must be hungry.

MASHA. I don't care, let Matryona feed it. [*Pause.*]

MEDVEDENKO. I'm sorry for him, this'll be three nights without his mother.

MASHA. You are a bore these days. You did have a little general conversation once, but now it's all baby, baby, baby, home, home, home. That's all you ever say.

MEDVEDENKO. Come on, Masha.

MASHA. You can go by yourself.

MEDVEDENKO. Your father won't give me a horse.

MASHA. Oh yes he will if you ask him.

MEDVEDENKO. Perhaps I will then. So you'll come tomorrow?

MASHA [*takes snuff*]. All right, tomorrow. Can't you leave me alone?

[TREPLEV *and* POLINA *come in.* TREPLEV *carries pillows and a blanket, and* POLINA *has some bed-linen. They put them on the ottoman, after which* TREPLEV *sits at his desk.*]

MASHA. Who's that for, Mother?

POLINA. Mr. Sorin asked to have a bed made up in Constantine's room.

MASHA. Let me do it. [*Makes the bed.*]

POLINA [*with a sigh*]. Old men are such children. [*Goes up to the desk, leans her elbows on it and looks at a manuscript. Pause.*]

MEDVEDENKO. I'll go then. Good night, Masha. [*Kisses his wife's hand.*] Good night, Mother. [*Tries to kiss his mother-in-law's hand.*]

POLINA [*annoyed*]. Well, go if you're going.

MEDVEDENKO. Good night, Constantine.

[TREPLEV *silently shakes hands.* MEDVEDENKO *goes out.*]

POLINA [*looking at the manuscript*]. No one ever dreamt you'd be a real author, Constantine, but now the magazines have started paying you, thank goodness. [*Strokes his hair.*] You've become good-looking too. Please be a bit nicer to my poor Masha, dear.

MASHA [*making up the bed*]. Leave him alone, Mother.

POLINA [*to* TREPLEV]. She's such a nice girl. [*Pause.*] A woman needs nothing, Constantine, just a few kind looks. I've learnt that.

[TREPLEV *gets up from the desk and goes out without speaking.*]

MASHA. Now you've annoyed him. Why go on at him?

POLINA. I'm sorry for you, Masha.

MASHA. A lot of use that is!

POLINA. My heart aches for you. I see everything, you know, I understand.

MASHA. Don't be so silly. Unhappy love affairs are only found in novels. What nonsense! The thing is, don't give way to it, and don't moon around waiting for the tide to turn. If love enters your heart, get rid of it. My husband's been promised a job in another part of the country. I'm going to forget all this when we move. I'll tear it from my heart.

[*A melancholy waltz is played in the next room but one.*]

POLINA. That's Constantine playing, he must be depressed.

MASHA [*silently does two or three waltz steps*]. The thing is not to keep seeing him, Mother. If only Simon gets that new job, I'll be over this in a month, take it from me. It's all so silly.

[*The door, left, opens.* DORN *and* MEDVEDENKO *push* SORIN *through in his bath-chair.*]

MEDVEDENKO. I've six mouths to feed now, and with flour at two copecks a pound.

DORN. He can hardly make ends meet.

MEDVEDENKO. All right, laugh—you're rolling in money.

DORN. Oh, am I? My friend, in thirty years of practice—a busy practice with hardly a moment to call my own, day or night—I managed to save only two thousand roubles and I just got through those on my trip abroad. I'm broke.

MASHA [*to her husband*]. Still here?

MEDVEDENKO [*guiltily*]. Can I help it if they won't give me a horse?

MASHA [*bitterly annoyed, in a low voice*]. Out of my sight!

[*The bath-chair comes to rest on stage left.* POLINA, MASHA *and* DORN *sit down near it.* MEDVEDENKO, *saddened, moves to one side.*]

DORN. You've made a lot of changes, though. You've turned the drawing-room into a study.

MASHA. It's better for Constantine's work, he can go in the garden and think when he wants to.

[*The watchman bangs.*]

SORIN. Where's my sister?

DORN. Gone to the station to meet Trigorin, she'll be back any moment.

SORIN. If you felt my sister had to be sent for, I really must be ill. [*After a short pause.*] It's a funny thing—I'm seriously ill, but I don't get any medicine.

DORN. What would you like? Valerian drops? Soda? Quinine?

SORIN. Oh, the speeches have started. This is the limit. [*Nods towards the sofa.*] Is that bed for me?

POLINA. Yes.

SORIN. Thank you.

DORN [*singing softly*]. 'See the moon floating by in the evening sky.'

SORIN. I'd like to give Constantine a plot for a novel. It ought to be called *The Man who Wanted—L'homme qui a voulu*. In youth I wanted to become a writer—I didn't. I wanted to speak well—I spoke atrociously. [*Mocks himself.*] 'And all that sort, er, of thing, er, don't yer know.' I'd be doing a summing-up sometimes, and find myself jawing on and on till I broke out in a sweat. I wanted to marry—I didn't. I wanted to live in town all the time—and here I am ending my days in the country and so on.

DORN. You wanted to become a senior civil servant—and did.

SORIN [*laughs*]. That's one thing I wasn't keen on, it just happened.

DORN. To talk about being fed up with life at the age of sixty-two—that's a bit cheap, wouldn't you say?

SORIN. Don't keep on about it, can't you see I want a bit of life?

DORN. That's just silly. All life must end, it's in the nature of things.

SORIN. You're spoilt, that's why you talk like this. You've always had what you wanted, so life doesn't matter to you, you just don't bother. But even you'll be afraid of dying.

DORN. Fear of death's an animal thing, you must get over it. It only makes sense to fear death if you believe in immortality and are scared because you've sinned. But you aren't a Christian for a start, and then—what sins have you committed? You've worked for the Department of Justice for twenty-five years, that's all.

SORIN [*laughs*]. Twenty-eight.

[TREPLEV *comes in and sits down on a stool at* SORIN'*s feet.* MASHA *stares at him throughout.*]

DORN. We're stopping Constantine working.

TREPLEV. No, it's all right. [*Pause.*]

MEDVEDENKO. Doctor, which town did you like best abroad, may one ask?

DORN. Genoa.

TREPLEV. Why Genoa?

DORN. The street life is so wonderful. Leaving your hotel in the evening, you find the whole street jammed with people, and you drift round in the crowd, going any old where in any old direction. You share its life, enter into its spirit and begin to think there really could be such a thing as a World Spirit, like the one Nina Zarechny once acted in your play. By the way, where is Miss Zarechny these days? Where is she and how is she?

TREPLEV. She's well, I presume.

DORN. I heard she was leading a rather odd life. What's it all about?

TREPLEV. That's a long story, Doctor.

DORN. Then make it short. [*Pause.*]

TREPLEV. She ran away from home and had an affair with Trigorin. You knew that?

DORN. Yes.

TREPLEV. She had a baby. It died. Trigorin tired of her and returned to his former attachments, as could only be expected. He never really gave them up in point of fact, but somehow contrived in his feeble way to keep a foot in both camps. Nina's private life has been a disaster so far as I can see.

DORN. And her stage career?

TREPLEV. Even worse, I think. She started off in a theatre at a resort near Moscow somewhere, then went to the provinces. I kept her under observation at the time, followed her about for a while. She always took leading roles, but her acting was crude and inept, with lots of ranting and hamming. She had her moments when she screamed superbly and died superbly. But moments they remained.

DORN. Then she must be some good after all?

TREPLEV. It was hard to tell. I suppose so. I saw her, but she wouldn't see me and the hotel servants wouldn't let me in her room. I knew how she felt and didn't insist on a meeting. [*Pause.*] What else can I say? Back home afterwards I had some letters from her—bright, affectionate, interesting letters. She didn't complain, but I sensed that she was deeply unhappy. Every line seemed sick, like a frayed nerve, and her mind was slightly unhinged. She used to sign herself 'Seagull'. Like the miller who calls himself a raven in Pushkin's *Mermaid*, she kept calling herself a seagull in her letters. Now she's here.

DORN. Here? What do you mean?

TREPLEV. Staying at an inn in town, she's been there four or five days. I was going to visit her and Masha here went over, but she won't see anyone. Simon Medvedenko claims he saw her yesterday afternoon somewhere in the fields a couple of miles away.

MEDVEDENKO. Yes I did, she was walking away from here towards town. I bowed, asked why she didn't come over. She said she would.

TREPLEV. She won't. [*Pause.*] Her father and stepmother will have nothing to do with her, they've posted look-outs everywhere to stop her even going near the place. [*Moves towards the desk with the* DOCTOR.] It's easy enough to be a philosopher on paper, Doctor, but how hard to act like one!

SORIN. She was a delightful girl.

DORN. What?

SORIN. She was a delightful girl, I say. Mr. Senior Civil Servant Sorin was even in love with her for a bit.

DORN. Ah, you old dog.

[SHAMRAYEV's *laugh is heard from off-stage.*]

POLINA. I think the others have just got back from the station.

TREPLEV. Yes, I hear Mother.

[*Enter* IRINA *and* TRIGORIN, *followed by* SHAMRAYEV.]

SHAMRAYEV [*coming in*]. We don't get any younger, we're all a bit weather-beaten through exposure to the elements—but you're still as young as ever, dearest lady, in that gay blouse, so lively and graceful.

IRINA. You'll bring me bad luck again, you tiresome man.

TRIGORIN [*to* SORIN]. Good evening, Peter. Why are you always unwell? It's very wrong of you. [*Seeing* MASHA, *delightedly.*] Masha!

MASHA. So you do recognize me? [*Shakes hands.*]

TRIGORIN. Married?

MASHA. Ages ago.

TRIGORIN. Happy? [*Exchanges bows with* DORN *and* MEDVEDENKO, *then hesitantly approaches* TREPLEV.] Irina says you've forgotten the past and aren't angry any more.

[TREPLEV *holds out his hand.*]

IRINA [*to her son*]. Look, Boris brought the magazine with your new story.

TREPLEV [*taking the volume, to* TRIGORIN]. Thank you, most kind of you. [*They sit down.*]

TRIGORIN. Your admirers send their best wishes. There's great interest in you in St. Petersburg and Moscow, and I'm always being asked about you—what's he like, how old is he, is he dark or fair? Somehow everyone thinks you're not all that young. And you publish under a pseudonym, so no one knows your real name. You're an enigma like the Man in the Iron Mask.

TREPLEV. Are you staying long?

TRIGORIN. No, I intend to go back to Moscow tomorrow, I have to. There's a novel I must finish soon, and then I promised to do something for a collection of stories. Business as usual, in other words.

[*While they are speaking,* IRINA *and* POLINA *put a card-table in the middle of the room and open it.* SHAMRAYEV *lights candles and places chairs round it. They take a game of lotto out of the cupboard.*]

TRIGORIN. The weather's not being very kind, there's a nasty wind. If it drops by tomorrow morning, I'm going fishing by the lake. And I must look at the garden while I'm about it, and the place where your play was put on—remember? I've a subject for a story and I only need to refresh my memory of the scene.

MASHA [*to her father*]. Father, can Simon have a horse? He must get home.

SHAMRAYEV [*derisively*]. Horse? Must get home? [*Sternly.*] They've only just been to the station, you can see for yourself. We can hardly have them out again.

MASHA. There are other horses. [*As her father does not speak, makes a gesture of despair.*] Oh, you're impossible.

MEDVEDENKO. I can walk, Masha, really——

POLINA [*with a sigh*]. Walk in weather like this! [*Sits down at the card-table.*] Come on, all of you.

MEDVEDENKO. Well, it's only four miles. Good night. [*Kisses his wife's hand.*] Good night, Mother. [*His mother-in-law reluctantly holds out her hand for him to kiss.*] If it weren't for the baby I wouldn't have bothered anyone. [*Bows to everyone.*] Good night. [*Goes out, walking in an apologetic way.*]

SHAMRAYEV. He can walk, can't he? He's not all that high and mighty.

POLINA [*bangs the table*]. Come on, everyone. Let's not waste time, they'll be calling us for supper soon.

[SHAMRAYEV, MASHA *and* DORN *sit at the table.*]

IRINA [*to* TRIGORIN]. In the long autumn evenings one plays lotto in these parts—look, the same old lotto that my mother played with us as children. Won't you have a game before supper? [*Sits at the table with* TRIGORIN.] It's boring, but not bad when you get used to it. [*Deals everyone three cards.*]

TREPLEV [*turning the pages of the magazine*]. He read his own story, but didn't even cut the pages of mine. [*Puts the magazine on the desk, then moves towards the door, left. Passing his mother, he kisses her on the head.*]

IRINA. How about you, Constantine?

TREPLEV. Sorry, I don't feel much like it, I'm going for a stroll. [*Goes out.*]

IRINA. The stake's ten copecks. Will you put up ten copecks for me, Doctor?

DORN. All right.

MASHA. Have you all staked? I'll begin. Twenty-two.

IRINA. Yes.

MASHA. Three.

DORN. Right.

MASHA. Have you put down three? Eight. Eighty-one. Ten.

SHAMRAYEV. Don't go so fast.

IRINA. I had such a reception in Kharkov, dears, I'm still dizzy.

MASHA. Thirty-four.

[*A sad waltz is played off-stage.*]

IRINA. The students almost brought the house down. I had three baskets of flowers, two bouquets and this. [*Takes a brooch from her breast and throws it on the table.*]

SHAMRAYEV. Yes, that's quite something.

MASHA. Fifty.

DORN. You mean five-oh?

IRINA. I was superbly turned out—that's something I do know, how to dress.

POLINA. Constantine's playing the piano—he's depressed, poor boy.

SHAMRAYEV. They're so nasty about him in the newspapers.

MASHA. Seventy-seven.

IRINA. He's a fool to let that bother him.

TRIGORIN. Things aren't going too well, he still can't find his real level. There's something vaguely odd about his stuff, and some of it even seems rather wild. None of his characters is ever really alive.

MASHA. Eleven.

IRINA [*looking round at* SORIN]. Bored, Peter? [*Pause.*] He's asleep.

DORN. Our senior civil servant's asleep.

MASHA. Seven. Ninety.

TRIGORIN. You wouldn't catch me writing if I lived in a house by a lake like this. I'd get over the urge and do nothing but fish.

MASHA. Twenty-eight.

TRIGORIN. To catch a perch or a ruff—what bliss!

DORN. Well, I believe in Constantine. He's got something, I tell you. He thinks in images, his stories are bright and vivid and I find them very moving. I'm only sorry he has no definite aims. He produces an effect, that's all, and mere effects don't get you all that far, do they? Are you glad your son's an author, Irina?

IRINA. You know, I've never yet read his stuff, never have time.

MASHA. Twenty-six.

[TREPLEV *comes in quietly and goes to his desk.*]

SHAMRAYEV [*to* TRIGORIN]. We still have that thing of yours, Boris.

TRIGORIN. What thing?

SHAMRAYEV. Constantine shot a seagull that time and you asked me to have it stuffed.

TRIGORIN. I can't remember. [*Reflecting.*] I can't remember.

MASHA. Sixty-six. One.

TREPLEV [*throws open the window and listens*]. Isn't it dark! I'm terribly worried, I don't know why.

IRINA. Do close the window, Constantine, there's a draught.

[TREPLEV *closes the window.*]

MASHA. Eighty-eight.

TRIGORIN. I've won, everybody.

IRINA [*gaily*]. Well done, well done.

SHAMRAYEV. Well done.

IRINA. The man's always lucky. [*Stands up.*] Now let's go and have a bite of something. The great man missed his lunch today. We'll go on again after supper. [*To her son.*] Leave your manuscripts, Constantine, and let's have supper.

TREPLEV. I won't, Mother, I'm not hungry.

IRINA. As you wish. [*Wakes* SORIN.] Peter, supper time. [*Takes* SHAMRAYEV's *arm.*] I'll tell you about my reception at Kharkov.

[POLINA *puts out the candles on the table. Then she and* DORN *wheel out the bath-chair. All go out by the door, left.* TREPLEV, *who is sitting at the desk, is left alone on the stage.*]

TREPLEV [*is intending to write and looks through what he has already written*]. I've talked so much about new techniques, but now I feel I'm gradually getting in the old rut. [*Reads.*] 'The notice on the fence stated.' 'A pale face, framed in dark hair.' 'Stated', 'framed'. Very second-rate. [*Crosses it out.*] I'll start when my hero's woken up by the rain and cut out all the rest. The description of the moonlit evening is long and forced. Trigorin's worked out his methods, it's easy enough for him. He gives you the neck of a broken bottle glittering against a weir and the black shadow of a mill-wheel—and there's your moonlit night all cut and dried. But I have a quivering light and the silent twinkling of the stars and the distant sound of a piano dying on the calm, scented air. This is agony. [*Pause.*] Yes, I'm more and more convinced that old or new techniques are neither here nor there. The thing is to write without thinking about technique—write from the heart, because it all comes pouring out. [*Someone knocks on the window nearest to the table.*] What's that? [*Looks through the window.*] Can't see anything. [*Opens the french window and looks into the garden.*] Someone ran down the steps. [*Calls.*] Who's there? [*Goes out and can be heard walking quickly along the terrace. Half a minute later he comes back with* NINA.] Nina, Nina!

[NINA *lays her head on his breast and sobs quietly.*]

TREPLEV [*very moved*]. Nina, Nina! It's you—you. I thought you'd come somehow, I've been terribly overwrought all day. [*Takes off her hat and cape.*] Oh, my dear, my darling. She's come! There now, don't cry.

NINA. There's someone here.

TREPLEV. No.

NINA. Lock the doors or someone may come in.

TREPLEV. No one will come in.

NINA. I know Irina Arkadin's here. Lock the doors.

TREPLEV [*locks the door, right, and goes over to the door, left*]. This one doesn't lock, I'll put a chair against it. [*Puts an armchair against the door.*] Don't worry, no one will come in.

NINA [*stares into his face*]. Let me look at you. [*Looks round the room.*] It's nice and warm. This used to be the drawing-room. Am I very changed?

TREPLEV. Yes. You're thinner and your eyes are bigger. It's somehow strange to be seeing you, Nina. Why wouldn't you let me visit you, why didn't you come and see us before? You've been here nearly a week, I know. I've been over every day several times and stood by your window like a beggar.

NINA. I was afraid you hated me. Every night I dream you look at me and don't recognize me. Oh, if only you knew! Ever since I arrived I've been going for walks—by the lake. I've been near your house lots of times, but couldn't bring myself to go in. Shall we sit down? [*They sit down.*] Let's sit down and talk and talk. It's nice and warm here, very cosy. Do you hear the wind? There's a passage in Turgenev: 'Lucky the man with a roof over his head and somewhere to be warm on a night like this'. I'm a seagull. No, that's wrong. [*Wipes her forehead.*] What was I saying? Oh yes, Turgenev. 'And may the Lord help all homeless wanderers.' Never mind. [*Sobs.*]

TREPLEV. Nina, you're crying again. Nina!

NINA. It's all right, it does me good. I hadn't cried for two years. I went in the garden late last night to see if our stage was still standing. And there it still is. I cried for the first time in two years, and it was such a relief, it did me a lot of good. See, I'm not crying any more. [*Takes him by the hand.*] So you're a writer now, you're a writer and I'm an actress, we've got caught up in this hectic whirl. I used to be as happy as a child and woke up singing in the morning, I loved you and dreamed of being famous. But now—. I have to go to Yelets early tomorrow morning, third class, along with the peasants. And when I get there I shall be pestered with the attentions of the more educated local businessmen. It's a rough life.

TREPLEV. Why Yelets?

NINA. I've taken an engagement for the winter. It's time I went.

TREPLEV. Nina, I cursed you, hated you, tore up your letters and photographs, but all along I've known that my whole being is bound up with you for ever. I can't help loving you, Nina. Since I lost you and began having my work published, life's been unbearable, sheer agony. It's as if I'd suddenly stopped being young, I feel as if I was ninety. I call upon you, kiss the ground you have trodden on. Wherever I look I see your face—the gentle smile that brightened the best years of my life.

NINA [*taken aback*]. Why does he say this—why, why?

TREPLEV. I'm lonely, I haven't the warmth of anyone's devotion. I feel cold, as in a vault, and all I write is so dry, stale, dismal. Stay here, Nina, I beg you, or let me go with you.

[NINA *quickly puts on her hat and cape.*]

TREPLEV. But why, Nina? For God's sake, Nina. [*Watches her put on her clothes. Pause.*]

NINA. My carriage is at the gate. Don't see me off, I'll manage on my own. [*Through tears.*] Give me some water.

TREPLEV [*gives her some*]. Where are you going now?

NINA. To town. [*Pause.*] Is Irina Arkadin here?

TREPLEV. Yes. Uncle was taken worse on Thursday and we telegraphed for her.

NINA. Why do you say you kissed the ground I trod on? I'm not fit to live. [*Bends over the table.*] Oh, I'm so tired, I need a rest, a rest. [*Lifts up her head.*] I'm a seagull. No, that's wrong. I'm an actress. Ah, well. [*Hearing* IRINA *and* TRIGORIN *laughing, she listens, then runs to the door, left, and looks through the keyhole.*] He's here too. [*Going back to* TREPLEV.] Ah, well. It doesn't matter. Yes. He didn't believe in the stage, he always laughed at my dreams and I gradually stopped believing too and lost heart. Then there were all the cares of love, jealousy and constant fears for the baby. I became petty and small-minded and my acting made no sense. I didn't know what to do with my hands or know how to stand on the stage, and I couldn't control my voice. You've no idea what it feels like to know you're acting abominably. I'm a seagull. No, that's wrong. Remember you shot a seagull? A man happened to come along, saw it and killed it, just to pass the time. A plot for a short story. No, that's wrong. [*Wipes her forehead.*] What was I saying? I was talking about the stage. Oh, I'm different now, I'm a real actress. I enjoy acting, I adore it. I get madly excited on stage, I feel I'm beautiful. And since I've been here, I've kept going for walks, walking round and thinking—thinking and feeling my morale improving every day. Constantine, I know now, I've come to see, that in our work—no matter whether we're actors or writers—the great thing isn't fame or glory, it isn't what I used to dream of, but simply stamina. You must know how to bear your cross and have faith. I have faith and things don't hurt me so much now. And when I think of my vocation I'm not afraid of life.

TREPLEV [*sadly*]. You've found your road and you know where you're going, while I still drift about in a maze of dreams and images, not knowing who needs my stuff or why. I've no faith and I don't know what my vocation is.

NINA [*pricking up her ears*]. Shush! I must go. Good-bye. Come and see me when I'm a great actress. Promise? But now—. [*Presses his hand.*] It's late. I can hardly stand—I'm so exhausted and hungry.

TREPLEV. Stay, I'll get you some supper.

NINA. No, no. Don't see me off, I'll go on my own. My carriage is quite near. So she brought him with her, did she? Oh well, what of it? When you see Trigorin, don't say anything to him. I love him—love him even more than before. A plot for a short story. I love him, love him passionately, desperately. Wasn't it nice in the old days, Constantine? Do you remember? What a life it was—so serene and warm, so happy and innocent. What emotions we felt—like exquisite, delicate blossoms. Do you remember? [*Recites.*] 'Men, lions, eagles and partridges, horned deer, geese, spiders and silent fishes, denizens of the deep, starfishes and creatures invisible—that is, all life, all life, all life—has completed its melancholy cycle and died. For thousands of centuries Earth has not borne one living creature, and in vain does that poor moon light her lamp. No longer do cranes awake and call in the meadows and no may-beetles can be heard in the lime-groves.' [*Embraces* TREPLEV *impulsively and runs out through the french window.*]

TREPLEV [*after a pause*]. It'll be a pity if anyone sees her in the garden and tells Mother. It might upset her. [*Spends two minutes silently tearing up all his manuscripts and throwing them under the desk, then unlocks the door, right, and goes out.*]

DORN [*trying to open the door, left*]. That's strange, the door seems to be locked. [*Comes in and puts the armchair back in its place.*] An obstacle race.

[IRINA *and* POLINA *come in, followed by* JACOB, *carrying some bottles, and* MASHA, *and finally by* SHAMRAYEV *and* TRIGORIN.]

IRINA. Put the claret and Mr. Trigorin's beer on the table here, we can have a drink with our game. Come on, everyone, sit down.

POLINA [*to* JACOB]. And please bring in the tea right away. [*Lights the candles and sits down at the card-table.*]

SHAMRAYEV [*takes* TRIGORIN *over to the cupboard*]. Here's the thing I was talking about just now. [*Takes the stuffed seagull from the cupboard.*] Your order, sir.

TRIGORIN [*looking at the seagull*]. I can't remember. [*After some thought.*] I can't remember.

[*A shot is heard from off-stage, right. Everyone gives a start.*]

IRINA [*terrified*]. What's that?

DORN. Don't worry. A bottle must have gone off inside my medical bag, don't worry. [*Goes out through door, right, and comes back half a minute later.*] As I said. A bottle of ether's exploded. [*Sings softly.*] 'Once more enchanted I appear before thee.'

IRINA [*sitting down at the table*]. Oh dear, I was frightened. It reminded me of when—. [*Covers her face with her hands.*] It made me feel quite ill.

DORN [*turning the pages of a magazine, to* TRIGORIN]. There was an article in this thing about two months ago, a letter from America, and I wanted to ask you, amongst other things—. [*Takes* TRIGORIN *by the waist and leads him to the front of the stage.*] Being extremely interested in this matter—. [*Dropping his voice, in an undertone.*] Get Irina out of here somehow. The fact is, Constantine has shot himself.

CURTAIN

APPENDIX I

PLATONOV

Platonov is the name often given for the sake of convenience by translators, literary historians and critics to the long, untitled four-act play by Chekhov preserved in the Soviet Central State Literary Archive. The manuscript, which is in Chekhov's handwriting, was acquired, together with certain other documents relating to Chekhov, by the Archive in 1920.

Platonov was first published in Russian as *Neizdannaya pyesa A. P. Chekhova* [*An unpublished play of A. P. Chekhov*] by the Central Archive in 1923, ed. N. F. Belchikov. This edition contains an appendix with variants consisting of passages still legible, but erased or altered by Chekhov in the course of several revisions of the manuscript. The general effect of the revisions, as was usual with Chekhov, was to tone down the more fanciful or outrageous elements and to cut rather than to expand. Though the text of these variants has been studied, it has been decided not to include them in the present edition in the interests of brevity and in accordance with the precedent of *Works*, 1944–51, xii, from which the present translation is made and in which Chekhov's final version is also published without the variants.

In the 1933 collection of Chekhov's works published by the Soviet State Publishing House for Literature, *Platonov* is given the title *Безотцовщина* which can best be translated as *Fatherless*. There is evidence that Chekhov did write a play with this title in 1878 or earlier: his *Fatherless* is criticized in a letter to him from his brother Alexander, dated 14 October 1878. But there is no conclusive evidence that *Fatherless* had any connexion with *Platonov*, apart from the general hopelessness of the 'fathers' (the older generation) in *Platonov* —a quality which, incidentally, the younger generation shares. *Fatherless* must therefore be presumed to have perished.

Platonov is, however, clearly the same play as that referred to by Chekhov's brother Michael in the following passage: 'While a student, he [Chekhov] wrote a long play, which he hoped to have put on at the Moscow Little Theatre. He even submitted it to the well-known Moscow actress M. N. Yermolova. The play was very top-heavy, with a railway train, horse-thieves and the lynching of a gypsy' (Michael Chekhov, in his introduction to Chekhov's *Letters*, vol. ii, Moscow, 1912–16). In another reference, clearly also to *Platonov*, Michael Chekhov says that his brother took the play to Yermolova while in the second year of his university course—i.e. in the academic year 1880–1 (*see* Gitovich, *Letopis zhizni i tvorchestva A. P. Chekhova*, p. 45). This dating of *Platonov* agrees with the calligraphic evidence. The exuberance of the style and the use of certain provincialisms in the Russian help to confirm the early 1880s as the period when the play was written (see Preface to *Neizdannaya pyesa*).

Despite the obvious need for cuts in an inordinately long text (so that previous translators have all either abridged it or indicated passages suitable for omission), *Platonov* has been produced on the stage in a number of countries. There are references to a production in German in 1928 and in Czech in 1929 (see *Literaturnoye nasledstvo: Chekhov*, p. 766). The first French production took place in Paris in 1956 and the first English performance at the Royal Court Theatre in 1960 with Rex Harrison in the title role.

APPENDIX II

IVANOV

1. The composition
2. The text
3. Variants

1. THE COMPOSITION

(a) First performance in Moscow

The evolution of *Ivanov* was long and complicated, involving extensive revisions between the play's first performance in November 1887 and its first appearance in print in early 1889, and also some further revision after that. But *Ivanov* was originally composed with great speed—within two weeks at the end of September and beginning of October 1887. It received its first performance in the provinces—at Saratov on some date between 10 and 19 November 1887 (*see* Gitovich, *Letopis zhizni i tvorchestva A. P. Chekhova*, p. 170). But the first important production was that given at Korsh's Theatre in Moscow on 19 November 1887, when *Ivanov* was staged as a benefit performance for the actor N. V. Svetlov, who took the part of Borkin. The performance created considerable stir and the reviewer for *Novoye vremya* [*New Time*] of 22 November commented that: 'There was a storm of applause, curtain-calls and hissing, so that no author of recent times has made his bow to such a hotch-potch of praise and protest.' That this was, if anything, an understatement is shown by references in Chekhov's letters, extracts from which are now given in chronological sequence, providing some indications of the planning of the play and a useful commentary on its first Moscow performance and the aftermath.

'I've twice visited Korsh's Theatre and each time Korsh has implored me to write him a play.... The actors claim that I shall make a good job of it because I know how to play on people's nerves.' (*Letter to M. V. Kiseleva, 13 Sept. 1887.*)

'The play's turned out light as a feather, with no dull passages and an original theme. I'll probably have it put on at Korsh's Theatre (if Korsh isn't too stingy).' (*Letter to Alexander Chekhov, between 6 and 8 Oct. 1887.*)

'I wrote the play more or less by chance after talking to Korsh. I went to bed, had an idea and wrote. It took two weeks, or rather ten days, as I had some days off or wrote other things. I can't tell how good it is. It's turned out suspiciously short. Everyone likes it. Korsh hasn't found anything wrong or un-stageworthy in it—which shows what fine, sensitive judges I have. It's my first play, so there are bound to be some mistakes. The plot's involved and rather clever. I finish each act like my short stories, conducting it quietly and peacefully, but with a punch on the nose for the audience at the end. I've put my entire energy into a few really powerful, vivid scenes, but the linking passages are weak, feeble and hackneyed. Still, I'm pleased. Bad as the play may be, I've created an important literary type and a part that only an actor as good as Davydov [the well-known actor V. N. Davydov] would take, a part for the actor to expand in and show his paces. . . .

'There are fourteen characters, including five women. I feel that my ladies aren't properly developed, apart from one.' (*Letter to Alexander Chekhov, between 10 and 12 Oct. 1887.*)

'Modern playwrights stuff their work with saints, scoundrels and comic types to the exclusion of everything else. But you can search Russia high and low without finding these things—that is, you may find some, but not in the extreme form required by playwrights. . . . I wanted to be original, so I haven't brought on one villain or saint (though I haven't managed to keep out the comic types). . . . I don't know if I've succeeded. Korsh and the actors are certain it will come off, but I'm not so sure. The actors don't understand, they bungle things, they take the wrong parts—while I struggle on, thinking the play's doomed if they don't keep my casting. If they won't do it my way I'll have to withdraw it, or we'll have a fiasco on our hands. The whole business is disturbing—in fact, highly unpleasant. I'd never have taken it on if I'd known.' (*Letter to Alexander Chekhov, 24 Oct. 1887.*)

'*Ivanov* will definitely be put on at the end of November or beginning of December. The contract with Korsh is signed. Ivanov himself will be played by Davydov, who, I'm very happy to say, is most keen on the play. He's really taken to it and he sees *Ivanov* just as I do. I was up till three this morning with him—he really is a tremendous artist, I was left in no doubt about that.

'To believe such judges as Davydov, I have the knack of writing plays. I turn out to have produced a completely finished article instinctively, by feel, without even knowing what I was doing—and haven't made *a single* mistake from the point of view of staging.' (*Letter to N. M. Yezhov, 27 Oct. 1887.*)

'Unexpectedly my damned play has taken so much out of me that I've lost track of time. I've gone off the rails and I'm heading for a nervous breakdown. It was easy enough to write, but staging it means a lot of nervous strain, quite apart from the waste of time and cab fares. Judge for yourself:

'1. There isn't a single sincere, truthful person in Moscow.

'2. The actors are spoilt, selfish, semi-educated and opinionated. They loathe each other and some of them would sell their souls to the devil to stop a colleague getting a good part.

'3. Korsh is a businessman who just wants a full house and doesn't care about the success of actors and play.

'4. There aren't any women in his company and I have two splendid female parts going begging.

'5. Of the men, only Davydov and Kiselevsky [I. P. Kiselevsky, who took the part of Shabelsky] will be all right. The rest will be no good.

'6. After signing the contract with Korsh I heard that the Little Theatre [a State Theatre] would have been glad to take the play.

'7. In Davydov's view, which I share, the play's the best one written for the present season, but it's bound to flop because Korsh's company's so rotten.

'8. Yesterday I wanted to take the play off, but Korsh kicked up an awful fuss. . . .

'There's material enough for another twenty items, but eight will do. You see what it's like to be an "aspiring" playwright who suddenly finds himself a square peg in a round hole.

'The one consolation is that Davydov and Kiselevsky will be brilliant. Davydov's got down to his part and is very keen.' (*Letter to N. A. Leykin, 4 Nov. 1887.*)

'I'm baffled by what you write about staging plays. You say an author only hinders a production and embarrasses the actors—that most of his advice is just silly. My answer is this:

'1. The author—not the actors—owns the play.

'2. The author must be responsible for casting—that is, if he's a responsible man at all.

'3. So far *all* my advice has been good and has been taken.

'4. The actors themselves ask me for advice.' (*Letter to N. A. Leykin, 15 Nov. 1887.*)

'Well, the play got by. I'll describe it in sequence. The main thing is, Korsh promised ten rehearsals, but had only four, and only two of those can really be called rehearsals because the other two were just occasions for the distinguished cast to indulge in slanging matches with each other. Only Davydov [as Ivanov] and Glama [A. Ya. Glama-Meshcherskaya as Anna] knew their parts. The others got by with the aid of the prompter and their own inspiration.

'*Act One.* I'm back-stage in a small box like a prison cell. My family sits in a baignoire in great trepidation. I'm unexpectedly calm and not at all nervous. The actors are tense and on edge and are all crossing themselves. The curtain goes up and an actor (the one who was having the benefit performance) [N. V. Svetlov as Borkin] takes a bow. What with them being so nervous and not knowing their parts and someone presenting a bunch of flowers, I fail to recognize my own play right from the start. Kiselevsky [as Shabelsky], of whom I was hoping a lot, didn't get one sentence right—literally *not one*, he was ad-libbing. Despite this and the producer's mistakes the first act went off well. Lots of curtain calls.

'*Act Two*. Lots of people on stage. Guests. They don't know their parts, get them mixed up and talk nonsense. Every word goes through me like a knife, but—luckily for my muse—even this act goes well, with a curtain call for everyone and two for me. I am congratulated on my success.

'*Act Three*. Not bad acting. A great reception. I have three curtain calls, during which Davydov pumps my hand and Glama . . . presses my other hand to her heart. Virtue and talent triumphant!

'*Act Four, Part I*. Goes quite well. Curtain calls. Follows a very long, exhausting interval. Unused to going to the bar between two parts of an act, the audience grumbles. Up goes the curtain. A pretty sight. Through an arch you see a table laid for the wedding supper. The band plays flourishes. Out come the groom's attendants—they're drunk, so of course they have to mess around and play the fool. It was a complete orgy, it quite horrified me. After this Kiselevsky came on. It's a poetic, soul-stirring passage, but friend Kiselevsky doesn't know his lines and is drunk as a lord—so a short, poetic dialogue turns into something sluggish and off-putting. The audience is baffled. At the end of the play the hero dies as the result of an insult too great for him to bear. The audience, bored and tired by this time, doesn't understand why he dies (the actors insisted I should keep this, I do have another variant). Curtain calls for the actors and me. During one of these there are sounds of unmistakable hissing drowned by applause and stamping.

'I was altogether exhausted and fed up. I felt disgusted, though the play went off pretty well. . . .

'Theatre people say they've never seen such a to-do on the stage, such a hotch-potch of clapping and hissing, and they've never heard so much quarrelling as they saw and heard at my play. And it's the first time the author's had a curtain call after the second act at Korsh's Theatre.

'The second performance is on the 23rd, with a variant and certain changes—I'm chucking out those groom's attendants.' (*Letter to Alexander Chekhov, 20 Nov. 1887.*)

'You'll never guess what happened. This play . . . this wretched piece of crap—it's got completely out of hand. As I told you, the first performance saw more excitement in the audience and off-stage than the prompter had ever known during thirty-two years in the theatre. There was a fearful racket, what with clapping, hissing and people nearly coming to blows in the bar. The students in the gallery wanted to chuck someone out and the police removed two of them. Everyone was very worked up. My sister nearly fainted. . . .

'The actors were on edge. . . . It turns out that the leading lady's daughter was dying, so how could she be expected to act under the circumstances?

'The second performance wasn't too bad, though there were a few little surprises. Instead of the actress with the sick daughter, another one took the part without rehearsing it. There were curtain calls again (two) after Act Three and Act Four, but no more hissing.

'That's all. *Ivanov* goes on again on Wednesday. Now everyone's calmed down and got into the swing of it.' (*Letter to Alexander Chekhov, 24 Nov. 1887.*)

'As I write, my play's being handed round and read. Having come to St. Petersburg in a state of panic and foreboding, I was surprised to find it making not a bad impression here on the whole. Suvorin [the writer and publisher A. S. Suvorin (1834–1912)] has conceived the keenest enthusiasm for my brain-child and keeps me discussing *Ivanov* for hours on end. Others do the same. There's a lot less talk than in Moscow, but enough for me to be bored with *Ivanov*. I can sum up my critics' opinions as follows:

'1. The play's carelessly written. So far as form is concerned, it deserves to be cursed with bell, book and candle. The language is flawless.

'2. No one minds the title.

'3. People are amused and puzzled by a certain immoral and brazen cynicism in it.

'4. The characters are sufficiently rounded, the personages come to life, the milieu carries conviction. So far I've heard of no misunderstandings or objections on this score, though I'm cross-examined on it in detail every day.

'5. Ivanov is *sufficiently characterized*—no need to add or subtract anything. But Suvorin has his own ideas on this: "I can make sense of Ivanov because I think I *am* an Ivanov. But the general public, which every author must keep in mind, won't understand. Why not give him a soliloquy?"

'6. Burenin [V. P. Burenin, a journalist] dislikes the fact that the plot doesn't thicken in Act One, which breaks the rules.

'7. The passage most fundamental to an understanding of Ivanov's character —or so most people think—is the bit in Act Four when he runs in to see Sasha before the wedding. Suvorin's very keen on that bit.

'8. The play feels a bit cramped because it has too many characters—to the detriment of Anna and Sasha, who don't get enough room, so are a bit pallid in places.

'9. The ending isn't untrue to life, but it is untrue to the stage. It can only satisfy the audience if played superlatively well. "If you're sure Ivanov will always be played by someone as good as Davydov," people tell me, "then leave the ending as it is. Otherwise we'll be the first to hiss you." In brief, the thing's got rather out of hand.' (*Letter to V. N. Davydov, 1 Dec. 1887.*)

'Everyone's quite delighted with the play, though they blame me for carelessness. My only offprint's being passed from hand to hand, and I can't get hold of it to send it to the censors.

'Suvorin's angry because I let Korsh have it. In his view neither Korsh's company nor a Moscow audience . . . can understand *Ivanov*. The Moscow reviews make people laugh here. Everyone's waiting for me to put the play on in St. Petersburg and they're sure it'll go down well. But I'm so fed up with it after Moscow, I just can't make myself think about it—I can't bother, I'm too disgusted. When I think how Korsh's people . . . mucked it up, mutilating and ruining it, it makes me sick. You feel sorry for the audience for leaving the theatre without getting its money's worth. I'm sorry for myself and Davydov.

'Suvorin's excited about the play. The funny thing is that after Korsh's production no one in the audience understood Ivanov—they blamed me and pitied me. But everyone here agrees that Ivanov's portrayed adequately and there's no need to add or subtract anything.' (*Letter to Michael Chekhov, 3 Dec. 1887.*)

(b) First performance in St. Petersburg

It was in October 1888 that *Ivanov* began to engage Chekhov's attention again, as the result of a proposal to stage the play at the Alexandrine Theatre in St. Petersburg for the benefit of the producer F. A. Fyodorov-Yurkovsky. This proposal was carried into effect on 31 January of the following year, when the play met with an enthusiastic reception.

Between first performance in Moscow and first performance in St. Petersburg, *Ivanov* was radically revised in two main stages:

(i) that of October 1888 to 19 December 1888, resulting in the version dispatched to A. S. Suvorin on the latter date and termed below (in section 2, on the text) 'Recension II';

(ii) that of late December 1888 to January 1889, resulting in the version performed at the Alexandrine Theatre and termed below 'Recension III'.

(i) First stage of revision (October 1888 to 19 December 1888)

This stage of revision is comparatively scantily documented in Chekhov's correspondence, where, however, there are four passages providing a useful commentary on work in progress.

In a letter to Suvorin dated between 4 and 6 October, Chekhov was already claiming that: 'I've radically changed Acts Two and Four of *Ivanov*. I've given Ivanov a soliloquy, touched up Sasha and so on. If people don't understand *Ivanov* even now, I'll chuck it on the fire and write a story called *I've had enough*! I won't change the title [it must be inferred that this question had been discussed between Chekhov and Suvorin]. That would be awkward. If the play had never been staged it would be a different matter.'

Chekhov was perhaps anticipating his own intentions in saying that he had already 'radically changed' Act Four, because a few days later he was again writing to Suvorin, as follows: 'I've been reading *Ivanov*. I think that if I write another Act Four, chuck out some stuff and insert a soliloquy that I've already worked out in my head, the play will turn out a finished article and a very effective one. I'll send it to the Alexandrine Theatre by Christmas.' (*Letter to A. S. Suvorin, 11–12 Oct. 1888.*)

Passages from two other letters mark the conclusion of this stage of revision: 'I've already got down to *Ivanov*. It'll be finished in two days and is turning out quite a smooth job, but not stageworthy. The first three acts aren't bad.' (*Letter to A. S. Suvorin, 17 Dec. 1888.*)

'I've finished my *Bolvanov* [a whimsical distortion of the word *Ivanov*] and am sending it to you at the same time as this letter. I'm fed up with it. . . . Master Ivanov's now much easier to understand. The ending doesn't satisfy me at all—it's too feeble, apart from the revolver shot—but I take comfort in thinking that it's not in its final form yet. . . .

'I cope with my plays pretty quickly, don't you think? I'd hardly touched *Ivanov* and the job was done. . . .

'I promise not to write any more of these damned intellectual plays like *Ivanov*. If *Ivanov* doesn't come off I shan't be surprised or accuse people of intriguing behind my back.' (*Letter to A. S. Suvorin, 19 Dec. 1888.*)

(ii) *Second stage of revision (late December 1888 to 31 January 1889)*

During this period Chekhov's comments on *Ivanov* in his correspondence are uniquely rich and circumstantial—more so than his recorded comments on any of his other works. They give an exact idea of his conception of the play and of its chief characters. As is shown by the following comprehensive extracts from the material, he was worried that the play might not be understood. He became irritated with it, and with V. N. Davydov, the actor who took the title role (after taking it earlier in Moscow, apparently to Chekhov's satisfaction at the time). Amongst other matters of interpretation, Chekhov makes it clear that Dr. Lvov was to be regarded as an unsympathetic character, as also—more surprisingly—was Sasha. Another interesting feature of Chekhov's correspondence is the material relating to changes made in Act Three (but later abandoned) in order to turn it into a more suitable vehicle for M. G. Savina, the actress who took the part of Sasha and who seems to have had a liking for horseplay on the stage.

'I've just got your letter. The fact that Sasha doesn't come on at the end of Act Four really shook you. Quite right too. Let her be conspicuous to the audience by her absence. You insist I bring her on, and you say it's bad theatre not to. All right, let's have her on. But what can she say? What lines? Spinsters like her—she's a spinster, not a girl—can't express themselves and shouldn't try. The earlier Sasha was articulate and likeable, but the new one will only annoy the audience if she comes on. She can't very well throw her arms round Ivanov's neck and say she loves him, can she? When she doesn't love him and has said as much? To bring her on at the end, I'd have to change her whole character from the word go. You say there are no women on stage and that this makes the ending dry. I quite agree. There are only two women who could come on at the end and stick up for Ivanov—those who really loved him: his mother and the Jewess. But they're both dead, so that's out of the question. He's bereaved, and let him damn well stay bereaved.' (*Letter to A. S. Suvorin, 23 Dec. 1888.*)

'You demand that I bring on Sasha. But *Ivanov* probably won't be performed anyway. If it is, all right—I'll do it your way. But in that case the little bitch is going to get it in the neck, sorry. You say women love and get married out of pity. . . . What about men? I don't like realist novelists to run women down, but I don't like seeing women put on a pedestal either. . . . I don't like people proving that even if women are worse than men, men are still swine and women angels. Men and women are worth a penny the pair, but men are the cleverer and less unfair.' (*Letter to A. S. Suvorin, 26 Dec. 1888.*)

'The producer thinks Ivanov an odd-man-out [superfluous man] *à la* Turgenev. Savina [M. G. Savina in the part of Sasha] asks why Ivanov's such a swine. You write: "You should give Ivanov some trait showing why two women throw themselves at him, why he's a cad and the doctor a hero." If you three all take it like that, my play's no good. I must have come a bit unstuck and not written what I meant at all. If Ivanov emerges as a villain or odd-man-out and the doctor as a hero, if you can't see why Anna and Sasha should love Ivanov, the play clearly hasn't come off and there can be no question of staging it.

'This is how I see my characters. Ivanov's a gentleman and a university man. He's not outstanding in any way. He's highly-strung, excitable, easily roused to enthusiasm like most well-educated gentlemen, he's decent and straightforward. He's lived on his estate and worked in local government. What he's been up to, how he's been behaving, how he's kept himself amused and occupied—you'll find all that in his speech to the doctor in Act One, Scene v:

' "Don't you go marrying Jewesses, neurotics or blue-stockings. . . . Don't take on thousands of people single-handed, don't tilt at windmills or batter your head against brick walls. And may God save you from things like scientific farming, cranky schools and wild speeches."

'That's what he has behind him. Anna, who saw his scientific farming and other adventures, tells the doctor: "He's a wonderful man, Doctor, and I'm only sorry you didn't know him a year or two ago. Now he's rather under the weather and doesn't speak or do anything. But in the old days—oh, he was so charming" (Act One, Scene vii).

'His past is marvellous, as with most cultured Russians. There's hardly a Russian squire or university man who doesn't boast about his past. The present's always worse than the past. Why? There's one thing about Russian excitability —it so quickly gives way to fatigue. The man's hardly left school when he's already bitten off more than he can chew—thrown himself into education, the peasant problem, scientific farming, the *Vestnik Yevropy* [*Herald of Europe*, a liberal monthly, St. Petersburg, 1866–1918], making speeches, writing to ministers, fighting evil, applauding virtue. He can't love in an ordinary, simple way, he must have blue-stockings, neurotics . . . even prostitutes that he rescues, and so on and so forth. . . . But at hardly thirty or thirty-five he's already tired and bored. He hasn't grown a decent moustache yet, but he's already laying down the law. "Don't get married, old man, learn from my experience." Or: "What is liberalism, actually? Katkov [M. N. Katkov, the well-known conservative publicist] was often right, between you and me." He's now ready to run down local government, scientific farming, love and learning. . . . Ivanov tells the doctor (Act One, Scene v): "You only left college last year, my dear Lvov, and you're still young and full of life, but I'm thirty-five, I've the right to advise you." That's typical of how they speak, these premature Weary Willies. He goes on to give the following advice, uttering authoritative sighs: "Don't you go marrying such-and-such girls," [see one of the extracts above] "but choose something nice and drab and ordinary. Don't go in for bright colours or unnecessary fuss and bother. In fact, run your life on conventional lines. The greyer and more monotonous the background the better. . . . But the life I've lived—what a trying business, oh, how exhausting" [see pp. 174–5].

'Physically tired and bored, he can't understand what's happening to him or what has happened. Horrified, he informs the doctor (Act One, Scene iii): "Now you tell me she'll soon die, and I don't feel love or pity, just a sort of emptiness and exhaustion. I suppose anyone would think I'm behaving terribly, but I don't know myself what's going on inside me." When narrow, unreliable people get in a mess like this, they usually put it all down to their environment or join the ranks of Hamlets and men at odds with society [superfluous men], and that comforts them. But Ivanov is a very straight person. He tells the doctor and the audience quite frankly that he can't make himself out, keeps saying he doesn't understand. That he really doesn't understand himself is evident in the long soliloquy in Act Three where he talks to the audience as man to man and actually bursts into tears while confessing.

'The change in him insults his sense of decency. He seeks reasons outside himself and can't find them, so he starts looking inside him, but can only find a vague feeling of guilt. This is a Russian feeling. A Russian always feels guilty when someone in his house dies or falls ill, and when he owes—or is owed—money. Ivanov keeps on about things being his fault, and feels guiltier with every jolt he gets. In Act One he says: "I suppose I'm very much to blame, but I'm so mixed up, I feel paralysed, half dead or something. I don't know what I'm doing." In Act Two he tells Sasha: "I feel so conscience-stricken all the time. I feel terribly guilty, but just where I went wrong I can't see."

'To exhaustion, boredom and guilt add another enemy—loneliness. If Ivanov was a civil servant, actor, priest or professor, he'd have got used to things. But he lives on an estate in the provinces, where people are drunkards or card addicts or resemble the doctor. . . . None of them cares how he feels or how he's changed. He's lonely. Long winters, long evenings, empty garden, empty rooms, that old geyser of a count, his sick wife. . . . There's nowhere he can go. So he's haunted by a problem—what to do with himself.

'Now for the fifth enemy. Ivanov's tired and doesn't understand himself, but life goes on regardless. It makes legitimate demands on him and he must try to solve his problems whether he likes it or not. His sick wife is one problem, his mass of debts is another. Sasha throws herself at him and that's a problem too. How he sets about these problems should be clear from the soliloquy in Act Three and from the content of the two last acts. People like Ivanov don't solve problems, they cave in under the weight. They're baffled, they make gestures of despair, they're all on edge. They complain and do silly things. And they end up giving way to their depraved, neurotic spinelessness, collapsing and joining the club of "broken men" that no one understands.

'Disillusionment, apathy, failure of nerve, exhaustion—that's what you must expect if you get over-excited, and such excitability is highly typical of young Russians. Take literature. Take the present day—socialism is a form of excitement. . . .

'Snivelling and boredom . . . aren't the only signs of exhaustion. An exhausted man's life isn't like this:

It's very uneven. Not all exhausted people lose their excessive excitability, but the bouts of excitement don't last long, and after each one even worse listlessness sets in. This can be shown thus:

'This isn't just sliding down a slope, as you see, it's a somewhat different process. When Sasha says she loves him, Ivanov's carried away and shouts about leading a new life. Next day he doesn't believe in this new life any more than in fairies (see soliloquy, Act Three). When his wife insults him, he goes off the deep end, gets terribly worked up and hurls a cruel insult at her. He's told what an unmitigated swine he is, and if that doesn't prove too much for his crumbling brain, he gets worked up again and denounces himself.

'I don't want to make you faint and weary, so I'll turn to Dr. Lvov. He's the decent, blunt, hot-headed type, but narrow and obsessive—what some wits have dubbed "the well-meaning fool". Breadth of vision and straightforward reactions are outside his scope. He's a walking cliché—tendentiousness personified. He looks at everything and everyone through narrow blinkers, and his opinions are all prejudiced. He adores anyone who yells "make way for an honest working-man"—thinks anyone else is a money-grubbing swine. There's no golden mean. . . . All men are sinners, but that's not enough for Lvov—he must see everyone in black or white.

'He arrived in the district already biased. He at once took all the richer peasants for profiteers, and Ivanov, whom he doesn't understand, for a crook. The man's wife's ill and he visits a rich woman of the neighbourhood, so what else can he be? He wants to murder his wife and marry an heiress. Obvious, isn't it?

'... Lvov's blunt and honest. He's a straight-shooter who doesn't spare himself. If need be, he'll throw bombs at a carriage [i.e. be capable of such acts as the assassination of Alexander II in 1881, killed during a journey by carriage], punch a visiting inspector on the nose or tell people what crooks they are. He'll stop at nothing, and he never feels a qualm—why be an "honest working-man" after all, if you can't give short shrift to the "forces of reaction"?

'Such people fill a need and are mostly likeable. To caricature them, even to make good theatre, is dishonourable and pointless. It's true caricatures are sharper, and thus easier to understand, but better to leave a bit unsaid than spoil things. . . .

'Now for the women. What attracts their love? Anna loves Ivanov because he's decent, spirited, brilliant—and as fiery a speaker as Lvov (Act One, Scene vii). She loves him while he's excited and interesting, but when she thinks he's growing dim and losing his special quality, she stops appreciating him and speaks out bluntly and harshly at the end of Act Three.

'Sasha's a modern young woman—well-educated, clever, decent and so on. She singles out the thirty-five-year-old Ivanov because he's the pick of the bunch and beggars can't be choosers anyway. She knew him when she was a little girl and had a good view of his doings before he faded out. He's a friend of her father's.

'She's the type of female that males conquer by moaning and groaning and bungling—not by being brave and supple and having bright plumage. She loves her men when they're going downhill. No sooner has Ivanov thrown up the sponge than up pops this young miss. It's just what she was waiting for—a great crusade, Lord save us! She'll bring him back to life, put him on his feet, make him happy. . . . It's her crusade she loves, not Ivanov. . . . But to Ivanov love's only one more snag, another stab in the back—that's what she doesn't know. What happens? Sasha gets to work on Ivanov for twelve whole months, but he still doesn't come to life—he only goes further downhill.

'My fingers ache and I must stop. . . . If what I've just written isn't in the play, there's no question of staging it—I can't have said what I meant and you'd better withdraw it. I don't want to propagate error from the stage. If the audience comes away from the theatre feeling that the Ivanovs of this world are villains and the Lvovs heroes, I can only give up and let my writing go to hell. Altering or inserting stuff won't help. No alterations can bring a hero down from his pedestal, and no insertions can turn a villain into an ordinary fallible human being. I can bring Sasha on at the end, but I can't add to Ivanov and Lvov, it's beyond me—and if I do add anything, I feel I'll only make matters worse. Trust my instincts—I did write the thing. . . .

'Frankly, it wasn't ambition or the thought of Savina appearing that seduced me into putting the play on. . . . I was counting on making the odd thousand roubles. But it's better to borrow a thousand than risk doing something silly. . . .

'I've read through what I've written. The word "Russian" often crops up when I describe Ivanov. Don't let that annoy you. When writing the play, I kept only the essence of the thing in mind—that is, the typical Russian traits. The over-excitability, the guilt complex, the tendency to fatigue are purely Russian. . . .

'Of course I haven't used such terms as "Russian", "excitability", "tendency to fatigue" and so on in the play, trusting my readers and audience to pay attention and not need every i dotted and every t crossed. I tried to write simply, without guile. I certainly never suspected that my readers and audience would try to catch my characters out and lay such emphasis on the talk about the dowry and so on.

'My play hasn't come off and of course I'm sorry. To my mind's eye Ivanov and Lvov look alive. I tell you truly, these people were conceived in my head. They didn't come out of thin air, they're not the product of prejudice, blind chance or being too clever by half. They're the result of observing and studying life. They're firmly fixed in my brain, and I feel I haven't deviated a hair's breadth from the truth or been in the least over-clever. So if they've come out limp and blurred on paper, don't blame them, blame me for not being able to put my ideas across. I'm not yet ready to write for the theatre, that's what it comes to.' (*Letter to A. S. Suvorin, 30 Dec. 1888.*)

'The play's already cast, but . . . I doubt if it'll be put on. I'm worried by faults so bad that I can't just ignore them. I posted a letter today listing certain conditions. If the play falls down on even one of them in the view of the people I was writing to, I've seriously asked to have it taken off. . . . I'm doing what you and Suvorin would have done—or any other self-respecting man who doesn't write many plays.

'The play's faults are beyond repair. It's not only me. People I trust completely and whose competence I rate above my own—they see them too. Wait till I write another play. To hell with *Ivanov*.' (*Letter to I. L. Leontyev* [*Shcheglov*], *31 Dec. 1888.*)

'I just don't care when you publish the play, in July or not at all—I dislike the thing. The later the better, actually, being nearer the next theatrical season. Besides, I've had a rather fiendish idea. When *Ivanov* flops in St. Petersburg I'll read a paper to the Literary Society against writing plays. I'll give extracts from my own, describing my characters—which, in spite of everything, I think new in Russian literature and so far virgin territory. The play's bad, but the characters live and aren't artificial.

'Somehow I feel *Ivanov* won't be put on. The producer's wish to stage it is flattering and touching, but I expect no good from this production. I've sent my frank opinion of the play to St. Petersburg and listed the conditions which it should meet—but doesn't, from what I hear. If my opinion isn't foolish, and if it prevails, the play won't be put on.' (*Letter to A. N. Pleshcheyev, 2 Jan. 1889.*)

'Of course I'm not my own worst enemy and I want my play to be put on. But between ourselves I don't like it and am sorry it was written by me, not by someone more sensible and rational.' (*Letter to A. S. Suvorin, 3 Jan. 1889.*)

'I've sent you two variants of *Ivanov* today. If the title role were to be played by an adaptable and energetic actor I'd have added and changed a lot. . . . But alas, Davydov's taking Ivanov. That means I must keep things short and dull, bearing in mind that any subtleties and nuances will be lost in drabness and boredom. Can Davydov be tender and furious by turns? When he plays serious parts, a sort of mill-wheel with a low, monotonous rumble seems to take over in his throat. . . . I'm sorry for poor Savina, playing that dead duck Sasha. I'd be glad to do anything for Savina, but if Ivanov means to mumble, Sasha's part won't come off however much I work it up. I'm downright ashamed that Savina will have to act such damned rubbish. If I'd known in good time that she'd play Sasha and that Davydov would take Ivanov, I'd have called the play *Sasha* and built it all round her, just tacking on Ivanov as an incidental. But who could have known?

'Ivanov has two long soliloquies vital to the play—one in Act Three and another at the end of Act Four. . . . The first one must be sung [*sic*], the second declaimed furiously. Both feats are beyond Davydov. He'll deliver both soliloquies in his "clever" style which means he'll sound more than half dead.

'I'd love to read a paper to the Literary Society about how the idea of *Ivanov* came to me. I'd make a public recantation. I conceived the daring ambition of summing up everything so far written about such Dismal Desmonds and of putting an end to these writings with *Ivanov*. In my view all Russian fiction-writers and dramatists have felt the need to portray despondency, but they've all done it by instinct, without any definite conception and view of the matter. I more or less hit my target in intention, but my execution's no damn good. I should have left it.' (*Letter to A. S. Suvorin, 7 Jan. 1889.*)

'Savina has agreed to play Sasha, but Sasha's part's very weak and pretty poor theatre. When I wrote it eighteen months ago I didn't attach special importance to it. But now the honour done to the play by Savina has decided me to alter her part radically. I've already done it in places, in so far as the play's general structure permitted.' (*Letter to F. A. Fyodorov-Yurkovsky, 8 Jan. 1889.*)

'I'm waiting for a copy of my play. I wrote Fyodorov a flattering letter, asking him to hurry up and send it—otherwise a lot of things won't get changed. You know, I have Sasha whizzing about the stage in Act Three? That shows how much I've changed it! I did it all for Savina. Tell her I'm so flattered by her taking a poor, unrewarding part in the play, I'm ready to lay down my life and shall change the part radically, as much as the play's structure allows. I'll have Savina buzzing about, jumping on the sofa and delivering soliloquies. Not to bore the audience with too much snivelling, I show Ivanov in one scene as cheerful, laughing and high-spirited and Sasha being gay with him. . . . I suppose it's not too much of a good thing, is it? I think I've hit it off just right . . . but being witty's a great chore. I tremble over every word I write in case I spoil Ivanov.' (*Letter to A. S. Suvorin, 8 Jan. 1889.*)

'I'm writing to you after a spot of real hard labour. Why, oh why did you pass *Ivanov* in committee? Why in the name of fiends and folly has Fyodorov taken it into his head to stage the thing for his benefit? I'm fed up. No fee can compensate for the strain of the hard labour I've put in this last week. I attached no importance to the play before, I was condescending and ironical about it, as if to say "the thing's written and to hell with it". But now it's suddenly unexpectedly got going, I see what a crude piece of work it was. The last act's remarkably bad. I've been fussing over the play all week—scribbling variants, corrections and insertions. I've done a new Sasha—for Savina. I've changed Act Four out of all recognition, given Ivanov himself a polish—and I'm fed up, I've come to loathe the play. . . .

'You need a special gift to write well for the theatre. (One may be an excellent fiction-writer, yet a hopeless playwright.) But to write a bad play and then to try and turn it into a good one by dint of sundry hocus-pocus, crossings out, additions, inserted soliloquies, bringing the dead to life and burying the living alive—for that you need much greater gifts. It's like buying an old pair of trousers from a soldier's uniform and trying your damnedest to turn them into a tail-coat. You don't know whether to utter tragic laughs or neigh like a horse.' (*Letter to A. N. Pleshcheyev, 15 Jan. 1889.*)

'I'll stay in St. Petersburg until Tuesday. . . . The actors are performing badly and no good will come of the play. I quarrel and make it up with the wretched Davydov about ten times a day. What a bore. There's absolutely nothing to be done about it. The play won't be put on more than four times—it's just not worth bothering with.' (*Letter to Michael Chekhov, end of January 1889.*)

(iii) *Aftermath of the first performance in St. Petersburg*

The following passages from Chekhov's letters show his reaction to the successful first season of *Ivanov* in St. Petersburg.

'The play had a terrific reception and I returned crowned with laurels.' (*Letter to D. T. Savelyev, 4 Feb. 1889.*)

'I don't care about your thrust at my author's conceit. You're quite right—Ivanov probably is clearer in my letter than on the stage. That's because a quarter of his part has been cut. I'd gladly sacrifice half my success if they'd let me make the play twice as boring. The public calls the theatre a school, so if it's not being hypocritical, let it put up with being bored. After all, schools aren't exactly fun, are they?' (*Letter to A. S. Suvorin, 6 Feb. 1889.*)

'The women in the play are superfluous. The great trouble was to stop the creatures becoming the centre of attention, which doesn't belong to them. If I'd managed to make them beautiful, I'd feel my job was done as far as they're concerned. Women contributed to Ivanov's downfall. . . . What of it? Am I really supposed to explain this contribution at length when it's already comprehensible and has been dealt with thousands of times before?

'I receive letters, both anonymous and signed, about *Ivanov*. Some socialist (apparently) writes an indignant anonymous letter, bitterly upbraiding me. He writes that some young person came to grief after seeing my play, that it's a bad influence and so on. The letters all interpret *Ivanov* in the same way. People have understood it, clearly, which greatly pleases me.' (*Letter to A. S. Suvorin, 8 Feb. 1889.*)

'Svobodin [the actor P. M. Svobodin (1850–1892)] came to see me. Amongst other things he said you'd apparently received a letter from some parent whose son shot himself as the result of *Ivanov*. If this letter isn't imaginary, please send me it and I'll add it to the letters I already have about *Ivanov*. . . . I'm frightfully bored with *Ivanov*. I can't read about it and I feel awful when people start giving ingenious explanations of it.' (*Letter to A. S. Suvorin, 5 March 1889.*)

2. THE TEXT

The present translation is based on the text of the play as printed in *Works*, 1944–51, xi, which is the same text as that in Chekhov's *Collected Works*, St. Petersburg, 1902, vii (second edition)—itself identical with the text given in the first edition (1901) of the same volume. This is here termed the 'final text'.

The final text was immediately preceded by two published drafts presenting numerous but relatively unimportant variants from each other and from the final text:

the '*Severny vestnik* text'—the play as it first appeared in printed form, in the magazine *Severny vestnik* [*Northern Herald*] for March 1889; and

the '*Plays, 1897* text'—the version printed in Chekhov's collected *Plays* (St. Petersburg, 1897).

The relationship between the texts of the above-mentioned documents is a fairly straightforward one. It is the previous history of the text—its evolution before its first publication in printed form—which makes *Ivanov* a fascinating and complex problem. The textual history of the play is complicated by comparison with that of Chekhov's other plays—or any of his other work—not only because he undertook repeated radical revisions, but also because unusually extensive evidence of these revisions has been preserved.

For the period preceding the first publication (that of the '*Severny vestnik* text') four versions (here termed 'recensions') of the play must be distinguished.

Recension I. This is the original text of the play, as first performed at Korsh's Theatre in Moscow on 19 November 1887.

Recension II. This is the version as extensively revised by Chekhov in October–December 1888 and sent by him to A. S. Suvorin on 19 December 1888 for transmission to A. A. Potekhin, Director of Repertoire at the Alexandrine Theatre in St. Petersburg.

Recension III. This is the play as further revised by Chekhov in January 1889 and performed on 31 January 1889 at the Alexandrine Theatre.

Recension IV. This is the play as altered by Chekhov (in a revision affecting the ending only) between its first performance at the Alexandrine Theatre and the preparation of the '*Severny vestnik* text'.

Recension I is that found in a lithographed publication of Ye. N. Rassokhina's Moscow Theatrical Library, marked as having been passed by the censor on 10 December 1887. This is not, however, the first extant draft of the play, which takes the form of a typescript preserved in the Central Library of the Russian Drama (no. 40393), and marked as having been passed by the censor on 6 November 1887. This typescript presents a text almost identical with that published by Rassokhina—the very minor differences between the two do not call for comment.

Unlike that of Recension I, the text of Recensions II, III and IV can in no case be equated with that of a single extant document. Each of these recensions can, however, be reconstructed by collating the evidence provided by the text (including the numerous insertions and passages erased, but still legible) in three drafts:

the 'Producer's text no. 4447'—partly in lithographed form and partly in manuscript, and preserved in the Central Library of the Russian Drama (no. 4447);

the 'Producer's text no. 4465'—in manuscript and also preserved in the above library (no. 4465);

the 'January 1889 text'—a lithographed version, marked as having been passed by the censor on 3 January 1889 and also preserved in the above library (no. 40394).

The relationship between the four recensions and five drafts, as just described may be recapitulated for convenience as follows:

Recension	Date	Drafts providing evidence on text of recension
I	19 Nov. 1887	November 1887 typescript. The lithographed text issued by Rassokhina.
II	19 Dec. 1888	Producer's text no. 4447.
III	31 Jan. 1889	Producer's text no. 4465.
IV	Early Feb. 1889	January 1889 text.

3. VARIANTS

The material given below, on variants of *Ivanov* in its pre-publication form, is based on the evidence contained in the Appendix to the play in *Works*, 1944–51, xi, as derived from the above-mentioned documents. However, in presenting this material a more selective approach has been adopted than that of the editors of *Works*, 1944–51—more selective also than has seemed appropriate in the case of *The Seagull* (in the present volume) and of the plays contained in vols. i and iii of the present edition. The sheer bulk of the material relating to *Ivanov* together with the comparative insignificance of some of the minor variants as evidence of Chekhov's creative methods, have combined to make the presentation of fuller details less desirable in the case of *Ivanov*. The variants given below have accordingly been chosen, after a careful study of the whole material, on the basis of their importance to the history of the play and to Chekhov's development as a playwright.

Chekhov's revisions of *Ivanov* present the following general features. Firstly, each successive revision tended to be less radical than the preceding one. Thus the revision of October–December 1888 recast large sections of the play, so that Recension II differs radically from Recension I. By contrast, the variations between the '*Severny vestnik* text' and that of the later printed versions are comparatively trivial. Secondly, the impact of Chekhov's revisions was felt with increasing severity towards the end of the play. Act Four—in particular its closing scenes—was altered again and again, whereas Act One remained comparatively intact throughout the whole process of revision, and Acts Two and Three represent an intermediate grade in the scale of revision.

Six stages of revision may be distinguished:

Revision	Leading to
1	Recension II
2	Recension III
3	Recension IV
4	'*Severny vestnik* text'
5	'*Plays, 1897* text'
6	'*Works, 1901* text' = final version

In the presentation of variants, below, a fairly full picture is given of Recensions I to IV inclusive. The relatively minor, though numerous, alterations which took place in the 4th, 5th and 6th stages of revision are only brought in incidentally.

One minor change, affecting the play as a whole, was the removal from the list of characters of 'DUDKIN, son of a rich manufacturer' in the first revision. From Recension II onwards Dudkin's part was distributed between the First and Third Guest. These and other variants are now considered under the Acts to which they relate.

ACT ONE

First revision (resulting in Recension II)

Few changes, and those mainly cuts, were made. The cuts were:

In Scene ii, after Borkin's words 'Shall I marry Martha Babakin?' (see p. 169), Recension I had:

Martha's a silly bitch, but I'll marry her if you like.

In Scene iii, after Borkin's words 'No more flower' (see p. 171), Recension I had:

[*Hums.*] 'Couldst thou but sense the trembling of my heart.'

In Scene iv, after Shabelsky's words 'the one like a washerwoman' (see p. 173), Recension I had:

who blows her nose like a cab-driver.

Second revision (leading to Recension III)

Two conversations were expanded. The exchange between Ivanov and Anna in Scene vi (see pp. 176–7) was given its final form in Recension III, having previously read as follows:

IVANOV. You must be sensible, Anna. We'll go and see them when you get better, but at the moment you need quiet. Well, good-bye. [*Goes up to his wife and kisses her head.*] I'll be back by one.

ANNA [*takes him to the front of the stage*]. Nicholas—. [*Laughs.*] Why not stay at home? We'll have a romp in the hay as we used to—have supper together and read. The old boy and I've learnt a lot of duets for you. [*Pause.*] Don't go out, we'll have some fun. [*Laughs and cries.*] What is it, Nicholas? Flowers come round every spring, but happiness doesn't—is that it? All right, go then.

IVANOV. I—I'll soon be back. [*Moves off, stops and thinks.*] No, it's too much. [*Goes out.*]

ANNA. Go away then. [*Sits by the table.*]

In Scene vii, Anna's comments to Lvov as adopted in Recension III and retained in the final version (see pp. 178–9, from 'There are lots of people ...' to '... What horrible thoughts I have') had been briefer in Recension II, where they read as follows:

There are lots of people, not better than me perhaps, who are happy and whose happiness costs them nothing. So why do I have to pay so dearly? Why charge me such a shocking rate of interest? [*Eagerly.*] What did you say?

LVOV. I didn't say anything.

ANNA. I've also started wondering why people are so unfair and cruel. Why can't they love those who love them? Why do they have to lie when they're told the truth? [*Shrugs her shoulders.*] You're not married, Doctor, so there's a lot you can't understand.

ACT TWO

First revision (resulting in Recension II)

The first revision included the distribution, as mentioned above, between the First and Third Guests of the remarks given to Dudkin in Recension I.

The following stage directions, occurring in Recension I after '*all under covers*' (see p. 181), were cut out in the first revision:

> *By the wall, left, is a sofa. In front of it a circular table with a large lamp on it. Armchairs to each side, and three armchairs in a row by the wall on the near side of the table. An upright piano, right, with a violin on it and upright chairs to both sides. A card table has been put up at the back of the stage near the door on to the terrace.*

The stage directions for Scene i were altered. Recension I had, in place of the words '*The young people are sitting . . .*' to '*. . . and* YEGORUSHKA' (see p. 181):

> *Opposite them, on upright chairs, are* DUDKIN, *the* FIRST GUEST *and five or six young ladies.* KOSYKH, YEGORUSHKA, AVDOTYA *and the* SECOND GUEST *are sitting at the card table playing cards.*

At the end of Scene i, in place of the Third Guest's speech 'It's no use having capital . . .' to '. . . in a worse fix these days than one who—' (see p. 182), Recension I had the following, attributed to Dudkin:

> Let's look at the thing sensibly. You get no profit nowadays, whatever you do with your capital. Stocks and shares are no good and lending money can cut both ways—you can so easily go bankrupt. The way I see it, anyone who has a bit of money put by may as well buy a revolver and put a bullet through his brains. Because capital's just a nuisance nowadays.

This was replaced in Recension II by a text corresponding with that in the final version, though slightly longer.

The following dialogue, occurring in Recension I after Mrs. Babakin's remark 'That's true' (see p. 182), was cut out in the first revision:

FIRST GUEST [*to the young lady sitting next to him*]. One man visits another, sees a dog. [*Laughs.*] 'What's the dog's name?' he asks. 'Same-as-yours', answers the other. [*Guffaws.*] 'Same-as-yours.' Get it? That's what the dog was called. [*Is embarrassed.*]

DUDKIN. At a warehouse in our town there's a dog called On-his-last-legs.

MRS. BABAKIN. What?

DUDKIN. On-his-last-legs.

[*Slight laughter.* ZINAIDA *stands up.*]

In Scene iii, Recension I read as follows after Sasha's words 'What harm did he ever do you?' (see p. 186):

ZINAIDA [*with a sneer*]. A decent, honest man——

FIRST GUEST [*sincerely*]. You don't really know him, Miss Lebedev, believe me. How can you call him honest? [*Stands up.*] Is this your idea of honesty? During the cattle epidemic two years ago he bought a lot of cows——

ZINAIDA [*interrupting*]. Bought a lot of cows, insured them, infected them with cattle disease and pocketed the insurance—call that being honest?

FIRST GUEST. Everyone knows all about that.

SASHA. It's not true, it's a lie. No one bought cows or infected them, it was all Borkin's idea that he went round boasting about. When Ivanov heard of the thing he had Borkin going round for a couple of weeks apologizing. Ivanov's only fault is being weak and generous, and not having enough go in him to chuck out friend Borkin.

FIRST GUEST. Weak! [*Laughs.*] That's only an act, Miss Lebedev, believe me.

ZINAIDA. Aren't you ashamed to stick up for someone like that?

SASHA. I'm sorry I joined in this conversation. [*Hurries towards the door, right.*]

LEBEDEV. Sasha, my little firebrand! [*Laughs.*] You spitfire!

FIRST GUEST [*blocks her way*]. I won't say it again, Miss Lebedev, really. I'm sorry—I won't, on my word of honour.

ZINAIDA. Don't show off in front of visitors, Sasha.

SASHA [*in a quavering voice*]. He's spent all his life working for others. He's had all his property pilfered and stolen. Everyone who wanted has made a packet out of his idealistic plans. He's never demeaned himself by lying or sharp practice, and I've never heard him run anyone down. And now what? Wherever you go it's 'Ivanov, Ivanov, Ivanov'—as if there was nothing else to talk about.

LEBEDEV. That's enough, you little spitfire.

SASHA. All right, so he sometimes makes mistakes. But every mistake made by someone like that is worth twenty of the things the rest of us do right. If you could only——. [*Looks round and sees* IVANOV *and* SHABELSKY.]

In Scene iv, Recension I had the following instead of Shabelsky's lines 'As for Sarah herself . . .' to '. . . jiggery-pokery' (see p. 189):

SHABELSKY. As for Sarah herself, she's a wretched Jewess. I don't believe a thing she says or does. Very sorry, yes plis, vy am I so unhappy? Nothing will make me believe her. I'm sorry, Nicholas, I'm not being particularly nasty, am I? To my way of thinking, if Sarah's ill she's ill because it's good business to be ill. I won't believe it if she dies—it'll just mean she thinks dying's good business too.

In Scene v, Recension I read as follows after Borkin's words '. . . tag, dancing, fireworks?' (see p. 192):

YOUNG LADIES. Dancing, dancing!

BORKIN. I'm ready. Let's dance, Dudkin. [*Moves the armchairs to the wall.*] Where are you, Yegorushka? Tune your fiddle.

> [YEGORUSHKA *shudders and goes to the piano.* BORKIN *sits at the piano and gives him an A.* YEGORUSHKA *tunes his violin.*]

IVANOV [*to* LEBEDEV]. Can I ask you something, Paul? The interest on my loan to you falls due in two days' time, but I can't pay it. Can I have a bit longer or add the interest to what I owe you?

LEBEDEV [*terrified*]. None of my business, old man. Talk to Zizi, I—I don't know anything.

IVANOV [*rubs his forehead*]. This is agony.

SASHA. What are you talking about?

IVANOV. I feel ghastly today.

SASHA. You look it too. Let's go in the dining-room.

> [IVANOV *and* SASHA *go out through door, right.*]

BORKIN [*shouts*]. The band's ready.

> [DUDKIN *invites* MRS. BABAKIN *to dance.*]

MRS. BABAKIN. No, I mustn't dance today, it's the anniversary of my husband's death.

> [BORKIN *and* YEGORUSHKA *play the polka* A propos Faust. *The* COUNT *plugs his ears and goes out on the terrace.* AVDOTYA *follows him.* DUDKIN *is seen trying to make* MRS. BABAKIN *change her mind. The young ladies ask the* FIRST GUEST *to dance, but he refuses.* DUDKIN *makes a gesture of resignation and goes out into the garden.*]

BORKIN [*looks round him*]. I say, what is all this? [*Stops playing.*] Why don't you dance?

YOUNG LADIES. There are no men.

BORKIN [*stands up*]. At this rate we'll get nowhere. Let's let off the fireworks, shall we?

YOUNG LADIES [*clap their hands*]. Fireworks, fireworks. [*They run into the garden.*]

BORKIN [*takes a packet and gives his arm to* MRS. BABAKIN]. *Je vous prie.* [*Shouts.*] Come on. In the garden.

[*Goes out. Everyone goes out except* LEBEDEV *and* ZINAIDA.]

The above was considerably shortened in the first revision.

Second revision (*resulting in Recension III*)

Scene vi had the following form in Recensions I and II (for the final version, as adopted, with one minor variant, in Recension III, see p. 193):

SASHA [*coming in through the door, right, with* IVANOV]. They've all gone in the garden.

IVANOV. That's how things are, Sasha. I don't do anything, I don't think about anything, but I'm exhausted, body, soul and spirit. I feel so conscience-stricken all the time. I feel terribly guilty, but just where I went wrong I can't see. Then there's my wife's illness, my money troubles, this non-stop backbiting, gossip and fuss. I'm sick and tired of my home, living there's sheer hell. [*Looks round.*] I don't know what's happening to me, Sasha, but I'll be perfectly honest with you—I can't even stand having my loving wife about, and my head's full of rotten, selfish thoughts such as I could never even imagine at one time. [*Pause.*] It's so nasty. Sorry, Sasha, I'm depressing you, but it's only when I talk to you, dear, that I can forget things for a bit. When I'm near you I feel like a dog warming itself in the sunshine. I've known you all your life, Sasha, I've always loved you and played with you. I'd give a lot to have a daughter like you.

SASHA [*joking, through tears*]. Let's run away to America, Nicholas.

IVANOV. I'm too lazy to get as far as that door and you want to go to America. [*They go towards the exit to the garden.*] It's not much of a life for you here, is it, Sasha? I can see that, I see everything. This atmosphere doesn't suit you.

Scene ix had the following form in Recensions I and II (for the final version, as adopted in Recension III, see pp. 194–5; in Recension II Dudkin's part is given to the First Guest):

DUDKIN. Just a moment, we'll sound out Yegorushka about the schnapps at once. I'll have a drink, old girl, and be off home. Confound him and to hell with everything! I'm so bored and starved, I'm ready to scream, and I'm not interested in any of your marriageable young women. How the hell can a man think of love when he doesn't get a drink after dinner?

AVDOTYA. It's not Sasha's fault, it's her mother's doing.

DUDKIN. But why are you trying to marry me to Sasha? That wishy-washy creature, she's too clever by half! I'm a solid citizen, a man of character. Give me something a bit more substantial.

AVDOTYA. Shall we go and look?

DUDKIN. Shush! Keep this under your hat. Martha would suit me, but she's frightfully, er, flighty. I went to see her yesterday and her place was crawling with actors and such. [*They go out through door, left.*]

Scene x was expanded. It has the following form in Recensions I and II (for the final, longer, version, adopted in Recension III, see p. 195):

LVOV. Why did we come here, I wonder?

ANNA. It's all right, they'll be glad to see us. No one here, they must be in the garden. Let's go in the garden. [*They go into the garden.*]

ACT THREE

First revision (leading to Recension II)

The following sentence was removed from the stage directions at the beginning of Act Three (see p. 198):

Book-cupboards, small tables, armchairs, sets of shelves, a pair of scales and a plough.

In Scene i, between Shabelsky's 'The man's a genius' and Lebedev's 'God knows, you do entertain us' (see p. 198), Recension I had:

He conceives thousands of schemes a day, tries to pull the stars down from the sky, but it does no good. He never has a penny to his name.

LEBEDEV. It's art for art's sake.

BORKIN. I don't do it for myself, it's for other people—out of philanthropy.

The above was cut out in the first revision.

In Scene i, after Lebedev's words 'the mere smell will make you swoon!' (see p. 199), Recension I had:

⟨LEBEDEV⟩ [*eagerly*]. Ever had caviare made of mushrooms—orange-agaric, I mean?

SHABELSKY. No.

LEBEDEV. Well, you shred your salted mushroom into tiny bits like caviare or porridge, see? Put in onion and olive oil, a spot of pepper and vinegar. [*Kisses his fingers.*] It's a knock-out.

The above was cut out in the first revision.

In Scene v, between Lebedev's words 'I'd take it from you, on my honour' and 'Are you awfully fed up?' (see p. 204), Recension I had:

IVANOV [*walks up and down*]. I don't care, I've no pride left. If you slapped my face now, I don't think I'd say a word.

LEBEDEV. Here it is on the table, eleven hundred roubles. Drive over today and hand it to her yourself. 'There you are, Zinaida,' say, 'and I hope it chokes you.' But for God's sake don't let on you got it from me.

This passage was recast to take its final form in the first revision.

Scene vi began as follows in Recension I:

IVANOV [*alone*]. I'll sign the papers and go for a stroll with my gun. I must tidy away this muck. [*Takes the snacks and bread on to a small table, squirming fastidiously.*]

In Recension II Chekhov substituted for the above the long soliloquy which remains in the final version, on pp. 206–7.

At the end of Scene vi in Recension II an insert (later removed) was made in which Dr. Lvov tells Ivanov that he is in love with Ivanov's wife. This appeared between 'LVOV. Oh, have you?' and '*Sees* SASHA *come in. She wears a riding habit*' (see p. 209):

⟨LVOV.⟩ If it comes to that, I may as well tell you I love your wife—I love her as much as I hate you. That's why I'm completely within my rights. When I first saw how unhappy she was, it broke my heart and——

The above was cut out in the revision for the '*Plays, 1897* text'.

The material corresponding to Scene vii in the final version (see pp. 209–11) had a somewhat different form in Recension I. It was rather shorter, was divided into two scenes (vii and viii) and brought on Ivanov's servant Peter. It read as follows:

IVANOV [*frightened*]. Is it you, Sasha?

SASHA. Yes. Weren't you expecting me?

IVANOV [*looking round*]. For God's sake, Sasha—this is most indiscreet. Your visit may have a very bad effect on my wife.

SASHA. I'm just going. I'm worried about how you are. Why haven't you been to see us?

IVANOV. For God's sake go. We mustn't meet until, until—oh, you know what I mean. [*Gently pushes her towards the door.*]

SASHA. At least tell me if you're well.

IVANOV. No, I've worn myself out and people never stop bothering me. I'm at the end of my tether, and I'd have put a bullet through my brain long ago if it wasn't for you. See how I'm shaking? Sasha, for God's sake take me away from here quickly. [*Presses his face against her shoulder.*] Let me rest and forget, if only for a minute.

SASHA. Make it quickly, Nicholas. Don't be downhearted—aren't you ashamed?

SCENE VIII

[IVANOV, SASHA *and* PETER. PETER *brings in some pasties on a piece of paper and puts them on the table.*]

IVANOV [*shudders*]. Who? What? [*Seeing* PETER.] What do you want?

PETER. Some pasties, sir, the count ordered them.

IVANOV. Oh, go away. [PETER *goes.*]

SASHA. Believe me, dear—here's my hand. Things will look up and you'll be happy. Please—see how brave and happy I am. [*Weeps.*]

IVANOV. It's as if we wanted her to die. What a shabby, rotten attitude, I feel so guilty.

SASHA [*in horror*]. Who wants her to die, Nicholas? Let her live on another hundred years. And what have you to be guilty about? Is it your fault you stopped loving her and that she's dying? Or that you love me? Think it over properly. Look [*weeps*], face the facts and cheer up. It's not your fault or mine—it's just the way things have turned out.

IVANOV. 'Please', 'a day will come', 'fell in love', 'fell out of love'—those are all clichés, hackneyed phrases that will do no good.

SASHA. I talk like everyone else, I don't know any other way of talking.

IVANOV. And this whole affair is so awfully commonplace. 'He became depressed and lost his sense of purpose. Along came She, high-spirited and strong, and held out a helping hand.' That's all right for novels, it fits in there, but in life—it's wrong, all wrong. You love me, you're mine, you've held out a helping hand—but I'm still as pathetic and helpless as before.

During the first revision the above Scenes vii and viii were combined into a single scene (Scene vii), in which the servant Peter does not appear, while the dialogue between Ivanov and Sasha corresponds closely with that in the final version as far as 'All very romantic and convincing in a magazine story, but in real life—' (see p. 210). Thereafter Ivanov's speech continued as in Recension I: 'it's wrong, all wrong. You love me, you're mine, you've held out a helping hand—but I'm still as pathetic and helpless as before.'

To this the following exchange (later removed) was added in Recension II:

IVANOV. But just look at yourself—you're shaking, you're pale and your eyes are full of tears. We're no good as heroes, you and I.

SASHA. You'll go on all day, I can see. Good-bye then. Listen—I love you and I'll follow you wherever you like, to Siberia if need be or wherever the storm is fiercest. I'm ready to die for you. Whatever happens to you, wherever you land up, I'll always be with you everywhere.

IVANOV. Yes, yes, yes, talk away. [*Presses his face to her shoulder.*] I've tortured you and myself. Sasha, in the name of all that's holy, take me away from here quickly. Let me rest and forget, if only for a minute.

Second revision (leading to Recension III)

Scene v was expanded. In Recensions I and II it ended shortly after Lebedev's words 'A genius, eh? Regular George Sand' (see p. 205) with the following brief continuation:

I thought it was only Borkin who had brainwaves, but now it turns out—. I'm going, I'm going. [*Goes.*]

In place of this, Recension III and later editions have the dialogue given on pp. 205–6, from 'IVANOV. Leave me alone, Paul, please . . .' to '. . . LEBEDEV. I'm off, I'm off. [*Goes.*]'

Scene vii of Recension III took the form in which it was rewritten 'for Savina' (the actress who played Sasha in the performance at the St. Petersburg Alexandrine Theatre; see p. 296, above). The text of this scene in Recension III is as in the final version (see pp. 209–11), but with the addition of certain passages which were cut out of later recensions. These are as follows:

After Ivanov's words 'All this rescuing and crusading zeal!' (see p. 210), Recension III had:

That's what Russian girls were always famous for—not being able to tell the difference between a good picture and a caricature.

After Ivanov's words 'All new babies will be snivelling neurotics, thanks to you' (see p. 210), Recension III had:

IVANOV. You are a funny girl. Now what are you laughing at? You're a bit young to start telling me what to do and trying to rescue me. Funny little thing.

SASHA. Good heavens, what a way to talk—don't overdo it.

IVANOV. Of course you're a funny little thing.

SASHA. Oh, spare us the irony.

IVANOV [*imitating her voice*]. I shan't spare you.

SASHA. All right, we'll find you a punishment. How about a little gentle exercise? [*Pushes his shoulder, then pulls him towards her by the hand as hard as she can.*] Limber up a bit. Heavens, what a clumsy old porpoise! Get moving, lazybones.

IVANOV. I didn't budge an inch. It'd take more than you to shift me, my girl, try as you like—rope in your mother too if you want. No, miss, you're not the only pebble on the beach. An entire widows' home and girls' boarding school wouldn't budge me.

SASHA. What, actually out of breath! Oh, confound you.

IVANOV. And you want to rescue me, you hussy, you naughty little black-eyed minx.

After Sasha's words 'asked for a drink' (see p. 211), Recension III had: [*Imitates him in a deep voice.*] Give me some water, please, Sasha dear.

After Ivanov's words 'I've just been grateful, that's all, there's no more to it' (see p. 211), Recension III had:

IVANOV. If only I could stop being such a jellyfish, damn me, I'd be a real man. Mind the train, you'll get run over! [*Chases* SASHA.] Grr!

SASHA [*jumps on the sofa*]. Go away, go away, go away.

IVANOV. O insignificant regiment of women! [*Roars with laughter.*] You are funny, little girl. I'm a silly ass myself. Do you know, there's a wretched, miserable, grey little bird living in the reeds by the Dnieper? It's called a bull-warbler and it sits in the reeds all day mooing in the most miserable way—moo-oo-oo, like a cow shut in a barn. I'm like that, I sit in my reeds disturbing the peace with my non-stop moaning and groaning. Moo-oo-oo. [*Moves off quickly.*] Please leave, Sasha, we're forgetting ourselves.

ACT FOUR

Recension I

Owing to Chekhov's repeated efforts to find a satisfactory ending for the play, Act Four was subjected to more radical revision than any of the other acts—in fact very little (approximately a quarter only) of the material of Recension I of Act Four survives, in considerably reshuffled form, in the final version. It is therefore essential to give the text of Recension I in full. As will be seen, its special features are: the division of the act into two Parts; the presence of much broad comedy peculiar to this recension and including the conversation between Dudkin and Kosykh about the dowry; Borkin's plan to buy a stud-farm and his proposal of marriage to Mrs. Babakin; the fact that (in Part II) the marriage between Ivanov and Sasha is to be understood as having taken place; the manner of Ivanov's death—the result here, not of suicide, but (presumably and somewhat implausibly) of a stroke brought on by the insult offered to him by Lvov.

ACT FOUR

(*Recension I*)

PART I

A small room in the LEBEDEVS' *house with antique furniture. Doors, right and left.*

SCENE I

[DUDKIN *and* KOSYKH. *Both wear tail-coats and gloves and have flowers in their button-holes. They stand near the door, left, snatching a quick smoke.*]

KOSYKH [*gaily*]. Yesterday I declared a little slam in clubs and got a grand slam. But once again friend Barabanov cooked my goose. We sit down to play and I bid one no trump. He passes. Then we go on to clubs. He passes and I bid two clubs—three clubs. He passes and—it's beyond the bounds of credence! I declare a slam and he doesn't show his ace. If he'd shown his ace I'd have declared a grand slam in no trumps.

DUDKIN. Wait, a carriage has arrived—it must be the best man. [*Looks through the window.*] No. [*Looks at his watch.*] It's high time he was here.

KOSYKH. Yes, the bride's been ready for ages.

DUDKIN. If I was the groom, old boy [*whistles*], I'd show them a thing or two! The bride's in her wedding dress and it's time to go to church—just the time, in fact, to turn up here and pitch into Zizi: 'Hand over a hundred thousand,' I'd say. 'Or the wedding's off. Come on!'

KOSYKH. You wouldn't get it.

DUDKIN. Oh yes I would—with everything ready in church and people waiting, she'd cough up all right. Ivanov won't get a sausage as it is—he won't get five thousand.

KOSYKH. He'll get the lot when she dies, though.

DUDKIN. It's all very well to say wait till she dies, but she'll bury all her money in the ground before she kicks off—she's a real old witch. I had an uncle like that, and before he died he chewed up all his share certificates and damn well swallowed them. The doctor comes to see him and his belly's this size! Ivanov thinks she'll fork out on the spot and be only too pleased. What a hope! He slipped up over his Jewess and found himself in queer street—and it'll be the same here. He's unlucky, that's all, he might as well curl up and die. He's a smart lad, though, a pretty slippery customer. There are no flies on him—he knows which side his bread's buttered. So it must be plain bad luck—fate is against him.

SCENE II

[*The above and* MRS. BABAKIN. MRS. BABAKIN, *dressed to kill, struts across the stage past* DUDKIN *and* KOSYKH. *Both of them guffaw into their hands behind her back. She looks round.*]

MRS. BABAKIN. Don't be silly.

[DUDKIN *touches her waist with his finger and clicks his tongue.*]

MRS. BABAKIN. Clumsy lout!

[*Goes out.* DUDKIN *and* KOSYKH *guffaw.*]

DUDKIN. The woman's off her rocker. She was all right before she set her sights on a title, but since she started this countess business you can't get near her. Time was, you could take a hamper of brandy and liqueurs, drive over to her place for two or three days—and have the hell of a good time, no end of fun and games. But now you have to watch your step. [*Imitates her.*] 'Clumsy lout!'

KOSYKH. The count's only having a bit of fun with her, you know. And you take it all as Gospel. He justs wants a spot of gossip and the odd free supper, he's been leading her up the garden path for the last twelve months. What I like about Martha, old boy, is that she's tough, really tough. Michael Borkin's sweated blood, played every trick in the book to get money out of her. But not one copeck have they had. He did get two hundred roubles out of her last year to fix up the marriage, but even that was sent back double quick by Ivanov. So Michael got nothing and wasted his efforts.

SCENE III

[*The above,* LEBEDEV *and* SASHA, *in her wedding dress.*]

LEBEDEV [*coming in with* SASHA]. We can talk in here. [*To* DUDKIN *and* KOSYKH.] Clear out, monsters, and join the girls in the ballroom. We want a private talk.

DUDKIN [*passing* SASHA, *winks and snaps his fingers*]. Pretty as a picture—very sparkling!

LEBEDEV. Move along, caveman, move along.

[KOSYKH *and* DUDKIN *go out.*]

LEBEDEV. Sit down, Sasha, that's right. [*Sits down and looks round.*] Listen carefully and with due reverence. The fact is, your mother told me to give you this message. Do you see? It's not my idea, it's what your mother told me to say. [*Blows his nose.*] Before the best man gets here and before we've blessed the bride, I must tell you once and for all—to avoid misunderstandings and possible argument later—that we, that is not we, but your mother——

SASHA. Can't you cut it short, Father?

LEBEDEV. Well, this is the point. Your dowry's to be fifteen thousand roubles in notes. Now look, we don't want arguments afterwards. No, don't speak, this is only the half of it, there are more treats in store. Your dowry's to be fifteen thousand, but as Nicholas owes your mother nine thousand, that debt's being deducted from the dowry, so you'll only get six thousand. *Vous comprenez?* I have to tell you all this to avoid argument later. Stop, I haven't finished. We set aside five hundred roubles to pay for the wedding, but as it's usual for the bridegroom to meet all wedding expenses, the five hundred's also being deducted from the six thousand. So it's five thousand five hundred all told, and you'll get it after the ceremony. Your good mother's also taking the chance to pass on some dud shares and bonds that don't fall due till the end of the century.

SASHA. Why tell me this?

LEBEDEV. Your mother told me to.

SASHA [*gets up*]. Father, if you had any respect for either of us, you wouldn't let yourself talk like this. [*Angrily.*] I don't want your dowry, I never asked for one and I'm not asking now. Leave me alone, and don't insult my ears with your cheap calculations.

LEBEDEV. All this about the dowry comes from your mother, not me.

SASHA. I've told you hundreds of times I won't take a penny. And we'll pay you back what we owe, I'll borrow some money and pay you. Can't you leave me alone?

LEBEDEV. Why pitch into me? Gogol's two rats had a sniff at each other and then left each other alone, but you're so much the emancipated woman, you lash out without even a sniff.

SASHA. Leave me alone.

LEBEDEV [*flaring up*]. Really, you'll all have me stabbing myself or cutting someone's throat. One of you's for ever yelling blue murder, nagging and counting pennies, while this one's so intelligent, humane and goddam emancipated, she can't understand her own father. I insult her ears. Why—before coming here and insulting your ears, I was being torn limb from limb out there. [*Points to the door. Walks about in agitation.*] She can't understand! [*Imitates her.*] 'Won't take a penny.' Who do you think you're impressing? How will you and your husband eat?

SASHA. We'll eat our own food, he's not a beggar.

LEBEDEV [*with a gesture of resignation*]. One's a shrew, the other a gas-bag, and I can't say a word to Nicholas—he's too clever by half. I don't know whether I'm on my head or my heels. Buck up and get married, and to hell with the lot of you. [*Moves towards the door and stops.*] I don't like you, I don't like anything about any of you.

SASHA. What do you mean?

LEBEDEV. Well, I'm not going to sit back and spout about it. I hate the whole thing, I can't stand the idea of your wedding. [*Goes up to* SASHA *and speaks kindly.*] I'm sorry, Sasha, your marriage may be all very clever, noble, starry-eyed and high-principled, but there's something wrong with it, there really is, you know. It's not like other marriages. You're young, pure, fresh as a spring morning, you're beautiful—and he's a shabby, frowsty widower aged thirty-five. Look, he'll be bored and have wrinkles in five years' time. [*Kisses his daughter's head.*] Sasha, I'm sorry, there's something not quite nice about it. There's a lot of talk about the way Sarah died and the way he was suddenly all set on marrying you because of this that and the other.

SASHA. He's a friend of yours, Father.

LEBEDEV. So he may be. Still, there's something a bit fishy about it, you know. [*With animation.*] I'm an old woman anyway, I really am, I'm a regular old grandmother. Don't listen to me, don't listen to anyone—listen only to yourself.

SCENE IV

[*The above and* ZINAIDA.]

ZINAIDA [*comes in wearing a new dress, with a wet towel round her head*]. The best man's just got here, I think—we must go and bless the bride. [*Cries.*]

SASHA [*imploringly*]. Mother!

LEBEDEV. That's enough of the waterworks, Zizi, God help us. You've been raising the roof for the last twelve months, if you don't mind my saying so. [*Pause.*] And you stink of vinegar.

SASHA [*imploringly*]. Mother!

ZINAIDA. If you've no use for your mother [*cries*], if you can manage without obeying your mother then—what do you need from me? I'll bless you, I'll do as you wish and give you my blessing.

LEBEDEV. You should be glad, Zizi——

ZINAIDA [*tearing her handkerchief away from her face and not crying*]. What for? He's marrying her for her money and to get out of paying what he owes me—and you're glad. [*Cries.*] We only have one daughter and God knows what she—. If he was as decent and responsible as you make out, he'd have paid his debts before proposing.

LEBEDEV [*to* SASHA]. Don't say anything, hold it. Just swallow it, old girl—it'll soon be over.

SCENE V

[*The above and* IVANOV. IVANOV *comes in noticeably overwrought, wearing tails.*]

Simultaneously {

LEBEDEV [*frightened*]. What's this? Where have you sprung from?

SASHA. What are you doing here?

IVANOV. I'm sorry, but please can I talk to Sasha in private?

}

LEBEDEV. You shouldn't visit the bride before the wedding. You should have been at church long ago.

IVANOV. Please, Paul.

[LEBEDEV *shrugs his shoulders. He and* ZINAIDA *go out.*]

IVANOV [*upset*]. Sasha, darling——

SASHA. You're upset. What's happened?

IVANOV. My treasure, my darling, listen to me—forget you love me, concentrate and listen.

SASHA. Don't try to scare me, Nicholas. What's the matter?

IVANOV. I was dressing for the wedding just now. I looked in the glass and saw grey hairs on my temples. Sasha, we shouldn't. Let's stop before it's too late, let's call it off. [*Clutches his head.*] Let's call it off. Leave me alone. [*Heatedly.*] You're young, lovely and unspoilt, with your whole life before you and I—have grey hair on my temples, I'm a broken reed, a man with a past, haunted by guilt. I'm no husband for you.

SASHA [*sternly*]. What is this sentimental rubbish, Nicholas? They've been expecting you at church for ages and you rush over here snivelling. None of this is new, I've heard it before and I'm fed up with it. Go to church and don't keep people waiting.

IVANOV [*takes her hands*]. I love and value you too much to dare stand in your way. You wouldn't be happy with me, I swear it. Give me up before it's too late, it's the decent, sensible thing to do. I'll go straight home, and you tell your family the wedding's off—make them understand somehow. [*Walks up and down in agitation.*] God, I feel you don't understand me, Sasha. I'm old, my day's over, I'm stale, I've lost my vitality for good, I've no future. I have such gloomy memories. I feel guiltier every hour, it stifles me. My doubts and forebodings—. Something's going to happen, I tell you—storm clouds are gathering, I feel it.

SASHA [*holds his hand, restraining him*]. You're talking like a child, dear. Calm down a bit. You feel downhearted and your strong, healthy mind is giving way to neurosis, but don't let it—pull yourself together. Stop and think— are there really any storm clouds? What have you done wrong? And what are you trying to do? You rush here to tell me you're an old man. So you may be, but I'm no child either. What has being old to do with it? If all the hair of your darling head suddenly went grey, I'd only love it all the more, knowing what turned it grey. [*Cries.*] Wait a moment, I'll—. [*Wipes her eyes.*]

IVANOV. Go on, go on.

SASHA. You're troubled by guilt. Everyone runs you down except Father. I had an anonymous letter yesterday warning me——

IVANOV. That's Dr. Lvov's doing, the man's persecuting me.

SASHA. Never mind whose doing it was. You have a bad name—but you're the best, the most decent and honourable man I know. In fact I love you, and love leaves no room for compromise and half-measures. I'll be your wife. That's what I want to be, it's settled and no argument! I love you and I'll follow you anywhere, and never mind those storm clouds. Whatever happens to you, wherever you may land up, I'll always be with you—otherwise my life has no meaning.

IVANOV [*walks up and down*]. Yes, yes, yes—. You're right, I'm being silly, I've let myself get in a nervous state, I've tortured myself—and now I'm making you unhappy. I really should settle down quick to do a job of work and live a normal life. My head's too full of useless ideas. There's nothing abnormal or remarkable about me marrying you—it's just that I'm so touchy, I've built the thing up out of all proportion. Everything's perfectly normal and all right. Very well then, I'll go to church——

SASHA. You go then and we'll come along at once.

IVANOV [*kisses her*]. I'm sorry, you're fed up with me. Today we marry, tomorrow we start work. [*Laughs.*] My lovely little philosopher, there was I boasting about how old I was, and you turn out to be ten years older, at least in wisdom. [*Stops laughing.*] Seriously, Sasha, we're the same as other people and we'll be as happy as they are. If we're to blame, we're no more so than they are either.

SASHA. Well, run along, it's time you went.

IVANOV. All right, I'm going. [*Laughs.*] How silly of me, what a child I still am. Really, I'm like a wet rag. [*Moves towards the door and bumps into* LEBEDEV.]

SCENE VI

[IVANOV, SASHA *and* LEBEDEV.]

LEBEDEV. Hey, come here. [*Takes* IVANOV *up-stage by the arm.*] You look me straight in the eyes. [*They stare at each other for a long time without speaking.*] All right, God be with you. [*Embraces him.*] Be happy, old boy, and forgive my evil thoughts. [*To* SASHA.] He's still quite a lad, Sasha. Look at him, he's no end of a fellow—quite the young guards officer. Come here, Sasha, come. [*Sternly.*] Come on.

[SASHA *goes up to him.*]

LEBEDEV [*takes* IVANOV *and* SASHA *by the hands, looking round*]. Look here, your mother can do what she likes, confound her. If she won't give you any money, never mind. Sasha, you always say you [*imitating her*] 'don't need a penny'. Principles, altruism, Schopenhauer and all that. Now that's a lot of nonsense, but you just listen to me. [*Sighs.*] I've ten thousand roubles stowed away in the bank. [*Looks round.*] Not a soul knows about it at home. It was your grandmother's. [*Letting go of their hands.*] Take it, take the lot!

IVANOV. Good-bye.

[*Gives a happy laugh and goes out.* SASHA *follows him.*]

LEBEDEV. Gabriel! [*Goes out and shouts on the other side of the door.*] Gabriel!

SCENE VII

[DUDKIN *and* KOSYKH. *Both run in and quickly light up cigarettes.*]

KOSYKH. Just time for a smoke.

DUDKIN. He's come to put the squeeze on over the dowry. [*Ecstatically.*] He's a hell of a fellow, I must say, one hell of a fellow.

CURTAIN

PART II

The drawing-room in the LEBEDEVS' *house. Furniture upholstered in velvet, bronze antiques, family portraits. An upright piano with a violin on it, and a 'cello standing near by. Plenty of light. A door, left. Right, a wide door into the ballroom from which comes a bright light. Servants are scurrying with dishes, plates, bottles etc. from the door, left, to the door, right, and back. As the curtain goes up, shouts are heard from the ballroom:* 'Good health to the bride and groom!'

SCENE I

[AVDOTYA, KOSYKH *and* DUDKIN *come out of the ballroom holding glasses.*]

A VOICE FROM THE BALLROOM. To the health of the groom's friends!

[*The band plays a flourish off-stage. Shouts of* 'Hurrah!' *and the noise of chairs being moved.*]

AVDOTYA. What a splendid marriage I arranged, they're a lovely couple—even in Moscow they'd make quite a splash. He's handsome, dignified, cultured, sensitive and as sober as they come. And Sasha's a little angel, a dear little flower. Matches like that aren't made in a hurry.

[*Shouts of* 'Hurrah!' *in the ballroom.*]

KOSYKH. } Hurrah-a-a-ah!
DUDKIN. }

AVDOTYA [*sings*].

> 'Don't sit around, Sasha darling,
> Open the window with speed.
> Is the sun riding high at the top of the sky?
> How does Nicholas look on his steed?'

Not bad! Oh, I am naughty, I've had a drop too much—really pushed the boat out.

[DUDKIN *makes to say something, but cannot.*]

KOSYKH. It's nice to see people happy. Please find me a wife, Avdotya. I'm fed up with being a lonely bachelor—at home I keep walking round the house, staring at the stove fittings. You fritter away your time, damn it, and life passes you by.

AVDOTYA. Why didn't you tell me before? I'd have fixed you up at once.

KOSYKH. It's different when you're married—you stay in your warm home with the lamp lit and this wife vaguely knocking around, God damn it, while you sit at table playing bridge with your friends. 'No trumps,' you say. 'Pass. One club. Pass. One heart. Pass. Two hearts. Pass.' You end up with a slam in hearts. Nothing but pass, pass, pass.

[DUDKIN *touches* AVDOTYA's *waist and clicks his tongue.*]

AVDOTYA. He's so tipsy he thinks I'm a young girl. Hey, what manners—and in someone else's house! Blind drunk, dead to the world!

A VOICE FROM THE BALLROOM. The health of Sergey Afanasyevich and Mary Danilovna!

[*The band plays a flourish. Cheers.*]

AVDOTYA [*goes into the ballroom and sings*].

> 'He is handsome, dear Mother,
> Most handsome of all.
> Now who would have thought
> That so low he could fall?'   [*Goes out.*]

DUDKIN. Come with me, Raisa Sergeyevna——

KOSYKH. What do you mean, calling me Raisa Sergeyevna?

DUDKIN. Oh, to hell! Come on, give the man on the door twenty copecks— I've no change. [*Shouts.*] Come on, Gregory!

KOSYKH. What are you yelling about? Who's this Gregory? [*Lights a cigarette.*]

DUDKIN. To hell! Let's go, let's really have a night out. [*Shouts.*] Come on, Gregory!

SCENE II

[*The above and* BORKIN, *in tails with a buttonhole.*]

BORKIN [*runs in from the ballroom out of breath*]. Why don't they serve champagne? [*To the* MANSERVANT.] More champagne and look slippy.

MANSERVANT. There's none left, sir.

BORKIN. What a damn disgrace—five bottles for a hundred people! Scandalous!

[KOSYKH *goes up to the 'cello and passes the bow over the strings.*]

BORKIN. What wine's left?

MANSERVANT. Some table wine—sparkling, sir.

BORKIN. I know—forty copecks a bottle. [*To* KOSYKH.] Do please stop nagging. [*To the* MANSERVANT.] Let's have some of this sparkling table wine, but be quick about it. Phew, I'm all in, I must have proposed twenty toasts alone. [*To* DUDKIN *and* KOSYKH.] Now we'll just announce the Babakin's engagement to the count. See here, gentlemen, you must cheer your heads off. I've an idea of my own to announce too, so we'll have to drink to that as well. Come on. [*Takes* KOSYKH *by the arm and goes into the ballroom with him.*]

DUDKIN [*follows them*]. Let's get a drink at the bar first, Simon, and then have one with everyone else.

[*Goes out. The band plays a march from* Boccaccio. *Shouts of:* 'Stop the Band!' *The march is interrupted.*]

A VOICE FROM THE BALLROOM. To the health of the bride's aunt, Margarita Savishna!

[*The band plays a flourish.*]

SCENE III

[SHABELSKY *and* LEBEDEV.]

LEBEDEV [*coming out of the ballroom with the* COUNT]. Oh, do come off it. Either you've worked yourself up into a bad temper, or it's indigestion or something. Who do you think you are—Mephistopheles? Why not put some old rags in your mouth, light them and blow fire on people?

SHABELSKY. No, seriously, I feel like doing something rotten and foul enough to make everyone else feel as sick as I do. And I will too, honestly. I've told Borkin to announce my engagement. [*Laughs.*] A dirty trick, but one that suits the times and the people concerned. They're all swine, so let me be one too.

LEBEDEV. I'm fed up with you. Look here, Matthew, if you go on like this you'll be carted off to the madhouse, if you don't mind my saying so.

SHABELSKY. Is the madhouse worse than any other house? Carry on, take me there now if you want, I don't care.

LEBEDEV. I tell you what, old man—get your hat and go home. This is a wedding, everyone's enjoying themselves, but you go on like a dying duck in a thunderstorm. Go away and don't bother me.

SHABELSKY. A wedding, everyone having fun, but there's something stupid and barbarous about it—all this music, noise and drunkenness, as if some vulgar businessman was getting spliced. I always thought you and Nicholas were civilized people, but today I see you're both on the same level of vulgarity as Zizi and Martha. This is more an orgy than a wedding.

LEBEDEV. Orgy? That's not my fault or Nicholas's. It's customary, you know, to knock back a few drinks, so knock 'em back they do. And custom, old boy, is the same as law. *Mores leges imitantur*—see, I still remember that from my student days. It's not for us two to try and reform humanity.

[SHABELSKY *bends over the piano and sobs.*]

LEBEDEV. Good Lord above! Matthew! Count! What's up? Matthew, my dear good friend, I've offended you. Forgive a silly old man, forgive an old soak. Have some water.

SHABELSKY. I don't want it. [*Raises his head.*]

LEBEDEV. Why are you crying?

SHABELSKY. It's nothing really.

LEBEDEV. Come on, old man, don't tell lies. What's the reason?

SHABELSKY. I happened to look at that 'cello and—and I remembered poor little Sarah.

LEBEDEV. Hey, what a time for reminiscences! May she rest in peace, poor woman, but this is hardly the time to talk about her.

SHABELSKY. We used to play duets together. She was a wonderful, marvellous woman. [*Leans over the piano.*]

A VOICE FROM THE BALLROOM. To the ladies! [*Noise and cheers.*]

SHABELSKY. They're all vile, petty, mediocre nonentities. And I'm an old bore myself, with my goddam posing, simpering and never saying what I mean. But everything's trivial, insignificant and sordid—don't you agree, Paul? I'm ready to love my fellow men before I die, but you can't really call them men—they're more like filthy, dirty microcephalous midgets.

LEBEDEV. Midgets—you're being silly, Matthew. Stupid they may be, but wait—their children will be clever. And if they're not all that bright, wait for the grandchildren. Don't expect everything at once. Intelligence needs centuries to develop.

SHABELSKY. Paul, you can be happy in a graveyard if the sun shines, and even old age is all right if you have hope. But I've no hope at all.

LEBEDEV. Yes, you really are in rather a bad way—no children, no money, nothing to do. Well, it can't be helped.

[*The band plays a waltz for half a minute, during which time* LEBEDEV *and* SHABELSKY *appear to be conversing.*]

SHABELSKY. We'll settle up in the next world. I'll go to Paris and visit my wife's grave. I've given a lot away in my time—I gave away half my property, so I've the right to ask. What's more, I ask as a friend.

LEBEDEV [*at a loss*]. I haven't a penny, old boy, honestly. *Omnia mea mecum porto.* I live on my wife, I don't earn a salary. I did have ten thousand stowed away, but I've just put that on one side for Sasha. [*Briskly.*] Wait, don't be downhearted. *Eureka!* I'll have a word with Nicholas—and you're as good as in Paris. Skip off to good old Paris. We'll let you have three out of the ten thousand. Or four. Buzz around for a year, then come home—and find yourself a great-uncle with luck. How about it? You have my promise.

SCENE IV
[*The above and* IVANOV.]

IVANOV [*comes in from the ballroom*]. You here, Uncle? My dear old boy, I'm laughing and grinning like the happiest of men. [*Laughs.*] Now, you cheer up and smile too, I sincerely beg you. Don't spoil our happiness by looking so down in the mouth. Take Paul's right arm and my left—we'll go and drink your health. I haven't been so happy and contented for ages. Everything's marvellous, wonderful, just right. I've had a glass of champagne [*laughs*] and I feel as if my happiness was making the world go round. [*Frightened.*] Have you been crying, Matthew?

SHABELSKY. Yes.

IVANOV. What for?

SHABELSKY. I was thinking of—Sarah. [*Pause.*]

IVANOV. Thank you for that, she was a marvellous, rare woman—there aren't many like her.

LEBEDEV. She was a nice woman, true enough. [*Pause.*]

IVANOV [*to the* COUNT]. Remember that trick I played on her when I was so upset and she came in my study? My God, we can refer to it casually now, but I was nearly scared to death at the time. For five days and nights I didn't have a wink of sleep, didn't eat a thing—and she did forgive me. She forgave all when she died. I seem to see her bright eyes looking at us now and forgiving us. Now she's in her grave, we're alive and the band's playing. But in good time we'll die too and then people will say we're in our graves. I like the way nature works, but I don't like nature itself. [*Laughs.*] I feel very fond of you today—you're a decent fellow, Paul. I mustn't have another drink, but you two go and have one.

LEBEDEV. A spot of brandy, eh, Count? Who shall we drink to?

SHABELSKY. Who cares?

IVANOV. I don't drink, but I like to see others drinking. [*Rubs his forehead.*] Happiness is all very well, but I've got so worn out these last few days, I can hardly stand. My whole body seems to ache. [*Laughs.*] Come on then.

SCENE V

[The above and BORKIN.*]*

BORKIN [*coming out of the ballroom*]. Where are you, bridegroom? They're looking for you. [*Seeing* IVANOV.] Ah—. Hurry up, they want you out there. But wait, I must tell you a marvellous idea—it'll cost each of you at least a thousand. Listen, Nicholas. Why don't you and I, Zinaida and the Babakin start a stud-farm as a joint stock company. How about it?

LEBEDEV. I must say, the boy has a screw loose.

IVANOV [*laughs*]. You're a clever, able fellow, Michael, I sincerely wish you good. Let's forget the past.

BORKIN [*very touched*]. You're a good chap yourself, Nicholas. I like you and I owe you a lot. Let's drink to our friendship.

IVANOV. There's no need, that would be silly. The point is—be an honest, decent man. Let's forget the past. You're to blame, and so am I, but we'll forget that. We're all sinful human beings, all guilty and all God's children. Only a man without hot blood and a heart can be strong and free from sin.

LEBEDEV [*to* IVANOV]. You've started talking like an evangelical preacher. Enough of this dirge! If we're drinking, let's drink—not waste good time. Come on, Count. [*Takes the* COUNT *and* IVANOV *by the arms.*] On, on! [*Sings.*] 'Let us three pick on someone else and beat the blackguard up.'

BORKIN [*blocks the way*]. Look, I wasn't joking about that stud-farm, it's a serious deal—both profitable and useful. It'll catch on here like a house on fire. Firstly, we've lots of pasture. Secondly, there are good watering facilities. And thirdly, we've room for the stables.

SCENE VI

[The above and MRS. BABAKIN.*]*

MRS. BABAKIN [*coming out of the ballroom*]. But where's my gentleman friend? [*Languorously.*] How dare you leave me on my own, Count? I've no one to clink glasses with. Oh, you horrid man. [*Hits the* COUNT *on the arm with her fan.*]

SHABELSKY *with* [*loathing*]. Can't you leave me alone? Go away.

[SHABELSKY, LEBEDEV *and* IVANOV *go into the ballroom.*]

MRS. BABAKIN [*flabbergasted*]. What does this mean, what right has he to—? Very grateful, I must say.

BORKIN. I'll come and see you tomorrow, Martha old girl, we'll go into details and draw up a contract. [*Out of breath.*] We shan't need much money at the beginning—if each shareholder puts in two thousand to start with, it'll be ample.

MRS. BABAKIN. How dare he? A lady comes up to him nice and friendly like, and he tells her to go away. What does it mean, has he gone off his chump?

BORKIN [*impatiently*]. That's beside the point—he doesn't want to marry, damn him. There are things more important than a title and getting married. Think, Martha old bean, there's only one stud-farm in the whole county, and that's up for auction. Good horses are frightfully hard to come by. If we open things up in a big way we can order two or three decent stallions from England.

MRS. BABAKIN [*angrily*]. Leave me alone, don't bother me.

BORKIN. She won't see sense! [*Heatedly.*] Given two or three thousand, we'd have a fortune in five or ten years. Firstly, we've lots of pasture. Secondly, there are good watering facilities. And thirdly——

MRS. BABAKIN [*cries*]. He's been coming over three times a week for a year— drinking, eating, taking my horses all over the place. But now his nephew's married an heiress, I'm not needed any more. Very grateful, I must say! Perhaps I didn't give him any money, but I'm not a millionaire, after all.

BORKIN [*throwing up his arms*]. I'm telling her something vital, and she kicks up this racket. What weird people, how can you do business with them? One lot doesn't want to listen and this one screams her head off. It's high time you stopped being so lazy and sluggish, ladies and gentlemen, you must get down to work some day. Can't you see your apathy's ruining us?

MRS. BABAKIN [*angrily, through tears*]. Leave me alone, I'll—I'll scratch out your eyes. I won't have any of you in the house—let none of you crooks dare show his nose there again! [*Weeps.*]

BORKIN. So my scheme's a dead duck and the deal's off. [*Sorrowfully.*] Thank you very much, everyone, I'm most grateful. You've money for clothes and madeira, but you grudge even a single copeck for a decent, useful business deal. Go on, bow down to the golden calf, worship Mammon——

[MRS. BABAKIN *makes to go.*]

BORKIN [*takes her by the arm, which she snatches away; decisively*]. All right, Martha, in that case I have another scheme. If you grudge two thousand roubles, how about me proposing? I'm popping the question.

MRS. BABAKIN [*angry and astonished*]. What!

BORKIN. Take my hand and heart, I love you passionately, wildly. Since first I saw you my life has had a meaning. To love you while not possessing you —it's sheer torture.

MRS. BABAKIN. No, no, no, no.

BORKIN. You've returned my affection, it's true, but that hasn't been enough. I want to be properly married, Martha, so I can belong to you all my life. [*Takes her by the waist.*] I love. I suffer. What more can I say? Marry me, that's all. You've lots of money that you don't know what to do with, and I'm a businessman, a solid citizen. Besides, I love you.

MRS. BABAKIN. But—you're joking, aren't you, Michael? You proposed once last year, but came along next day and said you'd changed your mind.

BORKIN. I'm not joking, honestly. All right, I'll kneel. [*Kneels.*] I'm crazy about you.

[*A servant passes through.*]

MRS. BABAKIN [*shrieks*]. Oh dear, the servant saw us.

BORKIN. Let them all see, I'll announce it at once. [*Gets up.*]

MRS. BABAKIN. But I shan't give you much money, Michael.

BORKIN. We'll see about that. [*Kisses her.*] Martha old bean, my little bit of fluff. We'll have some fun—we'll have such wonderful steeplechasers, I'll make a fortune in prizes alone.

MRS. BABAKIN [*shouts*]. Don't crease my dress, it cost two hundred roubles.

SCENE VII

[MRS. BABAKIN, BORKIN *and* AVDOTYA.]

AVDOTYA [*comes out of the ballroom and, seeing the two kissing, shrieks*]. Oh dear!

BORKIN. Congratulate us, Avdotya, we're engaged. I'm getting married. [*Goes to the door of the ballroom with* MRS. BABAKIN.] A bit shaken, eh? I'm getting married, I tell you. [*Kisses* MRS. BABAKIN.] Now I don't need shareholders, I'll build my own stud-farm.

AVDOTYA. My treasure, my lovely one. What wonderful news!

BORKIN. Wait, let me pass. [*Goes into the ballroom with* MRS. BABAKIN.]

AVDOTYA [*follows him, shouting*]. Look, all of you, I've arranged another marriage. Aren't they a lovely couple? [*Goes out.*]

SCENE VIII

[LVOV, *alone.*]

LVOV [*comes in through door, left, and looks at his watch*]. I'm a bit late, but everyone must be drunk anyway, they won't notice. [*Goes towards door, right, and rubs his hands in agitation.*] The great thing is not to get excited. [*Looks through the door.*] He's sitting next to her, grinning. He's deceived her, robbed her and he smiles at his victim. [*Hugs himself in agitation.*] Mustn't get too excited, though. There he is—happy, healthy and cheerful. And he's getting away with it. Thus virtue and justice triumph! He didn't get one wife's money, so he worried her into her grave. Now he has another victim, he'll play the same little game for her benefit till he gets his hands on the cash, when he'll dispatch her as he did the first one. It's an old story—some people will do anything for money.

A VOICE FROM THE BALLROOM. The health of all the guests!

[*The band plays a flourish. Cheers.*]

LVOV. He'll live happily to a ripe old age and die with a clear conscience. No, I'll show you up. I'll tear the mask off you. I'll wipe that grin off your face! You won't feel like grinning when I tell them just where you get off. [*Nervously buttons up his coat.*] I'm an honest man and it's my job to open a few eyes in the right quarter. [*Coughs nervously.*] I'll do my duty and leave this blasted neighbourhood tomorrow. [*Loudly.*] Nicholas Ivanov, I want everyone to hear this. You are the most unmitigated swine!

[*Hubbub in the ballroom.*]

SCENE IX

[LVOV, IVANOV, SHABELSKY, LEBEDEV, BORKIN *and* KOSYKH, *followed by* SASHA. IVANOV *runs in from the ballroom, clutching his head. He is followed by the others.*]

IVANOV. What's that for? Tell me, why? [*Collapses on the sofa.*]

ALL. Why? What for?

LEBEDEV [*to* LVOV]. For Christ's sake, why did you insult him? [*Clutches his head and walks about in agitation.*]

SHABELSKY [*to* IVANOV]. Nicholas, Nicholas! For God's sake—pay no attention. Show yourself above it all.

BORKIN. That was a rotten thing to say, sir. I challenge you to a duel.

LVOV. Mr. Borkin, I consider it degrading even to exchange words with you, let alone fight a duel. As for Mr. Ivanov, he can receive satisfaction any moment if he wishes.

SASHA [*comes out of the ballroom, staggering*]. Why? Why did you insult my husband? Just a moment, everyone, let him tell me—why.

LVOV. I didn't insult him without good reason, Miss Lebedev. I came here as an honest man to open your eyes. Please listen to me. I'll say what's on my mind.

SASHA. What can you say? What secrets do you know? That he drove his first wife to her grave? That's what everyone says. That he married me for

my money, and so he needn't pay Mother what he owes her? The whole
county knows that too. Cruel, trivial, wretched people! [*To her husband.*]
Let's get out of here, Nicholas. [*Takes his arm.*]

LEBEDEV [*to* LVOV]. As head of the household, as father of my son-in-law—
that is of my daughter, sir——

    [SASHA *shrieks and falls on her husband. Everyone runs up to* IVANOV.]

LEBEDEV. God, he's dead! Get some water! Fetch a doctor.

                           [SHABELSKY *weeps.*]

ALL. Fetch water, a doctor, he's dead.

CURTAIN

Recension II

  The beginning of Act Four (Scenes i to vi inclusive) was rewritten at this
stage to take almost the exact form which it has in the final version, except for a
few minor stylistic variants which affect Scene iv and will not be considered
here. The division of the act into two parts was abandoned, and the closing
scenes (vii to x inclusive, as numbered in Recension II) were rewritten to in-
corporate Ivanov's suicide, and also a feature of the plot peculiar to this recension: Sasha agrees to renounce Ivanov. The text of these scenes differs
radically from corresponding material in Recension I, and very considerably
from that in later recensions. It is therefore given in full.

SCENES VII to X of ACT FOUR

(*Recension II*)

SCENE VII

[*The above and* IVANOV.]

IVANOV [*comes in wearing a tail-coat and gloves, noticeably agitated*]. Sasha,
darling——

SASHA. Why in such a state? What's happened?

IVANOV. My treasure, my darling, listen to me—forget you love me, concentrate and listen.

SASHA. Don't try to scare me, Nicholas. What's the matter?

IVANOV. I was dressing for the wedding just now. I looked in the glass and
saw grey hairs on my temples. Sasha, we shouldn't. Let's stop before it's too
late, let's call it off. [*Clutches his head.*] Let's call it off. Leave me alone.
[*Heatedly.*] You're young, lovely and unspoilt, with your whole life before

you, and I—have grey hair on my temples, I'm a broken reed, a man with a past, haunted by guilt. I'm no husband for you.

SASHA [*sternly*]. That's not news, I've heard it before and I'm sick of it. Go to church and don't keep people waiting.

IVANOV [*takes her hand*]. I love and value you too much ⟨*the speech continues as in Recension I, Part I, Scene v; see p. 315*⟩.

SASHA. What do you want then?

IVANOV. You must give me up this instant without a moment's delay. Come on, make up your mind—I beg you, I implore you. You hesitate, you fear to speak the truth—I see it in your eyes. Do understand me, my darling, innocent lamb. It's not love that makes you talk like this, it's a stubbornness that comes from your own integrity. You set yourself to rescue me at all costs and make a new man of me—yes, yes, yes, don't try and deny it! Now you're ready to back out, but sentimentality stands in your way. Don't ruin your life! My treasure, listen to someone who loves you more than life itself. Well? Will you? Well? [*Pause.*]

SASHA. If that's what you want, all right—we'll put the wedding off for a year.

IVANOV. No, no, we must break it off this instant. I won't go away or leave you in peace till you give me up. Now, how about it? Say something. I'm so impatient, I shall burst. Well? [*Pause.*] Well?

[SASHA *nods.*]

IVANOV. You're so pleased, you actually smiled. [*Gives a sigh of relief.*] What a load off my mind. You're free, I'm free. You've certainly eased my conscience. [*Pause.*] So you give me up. If you hadn't agreed, I'd have—. [*Takes a revolver out of his pocket.*] I brought it with me just in case. [*Puts the revolver back.*] It's easier to kill myself than to ruin your life. You really are giving me up, aren't you? I'll go home. I feel so weak. I feel ashamed and hurt and—and a bit sorry for myself. Which door shall I take? [*Pause.*] But why don't you say something? Too shaken, eh? Look, the point is—. I had something to say, but I've forgotten what it was. [*Buries his face in his hands.*] I'm so ashamed of myself.

SASHA. Good-bye, Nicholas, good-bye. [*Goes towards the door.*]

SCENE VIII

[*The above and* LEBEDEV.]

LEBEDEV [*meeting* SASHA *by the door*]. Wait a moment, I want a word or two with you. [*Takes* SASHA *and* IVANOV *by their arms and looks round.*] Listen. Your mother can do what she likes, confound her. If she won't give you any money, never mind. Sasha, you say you don't need a dowry—something about principles, altruism, Schopenhauer and all that. Now that's a lot of nonsense, but you just listen to me. I've ten thousand roubles stowed away in the bank. [*Looks round.*] Not a soul knows about it at home—it was your grandmother's. So you take the lot. Only you must promise to let Matthew have about three thousand.

SASHA. Leave me alone! [*Snatches her hand away and goes out unsteadily.*]

LEBEDEV. What's the big idea?

IVANOV. The wedding's off, Paul. Finished.

LEBEDEV. What does this mean?

IVANOV. Tell the guests. The wedding's off, I got her to turn me down.

LEBEDEV. Is this just talk, or do you mean it?

IVANOV. I mean it, I'm leaving now. [*Pause.*] Oh God, God!

LEBEDEV. This makes no sense. You want me to tell my guests the wedding's off! Is that the idea? [*Pause.*] God is your judge, Nicholas, I mustn't judge you, but I'm sorry, we're no longer friends. Go where you like, I don't care. We'll never understand each other. Run along with you.

IVANOV. I would to God some frightful calamity might strike me, Paul—disease, famine, prison, disgrace, something of that sort. I can hardly stand, I'm so tired. I'm on the point of collapse. Where's Matthew? He can take me home. I love Sasha, I love her terribly. Now I love Sarah too, poor girl! Remember that trick I played on her when I was so excited and she came into my study? I was nearly scared to death at the time. For five days and nights I didn't have a wink of sleep, didn't eat a single thing—and she did forgive me. She forgave all when she died.

[*Guests gather in the ballroom.*]

SCENE IX

[*The above and* SHABELSKY.]

SHABELSKY [*comes in*]. Sorry, Paul, I shan't be at the wedding. I'm going home, I feel so exhausted. Good-bye.

IVANOV. Wait, Matthew, we'll go together. God, if only I could fall ill or destitute, I think I might come to life again.

VOICES IN THE BALLROOM. The best man's here.

LEBEDEV [*whispers angrily*]. You tell the guests yourself, I can't. How can I tell them, what can I say? Oh my God!

SCENE X

[The above, followed by BORKIN, *followed by* LVOV.]

BORKIN *[comes in with a bunch of flowers, wearing tails and the best man's button-hole]*. Phew! Where is he? *[To* IVANOV.] What brought you here? They've been waiting for you at church for ages, and here you are making speeches. You are a scream, honestly. Look, you mustn't go with your bride, but separately with me and I'll come back from church and fetch the bride. Don't you even know that? You really are funny.

LEBEDEV. What can I say, how can I put it? I'd rather die. *[Tugs* IVANOV's *sleeve.]* What are you standing around for? Be off with you, at least get out of my sight.

LVOV *[comes in, to* IVANOV]. So you're here, are you? *[Loudly.]* Nicholas Ivanov, I want everyone to hear this. You are the most unmitigated swine!

[General confusion.]

IVANOV *[clutches his head]*. Why? But why? Tell me what this is all about.

SHABELSKY *[to* IVANOV]. Nicholas, Nicholas, for God's sake! Don't pay any attention. Show yourself above all this.

BORKIN *[to* LVOV]. That was a rotten thing to say, sir. I challenge you to a duel.

LVOV. Mr. Borkin, I consider it degrading even to exchange words with you, let alone fight a duel. As for Mr. Ivanov, he may receive satisfaction when he wishes.

SHABELSKY. I shall fight you, sir.

IVANOV. May I, gentlemen? Let me say something. *[Shakes his head vigorously.]* I feel able to speak now, I can speak like a human being. I nearly died when he insulted me, but that's not his fault, is it? Try to see his point of view. Pretty funny, isn't it! He's known me over two years, but he's never been able to make me out, not for a single second. For two years he's been conscientiously trying to solve me. He's suffered and pestered himself, me and my wife, but a mysterious enigma I have remained. My wife, my friends, my enemies, Sasha, these gentlemen here—none of them have understood me. Am I a man of honour or a rogue? Intelligent or stupid? Sane or unhinged? Do I love? Or hate? Nobody knew, everyone was baffled trying to guess. The truth's as plain as a pikestaff, a child could see it—yet even clever men could make nothing of me. That means there was no truth in me. Oh, I understand myself well enough now, and pretty ridiculous I feel! I'm only too delighted to be called an unmitigated swine! *[Laughs loudly.]* Yes, I was a man of honour—enthusiastic, eager, tireless. I did three men's work. Indignation, grief, love, hate—I could feel them all, but only until I grew tired. Yes, I loved my fellow men, I loved women more than any of you, but my love only lasted a couple of years till I began to feel tired and lazy. I began to think that love was a fraud and any show of affection just sloppy sentimentality, that songs and fiery speeches were cheap and stale. I was very excitable and took on much too much, but I quickly caved in and lost heart. The great champion soon threw up the sponge! Now I'm thirty-five, and I've achieved less than nothing, but I've given in and collapsed. My miserable achievements and sacrifices have crushed me. I've no faith, the light of passion burns dim, I'm disillusioned and ill. Why? My ambitions were gigantic— but I had about as much strength as an earthworm. I had no discipline, no stamina. I'm a wretched nobody, a complete weed. I feel sorry for anyone who loves and admires people like me—puts us on a pedestal, worships us, finds excuses and sympathy for us. And it's a poor look-out for women who love spineless, cringing, snivelling weaklings instead of brave, high-minded, strong, healthy, handsome men. There spoke the old Ivanov! I despise, I hate myself—don't look at me, I'm too ashamed. Don't look. Waiting to see how I'll end, are you? Oh, I know what to do—why do you think I'm chattering with rage and self-hatred? Wait—now it comes. [*Takes out his revolver.*] So much for you! [*Shoots himself.*]

CURTAIN

Recension III

The revision which led to Recension III involved further radical alteration of the play's closing scenes (from Scene vii onwards), the main change in the plot being that Chekhov now abandoned the renunciation of Ivanov by Sasha—this being, as noted above, a feature peculiar to Recension II. Scene vii, as rewritten for Recension III, took its final, shorter form—in other words, the text of the scene is identical in Recension III and in the final version. The remainder of the play (from Scene viii to the end) was now brought closer to its final version, from which, however, considerable divergences remain. These include a difference in the numbering of the scenes: the material of Scene viii (Recension III) corresponds to that of Scenes viii and ix (final version); the material of Scenes ix and x (Recension III) corresponds to that of Scene xi (final version). The following other special features of the closing scenes of Recension III must also be noted.

Scene viii (*final version*) = Scene viii (*Recension III*)

Recension III contained the following sentence, between Ivanov's 'I carry boredom, gloom and despondency everywhere . . .' and his '. . . No, don't interrupt' (see p. 222):

IVANOV. I'm fed up with my life, but that doesn't entitle me to disparage other people's lives to them.

Recension III contained the following passage between Ivanov's 'I can't find other names for them . . .' and his '. . . I'm done for' (see p. 223):

IVANOV. How can I be saved then? Through love? A pretty dated notion, that! Love's only one more stab in the back—it only makes spiritual confusion worse confounded by adding new unhappiness to old. How about winning two hundred thousand roubles? The same's true of that. You can stimulate me till I feel on top of the world, but after the intoxication comes the hangover and I sink lower than ever. You must understand that and not try to run away from it. There's only one way out for my kind of snivelling neurotic, but we're unfortunately too clever to take that road to salvation.

Recension III contained the following passage, between Ivanov's 'I should have done as I intended . . .' and the stage direction '. . . LEBEDEV *comes in*' (see p. 223):

IVANOV. I just wanted to—. [*Shows her the revolver and puts it away.*] It's easier to kill myself than to ruin your life, but I thought you'd listen to the voice of common sense and——

SASHA. Give me that revolver.

IVANOV. No.

SASHA. Give it to me, I tell you.

IVANOV. Sasha, there's too much love for you in my heart for me to indulge in small talk, and I'm in too bad a temper anyway. Give me up, I implore— I demand it then, in the name of justice and common humanity.

Scene ix (final version) = *Scene viii (Recension III)*

The passage following Sasha's words 'So am I doing as my conscience tells me' (see p. 225) continued at greater length in Recension III as follows:

SASHA. I won't let you go, you can say what you like.

IVANOV. God, I'm on my last legs—I'm so weak, I can hardly stand. Where's Matthew? I want him to take me home.

A VOICE IN THE BALLROOM. The best man's here.

IVANOV. I'll go and tell the guests myself. I'm at the end of my tether, I'm at war with myself with no quarter asked or given.

SASHA [*holds his arm and stops him going into the ballroom*]. Nicholas, please— don't do anything silly.

Scene xi (final version) = *Scenes ix and x (Recension III)*

The main difference between the text of Recension III and that of the final version is that Ivanov's long speech, occupying nearly the whole of Scene x in the final version (see p. 225), appeared at a later stage in Recension III and in a somewhat different and more 'hypothetical' form ('If ever in your lives . . .', 'if you see . . .' etc.) In Recension III this speech led up more immediately to the final crisis of the play, which there ended as follows, continuing from Ivanov's 'What do you mean, come on?' (see p. 227):

SASHA. No, no, let's go.

IVANOV. Oh, get out of my way. Listen, all of you. I won't try to explain myself—whether I'm decent or rotten, clever or stupid, sane or mad. You wouldn't understand. All I ask is this. If you should ever meet a young man who is eager, sincere and intelligent, and if you see that he loves, hates and believes differently from other people, that he works and hopes hard enough for ten men, tilts at windmills and bangs his head against brick walls, if you see he's heaved a load on his back that has torn his muscles and cracked his spine—then tell him not to be in too much of a hurry to expend his youthful energy. 'Save it for the rest of your life,' tell him. 'Get drunk on love and hate, work, burn, thirst, suffer, get excited. But don't overdo it, or else fate will punish you cruelly. You'll wake up to yourself at the age of thirty and find you're an old man. Heavy-headed, dull-witted, worn out, without faith or love, with no aim in life, you'll moon around, more dead than alive, not knowing who you are, what you're living for or what you want. And you'll think that love's a fraud, that any show of affection's just sloppy sentimentality, that there's no point in working, that songs and fiery speeches are cheap and stale. And wherever you go you'll carry misery, indifference, boredom, discontent and disgust with life and you'll be past praying for—absolutely done for.' Say you've seen a man of thirty-five stand before you, wearied, disillusioned and crushed by his own pathetic efforts. Say you saw him bitterly ashamed and mocking his own weakness. Tell how his pride was wounded, how he was misunderstood, disliked and insulted—and what a stupid end he came to. Tell how he was choking with rage. But that's enough, I've had my say, I'm absolutely all in! I feel like a young man again, it's my old self that's speaking. Oh, I know how to end it all.

SASHA [*shrieks*]. I know what he wants to do! Stop him!

IVANOV. Who can stop me? I've been going downhill long enough, it's time to halt. I've outstayed my welcome. Stand back, all of you. Thank you, Sasha. Good-bye, Paul.

SASHA [*shouts*]. Nicholas, for God's sake! Stop him!

IVANOV. Leave me alone!

[*Runs to one side and shoots himself.* SASHA *faints. General confusion.*]

CURTAIN

A minor variant earlier in the same scene is the following exchange to be found in Recension III after Borkin's words 'You really are funny' (see p. 226):

SASHA. It doesn't matter, we'll go together now. [*Takes* IVANOV's *arm.*] Come on.

IVANOV. What energy! [*Laughs.*] You'd better send for the village constable.

Recension IV

Between the first performance in St. Petersburg (of Recension III) and the revision for the '*Severny vestnik* text', Chekhov undertook an interim revision, affecting only—and yet again—the ending of the play. This variant, here termed Recension IV, is to be found in 'Producer's text no. 4447' (see above, p. 299), where the relevant section of Recension III, from Sasha's words 'Say what you like' (see p. 225), was deleted and Recension IV, entitled 'altered ending of Scene viii and new Scene ix', substituted in Chekhov's handwriting (see *Works*, 1944–51, xi, p. 531).

The main feature of Recension IV is that Ivanov's long speech, which, in Recension III, immediately preceded the final crisis (see pp. 329–30) was transposed to an earlier position corresponding to that occupied in the final version by what is in effect the same speech (that in Scene x). But the *text* of the speech in Recension IV is almost identical with that in Recension III—especially in retaining the 'hypothetical' character mentioned above. It was only in the '*Plays, 1897* text' that this speech took its final shape, losing its 'hypothetical' character.

Recension IV also saw the removal of the passage 'IVANOV. God, I'm on my last legs . . .' to '. . . don't do anything silly' (see p. 331) and the substitution for it of the exchange (see p. 225):

⟨SASHA.⟩ I'm going to call Mother. [*Goes out.*]

LEBEDEV. I can't make sense of anything.

Later recensions

The main changes affecting Act Four in the later recensions (the printed editions) were cuts, including the following:

The passage from 'IVANOV. I just wanted to . . .' to '. . . SASHA. Give it to me, I tell you' was cut out of the '*Severny vestnik* text' (see p. 331). The immediately following speech by Ivanov ('Sasha, there's too much love for you . . .' to '. . . common humanity'; see p. 331) was cut out of the '*Plays, 1897* text'.

The passage 'IVANOV. How can I be saved then?' to '. . . road to salvation' was cut out of the '*Works, 1901* text' (see p. 331).

APPENDIX III

THE SEAGULL

1. The composition
2. The text
3. Contemporary reception

1. THE COMPOSITION

(a) Evidence of Chekhov's correspondence and of memoir material

The first reference to work on *The Seagull* occurs in a letter of 21 October 1895 from Chekhov to A. S. Suvorin: 'I'm writing a play which I probably shan't finish before the end of November. I'm quite enjoying the work, though I play fast and loose with stage conventions. It's a comedy with three female and six male parts, four acts, a landscape (view of a lake), a lot of talk about literature, little action and a hundredweight and a half of love.' On 2 November Chekhov again wrote to Suvorin about *The Seagull*, as follows: 'My play's growing, but slowly. . . . Still, I hope to finish it in November.' On 7 November Chekhov wrote to Ye. M. Shavrova, speaking of his intention to offer *The Seagull* to the Moscow Little Theatre, a plan which was later abandoned.

Other early references in Chekhov's correspondence reporting progress on *The Seagull* are as follows:

'My play's progressing. It's all going smoothly at the moment, but I don't know what will happen later, when I get to the end. I'll finish it in November.' (*Letter to A. S. Suvorin, 10 Nov. 1895.*)

'I've almost finished the play, there's a couple of days' work left. It's a comedy in four acts called *The Seagull*.' (*Letters to D. V. Garin-Vinding and I. L. Leontyev [Shcheglov], 14 Nov. 1895.*)

'I've finished the play. It is called *The Seagull*. It hasn't come off too well. In general I'm not much of a playwright.' (*Letter to Ye. M. Shavrova, 18 Nov. 1895.*)

'Well, I've finished the play now. I began it *forte* and finished it *pianissimo*, contrary to all the laws of the theatre. It's turned out like a story. I'm more displeased than pleased, and reading my new-born play has convinced me again that I'm not a playwright at all. The acts are very short and there are four. It's still only the skeleton of a play, a plan that will be changed a million times before next season, but I've ordered two copies to be typed on a Remington.' (*Letter to A. S. Suvorin, 21 Nov. 1895.*)

'Tomorrow I'll send you the play, but in manuscript. Read it and tell me what you think. There's plenty of time before next season, so it's still possible to make sweeping changes.' (*Letter to A. S. Suvorin, 7 Dec. 1895.*)

On 17 December Chekhov wrote to Suvorin expressing his concern that Trigorin in *The Seagull* might be regarded as a portrait of a friend, the writer I. N. Potapenko: 'My play has flopped without a performance. If it really looks as though Potapenko's portrayed in it, of course it can't be staged or published.'

From the evidence of Nemirovich-Danchenko it appears that an early version of *The Seagull*—presumably that current in late 1895, but no longer extant—contained the revelation (at the end of Act One) that Masha was the daughter of Dr. Dorn, a theme which was not taken up later in the play. 'I told him he must do one of two things—develop the theme or abandon it completely. All the more so if the first act was to end with it. He agreed and the ending was changed.' (V. I. Nemirovich-Danchenko, quoted in Gitovich, *Letopis zhizni i tvorchestva A. P. Chekhova*, p. 402.)

In a letter of 8 March 1896 to his brother Alexander, Chekhov wrote: 'I'm messing around with the play. I'm revising it.'

(b) *Evidence of Chekhov's* Notebooks

Evidence on the planning of *The Seagull* is to be found in the *Notebooks* which Chekhov kept between 1891 and his death. The entries are undated, those with a bearing on *The Seagull* being as follows (for more details on Chekhov's *Notebooks* and the method of quoting page references to them, see *The Oxford Chekhov*, vol. viii, Preface, pp. xiii–xiv).

Lokidin was a great drinker and ladies' man, which didn't stop him being a good obstetrician. (*Notebook* I, p. 37/7; see Dorn's words, p. 239.)

I scorn my material environment and all that goes with it. (*Notebook* I, p. 42/2; see Dorn's words, p. 246.)

A virgin pine-wood, or Mashka's Pine-wood. (*Notebook* I, p. 52/1; see Trigorin's words, p. 266.)

He was woken by the sound of rain. (*Notebook* I, p. 53/2; see Treplev's words, p. 277.)

To proclaim what is new and artistic is the function of the naïve and innocent. But you hacks have grabbed control of the arts. You don't recognize anything except what you do yourselves, everything else you crush. (*Notebook* I, p. 54/2; see Treplev's words, p. 263.)

She smokes and drinks, has red hair, lives with her lover and has her name bandied about in the papers. I've nothing against it, but I find all that very exhausting. (*Notebook* I, p. 55/1; the beginning of the entry refers to Masha, after which Irina is the subject—see Treplev's remarks on his mother, p. 236.)

A schoolmaster aged thirty-two with a grey beard. (*Notebook* I, p. 55/2; reference is to Medvedenko.)

If society makes a fuss of its actors and performers and thinks they're wonderful, that means it must be impregnated with idealistic urges. (*Notebook* I, p. 55/3; see Dorn's words, p. 239.)

Sometimes I can't help being a bit selfish and I'm sorry to have an actress for my mother. I feel I'd be happier if she was just an ordinary woman. Can you imagine anything more outrageous and idiotic, Uncle, than when masses of great actors and writers forgather in her house and you're the only nonentity among them? And they only put up with you because you're her son? I can tell what they're thinking when they look at me and I answer them with contempt. (*Notebook* I, p. 55/4; see Treplev's words, p. 236.)

In the country: he goes to bed at ten and gets up at nine. All this sleep has made his brain stick to his skull. Then he unintentionally fell asleep again after lunch, after which he had waking nightmares all afternoon. (*Notebook* I, p. 63/2; see Sorin's words, p. 234.)

The actress burst into tears on seeing the pond and remembered her childhood. (*Notebook* I, p. 63/4.)

We should show life neither as it is nor as it ought to be, but as we see it in our dreams. (*Notebook* I, p. 63/5; see Treplev's words, p. 238.)

Actors and writers back each other up. Once accepted by them, you become famous all over Russia. (*Notebook* I, p. 63/6.)

The writer: everyone writes the way he likes as well as he can. (*Notebook* I, p. 63/7; see Trigorin's words, p. 242.)

A provincial shopkeeper resident in Kiev. (*Notebook* I, p. 63/8; see Treplev's words, p. 236.)

If a well-known astronomer or politician dies, they publish an obituary only five lines long. But if an actor or writer dies, they knock off a two-column obituary and put it on the front page with a black border round it. (*Notebook* I, p. 63/9.)

I'm so old, I think I've even begun to smell like a dog-kennel, but you're still young, sister. (*Notebook* I, p. 64/1.)

The schoolmaster's always knocking about the house. In Act Three he makes conversation difficult and is asked to leave. (*Notebook* I, p. 64/2.)

About the schoolmaster and Kav. [?] They're nobodies, quite ordinary. Better if they were scoundrels or something. (*Notebook* I, p. 64/3.)

Sorin: I was very keen on being a writer. I wanted two things—to get married and be a writer, but neither of them came off. (*Notebook* I, p. 64/4; see Sorin's words, p. 237.)

He read his own story, but didn't even cut the pages of mine. (*Notebook* I, p. 64/5; see Treplev's words, p. 275.)

Trigorin (making a note): . . . takes snuff . . . is unhappy and dissatisfied, which is why she acts the fool. Drinks vodka. (*Notebook* I, p. 64/7; see Trigorin's words, p. 254.)

In Act Three: scrounger! Proletarian! Kiev shopkeeper! Mediocrity! (*Notebook* I, p. 64/8; see Irina's words, p. 263.)

Signed her letters 'Seagull'. (*Notebook* I, p. 64/9; see Treplev's words, p. 272.)

In Act Four Masha and her mother make the bed, and the mother keeps giving T. beer. (*Notebook* I, p. 64/10.)

De gustibus aut bene, aut nihil. (*Notebook* II, p. 11/1; see Shamrayev's words, p. 240.)

Only don't tell anyone I drink. Women drink more than you think. (*Notebook* II, p. 33/1; see Masha's words, p. 258.)

He went home and so on and sat down to dinner and so forth. (*Notebook* II, p. 35/2; an example of Sorin's conversational style.)

(c) Links between The Seagull *and Chekhov's biography*

The symbol of the shot seagull appears to have been suggested to Chekhov by an episode which occurred when the well-known painter Isaac Levitan was staying with him at Melikhovo in April 1892. The two men went shooting together and Levitan happened to wing a woodcock which fell into a puddle. Chekhov picked it up. 'It had a long beak, large black eyes and beautiful plumage. It looked astonished. What were we to do with it? Levitan grimaced and shut his eyes. "Knock it on the head, old man," he said with a shudder. I told him I couldn't do it. Levitan went on twitching his shoulders nervously, his head shook and he kept on at me, while the woodcock continued to look on in astonishment. I had to do as he said and kill it. And so the world was poorer by one beautiful, adored creature, and two fools went home and had their supper.' (*Letter to A. S. Suvorin, 8 Apr. 1892.*)

The eventual choice of a seagull, rather than a woodcock, as the symbolic bird in Chekhov's play, and of the lake which forms its setting, was perhaps suggested by a later episode, also involving Levitan. Chekhov visited him in 1895 when he was staying on an estate on the banks of a lake in the Novgorod area after an attempt to commit suicide (yet another inspiration to the plot of *The Seagull*?). This happened 'within 200 miles of the Finnish Gulf, where there are plenty of seagulls (they were certainly unknown in the Melikhovo area . . .). It seems likely that this trip provided both the lake and the seagull of the play which he [Chekhov] was then on the verge of writing' (see *The Seagull*, ed. Henry, p. 30).

In a letter, quoted above on p. 333, Chekhov expressed his concern that Trigorin in *The Seagull* might be regarded as a portrait of his friend, the writer I. N. Potapenko. In fact Trigorin, as he appears in the extant drafts, is much more of a self-portrait by Chekhov, at least in so far as his attitude to the craft of writing is concerned. But the episode of Trigorin's love affair with Nina was clearly suggested to Chekhov by the love affair which took place in real life between Potapenko and Chekhov's friend Lika Mizinova. Each resulted in the birth of a child, though there is no more reason to regard Nina as a direct portrait of Mizinova than to regard Trigorin as modelled in detail on Potapenko.

A more complicated biographical involvement is that which concerns Lydia Avilova, a minor writer and friend of Chekhov's who, long after his death, published memoirs in which she appears to have sought to exaggerate the intimacy of their relations. So far as *The Seagull* is concerned, the details of this friendship do not matter, except that they suggested the episode in Act Three, where Nina presents Trigorin with a medallion inscribed '*Days and Nights*, page 121, lines 11 and 12' (see p. 259). It will be remembered that the lines in question, from one of Trigorin's own works, turned out to read: 'If you should ever need my life, then come and take it' (see p. 264).

The following incidents from Chekhov's life have a bearing on this episode, though it should be borne in mind that the details derive partly from Avilova's memoirs, which do not appear to be in all respects reliable.

In early 1895 Avilova presented Chekhov with a pendant for a watch-chain in the form of a book inscribed '*Stories and Tales. Works of A. Chekhov.* Page 267, lines 6 and 7.' The reference was to Chekhov's own story *Neighbours* and the relevant lines read (as do those in *The Seagull*): 'If you should ever need my life, then come and take it.' Chekhov did not reply directly. But according to Avilova's memoirs he did eventually promise to answer her from the stage at the first performance of *The Seagull*, making the promise on the occasion of a masked ball in St. Petersburg on 27 January 1896. Eager to receive Chekhov's answer, Avilova duly attended the first night of *The Seagull* and recognized the 'page 121, lines 11 and 12' as the relevant message. It turned out to refer to a book of her own, the lines in question reading: 'it is improper for young ladies to go to masked balls'. A playful—perhaps rather unkind—snub had been administered.

2. THE TEXT

The present translation is based on the Russian text of the play as reprinted in *Works*, 1944–51, xi from vol. vii of Chekhov's *Collected Works, 1902*—the text in this (second) edition of Chekhov's *Collected Works* being identical with that printed in vol. vii of the first edition (1901). This itself had been preceded by three previous recensions, all differing from it, and from each other, in various particulars discussed below. These recensions were:

(*a*) the 'Censor's copy'—the first extant text of the play, being a typescript submitted to the censorship in St. Petersburg and now preserved in the Central Library of Russian Drama;

(b) the '*Russkaya mysl* text', being the first published text of the play, which appeared in the December 1896 issue of the magazine *Russkaya mysl* [*The Russian Idea*];

(c) the '*Plays, 1897* text', being the play as it first appeared in book form—in the volume of Chekhov's dramatic work entitled *Plays* and published in St. Petersburg in 1897.

These documents are now considered in sequence together with the variants which they contain.

(a) *Negotiations with the censorship and manuscript alterations in the 'Censor's copy'*

Over five months elapsed between 15 March 1896, when *The Seagull* was first submitted for censorship to the Press Department in St. Petersburg, and 20 August of the same year, when the typescript was finally passed as acceptable to the censor. This period was spent in somewhat dilatory negotiations between Chekhov and the censor concerned, whose name was Litvinov. The point at issue was the relationship between Irina Arkadin and her lover, Trigorin.

On 11 July Chekhov wrote to A. S. Suvorin: 'The censor has expressed his willingness to send me [back] the play, so that I can myself cut or change the passages which he finds dubious.' On 15 July the typescript was accordingly returned to Chekhov, and at the same time Litvinov wrote: 'The point is not that an actress and a writer are cohabiting, but the fact that her son and brother take the affair so casually. From the point of view of censorship it would be desirable not to mention the matter at all. But if artistic considerations do make it essential for you to describe the relationship between Trigorin and Mrs. Treplev [Irina], I trust you will manage it so that the censor's permission will be forthcoming without hitch.' (See Gitovich, op. cit., p. 419.)

On 11 August Chekhov sent the corrected typescript to Potapenko in St. Petersburg so that Potapenko could give any necessary explanations to Litvinov. 'On p. 4 [Chekhov wrote to Potapenko, the page references in this quotation being to the 'Censor's copy'] I have thrown out the phrase "lives openly with this novelist" and on p. 5 "can love only young women". If my changes . . . are accepted, then glue them in firmly in those places . . . but if they are rejected, then to hell with the play, I don't want to mess around with it any more and I advise you not to either.

'In Sorin's words on p. 5 ("By the way, tell me about her writer") the word "her" can be cut. Instead of the words in the same passage ("He's a bit of a puzzle, he hardly speaks"), you can put "you know, I don't like him" or anything, a text from the Talmud if you want, or: "What, at her age! Really, she should be ashamed of herself!"

'That the son is against the liaison is perfectly evident from his tone. On the offending p. 37 he also asks his mother: "Why, oh why has this man come between you and me?" On this p. 37 you can cut Irina's words: "Our intimacy can't of course please you, but". That's the lot.' (*Letter to I. N. Potapenko, 11 Aug. 1896.*)

In a letter to Chekhov of 23 August, Potapenko reported as follows: 'Your play has suffered minor alterations. I decided to make them on my own initiative as the play's fate depends on it and they don't add up to much anyway. I'll quote them from memory. In two places where the lady speaks to her son about the novelist: "I'll take him away" has been changed to "he will go". The words "she smokes, drinks and openly lives with this novelist" are replaced by "she does lead such an idiotic life, for ever taken up with this author of hers". The words "now he only drinks beer and can love only young women" are changed to "now he only drinks beer and all he asks from women is that they should respect him". Then there are two or three more very insignificant changes. The thing is, you completely missed what the censor was after. He required Treplev not to interfere at all in Trigorin's affair with his mother, and to remain in apparent ignorance of it—which is the effect of these alterations.'

The 'Censor's copy' does in fact contain handwritten alterations (not in Chekhov's own hand) corresponding closely to the material discussed in Potapenko's letter.

These changes were reversed in the '*Russkaya mysl* text', where the relevant passages read almost exactly as they had originally read in the 'Censor's copy' before the censor's objections had been taken into account. The process was once more reversed in the '*Plays, 1897* text', where the passages concerned have been changed back to read almost exactly as they had read in the 'Censor's copy' after correction. But the original phrase 'Now he only drinks beer and can love only young women', and another version of the same sentence ('Now he only drinks beer and requires no more from women than their friendship') are both absent in the '*Plays, 1897* text' and in subsequent recensions.

(*b*) *Comparisons of the 'Censor's copy' and '*Russkaya mysl *text'*

In addition to the restoration (mentioned above) of changes imposed by censorship, the '*Russkaya mysl* text' shows evidence of extensive revision when compared to the 'Censor's copy'. As was common with Chekhov, revision consisted chiefly in making cuts. The following are the main cuts concerned—passages appearing in the 'Censor's copy', but not in the '*Russkaya mysl* text' or later recensions.

Act One

After Medvedenko's words 'And tobacco?' (p. 233):

Yesterday we had to send for some flour, and searched high and low for a sack, but it had been stolen by beggars. We had to give fifteen copecks for a new one.

After Sorin's words 'My sister couldn't sleep again last night' (p. 234):

MASHA. Tell him yourself. There's some millet in the barn now, and he says thieves will break in if there's no dog.

TREPLEV. Oh, to hell with the millet.

After Sorin's words 'Even being an obscure writer must be quite nice, come to think of it' (p. 237):

Some time about ten years ago I published an article about trial by jury. It's pleasant to remember it now, you know. But when I start remembering that I worked in the Department of Justice for twenty-eight years, it's somehow not quite, er—[*Yawns.*]

At the beginning of Dorn's speech, before '*shrugs his shoulders*' (p. 239): There's quite a gap in your reasoning.

After the stage direction 'TREPLEV *appears from behind the stage*' (p. 240):

MEDVEDENKO [*to* SORIN]. And before Europe obtains results, humanity—according to what Flammarion writes—will perish as the result of a cooling of the Earth's hemispheres.

SORIN. God is merciful.

MASHA [*holding out her snuff-box to* TRIGORIN]. Have some. Are you always so silent, or do you sometimes speak?

TRIGORIN. Yes, I speak sometimes. [*Takes some snuff.*] Revolting! How can you?

MASHA. You have a kind smile. You must be quite easy to get on with.

After Irina's words 'I didn't mean to hurt his feelings' (p. 243):

NINA [*looking out from behind the curtain*]. Is it over already? Aren't we going on with it?

IRINA. The author's gone off. So it must be the end. Come down here, dear.

NINA. All right. [*Disappears.*]

MEDVEDENKO. This all depends on the existence of psychic matter and

After IRINA's words 'He's still charming, but in those days he was irresistible' (p. 243):

[POLINA *quietly weeps.*]

SHAMRAYEV [*reproachfully*]. Polina, Polina——

POLINA. It's all right. I'm sorry. I suddenly felt sad.

After Nina's 'Yes' (p. 244):

SHAMRAYEV. Bream and pike mostly. There are some zander too, but not many.

After Sorin's words 'Just one hour and so on. Surely you can—' (p. 245):
My darling girl, it's boring without you, honestly.

After Dorn's words 'Yes, that dear father of hers is a pretty thoroughgoing swine, give him his due' (p. 245):

MEDVEDENKO. A lamentable example of atavism, worthy of the attention of a Lombroso.

DORN. 'Lombroso—.' Can't you cut out the long words?

After Irina's words 'Well, come on, poor old thing' and the stage direction '*Takes his arm*' (p. 245):
There's a line in some play: 'Come to your senses, old man'.

Act Two

After Irina's words 'while you just stay put—you're only half alive' (p. 248):
MASHA. My mother brought me up like the girl in the fairy story who lived in a flower. I don't know how to do anything.

After Irina's words 'take me and Trigorin' (p. 249):
I didn't pick Trigorin out or lay siege to him or try to take him prisoner, but as soon as I got to know him I fell head over heels in love—came over all queer, darlings. I used to stand and look at him and cry—weep buckets, you know. How can you call that having things cut and dried?

After Irina's words 'Maupassant's *On the Water*, darling' (p. 249):
MEDVEDENKO. I've never read it.

DORN. You only read things you can't understand.

MEDVEDENKO. I read whatever books are going.

DORN. You read Buckle and Spencer, but you're no more knowledgeable than the average caretaker. You think that the human heart's made of gristle and that the earth rests on whales.

MEDVEDENKO. The earth's round.

DORN. Yes, but why sound so doubtful about it?

MEDVEDENKO [*taking offence*]. When you've nothing to eat, what matter whether the earth's round or square? Leave me alone, do.

IRINA [*annoyed*]. Stop it, you two.

After Medvedenko's words 'Mr. Sorin should give up smoking' (p. 250):

DORN. He should have stopped long ago. Tobacco and liquor are such loathsome things.

After Dorn's words 'that's just silly' (p. 250):

It's time to think of eternity.

[TREPLEV *walks past the house without a hat on, with a gun in one hand and a dead seagull in the other.*]

IRINA [*to her son*]. Come here, Constantine.

[TREPLEV *looks round and goes away.*]

DORN [*singing softly*]. 'Oh, speak to her, my flowers——'

NINA. You're singing out of tune, Doctor.

DORN. I don't care. [*To* SORIN.] As I say, sir, it's time you were thinking of eternity. [*Pause.*]

After Sorin's words 'Then there are cabs in the street and so on' (p. 251):

DORN. Say what you like, I can't manage without Nature.

IRINA. But what about books? Nature is much more moving and elegant in poetic images than it is on its own.

After Polina's words 'Put yourself in my place. What can I do?' (p. 252):

SORIN. He's going away. He's abandoning the farm at the busiest season and so on. I won't have it, I'll compel him to stay.

DORN. Show a bit of character, can't you Sorin?

After Polina's words 'now we're getting on in life?' (p. 252):

I've been your wife and friend for twenty years. Let me come and live with you.

After the stage direction 'NINA *appears near the house, picking flowers*' (p. 252):

POLINA [*to* DORN, *in a low voice*]. Did you spend the whole morning with Irina again?

DORN. I have to spend the time with someone.

POLINA. This jealousy is agony to me. Sorry, I'm being a nuisance.

After Polina's words 'being a doctor you can't avoid women' (p. 252):

That's how it is. But it's agonizing, I'd have you know. Spend your time with women then, but at least manage it so that I don't notice.

DORN. I'll try.

After Nina's words 'losing their tempers like anyone else' (p. 253):

They're modest. I asked him for his autograph yesterday, and he wrote some doggerel verse for a joke, deliberately making it bad to amuse everyone.

After Nina's words 'If you knew how I envy you' (p. 254):

TRIGORIN [*embarrassed*]. Yes, it's a world——

Act Four

After Treplev's words 'No, it's all right. [*Pause*.]' (p. 271):

MEDVEDENKO [*to* DORN]. May I ask you, Doctor, how much a ream of writing paper costs abroad?

DORN. I don't know, I didn't buy any.

After Trigorin's words 'my memory of the scene' (p. 274):

SHAMRAYEV [*to* IRINA]. Are they still alive?

IRINA. I don't know.

SHAMRAYEV. She was a very gifted actress, my word she was. They don't come like that nowadays! In *The Murder of Coverley* she was just—. [*Kisses the tips of his fingers*.] I'd give ten years of my life——

After Masha's words 'you're impossible' (p. 274):

SHAMRAYEV [*flaring up, in a low voice*]. All right, tear me in pieces! Hang me! I still say he must walk.

After Shamrayev's words 'He's not all that high and mighty' (p. 275):

DORN. Marriage changes a man. What's happened to Flammarion and all those atoms and substances? [*Sits at the card table*.]

POLINA [*bangs the table*]. Come on, everyone.

After Dorn's words 'An obstacle race' (p. 281):

POLINA [*following him in*]. You spent all the time looking at her. I beg you, I implore you by everything you hold sacred—don't torture me. Don't look at her, don't have long conversations with her.

DORN. All right, I'll try.

POLINA [*pressing his hand to her breast*]. I know my jealousy's stupid and senseless, I'm ashamed of it myself. I'm boring you.

DORN. No, it's all right. Carry on talking if you find it hard to keep quiet.

In several instances the '*Russkaya mysl* text' and its successors contain brief passages corresponding to comparatively lengthy passages cut from the 'Censor's copy', as follows.

Act Two

In place of Nina's words 'It's so boring' (p. 249): the 'Censor's copy' has Nina recite some lines of her speech from the stage in Act One (from 'Men, lions, eagles . . .' to '. . . no may-beetles can be heard in the lime-groves'—see pp. 240–1). To this Masha replies: 'How poetic!'

In place of Shamrayev's words from 'Carriage horses? . . .' to '. . . the bounds of credence!' (p. 251), the 'Censor's copy' has:

SHAMRAYEV [*upset*]. A carriage horse? Did you say carriage horse? Then go and have a look. Ginger's lame, Cossack Girl's been given too much water. And where am I to get collars? Where can I get them? This baffles me, it passes the bounds of credence!

POLINA [*to her husband*]. Oh, stop it, please!

IRINA. I'm not interested in horse-collars or rye. I'm going, that's all there is to it.

SHAMRAYEV. Have a heart, Irina! What horses can you use?

In place of Polina's words, from 'We have these mix-ups every day . . .' to '. . . I can't stand his rudeness' (p. 252), the 'Censor's copy' has:

He does what he likes. A couple of years ago he persuaded the old man to mortgage the estate. Why? What was the point? He bought some pedigree turkeys and piglets, but let them die. He set up an expensive bee-keeping outfit and let all the bees die in the winter. He spends all the income from the estate on buildings. Then he takes the old man's pension and sends Irina Arkadin six hundred roubles a year out of the old man's money, as her share of the income from the estate. And she's glad of it, being stingy.

Act Three

In place of the passage 'My manager takes all my pension . . .' to '. . . something wrong with me again' (p. 261), the 'Censor's copy' has:

My whole pension goes on raising crops, cattle and so on.

[MEDVEDENKO *comes in.*]

IRINA. Well, I do have some money, but I am an actress, you know. My dresses alone have ruined me.

MEDVEDENKO [*smokes a fat cigarette, addressing no one in particular*]. The schoolmaster from Telyatyev made a good thing out of buying some hay. Paid nine copecks a pood including carriage. And I had to pay eleven last week. It's hard to make ends meet. [*Examines the star on* SORIN'*s chest.*] What have you there? Well, well. I got a medal once, but I'd rather they'd sent me cash.

IRINA. Do me a favour, Simon, and let me talk to my brother. We'd like to be on our own.

MEDVEDENKO. Oh, all right, I understand. [*Goes out.*]

SORIN. He's been wandering about here since early this morning. Keeps walking around and talking about something. [*Laughs.*] He's a good fellow, but I must say he's very, er, boring.

Act Four

In the 'Censor's copy' Sorin remains behind at the point in Act Four where '*All go out by the door, left*' (p. 277), and is asleep in his wheel-chair throughout the ensuing scene between Treplev and Nina. After Nina's words 'It's time I went' (p. 279) the 'Censor's copy' has:

NINA [*with a nod at* SORIN]. Is he unwell?

TREPLEV. Yes. [*Pause.*]

After this the 'Censor's copy' continues as in the final text (p. 279): 'Nina, I cursed you . . .' etc.

After Nina's words 'completed its melancholy cycle and died' (p. 280), the 'Censor's copy' has the stage direction:

While she recites SORIN *wakes up and gets to his feet.*

In place of the passage from '*Embraces* TREPLEV *impulsively . . .*' to '. . . and tells Mother' (p. 281), the 'Censor's copy' has:

[*Embraces* TREPLEV, *then* SORIN *and runs out through the french window.*]

TREPLEV [*after a pause*]. We mustn't tell Mother she was here.

Two cuts made in the stage directions owe their origin to the disastrous first performance of *The Seagull* at the Alexandrine Theatre in St. Petersburg (see below, p. 348). These relate to a point (unfortunately only one of many) in the First Act where the audience laughed uproariously in the wrong place, and to another in Act Four where it was feared that the same thing would happen again, and the producer accordingly gave instruction, in the middle of the performance, to the actress playing Nina to disregard the stage directions in one particular. (See '*Istoriya pervogo predstavleniya "Chayki"*' [Story of the First Performance of *The Seagull*] by the producer, Ye. P. Karpov, *Chekhov i teatr*, pp. 240–1.)

The stage directions in question are embodied in the text of the 'Censor's copy', but are not present in later recensions. The first was:

Before Treplev's words 'O ye ancient, hallowed shades' (p. 240):

[*Bangs a stick. Two ghosts appear in the bushes on each side of the stage.*]

These ghosts then '*bow and disappear*' at the end of Treplev's speech.

The second of these stage directions came after Nina's words 'like exquisite, delicate blossoms. Do you remember' (p. 280):

> [*Sits on a bench and throws over herself a sheet which she has taken from the bed.*]

At the end of Nina's recitation, which follows, the stage direction '*Throws off the sheet*' occurred.

(c) Further Revision

The '*Plays, 1897* text' shows little evidence of revision apart from the restoration of certain passages almost exactly in the form which they take in the corrected censor's copy (see above, p. 340). A sentence was taken out of Sorin's speech on p. 235: 'Horace said: "*Genus irritabile vatum*".' A few other minor changes were made in punctuation, style and word order. In once more revising his text for his *Collected Works* (1901), Chekhov made some further minor changes, but these do not call for attention in translation.

3. CONTEMPORARY RECEPTION

(a) In St. Petersburg

Events conspired to make the first performance of *The Seagull* (on 17 October 1896) a painful experience to Chekhov and a fiasco memorable in the annals of the Russian stage. A sequence of unfortunate decisions contributed to the disaster. Chekhov decided to give the play to the Alexandrine Theatre in St. Petersburg after it had originally been destined for the Moscow Little Theatre. At this period the Alexandrine Theatre had the reputation of purveying light entertainment to lowbrow theatre-goers such as might never even have heard of Chekhov, or who remembered him only for his early comic work and short stage farces. Intellectuals—on whom the new techniques pioneered in *The Seagull* could most suitably make their first impact before being tried on a wider public—were rarely seen inside the Alexandrine Theatre at this time.

The cards were further stacked against Chekhov's play when one of the actresses at the Alexandrine Theatre selected it for her benefit performance. This was Ye. I. Levkeyeva, a well-known character-actress who was celebrated for portrayals of middle-aged women. The mere appearance on the stage of this grand old trouper is said to have been usually enough to put a typical Alexandrine Theatre audience into fits of laughter. But the trouble was that Levkeyeva was not to appear on the stage at all in this particular performance—simply because there was no part suitable for her in *The Seagull*, though at one time she was considered for Polina. On the first night the theatre was packed with her admirers, who had paid the special high prices normally charged for a benefit performance only to find themselves faced with something quite unfamiliar.

Thus the stage was set for catastrophe. In English theatrical terms it was as if an audience which had paid to see a 'Whitehall' (or, earlier, 'Aldwych') farce had found itself confronted with a play by T. S. Eliot instead. The situation was not improved by the hasty preparation of the play by the company. The actors and producer took Chekhov's lines seriously enough. But the decision to put on *The Seagull* at only ten days' notice was an unfortunate one—it was not until as late as 8 October that the play was first read through by the actors.

Chekhov himself was under no illusions about the prospects for the night of the 17th, having arrived in St. Petersburg early enough to attend the last rehearsals (from the fourth onwards) of *The Seagull*. But the result outstripped his most gloomy forebodings, and has been described by a number of eyewitnesses as a 'scandal without precedent' in the history of the Russian theatre—a turn of phrase which admittedly crops up rather frequently in Russian theatrical memoirs.

The trouble began in Act One, where Nina's speech (beginning 'Men, lions, eagles and partridges, horned deer' and particularly ill-adapted for the ears of Levkeyeva's fans) evoked jeers and derisive guffaws. As the play proceeded, members of the audience seated in the front rows demonstratively turned their backs on the stage, hissed, whistled, laughed and engaged in rowdy private conversations. The uproar in the theatre increased and much of the play became inaudible. But at least some of the visual effects could still strike home. Treplev's appearance (in Act Three) with his head bandaged, as the result of his unsuccessful attempt to shoot himself, evoked a particularly raucous storm of laughter and catcalls.

Chekhov left the auditorium during Act Two and sat in Levkeyeva's dressing-room. At the end of the performance he left the theatre, wandered the streets on his own and had supper at Romanov's, a well-known St. Petersburg restaurant. He did not return to Suvorin's house, where he was staying, until 2 a.m., by which time his sister Masha (who had come to St. Petersburg specially to see *The Seagull*) was becoming worried and attempts had been made to trace him all over town. That night Chekhov told Suvorin that he would never offer another play to be staged even if he lived another seven hundred years (Suvorin's Diary, quoted in Gitovich, op. cit., p. 432).

On the following day Chekhov left for Melikhovo, taking the noon train to Moscow. Had he remained in St. Petersburg he would have been able to confirm what his friends tried to explain to him by letter and telegram—that the later performances of *The Seagull* had an encouraging reception. The special conditions of the catastrophic first night were no longer operative. However, the management of the theatre, perhaps influenced by a delayed reaction to the original fiasco, and against the strong protest of the producer, Ye. P. Karpov, decided to take *The Seagull* off after eight performances. This decision was no doubt encouraged by the many viciously hostile reviews of *The Seagull* which appeared in the press—Chekhov's work being no exception to the tendency whereby superlative performance in any field sometimes attracts the malice of mediocrities. These reactions included notices in serious publications such as

The Petersburg Gazette and *Novosti* [*News*], as well as abusive doggerel verse making fun of Chekhov in the less edifying comic papers. This press campaign was later summed up as follows (in the magazine *Teatral* [*Playgoer*]): 'The press hurled itself at *The Seagull* and its author with relish. It got to the point where Chekhov was denied any talent whatever, and was written off as an enormous bubble inflated by his sycophantic friends. . . . The gloating of certain critics reached the point of downright cynicism' (*Teatral*, no. 95, 1896, quoted in *Works*, 1944–51, xi, p. 575).

The following extracts from letters written by Chekhov give an author's-eye-view of the above proceedings:

'If I heed Potapenko and give this part [Polina] to Levkeyeva, the audience may expect something comic and be disappointed. Levkeyeva's known as a fine comic actress, isn't she? So her reputation may swamp the part. It would be a good idea to give the schoolteacher to some little character-actor with a comic flavour.' (*Letter to A. S. Suvorin, 23 Sept. 1896.*)

'So far *The Seagull* isn't coming along very excitingly [in rehearsal]. St. Petersburg's boring and the season doesn't start till November. Everyone's bad-tempered, fussy and insincere. . . . The play's reception will be more sombre than enthusiastic. I'm not in too good a mood by and large. I'll send money for your journey today or tomorrow, but I advise you not to come.' (*Letter to Chekhov's sister Masha, 12 Oct. 1896.*)

'*The Seagull* will be performed on 17 October. Komissarzhevskaya [the well-known actress V. F. Komissarzhevskaya in the part of Nina] is acting marvellously.' (*Letter to Michael Chekhov, 15 Oct. 1896.*)

'Stop printing the plays. I'll never forget yesterday evening [the disastrous performance of *The Seagull* in the Alexandrine Theatre]. Still, I did sleep well and am leaving in a fairly tolerable mood. . . . I won't have the play put on in Moscow. I shall *never* write or stage any more plays.' (*Letter to A. S. Suvorin, 18 Oct. 1896.*)

'Yesterday's event didn't shock or bother me much, as I was prepared for it by the rehearsals, and I don't feel particularly bad.' (*Letter to Chekhov's sister Masha, 18 Oct. 1896.*)

'The play flopped—came a real cropper. Brooding tension, outrage and scandal in the theatre. The actors played vilely and stupidly.

'Moral: don't write plays.

'Anyway, I'm still alive and kicking.' (*Letter to Michael Chekhov, 18 Oct. 1896.*)

'In your last letter (of 18 October) you call me an old woman three times and say I behaved like a coward. Why such slander? I had supper at Romanov's after the play, then went to bed, slept well and went home next day without emitting a single squeak. If I'd really had the wind up, I'd have been rushing round to newspaper offices and actors, nervously begging them to be nice to me. I'd have been making futile, hysterical changes [in the text]. I'd have stayed on in St. Petersburg for a couple of weeks attending *The Seagull*, agitated, bathed in cold sweat and complaining. . . . When you came to see me that night after the play you told me yourself that I should leave, and you sent me a letter next morning saying good-bye. I can't see that I've been cowardly. I behaved rationally and coolly, like a man whose proposal of marriage has been turned down and who has no recourse but to take his departure. My pride was wounded—all right. But it wasn't a bolt from the blue, was it? I expected a flop. I was ready for it, as I warned you in all sincerity.

'When I got home I took some castor oil, washed in cold water—and now I'm ready to write another play. I'm not tired and irritated any more. . . . But please don't regret not having attended a rehearsal. Anyway, there was really only one proper rehearsal, and even then nothing made sense. The play was lost through the disgusting way it was acted.' (*Letter to A. S. Suvorin, 22 Oct. 1896.*)

'The play made a great stir, in that some people say it's meaningless and curse me up hill and down dale, while others claim it's "simply divine". This makes no sense, but I flew out of St. Petersburg like a rocket and I'm now getting masses of letters and even telegrams.' (*Letter to N. I. Korobov, 1 Nov. 1896.*)

'Of course I'm glad, very much so. Still, the success of the second and third performances can't wipe the impression of the first from my mind. I didn't see it all, but what I did see was dreary and extraordinarily odd. They didn't know their parts, they acted stiffly and hesitantly, and they all lost heart—even Komissarzhevskaya, who didn't play too badly. It was as hot as hell in the theatre.

'It looks as if all the elements were against the play.' (*Letter to V. V. Bilibin, 1 Nov. 1896.*)

'By all means let amateur companies put on *The Seagull*, but . . . as far as possible from Serpukhov [a town near Chekhov's home at Melikhovo], where I prefer to serve as juror or district councillor—as a citizen, not as a playwright. If they put *The Seagull* on in Serpukhov I shall lose my reputation in the county. What's more, a Serpukhov audience is so dim, clumsy, crude and tasteless. It doesn't need a seagull (doesn't even know the word) so much as a jackdaw.' (*Letter to Ye. M. Shavrova, 7 Nov. 1896.*)

'I only saw the first two acts of the play from the auditorium, after which I sat back stage, feeling all the time that *The Seagull* was being a flop. After the performance, on the night and next day, people assured me that my characters were all idiots, that my play was too cumbrous for the stage, that it was stupid, incomprehensible—totally meaningless even, and so on and so forth. You can think how I felt. This was a fiasco beyond my wildest imaginings! I was ashamed and annoyed, and left St. Petersburg full of all sorts of doubts. If I'd written and staged a play so blatantly crawling with egregious faults (I thought), I must have lost my touch—the works must have got completely gummed up. At home I received letters from St. Petersburg saying that the second and third performances were a success. Several letters, both signed and anonymous, praised the play and abused the reviewers. I enjoyed reading them, but still felt ashamed and annoyed. It occurred to me that if these kind people thought I needed comforting, things really must be in a bad way. But your letter really did impress me. I've known of you for a long time, have the greatest respect for you and trust you more than all the critics put together. You sensed this when you wrote to me, which is why your letter's so splendid and convincing. I feel relaxed now and I can think of the play and performance without revulsion.

'Komissarzhevskaya's a wonderful actress. She had many people in the theatre in tears at one rehearsal. They called her the best actress on the modern Russian stage. But on the night even she was infected by the atmosphere of hostility to *The Seagull* and seemed to take fright and lose her voice.' (*Letter to A. F. Koni, 11 Nov. 1896.*)

'Yes, *The Seagull* had a disastrous first night in St. Petersburg. There was an air of spite in the theatre, an atmosphere so thick with hatred that I flew out of St. Petersburg like a rocket, in accordance with the laws of physics—all your fault . . . for encouraging me to write a play. . . .

'My health's all right. So's my mood. But I fear I'll soon be in a bad mood again. Lavrov and Goltsev [the editors] insist on publishing *The Seagull* in *Russkaya mysl*, so now I shall catch it from the literary critics.' (*Letter to V. I. Nemirovich-Danchenko, 20 Nov. 1896.*)

'Not long ago I heard from Koni, who saw *The Seagull*. Your letter and Koni's have given me many happy minutes, but I still feel nauseated, still feel only disgust for my plays. It's as much as I can do to read the proofs. You'll tell me again how stupid and foolish I'm being, how it's all due to my conceit and pride and so on and so forth. I know, but I can't help it. I'd like to get rid of this stupid feeling, but I can't—really. The trouble isn't that my play flopped. Most of my earlier plays failed, after all, and that was all so much water off a duck's back. What failed on 17 October wasn't the play, it was me. What struck me right from Act One was this. People I'd been on easy, open, friendly terms with (up to 17 October), people I'd shared a carefree dinner with, people I'd stuck up for . . . they all had a funny look about them, a very funny look indeed. . . . I now feel relaxed and perfectly normal. Still, I can't forget what happened, just as I couldn't forget if someone was to hit me, for instance.' (*Letter to A. S. Suvorin, 14 Dec. 1896.*)

'I haven't forgotten promising to dedicate *The Seagull* to Anna Ivanovna [Suvorin's wife], but I deliberately haven't done so. The play's associated with one of my most unpleasant memories, it's repulsive to me. There's no point in dedicating it to anyone.' (*Letter to A. S. Suvorin, 4 Jan. 1897.*)

(*b*) *In Moscow*

After the fiasco in the Alexandrine Theatre *The Seagull* was performed successfully in several provincial towns, including Kiev, Astrakhan and Taganrog. But the most important event in its immediate future—and in that of Chekhov as a dramatist—was the first performance by the Moscow Art Theatre on 17 December 1898. This was the first season of the Moscow Art Theatre, which had been founded earlier in the same year by K. S. Stanislavsky and V. I. Nemirovich-Danchenko.

The inclusion of *The Seagull* in the Art Theatre's opening repertoire became possible through Nemirovich-Danchenko's persistence in persuading Chekhov to allow the play to be performed. Nemirovich-Danchenko wrote to Chekhov that *The Seagull* was the only modern play which really interested him as a producer, but Chekhov replied that he did not like to risk an experience similar to that which had caused him so much suffering two years earlier. In the end, luckily, he gave way (see *Works*, 1944–51, xi, pp. 576–7).

The new production was a much more serious affair than the old. The play was carefully studied by cast and producers—and also given adequate rehearsals, of which there were twenty-six in all. Chekhov managed to attend one of these before leaving to spend the winter at Yalta in south Russia, where ill-health from now on regularly marooned him in the cold weather.

The date of the first performance approached in an atmosphere of increasing tension, owing to the fears generally felt over the possible effects of failure on Chekhov's health. At the last moment his sister Masha appealed for the performance to be cancelled and Nemirovich-Danchenko had to take the responsibility of turning down her request. Stanislavsky describes with typical panache the mood among the actors just before the curtain rose: 'Standing on the stage, we listened to an inner voice, which whispered to us: "Act well. Act magnificently. Achieve success and triumph. And if you do not, know that on receipt of your telegram your beloved author will die, the victim of your own hands. You will become his executioners" ' (K. S. Stanislavsky, *Moya zhizn v iskusstve*, pp. 293–4).

It does not sound as if Stanislavsky himself (who played Trigorin in *The Seagull*) did much to calm down his junior colleagues on this occasion. Everyone had taken valerian drops (the tranquillizer of the period) and Stanislavsky himself was afflicted with a nervous twitch in one foot. To make matters more harrowing, the curtain came down at the end of Act One in total silence. This lasted for an agonizing few seconds before wildly enthusiastic applause broke out and showed that fears for *The Seagull* and for its author's well-being could be forgotten. It was on the demand of the audience that Nemirovich-Danchenko telegraphed to Chekhov in Yalta news of a truly triumphant reception:

'COLOSSAL SUCCESS PLAY CAUGHT ON SO WELL FROM FIRST ACT THAT SERIES OF TRIUMPHS FOLLOWED ENDLESS CURTAIN CALLS MAD WITH JOY.'

Next day Nemirovich-Danchenko (himself a playwright) sent a further telegram saying that the success of *The Seagull* had pleased him more than that of any of his own plays. He also informed Chekhov that:

'ALL PAPERS WITH SURPRISING UNANIMITY CALL SEAGULLS SUCCESS BRILLIANT UPROARIOUS ENORMOUS RAVE NOTICES.'

Chekhov later presented Nemirovich-Danchenko with a medallion inscribed: 'You gave my *Seagull* life. Thank you.' This was no more than justice, for Nemirovich-Danchenko had restored Chekhov to the theatre, and it is arguable that without him there might have been no *Three Sisters* or *Cherry Orchard*. Among those who also conveyed to Chekhov their admiration for *The Seagull* in connexion with the first Art Theatre production were Maxim Gorky and Fyodor Chaliapin. And to cap a pleasing episode in Russian theatrical history, a stylized seagull was adopted as the permanent emblem of the Moscow Art Theatre.

NOTES

The following notes, which have been kept as brief as possible, are designed to explain references in the text which might be obscure to English-speaking readers and to point out certain difficulties which have occurred in the translation.

Page

22 '*Russian national dress.*' See note to p. 104 of *The Oxford Chekhov*, vol. viii, p. 318.

23 'Mayne Reid.' Thomas Mayne Reid (1818–83), of Irish origin, author of children's adventure stories written in English and popular in Russia in Russian translation.

29 'the *Russian Courier.*' *Russky kuryer*, a Moscow daily paper (1879–91).

39 'Fonvizin.' D. I. Fonvizin (1745–92), the leading Russian eighteenth-century playwright.

57 'Pirogov.' N. I. Pirogov (1810–81), the famous surgeon.

57 'Kiev.' Large city in the Ukraine and site of the well-known Monastery of the Caves.

86 'Monastery of the Trinity and St. Sergius.' At modern Zagorsk, about 50 miles north of Moscow. One of the best-known Russian monasteries.

86 'New Jerusalem Monastery.' In the Zvenigorod District of Moscow Province, founded in 1656.

86 'Kharkov.' Large city in the Ukraine.

86 'Of course he does.' Literally: 'Of course—he's a Collegiate Registrar.' This was the fourteenth and lowest grade in the 'table of ranks'—the hierarchy to which all Russian officials, including schoolmasters in state schools, belonged.

88 'Sacher-Masoch.' The Austrian writer L. Sacher-Masoch (1836–95), from whose name the word 'masochism' is derived.

92 'Pushkins or Lermontovs.' Reference is to the poets A. S. Pushkin (1799–1837) and M. Yu. Lermontov (1814–41).

92 'Auerbach, Heine, Goethe.' Reference is to Bertolt Auerbach (1812–82), the German novelist; and to the German poets Heinrich Heine (1797–1856) and Johann Wolfgang Goethe (1749–1832).

98 'Ring out, ye peals of victory.' From a poem by G. R. Derzhavin (1743–1816). A misquotation—the original has 'thunder' in place of 'ye peals'.

100 'Nekrasov.' N. A. Nekrasov (1821–78), the Russian poet.

108 'Glinka.' M. I. Glinka (1804–57), the Russian composer.

108 'O shame! where is thy blush?' etc. *Hamlet*, Act Three, Scene iv. The Russian original is a paraphrase of these lines of *Hamlet*, or of others from the same speech.

116 'Sevastopol.' Reference is to the siege of Sevastopol (1854–5), the Crimean naval base, during the Crimean War.

136 'Krylov.' I. A. Krylov (*c.* 1769–1844), the best-known Russian writer of fables.

136 'Gogol.' N. V. Gogol (1809–52), the Russian writer.

159 'Theatre Square.' Large square in front of the Bolshoy Theatre in the centre of Moscow, now Sverdlov Square.

188 'In you I love. . . .' Two lines from Lermontov's lyric 'No, it is not thee I love so ardently' (1841).

188 'Dudkins and Budkins.' The first draft of *Ivanov* contains a character called Dudkin, whose part was later divided between the First and Third Guest (see above, p. 300).

193 'Manfred.' Reference is to Byron's play *Manfred* (1817).

205 'George Sand.' The French novelist (1804–76).

217 'Gogol's two rats.' The reference is to a speech in Act One, Scene i of Gogol's play *The Government Inspector* (1836) in which the Mayor describes his dream of 'two extraordinary rats'.

226 'SASHA [*to* LVOV] . . .' Sasha's entrance is not indicated in the original.

235 'Duse.' Eleonora Duse (1859–1924), the Italian actress.

235 '*The Lady with the Camellias.*' *La Dame aux camélias*, the play by Alexandre Dumas (*fils*; 1824–95), first performed in 1852.

235 'Odessa.' The large Russian port on the Black Sea.

236 'Maupassant.' Guy de Maupassant (1850–93), the French writer.

236 'provincial shopkeeper, resident of Kiev.' Literally, 'a Kiev burgher' (*meshchanin*), the burghers representing one of the social estates to which all Russians belonged in law. The translation attempts to preserve the disparaging flavour of the original, the estate of the burghers being, with that of the peasants, the least privileged.

237 'Tolstoy.' L. N. Tolstoy (1828–1910), the Russian writer.

237 'Zola.' Émile Zola (1840–1902), the French novelist.

237 'There were once two French Grenadiers.' *Die beiden Grenadiere* by Heine, set to music by Schumann.

239 'Poltava.' Town in the central Ukraine, a flourishing commercial centre in the nineteenth century.

239 'Rasplyuyev.' A character in *Krechinsky's Wedding* (1855), a play by A. V. Sukhovo-Kobylin (1817–1903).

239 'Sadovsky.' P. M. Sadovsky (1818–72), the famous Russian actor.

240 'O Hamlet, speak no more. . . .' *Hamlet*, Act Three, Scene iv. In the Russian, Treplev's reply is a paraphrase rather than a translation of Hamlet's lines and means, literally: 'And why did you yield to vice, and seek love in an abyss of sin?'

249 'Tver.' Town north-west of Moscow, now Kalinin.

249 '*On the Water.*' Maupassant's book of travel sketches *Sur l'eau* (1888).

255 'like the lunatic in Gogol.' Reference is to Poprishchin, the hero of Gogol's *Memoirs of a Madman* (1835).

256 'Turgenev's *Fathers and Children*.' Reference is to the novel *Fathers and Children* (1862) by I. S. Turgenev (1818–83).

264 'If you should ever need my life. . . .' The lines come from Chekhov's own story *Neighbours* (1892)—see further, above, p. 338.

266 'Yelizavetgrad.' A town in the southern Ukraine, now Kirovograd.

267 'the *Slav Fair*.' A large hotel in central Moscow at which Chekhov sometimes stayed.

268 '*A watchman is banging*.' In order to warn thieves that they were alert and show their masters that they were awake, Russian watchmen used to make a banging noise with a stick against a board or with some kind of improvised rattle.

272 'Pushkin's *Mermaid*.' Reference is to Pushkin's unfinished dramatic poem, *The Mermaid* (1832).

274 'The Man in the Iron Mask.' A French prisoner of state in Louis XIV's reign, whose identity was a matter of speculation and who died in the Bastille in 1703. He was in fact Mattioli, a minister of Duke Charles Ferdinand of Mantua.

277 'He gives you the neck of a broken bottle glittering against a weir. . . .' A very similar passage occurs in Chekhov's own story *The Wolf* (1886). Chekhov also mentions this device of evoking a moonlit night in a letter to his brother Alexander of 10 May 1886.

278 'Lucky the man with a roof over his head. . . .' The passage comes from the Epilogue to Turgenev's novel *Rudin* (1856).

279 'Yelets.' Town in central Russia, 70 miles north-west of Voronezh.

THE PRONUNCIATION OF RUSSIAN
PROPER NAMES

English-speaking actors do not usually attempt a phonetically accurate reproduction of Russian proper names on the stage. But where the less familiar proper names are concerned it is probably worth trying at least to preserve the Russian stress accent, and so an alphabetical list is appended of the proper names in the text, the stress being indicated by an acute accent over the relevant vowel. See also *The Oxford Chekhov*, vol. iii, p. 337.

Abramsón	Izmáylov	Polína
Aleútov	Izmáylovka	Poltáva
Arkádin	Kátya	Porfíry
Avdótya	Khárkov	Púshkin
Babákin	Kíev	Raísa
Balabálkin	Korolkóv	Rasplyúyev
Borís	Kosýkh	Sadóvsky
Bórkin	Krylóv	Sásha
Búdkin	Lébedev	Schrífter
Bugróv	Lérmontov	Sergéy
Chádin	Mánka	Sevastópol
Dárya	Márko	Shabélsky
Dmítry	Másha	Shamráyev
Dúdkin	Matryóna	Shcherbúk
Dunyásha	Medvedénko	Solomónovich
Fílka	Mílbakh	Sónya
Fonvízin	Molchánovka	Sórin
Gerásim	Múshkino	Súzdaltsev
Glagólyev	Nekrásov	Tálye
Glínka	Nílovich	Tolstóy
Gógol	Nína	Tréplev
Grékov	Odéssa	Trilétsky
Grokhólsky	Ósip	Trigórin
Ilyá	Ovsyánov	Turgénev
Irína	Pétrin	Vasíly
Iván	Pirogóv	Vengeróvich
Ivánov	Platónov	Voynítsev
Ivánovka	Platónovka	Voynítsevka
Ivánovna	Plésniki	Yegórushka

PRONUNCIATION OF RUSSIAN PROPER NAMES

Yeléts	Zaréchny	Zhílkovo
Yelizavetgrád	Zarévsky	Zinaída
Yusnóvka	Zaymíshche	

Note. One or two of the above have alternative stress—e.g. Medvédénko. And 'Treplyóv' is an acceptable alternative for 'Tréplev'. It has been thought better not to trouble the users of this volume with such refinements.

SELECT BIBLIOGRAPHY

I. BIBLIOGRAPHIES IN ENGLISH

Two most useful bibliographies, published by the New York Public Library and containing in all nearly five hundred items, give a comprehensive picture of the literature relating to Chekhov published in English—translations of his writings, biographical and critical studies, memoirs, essays, articles etc. They are:

> *Chekhov in English: a List of Works by and about him.* Compiled by Anna Heifetz. Ed. and with a Foreword by Avrahm Yarmolinsky (New York, 1949) and
>
> *The Chekhov Centennial Chekhov in English: a Selective List of Works by and about him, 1949–60.* Compiled by Rissa Yachnin (New York, 1960).

Bibliographies in English will also be found in the books by David Magarshack (*Chekhov: a Life*), Ernest J. Simmons and Ronald Hingley mentioned in Section III, below. Magarshack provides a bibliographical index of Chekhov's writings in alphabetical order of their English titles, Simmons includes a list of bibliographies in Russian, and Hingley gives a list of Chekhov's translated stories in chronological order.

II. TRANSLATIONS INTO ENGLISH OF THE PLAYS IN THIS VOLUME

(a) IN COLLECTIONS

Two plays by Tchekhof. The Seagull, The Cherry Orchard. Tr. with an Introduction and Notes by George Calderon (London, 1912).

Plays by Anton Tchekoff. Uncle Vanya, Ivanoff, The Seagull, The Swan Song. Tr. with an Introduction by Marian Fell (New York, 1912).

Plays from the Russian. Tr. Constance Garnett (London, 1923; New York, 1924). Vol. 1: *The Cherry Orchard, Uncle Vanya, The Sea-gull, The Bear, The Proposal.* Vol. 2: *Three Sisters, Ivanov, Swan Song, An Unwilling Martyr, The Anniversary, On the High Road, The Wedding.*

Plays and stories, Anton Tchekhov. Tr. S. S. Koteliansky (London, 1937; New York, 1938).
> Contains the following plays: *The Cherry Orchard, The Seagull, The Wood Demon, Tatyana Riepin, On the Harmfulness of Tobacco.*

Three Plays: The Cherry Orchard, Three Sisters, Ivanov. Tr. and with an Introduction by Elisaveta Fen (Harmondsworth, 1951).

The Seagull and Other Plays: The Seagull, Uncle Vania, The Bear, The Proposal, A Jubilee. Tr. and with an Introduction by Elisaveta Fen (Harmondsworth, 1954).

Plays by Anton Chekhov: Ivanov, The Seagull, Uncle Vania, Three Sisters, The Cherry Orchard, The Bear, The Proposal, A Jubilee. Tr. and with an Introduction by Elisaveta Fen (Harmondsworth, 1959).

A reissue of the preceding two items in one volume.

Six plays of Chekhov. New English Versions and Introduction by Robert W. Corrigan. Foreword by Harold Clurman (New York, 1962).

Contains: *Ivanov, The Wood Demon, The Sea Gull, Uncle Vanya, The Three Sisters, The Cherry Orchard.*

(*b*) SEPARATE TRANSLATIONS OF *PLATONOV* AND *THE SEAGULL*

(i) *Platonov*

Don Juan (in the Russian Manner). Tr. Basil Ashmore (London, 1952; New York, with a Preface by Sir Desmond MacCarthy, 1953).

A Country Scandal. Adapted by Alex Szögyi from *That Worthless Fellow Platonov* (New York, 1960).

Platonov: an Abridged Version of an Untitled Play in Four Acts. Tr. Dmitri Makaroff with an Introduction by George Devine (London, 1961).

Platonov: a Play in Four Acts and Five Scenes. Tr. David Magarshack (London, 1964).

(ii) *The Seagull*

The Sea-gull. Tr. Fred Eisemann (Boston, 1913).

The Sea-gull: a Play in Four Acts. Tr. Julius West (London, 1915).

The Sea Gull. Tr. Stark Young (New York, 1938).

The Seagull, produced by Stanislavsky: Production Score for the Moscow Art Theatre by K. S. Stanislavsky. Ed. with Introduction by S. D. Balukhaty. Tr. David Magarshack (London, 1952).

The Seagull: a Play. Tr. David Iliffe (London, 1953).

III. BIOGRAPHICAL AND CRITICAL STUDIES

Leon Shestov, *Anton Tchekhov and Other Essays* (Dublin and London, 1916).

William Gerhardi, *Anton Chehov: a Critical Study* (London, 1923).

Oliver Elton, *Chekhov* (The Taylorian Lecture, 1929; Oxford, 1929).

Nina Andronikova Toumanova, *Anton Chekhov: the Voice of Twilight Russia* (London, 1937).

W. H. Bruford, *Chekhov and his Russia: a Sociological Study* (London, 1948).

Ronald Hingley, *Chekhov: a Biographical and Critical Study* (London, 1950).

Irene Nemirovsky, *A Life of Chekhov*. Tr. from the French by Erik de Mauny (London, 1950).

David Magarshack, *Chekhov: a Life* (London, 1952).

David Magarshack, *Chekhov the Dramatist* (London, 1952).

Vladimir Yermilov [Ermilov], *Anton Pavlovich Chekhov, 1860–1904*. Tr. Ivy Litvinov (Moscow, 1956; London, 1957).

W. H. Bruford, *Anton Chekhov* (London, 1957).

T. Eekman, ed., *Anton Chekhov, 1860–1960* (Leiden, 1960).

Beatrice Saunders, *Tchehov the Man* (London, 1960).

Ernest J. Simmons, *Chekhov: a Biography* (Boston, Toronto, 1962; London, 1963).

Maurice Valency, *The Breaking String: the Plays of Anton Chekhov* (New York, 1966).

Thomas Winner, *Chekhov and his Prose* (New York, 1966).

Kornei Chukovsky, *Chekhov the Man*. Tr. Pauline Rose (London, n.d.).

IV. LETTERS AND MEMOIR MATERIAL ETC.

Letters of Anton Tchehov to his Family and Friends. Tr. Constance Garnett (London, 1920).

The Note-books of Anton Tchekhov together with Reminiscences of Tchekhov by Maxim Gorky. Tr. S. S. Koteliansky and Leonard Woolf (Richmond, 1921).

Letters on the Short Story, the Drama and Other Literary Topics. By Anton Chekhov. Selected and ed. Louis S. Friedland (New York, 1924).

Konstantin Stanislavsky, *My Life in Art*. Tr. J. J. Robbins (London, 1924; New York, 1956).

The Life and Letters of Anton Tchekhov. Tr. and ed. S. S. Koteliansky and Philip Tomlinson (London, 1925).

The Letters of Anton Pavlovitch Tchehov to Olga Leonardovna Knipper. Tr. Constance Garnett (London, 1926).

Anton Tchekhov. Literary and Theatrical Reminiscences. Tr. and ed. S. S. Koteliansky (London, 1927).

Vladimir Nemirovitch-Dantchenko, *My Life in the Russian Theatre*. Tr. John Cournos (London, 1937).

The Personal Papers of Anton Chekhov. Introduction by Matthew Josephson (New York, 1948).

Lydia Avilov, *Chekhov in my Life: a Love Story*. Tr. with an Introduction by David Magarshack (London, 1950).

Konstantin Stanislavsky, *Stanislavsky on the Art of the Stage*. Tr. with an introductory essay on Stanislavsky's 'System' by David Magarshack (London, 1950).

The Selected Letters of Anton Chekhov. Ed. Lillian Hellman, tr. Sidonie Lederer (New York, 1955).

V. OTHER WORKS USED IN THE PREPARATION OF THIS VOLUME

Neizdannaya pyesa A. P. Chekhova ['Unpublished Play of A. P. Chekhov'], ed. N. F. Belchikov (Moscow, 1923).

K. S. Stanislavsky, *Moya zhizn v iskusstve* ['My Life in Art'] (Moscow–Leningrad, 1941).

Polnoye sobraniye sochineny i pisem A. P. Chekhova ['Complete Collection of the Works and Letters of A. P. Chekhov'], ed. S. D. Balukhaty, V. P. Potyomkin, N. S. Tikhonov, A. M. Yegolin. 20 vols. (Moscow, 1944–51).

N. I. Gitovich, *Letopis zhizni i tvorchestva A. P. Chekhova* ['Chronicle of the Life and Literary Activity of A. P. Chekhov'] (Moscow, 1955).

Literaturnoye nasledstvo: Chekhov ['Literary Heritage: Chekhov'], ed. V. V. Vinogradov and others (Moscow, 1960).

A. P. Chekhov: rukopisi, pisma, biograficheskiye dokumenty, vospominaniya, teatralnyye postanovki, risunki, fotografii ['A. P. Chekhov: Manuscripts, Letters, Biographical Documents, Memoirs, Theatrical Performances, Drawings, Photographs'], compiled by V. P. Nechayev and Yu. M. Mirkina, ed. Yu. A. Krasovsky (Moscow, 1960).

Chekhov i teatr: pisma, felyetony, sovremenniki o Chekhove-dramaturge ['Chekhov and the Theatre: Letters, Articles and the Comments of Contemporaries on Chekhov as Playwright'], ed. E. D. Surkov (Moscow, 1961).

F. L. Lucas, *The Drama of Chekhov, Synge, Yeats and Pirandello* (London, 1963).

A. P. Chekhov, *Chayka: The Seagull*, ed. with an Introduction, Notes and Vocabulary by P. Henry (Letchworth, 1965).

PRINTED IN GREAT BRITAIN
AT THE UNIVERSITY PRESS, OXFORD
BY VIVIAN RIDLER
PRINTER TO THE UNIVERSITY